Building Effective Helping Skills

The Foundation of Generalist Practice

D. Mark Ragg

Eastern Michigan University

Allyn and Bacon

Boston ▪ London ▪ Toronto ▪ Sydney ▪ Tokyo ▪ Singapore

To Brenda, Jamie, and Devan
As I wrote about the importance of relationships for others, my relationship
with you has been compromised. Thank you for your patience and
understanding and the lessons in nonverbal expression whenever I said that I
needed to work on the book.

Editor-in Chief, Social Sciences: *Karen Hanson*
Editorial Assistant: *Alyssa Pratt*
Marketing Manager: *Jackie Aaron*
Production Editor: *Christopher H. Rawlings*
Editorial-Production Service: *Omegatype Typography, Inc.*
Composition and Prepress Buyer: *Linda Cox*
Manufacturing Buyer: *Julie McNeill*
Cover Administrator: *Brian Gogolin*
Electronic Composition: *Omegatype Typography, Inc.*

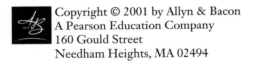
Library of Congress Cataloging-in-Publication Data

Ragg, D. Mark
    Building effective helping skills : the foundation of generalist practice / D. Mark Ragg.
       p. cm.
    Includes bibliographical references and index.
    ISBN 0-205-29802-8 (alk. paper)
    1. Social work education.   2. Social workers—Training of.   3. Communication in social
work. I. Title.

HV11+ 2001
361.3'2'071—dc21

                        00-040134

Printed in the United States of America

10 9 8 7 6 5 4 3 2 1   05 04 03 02 01 00

CONTENTS

PREFACE

In the literature on helping relationships and practice skills, one finds a myriad of skills and techniques for helping client systems. This can be confusing for students entering the helping professions as it often appears as if there are millions of minute skills that you must remember before you can engage in competent practice. This can be most disheartening as you read one book after another and learn of new skills and strategies for helping. If you read extensively, however, you will find that authors often apply different labels to very similar worker behaviors.

As workers' confidence increases, they discover that some of the initial confusion is due to differences in the way authors describe helping behaviors. More seasoned workers also begin to find that there is really little difference among the concepts described by different authors, and they come to realize that authors will choose different words to describe the same helping activity. There is also a tendency for different authors to focus on variations and nuances within a specific skill and discuss them as if they are different skills. These fine-tuned descriptions tend to be applications of a skill in different situations or toward different goals rather than entirely different skills.

This book approaches the development of helping skills from a very simple model that is based on a convergence between decades of practice experience and an extensive review of the practice literature. From this convergence, concepts are developed to help new workers develop the core skills of helping. The simplicity of the model is based on four skill sets that are necessary for effective practice. Each skill area speaks to an element of the helping situation that has been found to contribute to successful practice.

Each of the four skill sets builds on two component skill sets that must be mastered to begin effective practice. After the mastery of the core skills, workers continue to expand their application of the skills according to client needs and the helping situation. This creates tremendous variance in skills as workers advance in their careers. The four critical skill sets are:

1. *Developing the Professional Self*   Using oneself with professional purposefulness.
2. *Developing the Helping Relationship*   Establishing and maintaining the helping relationship.
3. *Developing an Accurate Understanding*   Achieving an accurate and unbiased understanding of the client situation.
4. *Developing Focused and Helpful Responses*   Responding to the client in a way that promotes mastery and change.

Often new or ineffective workers exhibit an uneven quality across the four skill areas. It is important that workers seek to develop their skills in all four sets. Uneven development leads to areas of practice weakness. Consequently, workers are encouraged to use the four skill areas to continually assess their abilities so they can develop conscious awareness of how they perform in each area.

Within the book's fifteen chapters, the skill areas and core skills will be explored in more detail, including strategies of combining and clustering skills to accomplish specific goals. But first, a brief description of the core skills for each area is necessary.

THE FOUR CORE SKILL SETS OF HELPING

The Skill of Developing the Professional Self

When in a helping relationship, the social worker is expected to behave in a professional and ethical manner. Many clients are in a vulnerable state when they enter service and often form a very intense relationship with the worker. Workers must be in control of their own impulses, tendencies, and beliefs to avoid taking actions that might interfere with the help that clients seek.

When workers are not in control of their feelings and reactions, clients often feel workers do not understand or care about them. Such perceptions can result when clients sense that the workers are attending to their own feelings rather than exploring the client situation. When workers begin to attend to their own feelings and agendas, it is impossible for them to function as effective professionals.

Concurrent with self-control, social workers are expected to maintain a sense of purpose in their interactions with clients. This requires workers to use their professional knowledge and theory base to guide interaction with clients. Each response to a client must be grounded in the worker's growing understanding of the client situation. This grounding leads to a well-conceived plan of action for helping the client effectively deal with their particular situation.

The two skills inherent in this skill set are:

1. *The ability to understand within the professional role.* This skill involves the ability to use professional knowledge as a guide for professional activity. Thinking helps the worker comprehend client situations and find direction for helping clients increase their competent functioning.
2. *The ability to respond professionally to client needs.* This skill involves the ability of workers to monitor, understand, and control their reactions and behaviors so action can be in response to the clients' actual needs rather than controlled by the workers' feelings, attitudes/beliefs, or reactions. The worker must maintain ethical standards of behavior with clients.

The Skill of Developing the Helping Relationship

Beyond professional self-control, competence, and ethical behavior, the worker must also be able to develop an accurate emotional connection with clients. Such a connection goes beyond simple understanding or imagining. An emotional connection allows effective workers to feel what the client is experiencing. This involves skills in extending oneself beyond personal experience to appreciate the experience of the other person.

The concept of establishing and maintaining a connection with clients has been central to the helping relationship ever since the beginning of the profession. The helping relationship is consistently argued to be the most important influence in client satisfaction and the perceived helpfulness of service.

The emotional connection between effective workers and their clients is not limited to the simple ability to feel what the client is experiencing. Although this is important, it is equally important that the worker be able to connect with the client's motivation to change and desired outcomes. This helps shape the relationship and provides a sense of purpose. The sense of purpose and the worker's ability to understand and help clarify the problem situation promote a strong helping relationship.

The two skills that help accomplish this sense of connection are:

1. *Tuning in and empathic responding.* This skill involves an ability to feel and understand the client's experience. An effective worker tunes in to the client's emotions, how the client interprets and responds to life events, and the impact of the client's current situation. This skill involves letting go of your own framework of understanding and adopting the framework of the client.
2. *Engaging the client in the helping relationship.* This core skill refers to the ability to motivate clients to participate fully in the helping relationship and activities designed to increase their competence within the presenting situation. This skill builds on tuning in through joining with the client's desires and motivations to improve the situation.

The Skill of Developing an Accurate Understanding about the Client Situation

In trying to understand client situations, workers must gather information to increase their understanding of the client's request for service. The information gathering helps to inform workers' thinking in a circular pattern. First, workers take in information. After taking in information, they use a framework of theories and experiences to interpret the meaning of the information. Based on this interpretation, they must seek additional information to validate their interpretation and to further advance their understanding.

Information is gathered through both passive and active skills. Passive gathering occurs through observing and listening to clients as they tell their stories. Active gathering of information involves seeking more information in response to these client disclosures.

The two critical skills associated with this skill area are:

1. *Sensory observation skills.* Sensory observation skills refer to the ability to use all five senses to gather information about a client's story. These same skills are used in conjunction with thinking skills to identify indicators of discrepancy and meaning associated with the client situation.
2. *Questioning/probing and reflecting skills.* Questioning and probing refers to the active skills when a worker observes or hears something in the client disclosure that

requires further clarification or information. This includes the worker responses that actively solicit information considered necessary for understanding the problem. Reflecting skills further exploration by making comments that capture important elements of the client story.

The Skill of Focused and Helpful Responses to Clients' Needs

In concert with the other three skill areas, workers must be able to respond to the client situation in a way that will help clients better resolve their situations. Often, helping clients to improve their life situations involves responses that help clients develop a different understanding of their situations. Consequently, workers often respond in ways that highlight patterns of thinking, feeling, behaving, or interacting.

In many client situations and in some forms of helping, the responses to the client require the worker to share information, intervene with third parties, or motivate some form of action. This requires a slightly different set of skills. These skills require the worker to be able to relate in a clear and concise manner, both orally and in writing.

The two core skills associated with this skill area are:

1. *Developing a working alliance.* Workers must work in concert with the client to maintain motivation and focus. Workers pace themselves with clients while promoting goal achievement. This requires ongoing attention and adjustment to the helping relationship.
2. *Goal-directed responding.* Workers must be able to clearly articulate their understanding, instructions, and observations so clients know and trust exactly what is being said. Good communication is clear, concise, and direct. Communication in the helping relationship is also goal directed with interactions focused on helping the client take more control over the situation.

USING SKILL SETS IN PRACTICE

The skill sets all work in concert with each other and cannot be separated out in practice. However, effective practice uses each skill set and each core skill continuously. Given that these are the core skills of practice, it is logical that a worker must achieve competence in each skill area for effective professional practice.

The skill areas and core skills are used differentially at different points in providing service. For example, gaining an understanding of the problem is important early in service so more information-gathering strategies are used. Later, the worker is attempting to help the client gain more control over the situation; consequently more reflective and direct communication strategies are used.

The skills described in this brief presentation are the core skills of generalist practice. However, variations on the skills occur as a worker begins to work with different sized client systems. For example, when working with an individual, a worker must tune in to the client's unique experience. With groups, tuning-in skills must extend to the group as an entity concurrent with individuals. When working with communities, the tuning-in skills extend even beyond groups. In communities, a worker must also tune in to political structures and organizations in relation to the community.

To help focus the skills in practice, an intervention framework is also provided in this text. This framework is referred to as *response systems*. It is assumed that most difficulties in client situations are associated with how the clients respond to their current situation. Responses are shaped by how the clients understand or process the situations as well as how the clients behave or are involved interactively with other elements of the situations.

Most of the skills within this text will be discussed through the response system framework to help students to focus on the application of the skill. The response systems will be discussed through two interrelated systems. The *processing system* refers to how the client thinks and feels about the situation. The *action system* refers to the client's behavior and interactions with others. These two systems influence the response.

Throughout the book, the response systems will be used to focus skill applications within each skill set. The framework will be used with client systems of different sizes to provide the broadest possible application for these core skills. As students practice each skill set, they will become accustomed to focusing on different elements of the client response systems. This should provide a solid grounding in applying these core skills. In future courses, students will learn more about different sizes of client systems. The frameworks provided in this book are designed to be sufficiently simple so the new knowledge can be easily integrated with the frameworks in this text.

ACKNOWLEDGMENTS

I would like to thank the following reviewers: Eileen Taylor Appleby, Marist College; Carol J. Bridges, East Central University; Michel A. Coconis, Grand Valley State University; Jean Nuernberger, Central Missouri State University; Ogden Rogers, University of Wisconsin, River Falls; and Jessica Van Gompel, Eastern Michigan University.

PART ONE

Toward Developing the Professional Self

The first part focuses on the core skill set that helps workers develop their professional identify. This involves how workers identify with their profession, how they maintain self-awareness and control, how they use their knowledge, and how they make ethical practice decisions.

In reading the chapters of this part, readers will develop skills in each of these areas. Written material and exercises are provided to maximize worker development. This part is quite different from many texts and materials used in other courses. The difference is associated with the focus on you, the reader. When reading the contents of these chapters, you will be encouraged to reflect on past experiences, feelings, thoughts, and motivations.

By the end of this part, the reader should be aware of typical patterns of thinking and responding to situations. Readers should also have a clear sense of the traits that must be monitored and controlled to assure they do not interfere with professional practice. This is critical to the professional use of self. If there are areas that seem particularly challenging, explore these with faculty advisors so the maximum abilities can be developed in the subsequent parts.

CHAPTER
1

Increasing
Self-Awareness

Effective workers demonstrate strong awareness of themselves and an ability to control how they respond to situations (Jennings & Skovholt, 1999). Self-awareness and self-control appear to dovetail with each other in creating interpersonal effectiveness. *Self-awareness* refers to the ability to "tune in" to yourself and maintain an ongoing knowledge of your emotional and cognitive reactions to external events. *Self-control* refers to the ability to control how your feelings and thoughts are expressed in interaction with others. Such control keeps your traits, emotional reactions, and personal issues from influencing your professional behavior with clients.

THE IMPORTANCE OF SELF-AWARENESS

The need for worker self-awareness in helping professionals is well established (Johnson, 1997; Spurling & Dryden, 1989). Self-awareness serves the following four critical functions for the helping professional:

1. *A source of personal power.* When people know what they are thinking and feeling, they stay fully informed on how they are influenced by others (Hedges, 1992; Rober, 1999; Tansey & Burke, 1989). When a person is not aware of how others influence feelings and thinking, there is a loss of control and personal power.

For example, a worker tended to get anxious when there was interpersonal tension. Other than this, he was a very effective worker. However, when people would raise their voices, he lost personal power through "backing off" to decrease the tension. This robbed his effectiveness with certain clients and allowed other workers to manipulate him into agreeing to do things he really did not want to do.

2. *Source of insight into differences.* When people are aware of their thoughts and feelings, they are also aware of the differences between themselves and other people (Arthur, 1998). A full awareness allows for differences to be explored without any feelings of threat (Manthei, 1997). People who are less aware often approach differences as threatening because they have no reference point for understanding the perspective of the other person. This creates risk of overidentification with the client situation. Alternatively, if people are aware of their own thoughts and feelings, they can

3

assess problem situations to determine whether they are doing something to create the problem or whether they need to explore the other person's experience.

For example, a worker was meeting with a family from an Indian reservation. When the family came in for the first appointment, the father appeared upset and not willing to talk with the worker. The worker began exploring the apparent reluctance with the father who expressed that the worker was asking too many questions. The worker mentally reviewed what had transpired and concluded that they had engaged in small talk with very few actual questions. The worker felt that there was probably something in this man's experience that might be interfering. In discussing this further, it appeared that the questionnaires sent out as part of intake were culturally offensive, and he had refused to complete the forms. The worker was able to explore his feelings with him and arrange a different way to gather the information needed for the intake.

In this example, the worker's awareness of what had transpired and how he had been conducting the work led him to the conclusion that the father's emotional state was not related to the content of the interactions. This opened up consideration that the worker and the client were having different experiences. Based on the awareness, the worker explored the situation without feeling that the difference was a reflection on him as a worker.

3. *A source of insight into reactions (hot spots and blind spots)* (Hedges, 1992; Rothman, 1999). Everybody reacts to certain situations. These reactions involve thoughts and feelings. If people are able to consciously monitor thoughts and feelings, they can separate their reactions from the client's story and proceed in a way that is most helpful to the client. However, when people are not aware, they may superimpose their reactions into the situation and proceed as if it is the client's reaction. This is a common threat as people are apt to react to themes in the client story that they would react to in their own life. If unaware, the worker is apt to avoid or possibly overreact to client themes, feelings, and issues that parallel themes in the worker's life. Concurrently, workers who are unaware of their feelings and are faced with differences may become defensive. Defensive workers are less effective in achieving client outcomes (Waldron, Turner, Barton, Alexander, & Cline, 1997).

For example, a female worker was working with a teenage girl who came from a background similar to her own. As they were exploring the girl's reactions to her mother's discipline, the worker began asking leading questions causing the girl to state reactions similar to her own. Whenever the girl expressed her reaction, the worker would respond "don't you think that you felt angry. . . ." Eventually the girl just agreed so she could move on with her story. The worker then framed her interventions based on this agreement. The relationship developed with the worker and the girl taking sides against the mother. The mother became alienated from the helping relationship, and the mother–daughter relationship deteriorated.

In this example, the worker's lack of awareness of her own feelings and reactions caused her to see her own issues in the client situation and respond as if they were the client's problems. This interfered with the development of service.

4. *A source of emotional connection with clients.* Workers' abilities to tune into their own strengths, vulnerabilities, sensitivities, and feelings provide a set of internal experiential "hooks" on which they can hang the experiences of others (Rothman, 1999). These experiential hooks are drawn on when others speak of their experiences. The worker listens to the other's experience and draws on these hooks to imagine the full experience of the client. The hooks, coming from self-awareness, consequently provide for empathic understanding of the client and a focus on improving responses (Manthei, 1997).

For example, several rebellious teens were starting service in a school-based group for high-risk youths. The youths were teacher-referred and knew that they might be expelled if they did not attend. The worker knew of the coercion to attend and was concerned about how the coercion might affect the group. The worker then reflected on past experiences when others had made her go places and do things that she did not want to do. Issues of resentment, passive defiance, and powerlessness filled her head as she thought about these experiences. In the first meeting, she used these experiences to make sense out of the attitudes presented by the group members. This allowed her to explore their feelings about their attendance.

In this example, the worker's awareness of her own reactions to similar situations allowed her to be open to the experiences of the clients. This is different from the earlier example, because the worker in this situation used the experience as an exploration guide rather than mistaking her reactions for those of her clients.

Building an Awareness of Your Response Systems

In building self-awareness, there are four areas of experience that affect how people react to any given situation. These four areas of experience provide a framework for monitoring reactions. Such frameworks are useful because it is impossible to monitor everything. The framework focuses the monitoring. The four areas of experience can be broken down into two domains, action systems and processing systems. Action systems refer to the things observed in interactions or actions occurring in response to a situation. Processing systems refer to the thoughts and feelings that occur in reaction to the situation. By concentrating on one or the other response system, people can scan and monitor how they react in different situations.

The Action System.   The action system governs what people say or do within a situation. There are two elements in the action system, interaction and behavioral responses. Although the two are closely related, it is worth considering each separately so the unique contributions of each can be understood.

The interactive domain of the action system focuses on how people speak to others in a situation. Astute students are well aware that how they speak and what they say changes from situation to situation. In some situations, they might feel compelled to talk more. In such situations, they may feel a tightening of the stomach or shoulders and a strong desire to do something about the situation. If they take notice that they are talking too much, a process of assessing the situation to determine the cause of this reaction can begin.

For example, Person A might feel pressure to tell Person B something. This is common when talking among friends; someone tells a story that causes another person to want to share a similar story. In such situations Person A focuses on telling the story in response to Person B. Consequently, Person A waits for an opening and mentally runs through the story while waiting for Person B to stop talking. If the conversation shifts, Person A may still wait to say what has been prepared and find that timing is lost because the statement no longer fits easily into the current conversation.

There are similar situations causing people to want to take some action or express themselves behaviorally. At times, people discover this reaction through their bodies. Gestures, feelings of pressure, and muscle tightening can tune people into the existence of such reactions. For example, when people hear that someone has been treated unfairly, they may experience a pressure to take some sort of action, such as calling someone or writing a letter. In such situations, it is important to identify the reaction and then assess how the reaction might influence the goals of intervention and the process of helping the client.

Awareness of your reactions within the action system is important in understanding what is occurring between you and the client. If a worker is feeling impatient to speak or to take action on behalf of the client, it is often a sign that the worker is reacting at an internal level to what the client is saying. Awareness of the reaction allows the worker to identify the pressure to do or say something as internal to the worker rather than as desired by the client. The worker can then let go of the impulse to take action and refocus on the client situation to see what might be needed.

The Processing System.   The processing system involves thinking and feeling. Often the action system is associated with the thoughts and feelings you have regarding a situation. Awareness of the processing system involves two areas of focus: what you are thinking and what you are feeling. The thinking elements include interpretations, attributions, frameworks of understanding, and applications of past experience. The feeling elements include the immediate emotional reactions to the client situation (e.g., sadness, helplessness, disgust, hopelessness) and your general affect at the time.

Awareness of cognitions and beliefs is vital because these become the interpretive frames for understanding the client situation. These frameworks filter and organize the client information and then guide the worker intervention and response. There are several systems of thinking that influence the interpretation of situations. Some systems include:

- *Meaning systems.* Systems of assigning meaning to statements, words, events, and situations. These are often based on past experiences with similar situations or past understandings of what situations/events meant.
- *Attribution systems.* Systems of assigning responsibility or control within situations. Often this is heavily influenced by past experience.
- *Interpretation systems.* Systems and frameworks for understanding and analyzing situations. Often values and beliefs (personal and cultural) surrounding definitions of right and wrong influence how a person interprets the situation.
- *Expectation systems.* Systems of thinking about what and how events should occur influence a person's reactions when situations either meet or disappoint expectations. This is also influenced by past experience, learning, and culture through the roles and other models that have existed in our development.

Without self-awareness of how beliefs and models of understanding are influencing their reactions, workers cannot truly understand the helping relationship. Responses to the client will consequently vary in their usefulness. For example, if a worker believes that arguing is "bad" and should be avoided, when members of a client system begin to argue, the worker might intervene to decrease the arguing. Although this might support the worker's beliefs about family life, it may not be useful for achieving the family service goals. However, if the worker is aware of these personal injunctions about arguing, it will be possible to control the impulse to stop the arguing and work with the family to bring an argument to fruition.

Concurrent with developing an awareness of their typical patterns of thinking and interpreting situations, workers need to be very aware of their feelings. Feelings are often automatic responses to situations. The automatic nature of feelings can easily communicate workers' reactions through their actions, interactions, or nonverbal communication. When clients see the feelings being transmitted, they are apt to interpret the worker's expression as a sign that they are doing something wrong. Clients may begin to edit their disclosures to spare the worker's feelings or avoid certain topics because they know the worker cannot handle the content areas.

For example, if a worker is dealing with a client in a very difficult situation, it is not unusual for the worker to feel helpless. The worker might be unaware of the feeling, feel pressured to do something to fix the situation, and may tell the client different things to try. Such a response is more effective in controlling the worker's feelings of hopelessness than in helping the client rectify the situation.

Self-awareness, however, can lead to the ability to reflect back feelings and allow the client to open up more. For example, a worker might say, "As you were talking, I found myself feeling overwhelmed and desperate to try anything to make things better even if it logically may not even work. Do you often feel this way?" This can lead to further exploration of the client's experience of the situation and eventually some help in understanding what can be influenced (and not influenced) in the situation.

TOWARD UNDERSTANDING YOUR RESPONSES

In trying to become aware of how you react to different situations, it is useful to explore the influences that underlie your response systems. Most of the events that influence your models of understanding come from life experiences and the cognitive constructions you use to make sense out of life. This often involves exploring how you have responded to, and made sense of, critical events and family history. Such exploration greatly increases your self-awareness.

The following sections provide an opportunity to explore your own life so you can begin to identify themes and patterns to monitor in your professional work. The exploration in this book is very brief and serves only as a beginning for your ongoing development. As you proceed with your professional career, it will be important to continue this work as new areas for understanding will frequently emerge in response to new client situations.

In guiding you through the brief self-exploration, three tools will be used to help you highlight patterns of thinking, feeling, acting, and interacting. The exploratory tools used in the next few sections are often used to explore client situations. As you use each of the tools, make note of your own experience of exploration. This experience will likely be somewhat similar to your client's experience during the assessment phase of intervention. The three tools used in this exploration include a genogram, a four-cell family model, and an eco-map.

The response systems are based on patterns of behavior developed in response to life events. We are all adaptive animals learning from life experiences and making sense out of life. Depending on our life experiences, we make sense out of life differently from others. In our most formative years, our life experience is dependent on our family and neighborhood. As we age, we integrate broader ranges of experience, but much of our response is still inherited from our families. To build self-awareness, we must concurrently build an understanding of how we have adapted to our family-based experiences.

The Genogram

A genogram is the first tool that you will use to make sense of your family experiences. The genogram was developed by Murray Bowen and has been broadly used in family-based practice (Marlin, 1989; McGoldrick, Gerson, & Shellenberger, 1999). There are many books that outline the use of genograms in practice. The following exercise will not provide a full exploration on how to use the genogram but will introduce you to the basics. In performing this exercise, first follow the instructions for constructing the basic genogram. After you have drawn your genogram, read the instructions for the family dynamics and document the dynamics on your genogram.

In the family genogram, circles represent females and squares represent males with their current age noted within the circle or square. Generational differences are indicated by vertical position with the parents (or even grandparents) on the top and offspring on lower lines. The lowest line in the genogram will be the youngest people in the family system you are assessing. Typically, the eldest offspring is on the left with a descending order based on age. The current family is always in the middle of the genogram with a dotted line around the family members. Multiple marriages or relationships are possible to draw. To depict such relationships draw lines between the adult and first partner. Then break the line and connect the next partner. Although this may sound complicated, the principles of drawing a genogram are fairly simple once you see how it is done.

In the genogram in Figure 1.1, you can see that both the current father and mother had prior marriages. One mother died (shown by an X) and the other mother had been divorced (shown by the slash breaking the line between the parent figures). The father in the current family had a son, who is now 18, with the female parent who died. The mother in the current family had twin girls who are 13 with her first husband. These girls are living in the current family, as shown by their inclusion in the dotted line. Children born from the current relationship (ages 9 and 6) are drawn with a line descending from the union line (the line connecting the two parents).

The genogram shown in Figure 1.1 is a two-generational genogram depicting parents and children. Often workers want to assess families using three-generational genograms, such as the one shown in Figure 1.2. Using the same principles, the three-generational genogram places the eldest family members on the top and the youngest on

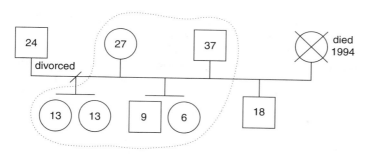

FIGURE 1.1   The Family Genogram

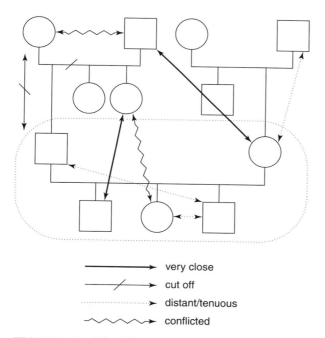

very close

cut off

distant/tenuous

conflicted

FIGURE 1.2   The Three-Generational Genogram

the bottom. The first (eldest) generation is represented by a third-generational line above the parents. This presents a bit of a challenge because the parents forming the current family system are also members of a sibling line. Typically, the children of the first generation who marry to form the next generation, are indicated by drawing them lower than the other siblings. A line can then be used to form the parent level of the next generation.

The relationships among the family members can also be depicted on the genogram using different types of lines, as shown in Figure 1.2. Typical relationship types included on a genogram are conflicted relationships, close relationships, distant or tenuous relationships, and cut off relationships (no longer talk to each other). Although many more types of relationships exist, these four are enough for the purposes of this example. If you want to include more, add more types of lines to the legend and use them in the genogram.

When using lines to show types of relationships, the direction of energy in the relationship is shown with arrowheads. If the feeling is mutual in the relationship, there are usually arrowheads on both ends of the line. If the feeling flows in only one direction, there is only one arrowhead (which points to the family member who receives the emotion). For example, if Person A was always angry with Person B but the feeling was not reciprocal, the arrowhead would point from Person A to Person B.

In Figure 1.2, the daughter in the current family has conflicts with an aunt on the father's side of the family. This same aunt has a very close relationship with the brother. The brother and sister have a distant or tenuous relationship. The father has a cut off relationship with his mother in which the emotional energy comes from him. The father's mother is divorced from his father and in a conflicted relationship with him. The mother has a very close relationship with her husband's father but her father is not close to her. The father seems to have a distant relationship with the youngest brother.

EXERCISE 1.1

Your Family Genogram

From the examples, it is clear that a genogram contains a depth of family information. It depicts who is in the family and how they get along with each other. To make sense out of your family, draw a genogram in the space provided. When drawing your parents, start with your father (or previous father figures) on the left and mother (or mother figures) on the right. Then draw in your brothers and sisters. After drawing the genogram, use the following types of lines to illustrate the relationships among the family members and use the arrows to indicate the direction of the relationships.

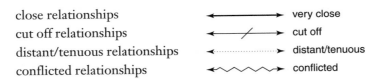

close relationships   ⟵——————⟶   very close
cut off relationships   ⟵——/——⟶   cut off
distant/tenuous relationships   ⟵·········⟶   distant/tenuous
conflicted relationships   ⟵∿∿∿⟶   conflicted

Your Family Dynamics. After completing your genogram, address the following dynamics about your family. You may want to make notes on the genogram to capture some of this information or just reflect mentally to ensure privacy. Make sure you address all questions and think about how these aspects of your family influence your action and processing systems.

1. *Support seeking.* You are entering a profession in which other people will be approaching you for support in many different ways. Sometimes, the methods clients will use to gain support are disguised and easy to miss if you have a predetermined belief regarding how people should ask for support. At other times, you may find that you have emotional reactions to a client's method of soliciting support from you. Both of these potential problems come from the historical models of support seeking you have developed through your family experience. Consequently, it is important to understand how people in your family achieved support. On the genogram you have drawn, make a dotted line (· · · · · · ·) between the people who tended to provide support to others and the people in the family that they tended to support. Look at the pattern of the dotted lines and think about the following questions. If you find any features of the support system that you think are important, write your observations in the margin of the genogram.

- *Identified support people.* Does the support tend to come from one or two sources? Are there any features of these people (e.g., sex, age, birth order) that might explain what the support system is based on? What do others do to activate these people in providing support?
- *Identified people receiving support.* Do some people in the family receive more support? What is it about these people (or the people not receiving support) that might explain this pattern?
- *Rules for whether or not one is worthy of support.* Do the people providing support place conditions on people such as expectations for how they should think or behave in order to receive support? What are the themes of these conditions that might operate as rules of standards?
- *Patterns of activating support.* How do people in the family activate the support-giving responses in others? Is it okay to directly ask others for help or do family members need to use indirect methods, such as being visibly helpless or increasing tension in the family (e.g., pouting or tantruming)?
- *Persistent unsolicited support.* Are there any family members who provide support even when others do not appear to want support? Are there patterns that might identify the rewards that the individual gets from this support giving? What is the impact of this support on others?

Based on the patterns of support giving in the family, identify some themes that might influence how you respond to clients. Perhaps there are experiences or modeling in your family that could cause you to be too abrupt when others seek support. There may be influences in some families that can cause a member to be too free with providing support. Do you find any such influences in your family?

2. *Influencing others.* All people in a family seek to influence others to assure that their needs are met. The strategies developed by family members to shape the responses of others often form a pattern or trend when a member wishes to influence people. Given that a component of your professional job will involve influencing the behaviors of others, it is important to be aware of the types of influence strategies that might be common to you. Look at the various members in your family genogram and try to determine the methods used by each to influence others. Some of the common influence strategies might include:

- *Logical argument.* Identify people in the family who believe that a person needs to be rational and logical and that these traits should guide behavior. How influential are these members of the family? Is this the primary source of influence?
- *Wearing down resistance.* There may be some people in the family who try to get their way via repeated requests, whining, pouting, or other "wear down" strategies. Identify these people on your genogram. How influential are they in the family? Are they the ones who get their way? How do you feel about the use of this strategy? Do you ever use this strategy?
- *Escalating tension.* Some people influence others by making them uncomfortable by expressing anger. Often people in a family use this type of strategy to control others. Sometimes people increase the volume of their voice, assume a condescending or angry tone, or become completely silent. Identify people in your family who use tension. Also identify how others respond them. How have you used tension to get your own way? How do you react when others use tension? Are there certain types of tension that you use more often? Are there certain types of tension that cause you to give in to others?
- *Induction of guilt.* Similar to tension, some family members may use guilt to influence the behavior of other people. Identify the people in the family who use guilt as a strategy of influence. Identify the people who are most susceptible to giving in when others use guilt. Think about how you use guilt in your relationships. Think also about how you respond when others use guilt to influence you. Do you give in? Does it make you feel things other than guilt?
- *Loss of approval.* Similar to guilt, some family members may use disappointment or disapproval to influence other people. In some families, loss of approval appears like a loss of love, while in others disapproval is more of a dirty look. How are approval and loss of approval expressed in your family? Identify the people who use this strategy. How do you respond when people express disapproval about what you are doing? How do you use disapproval to influence others?
- *Coercive sanctions.* In some families, coercion is used to gain compliance. At one extreme, this involves becoming violent or threatening harm. Spanking is one form of this strategy, but in more extreme cases, people may punch, kick, choke, throw things, grab, or push. If this has occurred in your family, identify the people who use this type of strategy. When this type of strategy is used, how do you react? How do you feel about the use of coercion? When you see people using this strategy, what do you want to do? In some families, there are more subtle coercive systems, such as being sent to bed, losing privileges, or grounding. How are these strategies

used in your family? How have you used different types of coercion in your life? What kinds of issues bring out a desire to use this type of strategy?

In reviewing the strategies of influence used in your life, identify types of clients that may evoke a strong response from you. Also identify reactions in yourself associated with the different types of strategies. How will you know when you are reacting to something? How will you know what you are reacting to if you find yourself using such strategies with a client? Spend some time developing a plan for monitoring and controlling your strategies of influence and reactions to people who may attempt to influence you.

EXERCISE 1.2

The Four-Cell Family Model

The second exploration strategy for developing self-awareness is to explore a four-cell model of understanding and responding that is inherited from one's family. The model uses four dimensions of development to explore your model of understanding. Each dimension is described in Figure 1.3. Read the descriptions and then use the blank form (Figure 1.4) to explore your own model. To help with this exploration, each cell will be described.

Cell 1—Genetic/Biological Influences.   This dimension explores the biological traits inherited from your parents. You most likely look similar to one of your parents. What are the similarities in the way you look? You also have inherited biologically based strengths and weaknesses such as learning abilities, physical abilities. Do these influence how you experience life? Did abilities make you proud or did aspects of ability create a different experience? The final type of inheritance is the manner of coping with pressure. What styles of coping might you have inherited? When completing this section, think about your similarities (physical attributes, abilities, and coping). Look at some of the inherited traits in Figure 1.3, and then list your inherited features in the square provided in Figure 1.4. After you have completed this, proceed to the square labeled "Environment."

Cell 2—Environmental Influences.   The environmental influence cell explores the immediate family and broader social environment that existed while you were growing up. As you think about environmental influences on your development, reflect on the questions and issues listed here. When you identify influences from your family or social environment, record them in the Environment cell of Figure 1.4.

Family Rules.   When thinking about the family environment, spend some time thinking about how rules were set. What were the formal rules? How about the informal rules (e.g., don't make Mom upset)? What rules resulted in the severest punishments? What rules were seldom enforced? Were the rules consistently enforced or did enforcement depend on people's moods? Could some people break rules and others not? Were there different rules for different people? Were the rules flexible and negotiable? What were

Genetics/Biology	Environment
• ability/disability • race • intelligence • attractiveness • temperament • neurological processing • parental identification • metabolism • aptitudes	**Family** • problem solving • alcohol/drug abuse • processing tension • self/other orientation • positivity/negativity • closeness/distance • violence/abuse • gender roles • autonomy/dependency • expressive/repressive • good/bad standards • culture/assimilation **Social** • oppression/privilege • discrimination/acceptance • ostracization/inclusion • economic options
Beliefs	**Behavior**
• tension values • similarity/difference values • gender values • self values • racial values • ability values • locus of control values • sex values • direct/indirect • standards of behavior • relational values • time values • cultural values	• affiliative responses • distaste of others • avoidance behavior and handling tension • side taking and triangulation • anger reactions and triggers • use of humor • reactivity and focus of fighting • ingratiating and validation seeking • discrimination (sex, age, ethnic, cultural, sexual orientation, economic, educational, attractiveness, able bodied, values) • acceptance/rejection patterns • flirting • performance expectations • punctuality/time beliefs • interpretation of behavior

FIGURE 1.3   Inherited Models of Understanding

the standards of behavior in the home? Did the standards change when other people were around? What were the standards about cleanliness, how you dressed, keeping commitments, how you talk to others, telling the truth, and punctuality? When people violated these standards, did the punishment cause anyone to lie to avoid volatile reactions? How might the rules and punishment systems influence your responses to clients who have different sets of rules from your family? How might the standards and rules of your family influence how you react to clients when they are late or when they come in dirty?

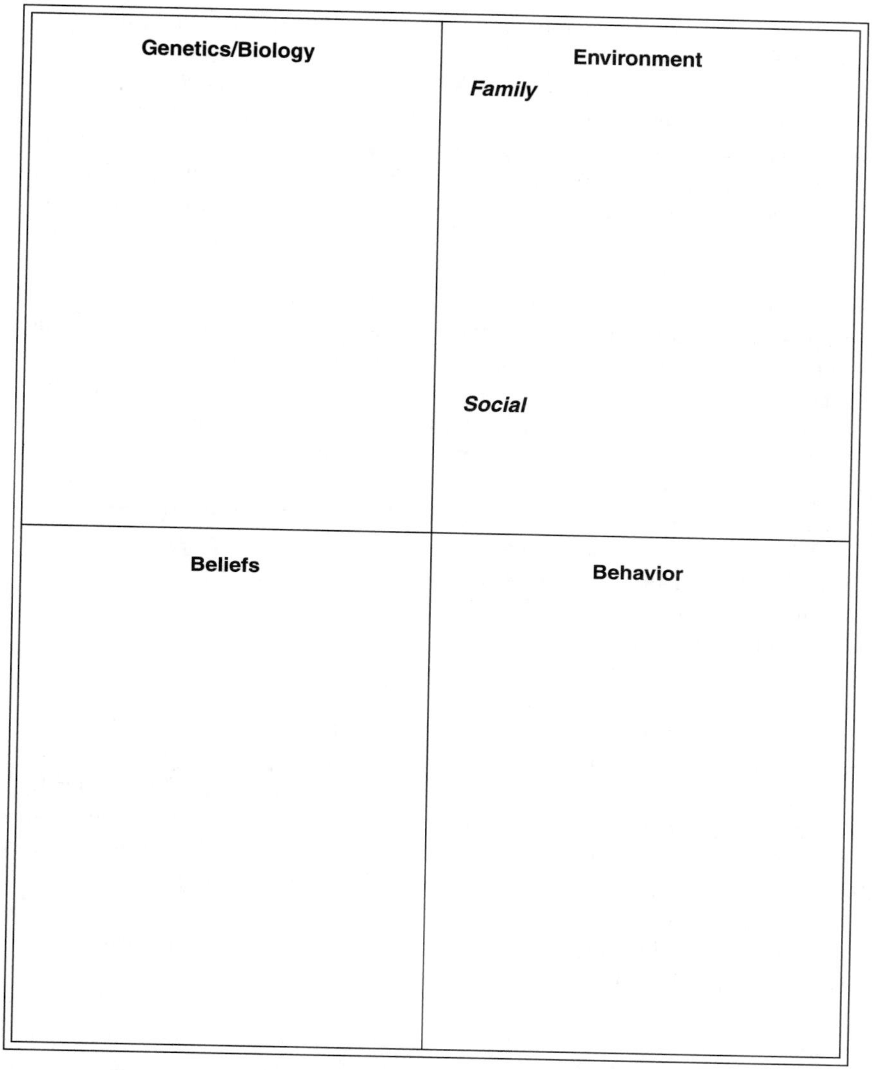

Genetics/Biology	Environment *Family* *Social*
Beliefs	Behavior

FIGURE 1.4   Family Model

Will such violations in rules cause you to think differently of them or make judgments about how rules are applied in their home?

Family Problem Solving.   Explore how problems were solved in your family. This includes the experience of differences and methods for solving difficulties. For example, did your parents fight or were problems hidden from the children? How were problems between parents and children resolved? How were problems raised in the family? Were problems openly discussed or did people hold them and later explode? Did people look for problems and pick at each other or did people avoid problems? How direct were people in confronting problems? Were there designated people who addressed or solved problems? Reflect on how the problem-solving systems in your family might influence how you work with clients who are struggling with problems. Will you want to take sides? Will you try to keep people from raising tension and avoid problems? If a client is upset or criticizes you, will you become defensive or will you be able to explore the situation with your client?

Emotional Expression.   Think about your family. How was emotion expressed among the family members? Were all emotions okay to express or were types of emotions hidden? Were feelings hidden or were they openly shared? Did this apply to all feelings? What about with the different people? Could you be open with everyone? Were there some people who you shared special feelings with and others you avoided? Were there people in the family who had trouble with certain emotions? Were difficult emotions such as inadequacy, powerlessness, hopelessness, and helplessness covered up with anger, or were people able to experience these feelings? Who supported the emotions of others in the family? Who supported emotions of others outside of the family? Based on your family system of expressing and supporting emotions, are there any emotions clients may express that could make you uncomfortable? Are there any reactions you might have that will interfere with the client relationship?

Family Roles.   Consider the roles that each family member played. Did the roles ever change or were people set in rigid roles? Were any roles burdensome for family members? Were there certain roles for people based on gender? Were there any roles associated with age or birth order? Did any roles conflict with others? Were the roles doable? Did some roles come with privileges? How did family members deal with the different privileges? Did some family members resent their roles? Were there competitions for roles with privileges? How did people get new roles? Were there any deviant roles that caused the family concerns (e.g., delinquent, troublemaker)? How did the deviant roles make other peoples' roles easier? Did any roles make other people look good because they did not have that particular role? Did some roles keep the family focused on individual problems rather than looking at how the family functioned? How might your roles in the family influence how you approach other families? How might your roles cause you to react when clients come in with different types of roles? Are there any roles, or ways that people approach roles, that cause you to be angry?

Relating to Others.   Think about the way people in your family related to each other. Did one family member make demands on others or was there equality? Were there expectations about how people can relate? Were people supposed to be loyal to family members and support them even when they disagreed? Were people free to disagree with each other? Did some members have more privileges or favors than others? Did people make demands on each other? What kinds of demands were made? What would happen to the relationship if one did not respond? Were there conditions placed on relationships requiring one to behave in certain ways to remain in the relationship? How did people influence each other (threats, tension, open communication, guilt, shame, or pouting)? How did you respond to these attempts to influence you? Did any influence strategies make you want to fight or give in? Did any make you second-guess yourself or need reassurance from others that you were all right? Given what you know about the relationship model of your family, how might the way people related affect how you relate to your clients? Are you apt to use guilt or shame? How comfortable will you be with clients who relate differently from your family? How will you react when clients start putting demands on you and your relationship with them?

Neighborhood. Identify nonfamily members who influenced what happened in your family. Were these people positive or negative influences? Who were the people influencing your family: extended kin, friends, neighbors, or professional types of people? When your family needed something (e.g., money, rides, baby-sitting) who were the most helpful people? How did the family keep favors balanced with these people? Which people knew exactly what was going on in the family? Did the family try to keep secrets? Could you trust the people living in your neighborhood or was there conflict? How did people talk about your family? Were you respected or did people tend to put you down for different things? What types of things brought you respect or disdain in the neighborhood? How safe was the neighborhood? If there was a lack of safety, did people in the neighborhood support each other to make it better? Who were the best supports? Given your neighborhood, how will you be able to understand the conditions that clients are living in? Can you see supports in difficult neighborhoods or will you be biased by the community problems?

Culture. Think about your culture and race and how these elements of you life fit into the larger society when you were growing up. All people, even the "dominant race," have race and cultural influences. These influences set a context for experience. What privilege or oppression did you notice resulting from your race, culture, or background (e.g., money, access to education, quality of life)? How did you make sense out of what you observed? Who helped you understand these elements of your life? When people of other cultures or races interacted with you, were there any barriers to understanding each other? Were you able to overcome these barriers? How did others react when you had relationships with people from different cultures, races, or backgrounds? What kinds of messages did you take in about your race/culture/background? What about other races, cultures, and backgrounds? What supports came as a result of membership in your race, culture, or background? How closely was your family involved with these systems of support? What values of right and wrong has your culture/background instilled in you? Do these values fit with the larger society values such as work ethic, democracy, competition, and equal opportunity? How might you respond to clients from different cultures, races, or backgrounds?

Institutions. Think about the societal institutions that influence the family (e.g., school, church, police, neighborhood organizations, social welfare institutions, economic institutions). What kind of relationship did these institutions have with your family? Did these institutions create stress or were they sources of support? Did people in your family feel judged by these institutions? Did people in your family feel like the institutions were fair or did they favor people who where not in the family? How did your family make sense out of the way people were treated by the institutions? Were relationships good with some institutions and not with others? Which were helpful and which hurtful? What kinds of things did parents say about the different organizations and institutions? How might these positions influence your reactions when you have to interact with these institutions and organizations as a professional? How might these experiences influence how you respond to clients who are having difficulty with different institutions?

After reflecting on these questions, make some notes in the Environment cell in Figure 1.4 that reflect some of the critical influences on your development.

Cell 3—Beliefs and Cognitive Influences.
Using the entries in the first two cells, think about how you have made sense out of your life. The experiences that you have had in your family and in your larger social environment have resulted in a framework of beliefs and cognitive structures through which you interpret and respond to situations. Reflect on some of the thoughts you experienced when filling out the first two cells. In the Beliefs cell in Figure 1.4, make some brief notes about the following types of beliefs.

Rules. What are the rules you developed to guide your own actions? What are the things that you feel you need to do in your day-to-day life? What are the things that you consider doing and what would you never consider doing? How rigid are these rules? How would it affect you if you violated these rules? Who in your life would be most affected? How do these affect your standards of punctuality, cleanliness, appearance, maintaining commitments, and so on? What would it mean about you if you could not maintain these types of rules? How important is it that other people maintain these types of rules and standards? What violations would cause you to end relationships with others? What rules form your creed for your own behavior? What feelings might you have if your clients held different rules/values from you? What rules may make you want to change clients who are different from you? Record the most important rules in the Beliefs section of Figure 1.4.

Self-Conceptions. What beliefs did you develop about yourself? Did you end up feeling good about yourself or were there events that created beliefs that there was something wrong with you? Do you feel that you should be better? How pervasive is this belief? Do you often feel that you must defend yourself or prove to others that you are all right? When you observe yourself to judge your actions, whose eyes or perceptions do you use to observe yourself? Are these people who are friendly or critical? Do you find you need other people to keep saying good things about you? If people criticize you, does it cause you to feel bad or forget your good points? When people tell you something about themselves, does it sometimes feel that they are making a statement about you? How might these traits cause you to respond if a client did not like you or something you did? How might these traits cause you to feel if you have been working hard to help several clients and things didn't improve? Will you feel some pressure to make things happen so you can feel effective? When clients don't feel good about themselves, will you try to talk them into feeling better or can you explore their feelings with them? How would you finish the sentence "There is something about me that . . . "? In the Beliefs section of Figure 1.4, write down a couple of words capturing the central features about yourself (e.g., "need approval" "set own path").

Relating to Others.   Based on your history, think about what you believe about other people. Are other people safe or must you be careful about trusting others? Is this belief extended to all others or are there differences? When considering these beliefs, are their differences according to gender, age, race, sexual orientation, or economics (e.g., Are all rich people selfish? Are welfare mothers different . . . how?). Can you trust others to do what they say or do you have to check up on them? Can you trust others to respect you, or do you have to analyze what people might mean by what they say (or don't say)? Do you feel others judge you harshly or want to bring you down? In the Beliefs section of Figure 1.4, write down a couple of brief phrases to capture your central beliefs about other people and relationships.

Problem Solving.   Consider your beliefs about problem solving based on your life experience. Is it good to identify problems or should you leave things alone? Is it important to identify every problem or are some more important? If there are priorities, what are the most important problems? When you raise problems, how are others likely to respond? Is there a right and wrong way to raise problems? When one raises problems, it creates tension. Is tension a good thing or should it be avoided? How strong is this belief? What might happen when problems arise? How do your mistakes affect you? When others disagree with you, what happens inside you? When the situation is tense, what happens to you inside and what does it mean about you? What feelings are evoked when you prefer one solution to a problem but people select a different solution? How is power used in problem solving? Is it okay to use threats and coercive strategies if the outcome is good? When should a person give in?

In your career, you will constantly engage in problem solving. What are the beliefs about tension and problems that might interfere with your work? In the Beliefs section of Figure 1.4, write a couple of brief words or phrases that can capture your important beliefs about tension and problem solving (e.g., "tension is bad," "a problem means someone screwed up," or "should not avoid problems").

Emotional Expression.   Spend a few minutes reflecting on what you learned from your family about emotions and the expression of emotions. Are there certain emotions that were avoided? Are certain emotions more important than others? Which emotions should be attended to first? What emotions are all right to express? When is it right to express emotions? When is it wise to keep emotions in? What are the acceptable methods for dealing with emotions? To whom should one express emotion? How can emotions be used to influence others? When is it okay to use emotions this way? When someone expresses sad or vulnerable emotions, what does that mean about that person? When someone expresses angry emotions, what does that mean about the person? What does it mean when someone is always expressing emotion? How much control should people have over their emotions? What emotional expressions might cause you to immediately act to make things better? What emotional expressions might cause you to want to withdraw from the other person? What emotions might cause you to react impulsively rather than in a thoughtful manner? In the Beliefs section of Figure 1.4, write down one or two words that capture the important beliefs you have about emotional expression.

Role Beliefs.   Reflect for a minute about the roles of the people in your family. What roles seem to be appropriate for different people? Are some roles more appropriate for men or women? What roles do you believe are important for a family to function? What roles might destroy a family if they are not there? Who should fulfill the caregiving roles? How do you know the roles are being properly filled? Who should fill the discipline roles? How do you know the person is doing a good job? Who should explain issues of right and wrong? How important is that role? Are roles that sacrifice the needs of one person for the good of the family all right? How do issues of age and gender fit into such roles? Which roles should come with power? How much power is too much? What kinds of power should come with different roles? How traditional are the roles you feel are important? What are the untraditional beliefs you support? What are the limits when you stop supporting untraditional roles? How might you react when working with clients who support vastly different role structures than the ones that you support? What role beliefs will make you want to try to change the other person? Write a couple of words in the Beliefs section of Figure 1.4 capturing your beliefs about roles and role structures.

Cell 4—Behavior.   Behavior is most often supported by a belief that validates and rationalizes the behavior (Ellis, 1996; Meichenbaum, 1997). To understand how your behaviors and beliefs operate together, look at the beliefs listed in the preceding cell. Spend some time considering how each word and phrase that you wrote into the cell influences your behavior.

Rules.   Look at the rules and values you wrote in the Beliefs cell. In the Behavior cell, write the behaviors that came from those beliefs and values. How much do the behaviors reflect your personality and the things you have learned through your life? How rigidly do you follow the rules? Take a minute and reflect on how these behaviors could be interpreted negatively by clients who live by a different set of rules. Write the behaviors that are most strongly influenced by your values and rules in the Behavior cell of Figure 1.4.

Self-Conception.   Review the words and phrases that capture your self-concept. How are your self-concept traits expressed in how you act with people? What are the actions you take to make yourself feel that you are all right? When others don't like you, how do you respond? Do you need to be liked and seek people out who might like you? Are you prone to defensive reactions with others? How might a client interpret your actions? Write the behaviors associated with your self-concept needs in the Behavior cell of Figure 1.4.

Relating to Others.   Review your comments and thoughts about relationships and other people. How do these beliefs influence how you approach other people? Do you keep control in the interactions or do you allow others to control the flow? Are you very direct or somewhat indirect in your interactions? Do you trust immediately or do people have to prove themselves to you? Do you look for strengths or is your radar tuned for problems? How consistent are your traits in relating to others? How might these ways of approaching others interfere with a helping relationship? In the Behavior cell of Figure 1.4, write the words or phrases that best describe your approach to relationships.

Problem Solving.   In the area of problem solving and tension, consider the following issues. How do you act around interpersonal tension? How do you approach problems? Do you immediately open up issues or keep things inside? How do you handle confronting others? How do you handle being confronted by others? How do you assign responsibility when approaching a problem? How might this interfere with developing a helping relationship? Write the words or phrases that best describe your approach to problem solving in the Behavior cell of Figure 1.4.

Emotional Expression.   After reviewing the statements you made regarding emotional expression, reflect for a minute on how you handle emotions. How controlled are you over your emotional expression? Do you express emotions easily or is it hard to identify and express emotion? Do emotions tend to control your thinking and actions? What emotions tend to influence your actions most? What emotions do you have control over? When certain emotions arise, do they trouble you? How do you respond to others who frequently express emotion? Do you try to fix things or withdraw from them? Do you ever get so wrapped up in another person's emotional problems that you stop taking care of your own responsibilities? How might your methods of dealing with your emotions interfere with a helping relationship? Could some of your responses interfere with people expressing their feelings? Write the words or phrases that best describe your central tendencies in dealing with emotions in the Behavior cell of Figure 1.4.

Roles.   Think about the beliefs that you listed about different roles. Spend some time reflecting on how your beliefs translate into behavior. Do you subscribe to traditional behaviors or tend to resist traditional expectations? How prominent is this reaction with you? Does your behavior broadcast your beliefs or is the influence more subtle? How do your beliefs affect your behavior with people ascribing to different role beliefs? Do you immediately challenge the person or do you tend to withdraw from such people? What happens when the differences are extreme? Might these types of reactions interfere with your ability to help certain clients? Write the behaviors that best express your beliefs in the Behavior cell of Figure 1.4.

Translating Your Personal Style into Professional Relationships.   After reviewing your family endowments, personal history, beliefs, and behaviors, spend time reflecting on the nature of the work for which you are training. If you found that your model has major areas that might interfere with serving clients, you may want to talk with your advisor and explore actions that can mediate the influence of your model. It is not unusual for people coming into the helping professions to have experiences and models that may interfere with the helping relationship. However, when models might interfere, it is important to develop systems to increase your ability to be in control of the effects of your model. As you read the other chapters in this part, you will discover guidelines for increasing your conscious control of what you do in the helping relationship. Begin monitoring your model and response systems now, so you can assess whether or not you might need additional support in controlling your model influences. If you think you might require additional support, discuss your concerns with an advisor in your educational program.

DEALING WITH PRESENT PRESSURES

Concurrent with developing an awareness of how you innately process and respond to situations, it is also important to understand how you operate at the current time. Methods of processing and corresponding actions change with different emotions. Emotions are strongly related to current life events and demands. If you are under high levels of stress, it is not unusual to revert to difficult or dependent coping methods. These are typically the coping methods used during early development. Given the relationship between current situations and coping, it is logical that you can monitor current events as an entry point to self-awareness. By knowing which situations are stressful, you can consciously tune into the thinking and behavior patterns, ensuring that the situation is not taking control of your responses.

EXERCISE 1.3

The Eco-Map

Taking stock of the sources of pressure and support in the environment can help a person tune into the current situation. An eco-map provides a visual image of the pressure points and supports in the current situation (Hartman, 1978). The final self-awareness exploration in this chapter involves using an eco-map to assess the relationships between you and the systems in your life.

Complete the eco-map in Figure 1.5, drawing a genogram of yourself in your current family situation in the large center circle. After the genogram is complete, use the legend to select relationship lines to connect the different systems to the people in the center circle. Use the full range of symbols to clearly document the positive/negative aspects of the relationships and the level of energy exchanged between you and the other systems.

Some of the circles on the eco-map in Figure 1.5 are empty so you can write in additional names of the people in each system who provide support or stress. Also, some labeled circles are provided to indicate typical sources of stress or support. You may have mixed relationships with a system, one supportive and one stress producing. In such situations, draw two lines to the circle, each line indicating whether it is a source of support or stress. When drawing the lines, use arrowheads indicating the flow of energy. For example, school may be a stressful relationship due to the demands placed on you. Given that the energy flow is typically from you to the school, the arrowhead would point from you to the school. However, if you were fighting with a professor or the department, the energy flow might go in both directions.

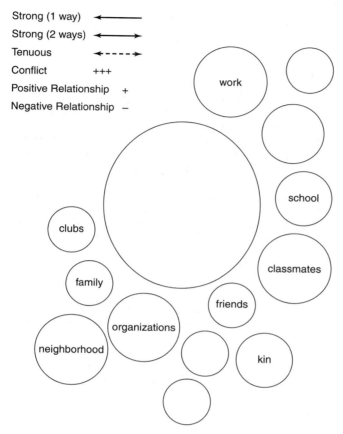

FIGURE 1.5   The Eco-Map

After you finish documenting the sources of stress and support in your environment, look at the final picture and assess whether your support systems are adequate to sustain you over the semester. If you conclude the supports are not sufficient, you may want to build some new supportive relationships. Student groups, peers in the program, and your departmental advisor are all sources of support.

Take time to consider the eco-map in concert with the information gleaned through the inherited family model and the genograms. Reflect on the influence that past models and relationships have on your responses to different situations. Are any of the pressures causing you to want to act or say things? Also think of the pressures influencing your feelings and beliefs. Think about your family relationships and models and how they have influenced your systems of support and your interaction with the stress-producing systems. Write notes on the eco-map about your understandings so you can use this information later in your career.

Critical Chapter Themes

1. It is critical for helping professionals to be very aware of themselves. Such awareness provides (1) a source of personal power; (2) awareness of differences; (3) insight into one's reactions; and (4) a source of emotional connection.
2. Self-awareness needs to focus on all four response systems to be fully aware of how one responds to situations (action, interaction, thinking, and feeling).
3. One's responses in all four systems of responding are heavily influenced by one's personal history. Models of understanding, interpreting, avoiding, and behaving evolve through one's adaptations to early family and community situations. One must understand past adaptations to be able to develop full self-awareness.
4. Using a genogram can help understand the patterns (action and processing) of support seeking and influencing others that one developed through family exposure. These are critical areas of awareness because helping professionals will always be dealing with support seeking and influence dynamics. The genogram also provides a tool for assessing client family patterns.
5. Using a four-cell model for assessing family influences can provide insights into the biological, environmental, cognitive, and behavioral influences that one has gleaned from family and community sources. Typically, models of thinking and interpretation will lead to behavior patterns. Knowing how one interprets and behaves is important in understanding one's responses. The four-cell model also provides a framework for conducting client assessments.
6. Using an eco-map provides one with insights into the pressures and supports in one's current situation. Considering the stress points and sources of supports allows one to see how environmental factors are influencing one's response to events. The eco-map is also a tool that can be used in assessing client situations.

RECOMMENDED READINGS

Marlin, E. (1989). *Genograms: The new tool for exploring the personality, career, and love patterns you inherit.* Chicago: Contemporary Books.

Rothman, J. C. (1999). *Self-awareness workbook for social workers.* Boston: Allyn & Bacon.

Waldron, H. B., Turner, C. W., Barton, C., Alexander, J. F., & Cline, V. B. (1997). Therapist defensiveness and marital therapy process and outcome. *American Journal of Family Therapy, 25,* 233–243.

CHAPTER

2

Conscious Self-Control and Ethical Behavior

As workers become aware of the models of interpretation and possible difficulties in the helping relationship, it is important to find methods of controlling the potential interference. Such control comes partially through the worker's efforts at self-awareness and understanding. To help workers refine their self-control, professions develop guidelines through value sets and codes of ethics.

Professional values, ethics, and legal rules all work together to provide direction for the worker. Values provide abstract goals or philosophies that influence the response systems of the worker. The abstract nature of values influences both action and processing systems. Ethics evolve from the values, providing principles that guide the worker's action systems. In addition to considering values and ethical principles, the professional must also attend to legal imperatives. The legal rules may relate to the values and ethics; however, they can result in civil or criminal action against the worker if the rule is violated.

THE ROLE OF PROFESSIONAL VALUES

In conjunction with thinking skills and self-awareness, professional helpers must establish professional self-control to maintain an effective practice (Johnson, 1997; Murphy & Dillon, 1998). Professional values and ethical guidelines are established to guide workers in developing this control. Through adhering to values and ethics, each worker establishes a range of behavior ensuring they maintain the client interest as central in professional activities. Although values and ethics are discussed in other courses and texts, the link to self-control makes them vital in skill development.

The social work value base has a long and integral history with the profession. Historically, there have been three important values guiding the social work profession. These values were an integral aspect of the founding of social work and have shaped the identity of the profession. The three core values are:

1. Relatedness and Mutual Responsibility
2. Self-Worth, Competence, and Dignity of the Person
3. Self-Directedness and Self-Determination

These values guide professional decision making and action. As such, they must be present at all times when workers respond to client situations. To integrate the values, workers build on their self-awareness by assessing how their values coincide with the social work value base. Any beliefs or behaviors that might not fit well with the professional values need to be adjusted so personal values and processing systems never interfere with professional activities.

Relatedness: Considering the Person-in-Environment

The value of relatedness maintains that people cannot be separated from their social context. All humans need to be understood within their life circumstances. Such understanding allows change efforts to be realistic and appropriate. If workers miss the context, they might blame their clients for things outside of their control. If workers consider problems occurring at the interface between the person and environment, intervention can be more appropriately targeted. Intervention may be directed at the individual, the environment, or at the interface between the two. Regardless of the ultimate direction, all three must be considered to accurately understand the client situation.

Inherent in the principle of relatedness, people and their environments are considered interdependent. This suggests that one needs the other to maintain the current system (e.g., the powerful need the subservient, parents need children, etc.). Through the interdependence, societies have common needs that should be considered basic rights for all. Given that these common needs are basic rights, society has a responsibility to assure these needs are met for all members of the society. Social work by its very nature is concerned with these common societal needs (Watt & Kallman, 1998).

Self-Worth, Competence, and Dignity of the Client: Maximizing Mastery and Strengths

The value of self-worth and dignity focuses on the uniqueness of the individual. Every person must be considered an individual rather than categorized or labeled. The individual becomes the primary concern for the worker regardless of classifications, problems, or larger issues. Although this value sounds very easy on the surface, it is often tested.

In situations such as domestic violence and child abuse, workers are tested when they must work with the people who violate others. In such situations, workers must constantly orient themselves to the worth of the individual to be able to provide quality service. If they cannot find this link to the worth of the other, anger toward the person may interfere with the quality of service.

Working with the self-worth of a client is a sensitive issue. Different clients will have different types of self-worth. Some receive their worth from outside of themselves and some find their sense of worth internally. Consider the following types of self-worth:

1. externalized self-worth (e.g., "If they say I'm good, I'm good")
2. social comparisons (e.g., "If he is bad, then I am good")
3. self-attributions (e.g., "I am a good athlete, therefore I'm good")
4. drawing on multiple traits to balance out negative elements (e.g., "I am not good at sports, but I am a great artist")

In working with different types of self-worth, the worker often prompts clients to have control over their own sense of worth. The worker identifies positive client traits, helps clients identify these strengths, and expresses confidence in their strengths. Ultimately, workers must make efforts to help individuals maintain control for their sense of self-worth rather than be dependent on the worker. This involves helping them to make their own decisions and take their own actions to increase self-efficacy.

Competence principles imply that all people have areas of competence they use in response to situations. Consequently, their efforts and actions are all adaptive. The worker must help clients achieve their highest level of functioning by building on their competencies. This is a primary concern for society, because if members are not able to, or are prevented from, achieving their highest level of competence, the functioning of the entire social system is compromised.

Given that competence comes from the inherent strengths in the individual, these strengths must be built upon to help clients overcome the challenges present in their lives. As such, workers must consider all individuals as expert in their own lives and competent to define their own struggles. The social worker joins with the clients in these struggles and enhances their competencies. As the clients begin to realize their inherent potentials, their competencies become equal to the environmental challenges.

Although easy to grasp as a value, the principle of competency is challenging in practice. The term *competency* can mean different things to different people. In human service professions, competency is assumed. Even with clients who have physical or mental disabilities, competency is assumed unless there has been a hearing that determines the person is not competent to make independent decisions (Hall & Jugovic, 1997). However, in the legal professions, competency is not assumed. A person is actually considered incompetent under the law until competency is established (Hall & Jugovic, 1997).

Given the different systems of determining competency, workers must be clear when dealing with different populations. Competency challenges may occur when working with children, adolescents, the elderly, and the disabled (Croxton, Churchill, & Fellin, 1988; Schmidt, 1988). Consequently, workers must know the competency laws that may impinge on this principle (Croxton, Churchill, & Felling, 1988; Hall & Jugovic, 1997; Schmidt, 1987).

Self-Determination: Empowering the Client

Self-determination builds on competence and self-esteem principles through allowing clients to make their own decisions and be expert on their own lives. Through self-determination, empowerment and growth occur. As such, social workers collaborate with the client rather than treat them. Collaboration infers that clients enter the helping relationship in an informed and equal manner (Corey & Herlihy, 1996). The collaborative relationship is different from treatment because treatment implies that the client is sick. Such conceptualizations disempower through labeling the client and implying exceptional power in the worker. Inherent in self-determination, the client's values and needs dictate the direction and extent of help.

The principle of self-determination is often a difficult value to maintain. Many elements of practice can challenge the worker in applying this principle. For example, there are pressures to remove the choice from the client through managed-care decisions (Clark, 1998; Watt & Kallmann, 1998) and empirically driven intervention protocols (Raw, 1998). Self-determination is further threatened by paternalistic approaches to service, social pressures, group decision making, and a lack of client awareness (Davitt & Kaye, 1996; Dolgoff & Skolnik, 1996; Stein, 1990). Finally, self-determination is curtailed by the decision being made. Determination is limited when the client wants to make a life or death decision, when competency is in question or when the decision may harm others (Clark, 1998; Wesley, 1996).

The principles contained in the professional values have direct implications for the worker's response systems. It is important as workers develop, that they continue to build an awareness of their responses. As this awareness increases, they need to examine their values and responses to determine how well the responses reflect professional values. Table 2.1 depicts the implications of each value principle for the worker's response systems.

THE IMPORTANCE OF PROFESSIONAL ETHICS

Although professional values provide general principles of professional activity, a clearer set of behavioral guidelines is needed. Professional ethics provide clear and concrete guidelines for professional behavior (Corey, Corey, & Callanan, 1998; Jackson, 1998; Murphy & Dillon, 1998). Ethics operationalize professional values with specific prescriptions for behaviors that are encouraged and prohibited. Most ethical guidelines focus on the worker's action systems through limiting the types of actions and interactions that may occur in the professional relationship. Such guidelines are developed primarily to protect the client from unethical workers. This is the most serious function of ethical guidelines and breaches could result in professional sanctions.

Ethical guidelines, in addition to client–worker relationships, govern inter-professional relationships, interactions in places of employment, and the advancement of the profession. Some codes of ethics also outline the professional role in challenging social patterns of oppression and abuse (Murphy & Dillon, 1998).

The range of ethical standards emanates from the centrality of the client in professional relationships and extends to agency and social situations. There is an expectation that ethical behavior be consistent in all situations. Social workers are consequently expected to display their values in all areas of living. To help understand how ethical principles operate in shaping behavior across the range of professional activity, review the code of ethics (see Appendix) to see how the specific domains yield concrete prescriptions for behavior. Codes of ethics from other professional associations can typically be purchased for a nominal fee.

Client-Focused Actions

One of the important ethical principles is the primacy of client interest (Corey, Corey, & Schneider, 1998), which insists that workers should keep all of their activities focused on achieving their clients' well being. Inherent in this injunction, workers need to avoid

TABLE 2.1   Social Work Value Implications for Worker Response Systems

	Action	Interaction	Thinking	Feeling
Relatedness	• Intervention directed not just at the client but also the environment and social systems • Target linkages between the client and other systems in change efforts	• Explore the social context for client problems • Expand the sphere of intervention by including other people and systems	• Think of problems within client's social context • Understand the multiple influences inherent in the client situation	• Sensitize oneself to the life situation of the clients
Competence	• Identify and use the strengths of the client system • Avoid taking over problems or doing things for people who can do for themselves	• Keep client strengths focal in the interaction so they can be used • Help clients identify their strengths and competencies	• Identify the adaptive elements in client situations • Think about how the adaptive behaviors can be used to achieve goals	• Maintain faith in the client's strengths and abilities
Self-Worth	• Efforts should be made to promote the dignity of the client in all actions and service systems • Advocate against any systems or procedures that compromise the dignity and self-worth of the client system	• Validate the worth of the client system • Avoid statements, judgments, or framing situations in a way that might undermine the self-worth of the client	• The worker must be able to identify strengths and adaptive elements that can be reflected back to the client in order to promote self-worth • Workers need to refrain from understandings of the client situation that undermine client self-worth	• Find elements of the client that they can like and begin to celebrate with the client
Self-Directedness	• Avoid taking action not endorsed by the client • Restrain impulses to take over the client's decisions	• Avoid telling clients what to do • Help clients identify options that they can then explore and select	• Identify options and choices for clients within their situation • Help clients find definitions of situations that allow for options and self-direction	• Control the desire to see the client do what the worker believes is best • Separate feelings of self-worth from the client outcomes so they can allow clients to make their own decisions

putting self-interest, career advancement, other relationships, and politics above the interests of the client. Specific guidelines focus on, but are not limited to, the following:

- *Self-determination.* Clients must never be coerced, threatened, cajoled, or otherwise pressured to take an action against their will. Clients should control the goals, direction, and procedures used in the provision of service.
- *Client rights.* Clients have a clearly stated set of rights including such things as:
  - a right to appeal decisions
  - a right to request a different worker
  - a right to effective, efficient, and accessible service
  - a right to nonintrusion
  - a right to respect
  Any violation of these rights constitutes unethical behavior by a worker.
- *Competence.* Workers are expected to provide the most competent service possible. This requires workers to continually increase their levels of competence through training, professional development, supervision, consultation/feedback, and continued reading of professional literature.
- *Privacy.* There is a client right to privacy that insists that areas of the client's life that are not related to the goals of intervention remain private. It is important to always keep the reasons for service in mind and refrain from asking questions about unrelated areas of the client's life.

Actions with Other Professionals and Systems

Workers are in constant contact with other professionals as part of serving clients. Consequently, there are ethical guidelines to govern the manner in which the worker relates to other professionals. These guidelines serve to keep the client interest primary in such interactions and also serve to maintain professional integrity within the service system. Some of the principles focused on interprofessional functioning include:

- *Maintaining high standards of personal conduct on the job.* Workers are expected to conduct themselves professionally at all times. They are to remain sober and appropriately behaved (e.g., no outbursts of anger, listening to others, direct communication vs. slander).
- *Maintaining confidentiality.* Workers are not to talk about their clients in an identifiable way without written and informed consent. Furthermore, in situations in which the worker discusses problem dynamics that allude to client information (e.g., discussing experiences in class discussions, training events), the worker must make sure the information shared does not cause the client to be identified.
- *Relate to colleague's clients with full professional comportment.* When interacting with clients of other workers, workers must assure their personal conduct is appropriate for their professional role. All clients of the service system deserve the full respect and appropriate responses of every worker in the system.

- *Community service.* Workers are expected to make their services available to the public. Even workers in private practice should make allowances so all people can access their services. Concurrently, workers are expected to live up to a commitment to make the community a better place for clients and nonclients.
- *Respect, fairness, and courtesy.* In working with others within the service system, workers are expected to treat colleagues with respect and fairness. Interactions containing slander, innuendo, and casting of suspicion are indications of unethical practice.
- *Maintain commitments to employing organizations.* Workers are expected to live by their commitments to attend work and abide by the conditions of employment. This includes such things as following the job description, honoring their contract, coming to work, completing documentation, and working while on the job.

Actions in Other Professional Domains

Workers are expected to contribute to the profession and advance the credibility of their profession. Worker contributions begin with assuring their highest level of competence in serving clients. Beyond service, workers should share their best practice principles, strategies, and knowledge with other professionals. This professional function is often inherent in professional associations and their annual conferences. Sharing at such events advances both the worker and the profession. Specific principles assumed in this area of ethics include:

- *Scholarship and research.* Workers are expected to contribute to the professional knowledge base through the unbiased documentation of client needs and service outcomes. Findings should be made public, allowing others to review and learn from such contributions.
- *Maintain the integrity of the profession.* Workers are expected to visibly follow professional values, ethics, knowledge, and missions. They are expected to take pride in the professional realms of competence and openly identify themselves as members of the profession.
- *Promote the general welfare of society.* Workers are expected to challenge the social conditions that maintain oppression and social-group vulnerabilities. Workers must be informed about social conditions and be able to contribute to societal improvement.

LEGALLY MANDATED ASSUMPTIONS AND DUTIES

Some ethical principles and values are enshrined in law as legal duties. Just as violations of the code of ethics can result in professional sanctions, violations of the following assumptions and duties can result in legal sanctions. For the purpose of clarity, this section will explore legally binding issues that pertain to the professional role. The discussion of legal issues will be followed by a description of some of the legal duties accompanying the professional role.

Legal Issues and Legislated Client Rights

There are several assumptions that are inherent in the provision of professional service. The fact that a worker is paid to provide a service in a professional setting should guarantee that assumptions are met. If a worker does not meet these assumptions, clients harmed by the worker's action (or inaction) could claim for damages. Some assumptions focus on the service quality, and others cover worker–client treatment in the professional setting. All workers should be aware of these assumptions as well as legally binding assumptions associated with specific jobs. Often, it is important to read the legislation, policies, and procedures carefully to see how different assumptions are operationalized with settings and job functions.

The Assumption of Worker Competence.   When a worker is hired to provide professional service, there is *a good faith assumption of competence.* This means clients should be able to assume a worker is able to provide client services as promised by the agency (Reamer, 1998). The client should also be able to assume that intervention will be delivered in an efficient and effective manner (Corcoran, 1998; Thyer & Myers, 1998). Workers must keep abreast of the literature and upgrade their training (Raw, 1998; Thyer & Myers, 1998). If a worker or agency promises to provide some service that staff cannot provide, the agency can be held legally responsible.

The assumption of competence infers ethical behavior by the worker. A worker who behaves unethically cannot competently fulfill his or her professional function. If a worker maliciously or punitively refuses services or otherwise compromises the quality of service (e.g., is impaired, is malicious toward the client, is neglectful), the worker can be held legally responsible for client harm.

The Assumption of Informed Consent.   Clients must give fully informed consent for many worker activities. Informed consent infers that the expectations, activities, and parameters of service have been described and written consent has been solicited. Informed consent is needed for activities such as:

■ *Entering the helping relationship.* Without a legal mandate (e.g., child protective services, guardian consent), treatment or service cannot begin without the client's awareness and permission. The worker cannot use professional information (e.g., clinical assessment) without the client's awareness and permission. Workers also need to advise clients of what they can expect to happen as a result of entering service (Corey & Herlihy, 1996; Prout, DeMartino, & Prout, 1999). Most agencies formalize this information into a "plan of care" or "treatment contract."

■ *Sharing information* (Dickson, 1998; Okun, 1997). Aside from legal reporting requirements, which will be discussed shortly, workers cannot, without written permission, share client information beyond the immediate service team (Prout, De-Martino, & Prout, 1999; Isaacs & Stone, 1999). This injunction includes members of other teams, friends, family, and other professionals. Prior to sharing any information, the worker must discuss what information is to be shared, the reason for sharing the information, and when sharing will cease. Based on this discussion, the worker must obtain signed permission to share the information.

■ *Altering the agreed contract.* Workers become very skilled at noticing areas of client's lives that may cause them problems. It is not unusual for workers to attempt to fix these areas even if the client did not enter service with such intervention in mind. This change of direction is unethical and could result in legal or professional sanctions. Once a client has entered service and established a plan of care (treatment contract, service agreement, etc.), any change in direction must be agreed on by the client.

■ *Expectations and procedures.* Clients have a right to know what will be expected of them (what they will have to do) as they enter the helping relationship. This includes the duration, procedures, limitations, expectations, potential risks, and anticipated outcomes of service (Corey & Herlihy, 1996). Only through the provision of such information can clients make an informed decision about participating in service. Concurrently, clients have a right to know generally what will happen while in service.

■ *Intrusion into private space.* The nature of human service work is somewhat intrusive because workers routinely ask questions and explore private areas of people's lives. Intrusiveness must be limited by the agreements made by the client when entering service lest it result in legal or corrective action (Smith & Fitzpatrick, 1995). Furthermore, workers have no right to look in a client's car, purse, or any other personal area without client permission.

Like other assumptions, the assumption of informed consent has some challenges. The assumption of confidentiality is often a challenge when working with children and youth because of their minor status (Isaacs & Stone, 1999). Similar challenges exist with dependent populations such as the aged or disabled because the worker may have frequent contact with caregivers. Confidentiality is also at risk in computerized or team environments in which networks allow broader access to client information (Goodyear & Sinnett, 1984).

The Assumption of the Least Intrusive Intervention. As clients enter service, there is an assumption that they will receive the least intrusive (intensive or drastic) intervention. This means the worker must attempt lesser intrusive interventions before proceeding with disruptive services (e.g., institutionalization, removal, or medically intrusive interventions). This assumption was instrumental in the closing of many residential institutions during the 1960s and 1970s when this assumption was used as part of several class action lawsuits.

Legal Duties

Legal duties are more specific and directive than assumptions. With the preceding assumptions, there are assumed conditions of service. If the worker or agency does not live up to the assumptions, the client can initiate legal proceedings and claim damages. With duties, there are clear guidelines that specify how the worker must respond every time a certain situation arises. If the worker does not respond appropriately, society or a third party may take punitive action. There are two types of duties common to the professional field: the duty to report and the duty to warn.

Duty to Report.   A worker who is aware of, or suspects, that there is abuse, exploitation, or neglect of someone in a vulnerable position must report the abuse to the proper authorities. This always applies to the abuse of children and disabled people who are dependent on the system. In some states, it also applies to spousal abuse, elder abuse, and suicide. It is important to know the reporting expectations for your state or province as you enter the field. As previously described in the informed consent section, the reporting duties should also be described to clients as they enter service.

Duty to Warn.   If a worker is aware that a client may do harm to another individual, or the worker reasonably can predict (based on past behavior) someone will seriously harm another person, the worker is obligated to warn the potential victim so safety precautions can be implemented (Sonkin, 1986). There have been several lawsuits in the United States as a result of failure to warn. Mental health professionals have even been found liable for the traumas experienced by family members witnessing a death due to the worker's failure to warn the victim.

RESOLVING ETHICAL DILEMMAS: THE WEIGHTING OF OUTCOMES

It is clear from the preceding discussion that professional self-control is much more complex than simply being aware of one's feelings. There are legal and ethical considerations in many areas of practice requiring workers to continually acquire new knowledge about interventions, legislation, and legal outcomes to shape practice responses (Dickson, 1998).

The overlap in values, ethical principles, assumptions, and duties can become confusing. Such confusion often accompanies worker attempts to apply professional values and ethics to group settings, management systems, and different types of client populations (Hess & Hess, 1998; Northen, 1998). Workers often must make decisions between two or more courses of action and need some system for deciding which action is most ethical.

Ethical dilemmas and confusion are compounded by competing priorities within the profession. For example, there are differing opinions between empiricists who want workers to use only validated and tested interventions and others who believe that intervention evolves through the interaction between the worker and client (Thyer & Myers, 1998; Raw, 1998). Each of these polarized positions can take a value or ethical principle and enshrine the argument within an ethical stance.

For incoming professionals, ideological professional debates and multiple choices can confuse. Many professionals are currently proposing that professionals attempt to balance and unify the values and principles rather than approach them as competing entities (Banks, 1998; Dean, 1998; Herlihy & Remley, 1995; Raw, 1998).

In attempting to provide clarity, this section provides a system for resolving dilemmas in which two possible actions appear to involve conflicts between two ethical principles. Challenges are inevitable when one ethical principle comes into conflict or competition with another. Often the values and principles can provide some guidance. The duty to warn tends to override the assumption of informed consent and confidentiality. Given legal ramifications, it is easy to resolve the dilemma as one is not responsible for the decision.

There will be times when a worker must weigh different ethical principles when trying to decide which action to take with a case. The following weighting or prioritization system helps with this decision making. The weighting system has five levels of priority beginning with life-and-death issues and ending with subjective judgments of what might yield the best benefit for the client. The five levels are:

1. *Issues of life and death.* When situations have implications for life and death of any person, the worker must give this the highest possible priority regardless of other ethical considerations. Although maintaining the service relationship with a client is important, it falls under the maximum benefit (or fifth) category. As such, the relationship becomes a lesser priority to a higher priority issue. Most often situations covered in this category are considered legal duties that require the worker to warn and/or report that someone is at risk.

2. *Issues of abuse and violation.* Situations of abuse are ranked second because they can compromise safety and well being even if death is not an imminent risk. As in the first category, many of these situations will be covered under the legal duties and assumptions. However, there may be situations in which a worker must make an independent decision. If abuse occurs concurrent with other issues, workers should always prioritize issues of abuse over less damaging issues.

3. *Issues of rights.* The third tier of decision making focuses on violations of client rights. Such situations include many of the assumptions and civil rights previously described. Rights issues can be difficult to resolve because many dilemmas occur among different rights. For example, one worker might need to choose to violate a client confidence in order to report another worker who violated the client's right to competent service (e.g., refusing to see the client). Given the equal ranking of these rights, a worker cannot ethically make such a violation without permission from the client. If the situation included abuse or a risk of suicide, a violation of confidentiality would be warranted.

4. *Issues of restricted freedom.* The fourth level for decision making focuses on restriction and freedom. Workers will be confronted with situations in which they want to take action to help clients who are in oppressive situations in their personal relationships, living situations, or other situations. Workers must attend to the first three levels of consideration first. For example, a worker may work with an abused woman and want to talk to her boyfriend to try "straighten him out" or engage the couple in service. This, however, may put her in danger. Given the potential for danger, the worker must first attend to the first (life/death) and second (abuse) priorities before attempting to challenge the oppression of the woman. These levels would need to be explored and the woman would need to give permission before any contact with the partner would be appropriate.

5. *Issues of maximum benefit.* The fifth category in this system is the principle of maximum benefit. This weighting category asserts that when two alternatives of equal value are considered, workers should use a cost-benefit analysis. One should take the path of maximum gain with the least potential damage. Workers should do their job efficiently, with competence and appropriate consultation, and keep the client's best interests primary. This is a principle that is often violated by pressuring clients, speaking badly about clients, inappropriate closures of service, or taking more intrusive types of interventions than are warranted. A worker must be able to demonstrate that the chosen course of action will have the best potential for a positive, safe outcome.

Weighting Alternatives

To resolve an ethical dilemma, workers can use the five categories to consider alternative actions and decide a plan of action. When confronted with an ethical dilemma, proceed through five basic steps to resolve the dilemma.

1. Identify the options creating the dilemma.
2. Assess the critical information to determine the weighting category of each option.
3. Proceed with the option to resolve the risks associated with the highest weighted category.
4. Assess the ethical and service implications of the chosen direction.
5. Work with the client and other individuals impacted by the option to mitigate any potential problems associated with the action.

In reviewing these five steps, it is clear how the different levels of the weighting system work in conjunction with each other. The earlier steps find the appropriate weight to guide the decision, and then the worker assesses the ramifications of the decision. The worker can then assure the principle of least harm guides attention to possible reactions. The attention to multiple perspectives is an important part of resolving ethical dilemmas.

Although the final step in resolving the dilemma can only be explored at the theoretical level at this point, it is helpful to practice resolving practice dilemmas. The following few pages have exercises designed to allow you to explore different ethical dilemmas from practice. Complete the work sheets associated with each dilemma and practice walking through the steps of resolution.

EXERCISE 2.1

The Women's Shelter

You are a worker in a shelter for battered women. There is a young woman in the shelter who has described horrendous abuse. In her marriage, there was ongoing violence that often resulted in the need for medical care. She never reported the abuse to the police because her partner threatened to kill her. Just prior to admission, she had been held for three days by her husband at knifepoint and repeatedly raped. She escaped when he fell asleep.

Along with this young woman, you work with several other women at different stages of leaving or reconciling with their partners. You have just become aware of another young woman who left her abusive partner and began dating another man. They are thinking of living together, and she has approached the center requesting donated furniture and supplies for setting up the new apartment.

You discover that the woman setting up the new apartment is planning on moving in with the ex-partner of the first woman. The man has admitted to knowing the staff at the center but has presented himself as a volunteer who helped with fundraising. He even stated that he knows you but, due to ethical guidelines, you said nothing about him. The second young woman keeps informing you that he has told her to say "hi" for him when she comes in for meetings. You want to warn this woman, but you know he would sue or take some action against the agency. You are also concerned that furniture and supplies meant to help battered women are going to be given to a batterer.

1. Rank the following options on the weighting system: (a) warning the second woman by breaching confidentiality of the first woman, (b) saying nothing, and (c) withholding the furniture with no explanation.

2. Explore the ethical dilemma and outline the ethical principles keeping you from immediately warning this woman.

3. Using the weighting system, try to find a way to use ethical behavior guidelines to resolve the dilemma without violating any ethical guidelines.

EXERCISE 2.2

The Job Offer

You are graduating from a university and have focused your studies on treating perpetrators of domestic violence. You are well versed in the research literature and know that many anger-management programs are not successful using short-term intervention with a limited focus. You have just read reviewed research on many promising programs.

The literature you have been reading suggests that combined cognitive-behavioral and mutual aid strategies of group work should be combined for long-term results.

You have been interviewed for a job doing group work with batterers and impressed your interviewers with your knowledge of the field. The supervisor has just called to offer you the job. When you shared your thoughts about the best treatment based on the current research, the supervisor stopped you and explained the program. She stated that the agency offers an eight-week anger-management program to the men and that is the extent of the program. She further stated that the community is counting on the agency to do something about this pressing problem.

When you mentioned some of the research, she again stopped you and explained that the agency has been funded for the past two years to provide this service but, due to internal problems, has only offered three group series. She stated there was a waiting list due to worker turnover and a need to let the community see that the agency was doing something about the problem. Consequently, this program will run as is, and you will be videotaped to assure compliance with the program. You really want this job.

1. Using the code of ethics, what ethical principles are at risk of violation if you accept the job?

2. What would your ethical obligation be if you were to accept the job?

3. Using the weighting system, what would be the best course of ethical action?

EXERCISE 2.3

The Child Guidance Clinic Lunch Room

You work in a children's guidance clinic and were having lunch with some of the other staff members. A coworker came into the break room and began to tell people of a case that he was proud about. He described a case of a 14-year-old boy who came in expressing some sexual confusion. He had been turned off by girls and very interested in sexual contact with boys. The worker went on to describe that this boy was clearly gay, but that he had been able to "cure" him by convincing him that "these things develop slowly and he was really heterosexual." He spoke in great detail of how he had convinced this boy that he had not yet developed his interests in women that he will in the future. The boy was told to come back to explore these interests and develop the heterosexual side of his personality.

1. What ethical guidelines were violated in this case?

2. Using the code of ethics, what are your ethical obligations to the client, your coworker and the agency?

3. Using the weighting system, how would you proceed in this situation to resolve the ethical conflicts?

EXERCISE 2.4

The Case Flow Problem

You are a worker in a government-funded children's center. This center serves families and children mostly living well below the poverty line. You were hired into a position that had been vacant for about one year. The technology in the agency is clearly at the cutting edge. All note taking is computerized, appointments go into the computer, and reports are automatically generated. All computers are top-of-the-line, and there is one photocopier and laser printer for every ten staff. Furnishings are top notch with oak bookcases, desks, and nicely decorated meeting rooms. These supplies and equipment were purchased at the end of the year through surplus funds.

After a while, you notice that most positions in the agency are left vacant for at least one year before being filled. You also notice that many positions are never refilled and often become nonexistent after somebody leaves the agency. The work from the empty positions is redistributed to the other staff. To ease pressures, the agency has moved to a short-term treatment model in which families receive a maximum of six months of service. Treatment is guided by a clearly written contract outlining the goals and time frames. If families want more than six months of help, they have to formally apply for additional treatment.

1. Using the code of ethics, what are the ethical issues inherent in this agency system?

2. What are your ethical obligations to the agency, the profession, and the clients?

3. Given the ethical principles and weightings, what might you do about the ethical dilemma?

EXERCISE 2.5

The Street Kid

You are working in a center-city with street kids and homeless young adults. You have been serving a young, gay male who gets his spare money as a prostitute. He looks young and is able to make lots of money on the street. In his last conversation with you, he told you that he makes double the money when he agrees not to use a condom. Apparently, the men purchasing his services prefer skin-to-skin contact and pay extra. When you expressed concern, he grinned stating, "They are the ones at risk, not me. If they are so stupid, they deserve what they get." This caused you to think that he might be HIV-positive and presenting a risk to the community.

1. Using the code of ethics, what are your ethical obligations in this situation?

2. Make recommendations of how you might proceed with this case.

3. Use the weighting system with each action outlined in number 2.

A FRAMEWORK FOR SELF-CONTROL

It is inherent in the code of ethics, values, and principles that workers must have clear control over their own behavior. Control over one's action systems often comes through the processing systems. Although values provide guidelines, they do not provide a framework that is immediately useful for understanding one's response systems and generating injunctions to curb behavioral impulses to act. To be useful in placing controls on one's behavior, frameworks must be easy to use and provide a system for curbing one's expectations and actions. *Spheres of control* is a helpful framework for developing self-control.

The Spheres of Control

The spheres of control framework is based on a series of three concentric circles: the circle of control, the circle of influence, and the circle of no control (see Figure 2.1). Workers need to be clear on which sphere every situation falls into in order to maintain clarity on the limits to their behavior.

Workers can use the circles to assess whether or not they are trying to control their clients. The spheres of control model assumes that people can only control their own response systems. If people try to limit control efforts, there is a clear focus and ease with events. However, when people attempt to exercise control beyond their response systems, there will be internal tension and feelings of pressure. Inherently, the spheres of control build on self-awareness so people can "tune into" their feelings to assess whether or not they are extending control beyond their ability to control things.

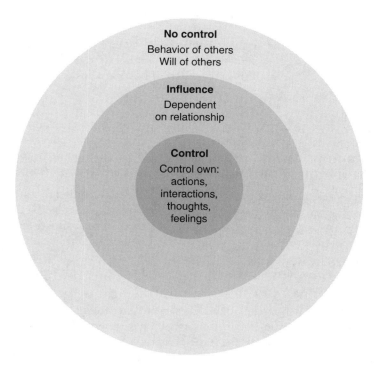

FIGURE 2.1   The Spheres of Control

When people feel pressure or some sense that they should be influencing things beyond their control, the spheres of control can be used to help them understand the feelings of pressure and curb their impulses to act. In the center of the model is what is known as the circle of control. This refers to the areas of life that people legitimately have full control over, their response systems. This circle is fairly small because people really can control little in their lives. They can only control what they do, say, feel, and think. Anything else is beyond their circle of control.

The Circle of Control.   People's ability to control is limited to their response systems. If they are truly in control of their processing and actions systems, they can be proactive in their behavior and stable in their reactions. This is a powerful position to be in. Many people experience life with others controlling aspects of their response systems. Everyone has had someone make him or her feel badly or react in unintended ways. In such situations, people are not in control of their response systems, and one (or more) of the response systems is under the influence or another person. In such situations, people lose control of elements of their response.

Often when people lose control over one element of their own response, they attempt to control elements outside of themselves to compensate for their feeling of discontrol. For example, workers who doubt their ability need clients to respond to them in ways that make them feel competent. This position shifts effective control to the external source. Now, in order to feel adequate, the worker is likely to pressure clients into appearing better so feelings of adequacy can be maintained.

The Circle of Influence.   Beyond the circle of control lies the circle of influence. People can use their action systems (acts, statements) to cause another to respond in certain ways. There are several ways a person influences others. The mechanisms of influence include (but are not limited to):

- ■ *Relationship.* Formal, familial, hierarchical, functional, and supportive relationships provide power for the individual through shared experiences and expectations. For example, when people are in relationships in which another is dependent on them for some outcome (e.g., children rely on parents for many life functions), influence increases.

- ■ *Outcomes of behavior.* There are many ways that a person's actions and interactions create outcomes that can influence others. Another's dependence, obligation, and desires to make a person feel good are examples of such types of influence. In such situations, the other yields some control over responding to gain a desired outcome. It is like control over responses is bartered away. In some organizations, this type of influence is used when a worker's output or performance becomes important to goal achievement. Such workers can often have great influence over their superiors.

- ■ *Requests/appeals.* Sometimes, people can influence others to alter their responses as they would like simply by asking or creating feelings of obligation in others. When a person feels obligated, influence is given away through the obligation to live up to a verbal commitment. For example, when people ask for a favor, one must either decline their request, lie, or form an obligation to alter normal responses until the obligation is fulfilled.

■ *Contracts.* Mutually negotiated roles and behaviors create a system of influence in which one person agrees to give up some control to the other to achieve some benefit. We all make such contracts when we accept a job. We agree to allow the new boss to have influence over our response systems, and the boss agrees to provide resources that will allow us to achieve our personal goals.

■ *Coercion.* Threats and negative sanctions can be used to increase the power to influence other people. Most often, coercive strategies are intended to control others. In such situations, the "payoff" for the coercive individual is perceived as critical. As such, people have most often extended elements of their processing system (e.g., feelings) to the other person. For example, many batterers are emotionally dependent on how their partner responds to them to maintain feelings of self-worth. They consequently try to coerce the partner into responding in ways that will take care of their feelings.

■ *Presence.* Sometimes people behave in a certain way as long as a particular person is present. This is common with children and parents. It is also common in work situations when a supervisor is present. This is a weak form of influence as it always relies on the conjoint presence of the two parties.

Inherent in the mechanisms of influence is an exchange in which the control over someone's response systems is adjusted to accommodate the influence of another person. As such, part of one person's power is relinquished (either voluntarily or involuntarily) to another as the source of influence.

When working with others in a helping relationship, workers must always be wary of the exchanges of power and influence in the relationship. If the client is giving away his or her power, the worker must resist taking too much power from the client. Remember, the goal is to empower clients rather than create dependency that would disempower them. The worker must also be careful to guard against being influenced too much by client behaviors and outcomes. Some workers draw their self-worth from the client's improvement or appreciation.

The Circle of No Control.   The final ring in the spheres of control is the circle of no control. This circle encompasses the areas of life over which people have no control or influence. The circle of no control includes the behavior of others and social conditions. Nobody ever has control over such situations. This is the largest circle in everyone's life.

At times, people become frustrated when they attempt to control elements of a situation that is outside their circle of control. This is very common with parents who, as their children grow up, must accept that their children will make their own decisions about their lives. Many marital partners often experience these same frustrations. At best, a person can move situations in this circle into the circle of influence, but a person can never achieve control of someone else.

When a worker feels impatient with a client to make some change, this is often an indication that the worker is attempting to control the client. Such feelings alert a worker to rethink what is occurring. The spheres of control can be helpful by first helping to identify what is trying to be accomplished. Workers can identify potential problems by placing their desired outcome on a picture of the spheres of control.

For example, if trying to change a client behavior, workers would put a dot in the circle of no control. If frustrated, workers can also draw a dot in the circle of control and then extend a line from the dot in the circle of control to the other dot. Such visualization strategies allow workers to see how they are relinquishing some of their control into an area where they have no control. When workers find they have extended beyond their circle of control, they can review the goals and explore what the client wants to accomplish (rather than the worker).

EXERCISE 2.6

Analyzing Frustration

Think about a time when you were very frustrated with another person and found yourself becoming angry. Use the spheres of control in Figure 2.2 to identify the following:

1. Where in the spheres was the control of your feelings? What kinds of thoughts or interactions led to the control being placed in that situation?
2. What did you do to try to control the feelings (e.g., Did you try to get the other person to change the behavior? How?).

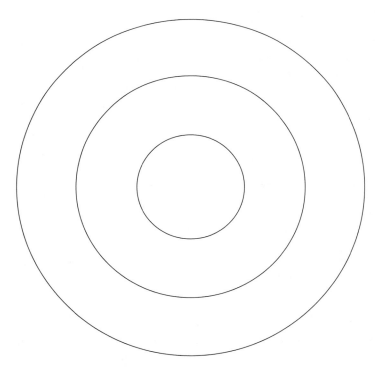

FIGURE 2.2   Spheres of Control for Analyzing Frustration

3. Locate the focus of your attempts in one of the circles.
4. How might you use such feelings and thoughts to identify potential problems when working with clients?
5. What alternate thoughts can help you maintain your emotional control?

Critical Chapter Themes

1. Workers must be in professional control of their actions and interactions at all times. Values, ethics, and legislated protocols have been developed as guidelines for professional self-control.
2. The social work profession has been guided by the values of relatedness, dignity/worth of the individual, and client self-determination. Adherence to these values differentiates social workers from other professionals.
3. Within the framework of values, there are important ethical principles within which guidelines are outlined. The ethical principles govern behavior in three areas of professional practice: (1) client-focused actions (e.g., client self-determination, adherence to client rights, competence); (2) professional interactions (e.g., high standards of conduct on the job, confidentiality); and (3) commitment to the profession (e.g., scholarship, maintaining the integrity of the profession). Workers can be held professionally accountable for failure to follow ethical guidelines.
4. Some behavioral guidelines have legal implications. These include legal issues that are assumed in the provision of service (e.g., professional competence, use of the least restrictive alternative, informed consent) and legal duties (e.g., the duty to warn and report). Workers can be sued for violations of these guidelines.
5. When different principles are in conflict with each other, workers use a system of weighting different alternatives to identify the best choice for action. The weighting system protects life as a top priority and extends to choosing the least harmful alternatives.
6. Workers must be clear about the things they can control (their response systems), things they can influence, and things over which they have no control to help them operate within the professional guidelines.

RECOMMENDED READINGS

Banks, S. (1998). Professional ethics in social work—what future? *British Journal of Social Work, 28,* 213–231.

Clark, C. (1998). Self-determination and paternalism in community care: Practice and prospects. *British Journal of Social Work, 28,* 387–402.

Davitt, J. K., & Kaye, L. W. (1996). Supporting patient autonomy: Decision making in home health care. *Social Work, 41,* 41–50.

Dickson, D. T. (1998). *Confidentiality and privacy in social work: A guide to the law for practitioners and students.* New York: The Free Press.

Northen, H. (1998). Ethical dilemmas in social work with groups. *Social Work with Groups, 21,* 5–18.

Watt, J. W., & Kallmann, G. L. (1998). Managing professional obligations under managed care: A social work perspective. *Family & Community Health, 21,* 40–49.

CHAPTER
3

Acquiring a Knowledge Base

In Chapter 2, the need to acquire information was explored as an ethical concern. Workers clearly need to understand the legal aspects of their jobs and keep up on the laws and legislation (Dickson, 1998; Prout et al., 1999). Workers must also learn effective interventions (Thyer & Myers, 1998). Together, these requirements make it imperative for workers to develop a strong knowledge base. This chapter explores elements of the knowledge base and provides a conceptual framework for applying this knowledge.

THE PROFESSIONAL KNOWLEDGE BASE

The knowledge base is instrumental in helping workers understand and plan intervention into client situations. Effective workers are driven to learn and expand their ability to understand client situations (Jennings & Skovholt, 1999; Spurling & Dryden, 1989). Through such understanding, a direction for service evolves. Without direction, workers may drift ineffectively from subject to subject with no purpose.

To establish understanding and purpose, workers use their professional knowledge base to guide their thinking. Much of the knowledge base comes through research or professional observations. The knowledge base promotes competence in workers (Staller & Kirk, 1998). As workers contribute new knowledge, the profession itself is advanced.

Theory lies at the root of professional knowledge. Most research is theoretically driven. Furthermore, theory shapes worker thinking as the worker begins to explore the client situation (McGovern, Newman, & Kopta, 1986).

The Role of Theory

There are three types of theories that guide professional practice: developmental, systems, and motivation/change theories. Developmental and systems theories guide thinking about clients, while change theories guide technique. *Developmental theory* explains problems and issues based on stages of development. Typically, a stage includes a task that must be mastered before the next stage can be completed. An optimal direction for growth is inherent in developmental theories. If growth stops or strays from this direction, problems occur. Developmental theories have been applied to biological, psychological, sexual, cognitive, group, family, agency, and community development.

46

The second type of theory is systems theory. *Systems theories* focus on subcomponents combining to create a whole system. In the system, component parts interact and influence each other. Typically, each system is viewed as a subcomponent of larger systems. For example, the family is a system that is also a subcomponent of the neighborhood, which in turn is a subcomponent of a town. The way that an individual system and its component parts function is the concern of professionals using this theory. Systems theories are commonly used to understand families, organizations, communities, groups, and societies.

The third theory type is *theories of motivation and change.* This is a unique type of theory that explores mechanisms for motivating and creating change in client systems. The first two theoretical types promote an understanding of the client situation. Motivation and change focus on influencing change. Motivation and change-focused theories attempt to explain how people change and how to capitalize on natural processes to promote change. Like the other two types of theories, there is a strong clinical and empirical knowledge base that supports motivation and change theories.

Developmental and systems theories primarily influence workers' assessments of the client situation. Motivation and change theories influence intervention. Given the influence of knowledge and theory in planning and understanding practice, workers must remain current in reading the professional literature to assure competence. Bachelor-level professionals should read about two chapters or articles every week, and master's-level professionals should average three chapters or articles per week. This reading should include both clinical and empirical works to assure a broad knowledge base. Along with reading, workers need to attend professional-development activities.

To illustrate the contributions of theory and knowledge to professional practice, Table 3.1 outlines the knowledge base, elements of knowledge, theories, and the areas of practice influenced by different knowledge elements. Effective workers will have a working knowledge of most of these content areas so their knowledge can be differentially applied to client situations.

The Role of Research

In addition to using theory, workers need to learn how to apply research findings in their work. Research has an important role in the identification phase of effective service (Thyer & Myers, 1998). Most research builds on theory through theoretically grounded questions about problem situations. There are two types of research informing the profession, quantitative and qualitative. *Quantitative research* uses statistics to assess relationships, trends, and differences. *Qualitative research* uses themes as indicated in spoken or observed exploration to understand situations.

Sources of Quantitative Research.   Most sources of quantitative knowledge are studies exploring or comparing different client groups or intervention methods. These studies are important sources of information and provide empirically tested foci and methods for intervention. There are five types of quantitative research contributing to the professional knowledge base.

TABLE 3.1   Elements of the Professional Knowledge Base and Professional Practice Influences

Knowledge Base	Knowledge Elements	Theories	Influences
Individual/ Human Knowledge Base	• Individual development • Socialization • Attachment and loss • Trauma and stress • Self-conception • Cognition • Adaptation • Biological functioning • Ability/disability • Psychopathology	• Freudian • Neo-Freudian • Object relations • Piaget • Stress/coping • Attachment • Learning • Locus of control • Constructionist • Biopsychosocial development	• Understanding of the problem • Focus of intervention • Intervention goals • Intervention strategies • Focus of questions • Flow of session • Inclusion of collateral contacts • Prognosis
Systems Knowledge Base	• Relationships • Family systems • Groups • Community systems • Political systems • Ecosystemic systems • Cultural systems • Social systems • Power/oppression • Discrimination/ differences	• Exchange theory • General systems theory • Family systems theory • Family development theory • Field theory • Game theory • Economic theory • Political theory • Cultural transmission theories • Sociological theory	• Understanding of the problem • Client system focus • Intervention goals • Intervention methods • Flow of intervention • Membership of the intervention • Scope of the intervention • Inclusion of other systems • Contextual elements
Motivation/ Change Knowledge Base	• Change dynamics • Motivation • Equilibrium/dis-equilibrium • Problem solving • Decision making • Solution focusing • Interpersonal processes • Political account-ability structures • Service system availability • Advocacy groups • Large-group mobilization	• Intrapsychic theory • Learning theory • Narrative approaches to intervention • Family systems theory • Constructionist theory • Field theory • Mutual aid theory • Exchange theory • Political theory • Economic theory	• Involvement in the client system • Intervention plan • Choice of strategies • Sessional focus • Inclusion decisions • Assumptions of intervention • Expectations of the client system • Worker authority

- *Outcome research.* Outcome research often assesses the effectiveness of new or different intervention techniques. Subjects in these studies often have similar problems or experience some situation requiring intervention. Such research can be very useful and immediately applied when working with similar client groups.
- *Program evaluations.* Program evaluations are similar to outcome research in trying and assessing an intervention system. With program evaluations, a broader type of intervention is studied, often a new approach or model (such as Family Preservation Programming). Program evaluations often focus on interventions that use a manual to assure that all workers use the same approach. This source of knowledge is important for providing intervention ideas and useful manuals.
- *Cross-sectional research.* When researchers want to understand the impact of an event or experience, cross-sectional research is used to take a close look at effects. Cross-sectional research provides important information on effects, thinking styles, and other traits that can focus intervention. Cross-sectional research is useful when a worker wants to learn about different populations.
- *Comparative research.* A large body of research that compares two (or more) groups of people or types of interventions is called comparative research. This allows workers to see if the impact on one group is really different or if one intervention is better than another for certain situations.
- *Epidemiology.* Epidemiological research focuses on the frequency, prevalence, and patterns of different types of problems. Most people can report that one in four women experience unwanted sexual attention by the age of eighteen even without knowing the actual study. Such epidemiological information frequently anchors our knowledge base about social problems.

Quantitative research is often difficult to read and apply to practice. The analyses are often complex and difficult to understand. Many practitioners pay close attention to the literature review, the description of the method, and the discussion section when the analysis is beyond their understanding. When taking the research courses in your program, also read professional articles to promote an understanding of how research can be applied.

Sources of Qualitative Research. Although there are some qualitative articles coming out in journals, the richest sources of qualitative learning are books in which a researcher becomes immersed in situations that can help inform practice. There are five types of qualitative research frequently used to build professional knowledge.

- *Ethnographies.* Ethnographies are most often stories of a single person or situation that are developed in great depth and detail. Such stories can provide insight and inspiration to workers. Such in-depth documentation helps workers at a deeper level than they can get in quantitative research.
- *Grounded theory.* This approach to qualitative data begins with letting a person or group tell his or her story without a specific question guiding the research. As the

story unfolds, the researcher categorizes and compares themes to come up with the strongest explanatory theory.

- *Participant observation.* With participant observation, researchers act as if they are one of the subjects. They observe situations and events from the point of view of the people being studied. The observations are often followed by reflections on their experience and observations.
- *Narrative interviews.* Narrative interviews involve an unstructured approach to interviewing people about their stories. The researcher then analyzes the content of the answers and uses content themes and presentation styles to make sense out of the situation or story.
- *Focus groups.* Focus groups involve several people responding to a set of questions—similar to an interview. The researcher tracks the themes and consensus of the group and reports them as findings.

Qualitative research is often easier to read than qualitative research because the report provides a full story. Consequently, the research is very similar to a book. There is very little abstraction, such as statistics, which make it easier for practitioners to digest. However, the findings are often based on very few subjects making it hard to generalize.

THE RESPONSE SYSTEMS: A CONCEPTUAL FRAMEWORK

In applying knowledge in practice situations, it is useful to have frameworks through which the knowledge is applied. The response system framework is one such system for focusing the application of the knowledge base. The response system framework focuses on understanding and influencing how the client system responds to situations. The conceptual framework is different from theory. The framework builds on concepts common to many theories, generating a broadly applicable structure through which theories can be applied. The focused application of knowledge can also help organize client information for assessment purposes.

The response system framework consists of two subsystems, the action systems and the processing systems. *Action systems* focus on behavior and interaction. Although action is important, so too are feelings and thinking (Johnson, 1996; Peile, 1998). Consequently, *processing systems* (feelings and thoughts) provide a second set of response systems. The two broad systems work simultaneously to form the responses of the client system.

The two subsystems should be somewhat familiar. The self-awareness chapter (Chapter 1) used this framework in the four-cell family assessment model. If you refer back to the family model exercise completed in Chapter 1, you can see how one cell focused on beliefs, which are governed by processing, and the final cell focused on behavior and interactions. This exercise used the framework in conjunction with developmental theories. Chapter 2 also contained response system concepts in the spheres of control. In the spheres of control, the framework concepts are used as part of a systems theory. Having already used these concepts in exercises, it is useful to understand how the framework can be useful in focusing practice skills.

The Action Systems of Responding

When working with action systems, workers focus on the content of the client story by exploring behavioral and interaction themes. These action systems often provide the story line, relationship information, and the drama/interaction among the characters in the client's story. There are two action systems within the client story, the behavioral response and interaction systems.

The Behavioral Response System: The Things People Do.   The behavioral response system focuses on client behavior, or lack of behavior, in response to the client situation. Behavior is typically observable and measurable, allowing the worker to count the number of times the behavior occurs and assess the intensity of behavioral responses in given situations. Often workers are called to focus on many difficult behaviors, such as child abuse, battering, and other offensive acts. Workers are also called to work with nonbehaviors, such as low assertiveness, child neglect, and low levels of self-care.

In working with difficult behaviors or inaction, workers often focus on patterns of behavior repeated over time. Inherent in the repetition, the worker can begin to see what situations contribute to the action responses of the client system. It is important to understand that the client action does not occur in a vacuum—actions are typically in response to some situation. Consequently, workers must consider the client system within the environment to understand the context of the behavior.

For example, consider a client who stole some jewelry. If the worker just looks at the behavior, it is a simple act of breaking the law. However, consider three possible contexts. First, there may be a client who stole the jewelry because she wanted to own the piece. She has enough money but decided to steal the jewelry rather than buy it. Second, consider a youth stealing the jewelry to give to his mother for Mother's Day. The youth has no job and really wants to get something for his mother. Third, consider a person who stole the jewelry to sell so he can feed his family. Perhaps the father has been cut off welfare and is losing his home.

Although all three people in the example broke the law, the contexts say something very different about each person. Clearly, the context of action responses is important in assessing the client situation. The worker also considers the history of the client system. Recall the family model exercise in Chapter 1, and recall that beliefs and behaviors are typically adaptive to life experiences.

Returning to the examples, consider the possibility that the first woman grew up in a home where everything she did was unconditionally supported whether she was well behaved or not. Such a background may guide the worker to understand the action as part of a life pattern. With the youth, consider that he is from a divorced family, and the mother has been working three jobs to support him and his four siblings. Such a history certainly shapes the understanding of his behavior. Finally, consider the parent stealing to feed his family. Consider that he may be a member of a racial group that has experienced a long history of employment discrimination and that he was injured two years ago in an industrial accident. All of these historical contexts shape the under-standing of the actions.

Like individuals, larger client systems also have action responses. For example, families have action systems through which they assure that basic needs are met, disci-pline is enforced, and nurturing is supplied to family members. Within the family, role designations and the assignment of discrete tasks assures that necessary actions are per-formed. In response to external events, families also engage in action responses to deal with events and information crossing the family boundaries. For example, when a single parent must go to work as a condition of receiving welfare, it is not unusual for the older children to miss school to care for the younger siblings. Such action is adaptive within the situation.

Interaction Systems: The Things People Say.   Within a client story, clients interact and operate in relation to others. Typically, the difference between understanding the behavioral response system and the interaction system is understood by the exchanges between two parties. In behavioral/response, the worker looks at the overt behavior of the system. In interaction systems, the worker looks at the reciprocal communication between one system and the other, and at the relationships among people within the situation.

With individuals, communication occurs both verbally and nonverbally when information is exchanged between one person and another. Even when working with an individual client, there are interactive themes in the client story. When clients describe the interaction, the worker can gain information about the relationships between the client and others in the situation. Effective workers explore these elements to broaden the understanding of the client situation.

With larger systems, the worker is in the position of observing interaction among members or constituency groups in the situation. With groups and families, the worker can often watch interactions and assess how different members of the system relate to each other. Working with the interactive processes is often a central element of the work with larger systems.

The Processing Systems of Responding

The processing systems focus on how events and situations are interpreted. Interpreta-tion can be based on emotions or thoughts. Consequently, there are two elements of the processing systems, affect and cognitions. Although the two systems heavily influence each other, they are most easily understood through separate explorations.

The Affective Processing System: The Things People Feel.   The affective system of processing is very much feelings based. Feelings can generate almost instant responses to situations and events. Everyone can recall times when an action was taken or some-thing was said based on feelings, even though logic cautioned against such action. Some feelings, such as powerlessness, hopelessness, inadequacy, euphoria, and joy can exert powerful effects on behavioral responses.

Often emotions (e.g., anger, happiness) involve a combination of thinking and feel-ing, creating a secondary emotion. For example, when a person feels inadequate, anger evolves in the response. The anger links up with the underlying feeling because it is action focused and can generate a response. In the response, cognition is often later combined with the feeling to justify the reaction. In such complex affects, it is important to understand the primary (underlying feeling) and secondary feeling (anger) as related elements in the situation, and both must be explored.

For example, in preparation for Halloween, a father was trying to complete several tasks while his partner, just getting off shift, was sleeping. He expected to be able to accomplish more tasks than was possible. He expected to do all of the dishes, clean the kitchen, do some yard work, get the children ready, and carve the Halloween pumpkins. He began to feel some pressure as the morning elapsed and many tasks were not complete. He began to feel upset that he could not achieve his goal. When his partner awoke, she came downstairs and noticed the pumpkins had not been carved. When he saw her look at the pumpkins, he felt badly that he had not been able to complete everything he wanted. She said, "Oh . . . the pumpkins are not done yet!" With this statement, the feelings of inadequacy erupted into defensive anger, yielding an angry tirade.

In this example, the man's thinking had set him up to feel inadequate. When the woman made the comment about the pumpkins, the thinking and feeling combined, generating anger. In this response, the anger is secondary to the feeling and results from the combination of thinking and feeling. The woman's statement was not received as intended, due to the feelings and interpretations.

Larger client systems also exhibit affective processing. Affective processes are noted in families and groups in such dynamics as taboo topics or tense/anxious moments when everyone in the family experiences some affect. Larger systems consequently develop responses influenced by the affect such as avoidance of topics and scapegoating.

The Cognitive Processing System: The Things People Think.   The wise reader will have already noted that cognition and affect are often closely associated with each other. It is not unusual for thinking to generate feelings and for feelings to produce thoughts. For example, if a student believes a professor does not like her, feelings of persecution are likely to be generated. Likewise, if the student believes a professor respects her opinion, feelings of confidence are engendered. The combined effect can influence the response that occurs in different situations.

The link between cognition and action responses often lies in the interpretation that provides the rationale for action. Such rationales are often embedded in explanations of reasons, excuses, and thoughts that occur before the event. In the Halloween example, the man's expectations of what he could achieve set the tone for problems. He also tended to feel that if he could not achieve such goals, he was somehow inadequate.

Larger systems also have cognitive types of processes forming the systemic interpretations. For example, groups and families develop rules and beliefs that serve the system and help interpret members' behaviors. For example, nonmembers may be viewed as hostile. A member's violence toward a nonmember may be viewed as an act of loyalty. However, in a support group for abusive parents, an act of aggression is interpreted as a need for additional support. Unlike families, groups often have an expressed purpose that shapes the beliefs.

CULTURAL INFLUENCES ON RESPONSE SYSTEMS

The astute reader will have already noted that the cultural background of client systems influences the response systems. Response systems flow from life experience and family background. Given family is often the vessel of cultural transmission, one must consider culture when discussing response systems. Culture has an indelible impact on the development of both action and processing (Lum, 1992; Pangagua, 1995). Figure 3.1 depicts some of the cultural influences on the response systems. Although this figure is not able to show every cultural influence, it does provide a simple method of understanding multiple influences occurring within the cultural context.

Cultural Influences on the Development of Processing Systems

There are four aspects of culture that have immediate implications for the development of the processing systems: abstract mindedness, values and religion, experience of difference, and the collective versus individualistic nature of the culture. Although Figure 3.1 shows these in approximation to either affective or cognitive processing, the influence can be broad and overlap between the thinking and feeling systems. To help understand

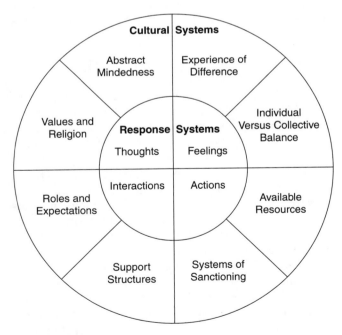

FIGURE 3.1   Cultural Influences on People's Response Systems

each element, they are discussed separately. When working with clients, the worker will find that these elements are heavily related to each other and exert simultaneous influences.

Abstract Mindedness.   Often people make sense out of events and situations through mental frameworks. These frameworks can be heavily influenced by culture. Some cultures process information in abstract ways, whereas others are quite concrete. This is often an important dimension to consider when working with people from differing cultures (Helms, 1995). Some cultures (e.g., Native American) use stories, legends, and their oral traditions to provide guidance to members of the culture. Embedded in the stories are the principles for living, such as harmony with nature and community. This is a fairly abstract system of sharing an understanding of the world.

Not all cultures interpret situations and pass knowledge through abstract principles. Many cultures are concrete. Such cultures are often rule bound with strict codes of acceptable and unacceptable behavior. The rationale for the behavior may not be important in the culture; rather, rules or customs are accepted with no discussion of why, there is simply a rule or expectation. Some such cultures do not allow people in certain circumstances to look others in the eye, speak, or dress in certain ways. Situations are interpreted through the rules and are often judged as adhering to, or violating, the rule.

There are often challenges when a worker from one position on this continuum begins work with clients from a different culture. People have a tendency to understand and interpret situations based on their framework for understanding. This will influence the direction that they will eventually take in response to the situation. A worker who is abstract minded may attempt to engage the client in abstract discussions. Conversely, a worker from a more concrete culture may simply expect the client to follow some direction because it is the right thing to do. In either situation, the worker may feel the client is resistant when the cultural difference inhibits engagement. Such exchanges can prove frustrating for both the worker and the client and can lead to ineffective service.

For example, a worker was providing family support in an agency for people with developmental disabilities. A family referred their developmentally disabled son due to "excessive masturbation." The worker explored the frequency of touching and concluded that such touching occurred on two occasions. The worker began to explore the rights of disabled people to be sexual and principles of appropriate versus inappropriate places to engage in sexual touching. This direction yielded frustration and argument from the family. The family maintained that the behavior was "wrong" and must be stopped. In discussing the situation with a supervisor, the worker began to understand that the family had strong and very concrete beliefs about the behavior. When the supervisor pointed out the differences in abstraction, the worker allowed the family to describe the rules that seemed important. This shift from abstract principles to concrete rules promoted engagement by the family.

Values and Religion.   Values and beliefs about right and wrong influence how a situation is interpreted. Cultural beliefs and religious affiliations exert a strong influence on a person's values and, consequently, on a person's thinking in response to situations. Such affiliations are often culturally influenced (Betancourt & Lopez, 1995). For example, in American society, efficiency and hard work are valued. A person who is hardworking with good outcomes is often considered worthwhile. This is true in most employment situations and extends subtly into other areas of life. Consider how friends often expect each other to provide help and invest energy in the relationship. A friend who does not help when needed will become a less valuable friend.

Cultural institutions, such as the church, the government, and the economic system, are inherent in the cultural values. People hold beliefs about social institutions that are passed on to others within the cultural group. Within a cultural group that values religion, people often use religious teachings for guidance in their response to a situation.

In a less obvious way, people are influenced by their culture's economic system. This often occurs through the package of beliefs accompanying the system of economic distribution. For example, many people believe that capitalism is the best economic system. This is couched in the values of freedom, efficiency, and accumulation of wealth. People from other cultures hold a different set of beliefs associated with their economic background. Some feel that communism is superior with its values of fairness, reciprocity, and the common good.

At the individual level, the influence of the cultural institutions shapes different values. Some cultures reinforce the values of competition and others promote cooperation (Sue & Sue, 1990). Some value material goods and others tend to hold more spiritual values. Such values provide a framework for interpreting good (valued) and not good (not valued) within each culture. These values are often indelible and unconscious in the minds of people raised within a certain culture. Most often the influence of the values is never noticed, but it is expressed in the interpretations and choices made by the individuals within the different cultures.

When people from different cultures come together, value conflicts can emerge. For example, an American job coach who values competition and output will have a difficult time motivating someone from a culture who values harmony and cooperation. The person may not produce at his maximum capacity and the interpretation of the job coach might be that the client is underachieving or lazy. Such interpretations are culturally insensitive as the job coach imposes her personal cultural values to judge someone from a different culture. Cultural conflicts are common in social work. They often surface when someone comes from a culture that has different beliefs about work, money, family, children, gender, and numerous other areas of life. Social workers can perform a serious disservice by intervening without first being sensitive to the client's beliefs and values.

To avoid value conflicts associated with culture, social workers need to expose themselves openly to the differences that exist among cultures. Workers must also plan pathways to increase their knowledge of different cultural groups (Sue, Ivey, & Pedersen, 1996). This is an easy suggestion that is difficult to achieve given the many differences within cultures. Workers must consequently seek to gain knowledge while avoiding stereotypes and over-generalization. This usually requires workers to expose themselves to different cultures exploring the differences in common values between the two cultures. In this exploration, workers also need to explore the differences among people within each culture. When meeting with clients from different cultures, competent workers allow the clients to tell their own stories. As cultural themes emerge, workers can explore the culture and avoid potential conflicts.

Processing of Differences.   When a cultural group is visibly, socially, or economically different from the dominant culture, differences are highlighted and hard to ignore because one can immediately identify the different culture or race. Multiple differences accentuate the need for members of a cultural group to work with their young to help them understand the differences at each stage of development.

Regardless of the extent of difference, members of each cultural group develop methods of teaching young members the meaning of cultural differences. This provides a framework for young people to interpret interactions with the dominant culture. If the difference is slight rather than multidimensional, this is often a fairly simple task of exploring the differences and similarities across the cultural groups.

When members of the cultural group are different from the dominant culture and experience racism and oppression, the task of helping young members of the culture understand the difference becomes more difficult (Fiske, 1995). The all-encompassing judgments inherent in racism cannot be easily explained nor can the inconsistencies among the members of the dominant culture. Members of such cultural groups have enormous challenges interfacing with the dominant culture. One cannot predict whether the response will be overtly racist, covertly racist, or open and accepting. Distrust arises as people who have been oppressed and discriminated against develop screening systems for detecting racism and bias in their interaction with the dominant culture.

Economic oppression can greatly complicate the processing of cultural differences. When members of a nondominant culture notice that their economic resources are not equal to that of the dominant culture, resentment results. It is difficult to explain to young members of a culture why one group has high-paying positions and another must perform menial tasks for long hours with little pay. Along with the social impacts of poverty and economic oppression, economically vulnerable groups are also exposed to higher levels of pollution, environmental stress, and health risks (Anderson & Armstead, 1995; Link & Phelan, 1995). It is difficult to find positive frames for understanding such differences.

For some cultural groups, these challenges are exacerbated by broad public acceptance of an unfair situation. Such acceptance of the dominant culture is often interpreted as purposeful indifference that supports and legitimizes the oppression. This leads to stigma and anger as members of the nondominant culture feel hopeless and powerless about the overwhelming differences.

These experiences of difference can greatly influence how situations are processed. Given that helping professionals often come in contact with members of nondominant cultural groups, workers can expect some processing that reflects a lack of trust in the helping systems. Depending on the cultural group of the worker, this can increase or decrease depending on the cross-cultural experiences and methods of processing the differences developed by the client.

Collective versus Individualistic Cultures.   Some cultures have high levels of obligation to the collective group whereas others tend to be very individualistic. This cultural dimension often leads to differences in processing that can create problems in the provision of service (Sue & Sue, 1990). Individualistic cultures tend to be competitive and view success through individual achievements and acquisitions. Collectivist cultures are more collaborative and view success based on the conditions of the larger group. In

North American society, the individualistic elements of the culture are clearly expressed in the political debates about tax cuts, individual responsibility, and property acquisition.

When working with people from collectivist cultures, workers often find that clients will acquiesce to the larger group when making decisions. Concurrently, their self-judgments may be heavily influenced by the obligations and attitudes of others within the cultural group (Triandis, 1995). This can present challenges to workers of an individualistic culture trying to help clients empower themselves. The concept of empowerment may not be interpreted as an individual achievement but rather as a group accomplishment. Workers may also find that clients will sacrifice individual achievements to attend to the needs of others within the cultural group.

For example, a family service agency participated in a work project and hired a Native American who had been on welfare as a maintenance person. The man was very competent in his job and was well liked; however, he would often not come to work. Reasons for his absence included his sister needing his car to take her son to a hockey tournament, fixing his cousin's truck, and helping his brother butcher a deer. This was a source of frustration for one of the managers in the agency who advocated letting the man go for not coming to work. Luckily, other managers were more culturally aware and could see that there was a conflict between the collective culture and the individualistic culture.

Cultural Influences on the Development of Action Systems

In addition to influencing client processing, culture exerts direct influence on the action response systems. For the purposes of this discussion, four cultural dimensions have been highlighted to help understand the influence on action systems: roles and expectations, systems of support, social and economic resources, and systems of sanctioning behavior. Each of the dimensions influences client behavior.

Roles and Expectations.   One of the strongest cultural influences on behavior is culturally determined role prescriptions. Culture heavily influences social, family, and gender roles through culturally determined expectations of how such roles should be performed (Devaux, 1995).

Understandably, the first culturally influenced roles are family roles. These roles provide the foundation for modeling the family. Every culture has a model of the ideal family (Montague, 1996). Through this model, cultures dictate how men and women act, family structure, and the expected family functions. In addition, images of mothers, fathers, and children are set (McCollum, 1997). In some cultures, clear distinctions and divisions of labor exist within the different roles in the family. For example, in some cultures women are expected to defer important decisions to the male head of the household. Such cultural models invest power in the male role and expect interaction and action to be controlled by the male. This cultural model is very different from the North American egalitarian model of families and often produces conflict if a person is not sensitive to the nondominant culture.

Inherent in family roles, culture exerts influence on the tasks and expectations associated with gender. Images of maleness and femaleness are largely culturally determined. In male-dominated cultures, there is a prescription for males to be assertive and decisive with concurrent female prescriptions of submission. Each of the gender role prescriptions has implications for allowable gender-specific behaviors and interactions within the culture. Notably, prescriptions are accompanied by power, autonomy, and prestige differences across the genders.

In addition to family and gender roles, cultures influence the power and prestige associated with work and social roles. In some cultures, religious roles are highly respected, whereas in others secular priorities (e.g., business) are more esteemed. With such roles, there are often social expectations within the culture that attempt to emulate the traits of the highly valued roles.

For example, business roles are highly valued in North American culture. Consequently, efficiency and directness are behavior traits that are encouraged. In a culture in which religious roles are more highly valued, caring and sacrifice are behaviors that are likely to be respected.

Systems of Support.
Associated with roles, cultures often influence the systems of support available for individuals and families. Some cultures promote kinship groups as the first level of support (Scannapieco & Jackson, 1996; Weaver & White, 1997). Such cultures expect that families will provide resources and services. In other cultures, other institutions such as government or charities might provide the same functions.

Some cultures have internal systems of support through which people within the cultural group are expected to provide help for each other. In such cultures one often finds assistance in establishing businesses or other systems through which cultural members can enhance the success of the group. Some cultures even have their own agency systems (e.g., Jewish Family Services).

Concurrent with provisions of cultural support systems, cultures may have injunctions about using other supports. For example, using formal supports may be viewed as a selling out or a sign of failure. Such injunctions can present problems when a client is referred to a formal system or is mandated to attend service through a court order. This is also problematic when limited cultural supports for people from a non-dominant group exist. Such cultural influences must be considered when attempting to engage members of a nondominant cultural group in service.

Social and Economic Resources.
Although cultural support systems provide supportive resources, there are broader resource issues associated with culture. Everyone has a minimum resource requirement to meet personal and family goals. Culture impacts the minimum requirement in two ways. First, some cultures promote exceeding the basic requirements by acquiring many items of wealth. A person who does not achieve the optimal level of wealth held by the culture may feel unsuccessful. The second impact is associated with economic disparities among cultural groups. If some groups do not have enough resources to achieve their goals, they must work extra hard to increase their resources (e.g., take two jobs) or compromise their goals.

With sufficient resources, it is easy to meet goals, like having a comfortable and secure home. With some additional resources, a person can develop new goals, such as extracurricular activities for the children or enhancements, like boats and outings. With very high resources, a person can influence events beyond the family by donating resources to politicians and lobbyists. Although the relationship is not direct, there is clearly a tendency for members of the dominant culture to have a much higher level of resources.

Many people in nondominant cultural groups do not have resource levels sufficient to meet their personal and family goals (Falicov, 1998). Consequently, there are no enhancements or ability to influence political and economic decisions. Lower levels of resources also mean that members of the cultural group must compromise their goals. Many families work long hours doing undesirable work just to meet the basic needs of the family members. In such situations, assuring resources for the family forces adult authority figures out of the home for extended periods of time. Energy is consequently invested in survival with limited time for other family functions.

In such families, the potential action responses of cultural group members are limited (Fiske, 1995). They do not have the resources needed to extend influence and have little time to invest in areas of life beyond subsistence. Many service systems seem to overlook the resource pressures on such families when scheduling services and establishing service protocols.

Systems of Sanctioning.   The final cultural influence on action systems involves sanctioning behavior. Some cultures prohibit or limit certain behaviors that may be normal in another culture. The sanctioning systems are associated with values and processing systems but are also somewhat independent in that the manner in which behavior is sanctioned often influences behavior within the cultural group (Denby & Alford, 1996).

Some cultures sanction behavior through resources (e.g., dowries, inheritances), some through relationships (e.g., disowning, ostracizing), and some through corporal systems (e.g., cutting off limbs, caning, killing). Some of these systems of shaping behavior are very extreme. Members of more extreme cultures are often more repressed in their behavior and prone to use corporal systems of control. People within an abstract and permissive culture are more likely to be lenient and flexible in their approach to situations.

Along with punitive systems of sanctioning, cultures provide models of desired behavior for people to emulate. Some cultures revere brave warriors and others revere the shrewd businessperson. These cultural ideals interact with some of the other influences on action systems and often result in subcultural models. The popularity of gangster rap artists is one such emerging icon that provides models of strength within the limits of resource scarcity and oppression. Notice that aside from the subcultural elements, the gangster rap artists comply with the choices of automobiles and possessions that are consistent with the dominant class. This provides an interesting blend of achievable models for members of oppressed groups.

When working with clients from a different culture, workers are often confronted by sanctioned behaviors foreign to their culture. This is most difficult when youth adopt subcultural icons that challenge the status quo. It is imperative that workers are both aware of the culturally sanctioned behaviors and the subgroup differences that might cause worker reactions to the client situation.

The influence of culture is inherent in many professional situations. In the cases used throughout the book, try to consider how cultural backgrounds might affect the experience of the client coming to see you. Most of the cases have no indication of race or culture. This is to allow you to consider cultures and races different or similar to your own when reflecting on the case situation. Allow yourself to experiment with different combinations to see the powerful impact that culture might have on the case.

USING THE FRAMEWORK AND KNOWLEDGE BASE TO ASSESS AND PLAN

The framework described in this section provides students with an easy-to-remember system for understanding the client situation. By using the response systems and understanding actions in their social and historical contexts, workers can develop an understanding of the situation that can guide the direction of service.

Assessment Components

Given the utility of the framework for understanding situations, developing skills using this framework can foster the development of assessment skills. The framework, if used within the context of the client situation, provides four elements to promote understanding. These elements provide a basic framework for assessing the client situation. Different books and agencies have various formats for making an assessment, but most assessments focus on these elements.

Although this book will not concentrate on writing up assessments, the skills focused on using the knowledge base, thinking, observing, and questioning will provide the core skills needed to explore and make sense of the client situation. Mastery of these skills will allow workers to use different assessment formats, most of which base decisions on similar components. The dimensions provided here are useful in organizing assessment-based thinking.

Background and Context.   In conducting the assessment, workers often begin with a history of the people and the situational elements. In the history taking, there is often some exploration of what has been done in the past about the situation. As the worker explores the situation, there is typically a full exploration of the environmental and cultural contexts in which the problem is occurring. The following three background components provide workers with a fairly full context upon which to base assumptions.

- *History.* The personal and situational histories associated with client request for service concurrent with past adaptations to the problem.
- *Environmental context.* The situation to which the client is attempting to adapt and the elements that appear to be stressing the adaptive abilities of the client system.
- *Culture.* The historical and current influences on client adaptation, cultural supports, and strengths of the cultural systems.

Problem Parameters.   In addition to exploring the background of the client and the problem situation, the worker explores the nature of the problems. The response system framework is useful in guiding this exploration. The four cells of the framework provide ample information on the different aspects of the situation. In this exploration, the worker also wants to explore how different people in the situation experience the problems.

- *Action systems.* The behaviors, interactions, context, and links to personal history. The worker also explores for indicators of strength and adaptation.
- *Processing systems.* The feelings, thoughts, context, links to history, and links to action systems. The worker also explores for indicators of strength and adaptation.
- *Problem perspectives.* The different experiences of the problem situation and how it is a problem for each person.

Hypothesis and Direction for Service.   Based on the exploration, the worker uses thinking skills, theory, and knowledge base to integrate the different elements of the client story into an integrated understanding of the situation. In this component of the assessment, the worker reflects on all of the information to think through what may be creating difficulties and what elements of the situation will need to change for the situation to be resolved. This is a critical component of the assessment as it provides the rationale for the intervention. There are two critical components to the hypothesis: first, an understanding that integrates information; second, a sense of direction.

- *Integrated understanding.* The worker forms a hypothesis on how the elements fit together as an adaptive response by the client system. The worker integrates client strengths associated with the adaptive elements.
- *Direction.* The worker indicates what needs to happen to help the client achieve the goals of service. In this direction, the worker identifies how the strengths and adaptive abilities can be used to achieve the client goals.

Developing Goals from the Professional Understanding.   From the professional understanding of the situation, workers develop goals and objectives to guide their intervention. This is discussed fully with the client, who shares in the development of the hypothesis and understanding. As the understanding is mutually agreed upon by both the worker and the client, the task of moving from the understanding to clear goals and objectives becomes necessary so the client has an informed understanding of what services will accomplish.

When developing goals, there are different levels of abstraction the worker and client must progress through to clearly understand how service will proceed. There are four components of a goal statement that must be worked through to arrive at a service plan (often called a treatment plan or contract).

1. *The goal statement.* The goal statement is the most abstract statement outlining what the client wants to achieve as a result of service. The statement must reflect an accomplishment for the client and have a direction for the change. Services are not adequate goal statements. For example, if working with a violent family, attending an anger-control program would not be an appropriate goal. It is a service rather than an accomplishment and indicates no direction for change. The plan would need to identify and state a goal, such as stopping or decreasing the violence. Such a statement would indicate an accomplishment and has a clear sense of direction to guide services.

2. *Measurable goal outcomes.* From the general statement of accomplishment, workers use the direction implied in the goal statement to identify a way to tell when the goal is accomplished. It is important to be able to identify when the work is done to avoid promoting dependence on service. This also allows the worker to illustrate movement for motivating clients. In making the goal outcomes measurable the worker must explore the current level of the problem and develop the level at which the client can feel that the work is accomplished. In the example of a violent family, the first step is to gain some sense of the types, frequency, and severity of the violence and the second is to identify outcomes that the client will attempt to achieve through service.

For example, a Child Protective Service worker found that during the past week a parent slapped her children about four times a day, punched them about once, and swore at them at least ten times a day. In exploring the severity, it was determined that the slaps leave red marks about half of the time but the punches leave bruises every time, and the swearing tends to cause the children to cry about half of the time. In developing goals, the worker and parent established that punching and hard slaps (ones that leave welts) would be brought to zero. The other slaps had to decrease to once per month and the swearing to once every other day. Once these goals are achieved the services can decrease in intensity.

In this example, it is clear how the direction for change was very abstract compared to the outcomes. In developing the goals, specific behaviors were targeted and baselines were developed so progress could be measured. Concurrently, the worker and client identified specific benchmarks for indicating success. They could then monitor the situation to see how service was helping.

3. *Objectives.* After establishing the goal statement and the outcomes, the worker and client remain on a concrete level and try to determine what must change to accomplish the goals. This often involves thinking through both what must decrease (hitting, etc.) and also what must increase (e.g., use of nonviolent discipline, stress reduction, parental self-care, and developing mechanisms for the family to have fun). Once accomplished, the objectives should result in achieving the outcomes.

4. *Services to be provided.* The last component to think through is what services will be used to accomplish the goal outcomes. In this component, the worker and client think through the types of services (counseling, supports, big brothers, etc.) that can be put in place to accomplish the objectives.

These components of the assessment and goals use many skills. The exploration will use questioning, reflecting, listening, engaging, tuning in, and the other interpersonal skills developed through this book and the classroom activities. The hypothesis and direction will use the thinking, tuning in, and engagement skills to work through with the client. In future classes and courses, you will learn the strategies for developing the service sections, and in your placement, you will get some practice in negotiating and writing up the assessment.

EXERCISE 3.1

The Case of Cecil

In this exercise, you are a worker for a child protection agency in a small city. You are new in the agency and preparing to meet with an adolescent placed on your caseload. The youth needs a placement and seems to be frequently in crisis. To make sense of his situation, read the background material provided here and answer the questions to begin using the framework as a tool for understanding this youth.

As a young infant, Cecil lived with his paternal aunt and uncle, the Greenbirds. They lived on an Indian reservation in a rural area of the state. Reportedly, Michael and Deloris Greenbird were planning to adopt Cecil when he first came into their home. His biological parents believed that this would be best for Cecil, but after six months, Cecil's mother rescinded the adoption agreement and took Cecil to live with her and her common-law boyfriend, Steve Whitefeather. Contact with the Greenbirds was terminated at this time.

While living in his mother's home, Cecil was witness to, and a victim of, multiple forms of family violence. He was cut by Mr. Whitefeather, burned, and witnessed several incidents of physical and sexual abuse of his mother. Cecil also witnessed Mr. Whitefeather burning his sister with a lighter. Both Mr. Whitefeather and Cecil's mother were alcoholic, resulting in a chaotic and abusive home atmosphere. Cecil lived in this setting until the age of 5 when he was taken into care by Child Protective Services.

After coming into care, Cecil's biological father explored taking custody, but at the time, courts were reticent to release dependent children into the care of single males. There was also a tendency to move Native American children into adoption with Caucasian families. Cecil consequently lived in a series of foster homes. Although Cecil was taken into care along with two female siblings, they were initially separated and then reunited as they changed foster home settings. Eventually, the three siblings were adopted by John and Sarah Smythe and moved to a town about three hours from the reservation.

Immediately after adoption, Cecil worked very hard to please the new adult authority figures in his life. He was outgoing and eager to avoid raising any form of anger in the home. Cecil also seemed to function as the caregiver for his siblings. Reportedly, he had fulfilled a caregiving and protective role in the maternal home by scrounging for food and making sure his siblings were okay.

The caregiving role he historically fulfilled with his siblings tended to create difficulties in the adoptive home through his resistance to parental authority. This peaked in adolescence when he tended to get into power struggles with John and Sarah. Also, as an adolescent, Cecil experienced increased freedom because the high school was in town and the home was in the country. Cecil discovered that he could leave school and go downtown. Cecil also began teaming up with friends willing to leave school with him. One such friend was a Native American youth who was also adopted into a Caucasian family. The new peers provided pressure for each other and became partners for exploring some confusing identity issues.

Identity confusion seemed to be a theme in Cecil's adolescence. Cecil reported that the Smythes were very good to him and imparted strict Christian values. However, he never felt he fit into the family. Cecil was acutely aware of his Native American heritage but was being raised as a religiously conservative Caucasian child in a predominantly white community. His friendship with the other Native American child gave him an outlet to share his confusion.

At the age of 14, Cecil became defiant, began running away, and started using mind-altering substances. Cecil began stealing and missing school on a regular basis. Missing school was done primarily with his Native American friend. The police became involved because of two incidents of stealing. Police involvement prompted extreme family tensions in the Smythe household.

Cecil reported that he was angry during this time of his life. He felt angry about his lack of fitting into his life situation. Cecil railed against the child welfare system and other Caucasian social structures, blaming them for his loss of a Native American identity and poor fit in the world. This did not promote a strong working relationship with the adoptive parents, school, or other authority figures during this time.

The family tensions led to flare-ups between Cecil and another adopted child (non-related) by the name of Cindy. Reportedly, Cecil and Cindy had a kind of "love–hate" relationship that was close one day and explosive the next. At one point, during a volatile and stressful period, Cindy approached the Smythes and disclosed that Cecil was having sexual intercourse with her. Even though the sexual relationship was consensual, the disclosure resulted in family tensions escalating to the point when John Smythe slapped Cecil, causing a nosebleed. Cecil was consequently taken into care through "care-by-agreement" procedures (the foster parents agreed to entering care rather than proceeding in court).

First use the processing systems (feeling/thinking) to understand how Cecil interprets his situation.

1. When dealing with the helping systems, list at least two beliefs or cognitions that help explain how Cecil relates to the helping systems.

2. What tends to be the central feeling about himself that promotes his anger?

Second, given the way that Cecil processes situations, what are the patterns of behavior and interaction (action systems) used to adapt to his situation?

3. What behaviors seem to producing problems in the situation?

4. What is the general style of interaction with other people?

5. How do the processing systems support these difficult behaviors and interactions?

6. What elements of this young man's personal history might contribute to this style of processing?

7. How would each of these elements lead to such difficult processing styles?

8. Given your position and cultural background, how might Cecil experience you when he first meets you as a new worker?

9. What other cultural issues are evident in this situation?

10. What is there about your job that might cause Cecil to distrust you?

Critical Chapter Themes

1. Workers use knowledge gleaned from research and practice in developing interventions with clients.
2. The application of knowledge is guided by theory. There are three types of theories. Developmental theory and systems theory guide the assessment and the worker understanding of situations. Motivation and change theories influence the intervention strategies of workers.
3. The response systems (action, interaction, thinking, and affect) provide a framework through which theories can be applied to client situations.
4. People's response systems are heavily influenced by cultural background. When working with people's responses, the worker must consider the cultural influences in order to develop an understanding of the situation.
5. As workers develop an understanding of the situation, they organize information into an assessment. The assessment will typically contain background information, problem parameters/dynamics, and an integrated understanding of what the worker believes is occurring.
6. The understanding of the situation develops goals for service. The service goals involve a goal statement, identification of measurable outcomes, objectives, and services to be provided.

RECOMMENDED READING

Anderson, N. B., & Armstead, C. A. (1995). Toward understanding the association of socioeconomic status and health: A new challenge for the biopsychosocial approach. *Psychosomatic Medicine, 57,* 213–225.

Devaux, F. (1995). Intergenerational transmission of cultural family patterns. *Family Therapy, 22,* 17–23.

Peile, C. (1998). Emotional and embodied knowledge: Implications for critical practice. *Journal of Sociology and Social Welfare, 25,* 39–59.

Sue, D. W., Ivey, A. R., & Pedersen, P. B. (1996). *A theory of multicultural counseling and therapy.* Pacific Grove, CA: Brooks/Cole.

4

Thinking Skills

From the previous discussion on assessment, it is clear that knowledge and theory cannot guide practice without application. The professional knowledge base is dependent on thinking to apply knowledge to the client situation (Badger, 1985; Gambrill, 1997). Without the ability to think and apply knowledge, the professional information would be trivialized. Effective workers are able to think, conceptualize, and apply knowledge (McLennan, Culkin, & Courtney, 1994).

For the purposes of this book, five types of thinking skills are considered central to good practice. Each of these abilities helps keep workers grounded and purposeful in their interaction with clients. Thinking is enhanced through the use of frameworks for applying professional theory and knowledge. This chapter will briefly explore the five styles of thinking and then discuss how the inability to think effectively leads to worker mistakes and faulty assumptions.

FIVE STYLES OF THINKING

Logical Thinking Abilities

Logical thinking is central to understanding the problem that is being presented by the client. In logical thinking, workers use client information and their knowledge base to infer linkages among events (Freeman, 1993). The understanding that evolves through establishing the linkages guides the worker in selecting theories to apply and questions to use while exploring the situation (Baron, 1994; Brown & Keeley, 1994; Kassierer & Kopelman, 1991). You used logical thinking in the Cecil case in Chapter 3 when understanding how his personal history contributed to the problem situation. There are many dimensions of logic and rational thinking that are critical to effective practice.

Cause and Effect Linkages. Often problems are caused by a prior event. To help clients understand how problems have evolved, the worker explores the history of the problem to identify how one event contributes to the next. Such thinking is linear with clear sequencing of events and outcomes (e.g., A leads to B). For example, a family came into service complaining of parent–child conflict with their teenage daughter. When the worker explored the fighting, the parents shared that about a year ago another relative told them they were too lenient with the daughter. In response, the parents tightened up on their expectations. This led to a power struggle as the daughter tried to re-establish her freedom associated with the initial rules.

Establishing Problem Parameters.   Workers must use logical thinking abilities to identify the beginning, end, and dynamics of a problem. Many problems are matters of degree. For example, it is normal for couples to argue once in a while. However, arguments become problematic when the severity or frequency exceeds client tolerance. Workers must be able to identify the thresholds and parameters of problems. This helps in defining the problem, identifying when the problem is solved, and establishing measures of success.

Partializing Problems.   When clients approach helping systems, often their problems seem overwhelming. The overwhelming nature of such problems is often due to several smaller problems combined in the situation. Effective workers separate out the smaller problems, or problem components, making the situation more manageable. This skill is critical to setting goals in the assessment.

For example, a couple was arguing about whether or not to replace the family dog who had just died. As they discussed the situation, it was apparent that the mother wanted to take some action to ease her children's pain. The father, on the other hand, was concerned that nobody in the family would assume responsibility for the dog, and it would fall on him. He was not willing to assume responsibility for the new pet. The worker helped the couple to see there were really two problems, caring for the children's grief and managing the father's concerns. Once they were separated, the couple was able to solve them as separate problems.

Identifying Objectives.   As clients come into the helping situation, workers listen to their stories, extrapolating areas in which change can increase client mastery of the situations. This act of extrapolating areas for change establishes goals. Goals are a general statement of the change or changes that need to occur.

For example, when serving neglectful parents, a goal might be to increase parental attention to child needs. Such goal statements are broad and abstract. Consequently, workers must break the goal down into smaller changes or objectives. When the client achieves the combined objectives, the goal will be met. The objectives address specific elements that maintain the problem. If a parent feels overwhelmed by multiple demands, one objective would focus on managing external demands.

Making Goals/Objectives Measurable.   When clients are working to resolve imperfect situations, it is important to help them identify when the problem will be resolved to their satisfaction. Identifying such progress and resolution requires workers to help clients identify indicators of success (Bloom, Fischer, & Orme, 1995). For example, if a client wants to decrease anxiety, the worker needs to help the client identify observable behaviors associated with the anxiety (e.g., talking too fast in new situations, thinking that people are talking about him or her). The worker must also explore the frequency and intensity of his or her responses that appear problematic. Finally, the worker needs to explore acceptable levels in order to monitor progress toward the goal.

Reflective Thinking Abilities

The linear strategies of logical thinking are appropriate for understanding many client situations. However, client situations with no clear cause and effect defy linear logic. Workers are often confronted with situations involving a myriad of divergent influences that may cause or aggravate the problem. These situations demand circular thinking. Such thinking begins with intuition and hunches and then reflects back on the situation to confirm the hunches. The confirmation or nonconfirmation then builds a new set of hunches to be confirmed. You used this thinking in the Cecil case when considering how cultural backgrounds might impact the client.

The use of intuition and hunches in practice requires significant rigor from social workers, because they must follow their hunches until they are validated in the worker–client relationship. This sets up a circular thinking pattern in which the worker first establishes an assumption or hunch about the client situation. The worker then takes some action based on the hunch to test whether or not it is operational in the situation. After action, the worker monitors client reactions to determine whether the hypothesis is supported. The support, or lack of support, is then fed back into the thinking to change or confirm the assumption held by the worker. There are four critical skills associated with this reflective thinking.

Maintaining Sense of Purpose.   The worker must always stay focused on the agreed-upon work. Reflective thinking helps assure the sense of purpose as the worker hears elements in the client story that may be associated with the problem. The worker consequently takes some action or begins an exploration to assess possible connections. If there seems to be no connection, the worker proceeds in a slightly different direction. Less effective workers often fail to complete the circle and will pursue many content themes that are unrelated to the client goals and purpose.

Identifying Operational Assumptions.   Concurrent with maintaining a sense of purpose, the worker needs to be aware of assumptions that underlie the interventions. Effective workers use reflective thinking as they begin to take action with clients. Often workers begin with an assumption of what must change to help the client. As they proceed, they test the assumption; when the assumption is confirmed, they make a conscious note of what they believe is occurring in the client situation.

Ineffective workers are often unaware of their assumptions. For example, a child protection worker was having difficulty with a family. There was a high level of distrust in the relationship and the client seemed very evasive. When describing the family to the supervisor, the worker presented the client as highly manipulative. The supervisor highlighted the assumption that the client was manipulating the system. In the supervisory exploration, it was clear that the assumption was causing the worker to question and challenge statements made by the client. The client consequently attempted to stop making statements that would yield such challenges.

Separating Intuition from Reactivity.   In the reflective loop, workers also reflect on their responses to the client situation. Such reflection helps identify worker priorities and concerns from client concerns. Consequently, workers must build in hunches both about their responses, and about the client situation. Such self-reflection assures that responses are based on client goals, rather than on the worker's emotional response to the client story. This skill is highly dependent on the self-awareness skills developed in Chapter 1.

Incorporating Feedback into Assumptions. Reflective thinking must keep informing the worker about the client situation in order to be useful in practice. Consequently, workers must act on their hunches (e.g., share the insight, suggest some alternatives). After action, the worker monitors the client feedback to assure accuracy and then, based on the client reaction, revises or refines the assumption.

For example, a worker was discussing a client's negative self-feelings. Based on a pattern of extreme negative feelings, the worker suspected there was some sexual abuse in the background. The worker stated, "I have a question in my mind that may seem weird to you at first. I would like to ask it because it may have some influence on what we are discussing." After the client agreed to answer, the worker stated, "When you were talking, I had a feeling that someone did something to you when you were little that made you feel lousy about yourself." The client responded, "No . . . never to me. But my dad used to hit my mother a lot." The worker incorporated the information and then asked, "How were you involved?" The client began to share how most of the mother's beating occurred when the client had done something wrong. Apparently, the father would start berating the client, and then when the mother attempted to defend her, the father would become violent to the mother.

In this example, see how initial action yielded information that the hunch was wrong. The worker consequently incorporated the feedback and altered the path of exploration, still believing the client was involved in some type of abuse. The question about how the client was involved yielded confirmation that there was some trauma (witnessing spousal abuse) that impacted her self-concept (the fights were about her).

Critical Thinking Abilities

Given that workers spend much time engaged in firmly entrenched problems, critical thinking is a necessary skill. Critical thinking is an integrative skill using emotional as well as logical processes (Brookfield, 1987). Critical thinkers are able to go beyond current understandings and see situations from new perspectives (Brown & Hausman, 1998). This allows them to find new and innovative understandings of problem situations. Critical thinkers tend to remain hopeful that every problem can be solved once the right solution is achieved.

Critical thinkers tend to mentally turn the problem around in their heads exploring new interpretations that might create new directions for action. Even if there is no problem, critical thinkers are always trying to find new and better ways to do things. This is the type of thinking you used when thinking about what elements of the job would need to be confronted to gain Cecil's trust. There are four traditional attributes of critical thinking (Gambrill, 1997; Gibbs & Gambrill, 1999).

Questioning Assumptions.   Critical thinkers never take assumptions for granted; instead, they tend to question how the assumption came to be and whether it applies in this situation. As such, each assumption must logically fit the situation. Such workers are always attempting to find new definitions of problems and new solutions to better fit the situation. Critical thinkers do not discount other people's ideas; however, rigorous scrutiny is applied to assure it is the best understanding of the situation.

Attending to Person and Context Simultaneously.   Many workers tend to interpret situations from a single perspective. For example, some workers view the problem as coming from the client. Other workers view problems as originating in the environment. It is not unusual for workers from these different orientations to debate about the "true" cause of client problems. Critical thinkers tend to include both person and context in their attempts to understand the client situation (Brookfield, 1987). This allows all elements of the situation to be considered at once (Gibbs & Gambrill, 1999). The inclusiveness of critical thinking often provides a novel understanding of the problem.

For example, a client diagnosed as both developmentally and mentally disabled was referred for help because of volatile outbursts. The worker wanted to observe the client to better understand her behavior. He followed her around at the sheltered workshop to observe her within the problem context/environment. Observations indicated that prior to volatile outbursts, the client was most often trying unsuccessfully to get the attention of a staff person. At one point, the staff member left the room and the client pulled the door off the hinges. Other staff intervened at this point, escalating the situation. By including the contextual elements he observed, the worker intervened both with staff and the client, changing staff responses concurrent with client behavior.

Identifying Alternative Interpretations.   Critical thinkers do not readily adopt the most expedient or readily apparent interpretation of an event. Instead, they experiment with alternative interpretations of the situation. This allows for them to see different aspects of the situation that can be helpful in working with clients (Brookfield, 1987; Gambrill, 1990, 1994). This is a necessary skill when using the "strengths perspective" because the worker must explore alternative definitions of situations to find one that reflects client strength.

For example, a family was referred to the children's mental health center. As they came into service, they were very angry at the system. Apparently, the family had been fighting with a child protection worker and a hospital social worker to get them to understand their situation. These workers interpreted the fighting as hostility and manipulation. Client behavior was interpreted as confirming the worker assumptions. The children's mental health worker adopted a different interpretation. His interpretation was that the family was working hard to master very difficult losses. The fighting was incorporated into this interpretation as family attempts to keep others from taking their control away. This interpretation created a positive relationship with the family, who began to work cooperatively with the new worker.

Maintaining Skepticism.   Critical thinkers are never satisfied that they have reached the final conclusion (Brookfield, 1987; Gibbs & Gambrill, 1999). They always review past actions to learn what they can do differently next time. They also review every situation with an element of skepticism that anyone truly knows the right answers. This skepticism keeps them searching and questioning to find better, more effective ways to do almost everything. Statements of certainty are met with "Well, I'm not so sure," or "Yes, but . . ." responses.

Correlational Thinking Abilities

Correlational thinking is central to identifying connections in the problem situation and translating theory into helping behaviors. It is also a necessary ability for formulating assessments in which the worker must take background or environmental events and identify how they contribute to the presenting problem. You used correlational thinking to identify connections between the history and processing systems in the Cecil case. There are five common types of correlational thinking.

Identifying Connections.   Workers often are challenged to understand current difficulties that originate in other areas of the client's life. Many people adapt to past events only to find later that the adaptations can contribute to problems. Similarly, many find that events outside of the situation can contribute to the problem. Effective workers are able to make the connections among different elements of a person's life and complete the problem understanding by drawing linkages. For example, a chaotic lifestyle may be correlated to living in poverty. Workers need to identify these connections to determine where to and where not to intervene.

Identifying Themes.   Often there are themes inherent in client discussions about their stories. Workers need to be able to identify the client themes to understand the current problem. For example, a parent working to decrease volatility with his children described several volatile incidents in which the parent wanted something to occur to reinforce that he was a good parent. In each of the examples, the children did something different, causing the father to feel inadequate. The parent then berated the children, making himself look and feel worse. By identifying the themes in the descriptions, the worker and parent were able to explore the problem at a very meaningful level.

Identifying Parallel Processes.   Similar to identifying themes, there are often sequences of interaction that occur at different levels of the client's life (Shulman, 1999). A common example is the pattern in which abused children grow up to abuse their own children. This is an intergenerational parallel process. Similarly, workers in agencies that have a poor tolerance for differences usually do not perform well with clients who are very different. Many clients who have been rejected by parents fear rejection by workers. All of these parallel processes involve themes occurring at different levels of the situation.

Identifying Interactional Patterns.   Often problematic behaviors follow similar patterns each time they occur. As with the content themes, workers can identify interactional themes. For example, during a group for child witnesses of spouse abuse, members would become very agitated and change the subject every time the worker mentioned violence. After several instances of this pattern, the worker pointed it out to the children. After the theme of discomfort was highlighted, the children began discussing their feelings about the violence.

Producing Analogies/Metaphors.   Effective workers often introduce discussions of change or introduce information through telling stories paralleling the client situation. The parallel between the client story and the shared story allows the client to make connections yielding understanding and change. Concise correlational thinking is important when developing metaphors. Correlational thinking assures similar meanings and patterns. The worker will look foolish and distracting if the intervention is indirect or confusing.

Predictive Thinking Abilities

Similar to correlational thinking, predictive thinking is focused on relationships among current actions and future outcomes. In predictive thinking, a worker is attempting to predict how one situation or action will affect others in the future. This is most useful in selecting interventions and preparing clients for generalizing changes. There are four types of predictive thinking.

Predicting Thoughts.   Effective workers are able to predict normally occurring sequences of events. By sharing these with clients, workers can identify potential resistance or reactions that are likely to occur. Effective workers are able to predict such normal outcomes and discuss them to prevent potential problems.

For example, a worker was counseling a mother who had an anger problem. The mother was making progress and becoming optimistic. The worker worried how a slip in progress might affect her and stated, "In the next little while, you will lose it again and yell at your kids. Right after the yelling, you will get down on yourself and want to give up. I want you to know that slipping is normal. When you slip, even though you will feel like we are failing, you need to think about how well we have done for four weeks. How can we keep things hopeful when this occurs?"

Predicting Outcomes.   Workers make statements, suggestions, or take action to help clients achieve their goals. In taking such action, workers are required to predict how their intervention will affect the client. Such prediction includes predicting positive outcome or progress toward the goal and potential negative outcomes. The predictive thinking is instrumental in minimizing the negative outcomes of interventions while maximizing progress toward the goals.

Identifying Challenges.   In conjunction with other types of thinking, effective workers are able to project forward and identify challenging situations. Such prediction is instrumental in relapse prevention in which the worker identifies challenging situations and engages the client in exploring how to maintain changes within the situation.

Sometimes this involves identifying a series of events that can be problematic. At other times, it might involve instructing the clients to engage in behaviors to test the changes. Predictive thinking is often used in relapse-prevention planning when ending service.

Expanding Change to New Situations. Similar to projecting challenges, effective workers help clients project success into the future by predicting situations in which the new skills or abilities will be useful. Such prediction occurs through expanding the current changes and new abilities to new situations that are likely to occur. The abilities and situations the prediction is built upon must be readily identifiable for the client. This requires using information about the client situation to develop the prediction.

EXERCISE 4.1

The Peter Case Study

This case is provided to help you practice the different styles of thinking. In using this case study, read each section and then answer the questions. Upon completing each section, proceed with the next section until the case study is completed. After completing the case study, share your answers either with your instructor or your classmates to glean feedback on the outcomes of your thinking. With this feedback in mind, read the thinking styles again to determine which thinking styles are natural to you and which styles need more development.

Section 1. The worker in this case is Glenna, a case manager working in a center for people with developmental disabilities in a rural southern state. The center has educational, prevocational, vocational, and residential programs serving clients of all ages. Glenna is a 29-year-old Caucasian woman living with the supervisor of the residential services (named John).

The client in this case is Peter, a 27-year-old Jewish male of Russian decent who has a rare handicapping condition that causes him to have a small and somewhat frail stature. Intellectual disabilities are minimal with this syndrome, but there is difficulty processing on the abstract level. Peter was diagnosed as a young child and immediately placed in an institution for the developmentally disabled. He remained in the institution until two years ago when it was closed. He has neither seen nor heard from his family since his placement in the institution.

Peter has consistently done well in the sheltered workshop where he is employed. He is brighter than most of the other clients and consistently produces at a high rate. He has a fairly good relationship with the staff in the workshop and often comes to visit the case managers in their offices. Glenna sees him probably four to five times per day as he drops in to chat and then returns to work. Even with this pattern of chatting, Peter has high productivity at work. Given that he is paid piecework, his high production benefits him with money. Peter is able to take the bus downtown and use his money well. He has bought season tickets to the little theater and loves to read books. He is being considered for competitive employment (part of the general workforce) at a local department store where he will be stocking shelves and sweeping floors.

The problem area for Peter is maintaining stability in his residential placements. Peter does not do well in group-living situations and will rant and rave for days on end if placed in a group home. Consequently, he was placed in a specialized foster home. Peter has had several foster home placements since coming to the agency. Although he is bright and participates in community activities, he is demanding of people in caregiving roles. If Peter does not feel his needs are met, he will storm into the room, pound tables or desks, and demand that people do what he wants.

Peter's demandingness is not a constant type of behavior. There are often times when Peter functions well in all areas of his life. During these times, he is helpful around the home, engages in conversation, and is pleasant company. During these periods, he is rewarded with increased freedom and responsibility. One of the rewards during calm periods is a TV for his bedroom. This allows Peter total control over program choice and an opportunity to spend unlimited time in his room watching TV. He is also allowed to go out in the community without restrictions. This is a positive time for the foster parents who feel free to leave him at home alone and resume their own lives.

Inevitably, Peter's good periods seldom last longer than four to six weeks, after which he will "blow up" at the foster parents. Typically, there are no warning signs. The foster parents, after being out, are greeted by pounding and swearing when Peter sees them coming into the home. Such behavior jeopardizes his residential placement, given that he is most unkind in the things that he yells. Peter also has smashed items but never attacked a human being.

When Peter gets in his angry state, he generalizes his anger and becomes demanding of everyone in roles of authority. He has gone into the executive director's office ranting and raving about how people in this "f_ _king dump need to pay attention to what I want." During these periods, Glenna builds in extra supports for the residential providers until things stabilize. It takes about two to three weeks to get him stabilized and about another month or two before the additional resources can be withdrawn.

1. Using the theories you know, what might be causing Peter's problem?

2. What are the parameters of the problem (when, where, how, etc.)?

3. What are the elements of the problem (can you identify components or smaller problems inside this larger problem)?

4. What is the pattern of the problem?

5. Based on the pattern, what do you think is associated with the problem behaviors?

6. What would you select as a goal in this case?

7. What smaller changes might you make that combined would accomplish this goal?

8. How would you know if your attempts to make this change were successful (what would you see that was different)?

Section 2.   After the last volatile incident, Glenna met with Peter and discussed the problem of his volatility. He had gone into the executive director's office and called her several names. Many of the names and phrases incorporated observations about her obvious weight problem. Peter had made some suggestion that she would do better if she were seated less and did her job taking care of clients like him. Glenna received a call shortly after his visit with the executive director.

Glenna took a firm stand with Peter. She stated that he was going to have to "redeem himself this time." Peter was consequently prohibited from visiting staff during working hours. He could only come to see the staff members on coffee breaks, and this was only with workshop staff permission. Peter stated this was not fair to him. Glenna responded that his behavior was not fair to others and stressed that he needed to learn how to work with others.

1. What goal does this intervention seek to achieve?

2. What is the assumption underlying this intervention; what is the leverage to make it work?

3. When Glenna said, "you have to redeem yourself," what do you think was going on for her?

4. What assumptions do you think might work better in this case?

5. What type of intervention would this lead to?

6. How do you think this would change the relationship?

7. Based on what you know about the client, what is likely to happen with Peter as a result of Glenna's intervention?

Section 3.   When Glenna told Peter he was prohibited from visiting, he became irate. He yelled at her, swore, and called her names. He then escalated and began kicking her bookcase and yelling, "You don't care. Nobody cares about me. You might as well just get rid of me." He then ran out of the workshop and left for the day. Glenna called John and told him of the escalation in volatility in Peter's final statement before leaving. John phoned the consulting psychiatrist, and they agreed that Peter should be hospitalized for his own safety. It was arranged for him to be picked up by the police when he arrived at the foster home.

1. What was Glenna's interpretation of Peter's statement, "You might as well get rid of me?"

2. What alternative interpretation is there for Peter's statement?

3. If Glenna took this alternative interpretation, how would it change intervention?

4. What are the parallel processes evident in this section?

5. What do you think the client's experience of intervention is?

6. What do you think the outcome of this will be for the worker–client relationship?

7. What might be done at this point to salvage the worker–client relationship?

Section 4. After getting out of the hospital, new supports were put in place and Peter was stabilized again. He did well in both residential and workshop settings. The supports included ongoing counseling, a community/respite support person (to take him out), and an independent-living group at the workshop. The period of stability lasted more than four months, leading Glenna to put his name forward for a supported independent-living apartment and competitive employment. Her plan was to move him into the new services and then pass his case on to a different case manager.

1. What is likely to happen to Peter in this transition?

2. What is the parallel process in this situation?

3. What might be done differently to help the plan (apartment and work) succeed?

ASSUMPTIONS: THE FOUNDATION OF WORKER MISTAKES

Most worker mistakes are based in their assumptions and interpretations of the client situation. A worker who has negative interpretations of client behaviors will respond based on negative assumptions. Alternatively, if the worker forms positive assumptions, a totally different response will be generated to the identical client behaviors. When mistakes arise, the worker must try to understand the assumptions and thinking that led to the mistake.

In the preceding exercise, it was obvious that Glenna made assumptions about client motivations and intent. Based on her interpretations of the client, Glenna intervened. As you explored her thinking and had opportunities to rethink situations, alternative interpretations became evident. In professional practice, workers must use the thinking skills outlined in this chapter to scrutinize their interpretations and assumptions. This can prevent mistakes. In such scrutiny, they must consider the core professional values and ethics as guides for assessing assumptions.

The following pages contain exercises to challenge thinking about client situations. The exercises focus on the thought processes behind mistakes in working with clients. Each client scenario contains three mistakes made by the worker. The mistakes are associated with an assumption or theory upon which the worker is basing his or her action. In these exercises, read the client scenario to find the mistakes. Then determine the assumption or theory leading to the mistakes. After identifying the assumption that created the problem, identify alternative assumptions and how this might improve the client situation.

EXERCISE 4.2

The CPS Worker

1. A Native American male age 36 met with the 27-year-old Caucasian worker assigned to him through Child Protection Services. This single-parent father lives on a local Indian reservation. In the meeting, he sat quietly and nodded as she told him that he needs to make sure his children are supervised while he is working. The children are 8, 9, and 10 in age. The caseworker told him that the children had informed her that when they got off the school bus, there was often nobody home. He responded that his sister and mother live in the area and look out for the kids. The worker continued that often the children stay all night at relatives' homes rather than in his home. He confirmed that this was true. The worker confronted the father stating that he did not seem concerned about the welfare of his children and that she should take the kids away from him. He responded, "You are going to do what you are going to do anyway." She then became angry and told the father that she was picking the children up at the school and he was being charged with child neglect.

    a. What are three mistakes made by the worker?

    b. What are her assumptions that led to the mistakes?

    c. What would a better set of assumptions be?

    d. What is the first spot in the case description that this would change? What would the difference be?

The Shelter Worker

2. A 27-year-old Caucasian woman had been staying with her sons, aged 8 and 10, in a shelter for battered women. The youngest son appeared to be hyperactive or having some sort of attention deficit. This woman met with her shelter worker, a 55-year-old African American woman who was herself battered when younger. The client wanted to return home, which prompted the worker to state this would not be wise because her husband would beat her again. The worker then described her own abuse and how she finally had to just leave her partner. The woman responded, "But Ben is different. He really is a good father and tries really hard to keep the boys in line. The problem is that I don't always support his decisions. That is what happened, I butted in when he was disciplining the children. I just didn't think he should be so hard on them. When I said that, he went off on me. If I didn't do that, he wouldn't have hit me." The worker responded, "You know that is not true. A batterer will hit you regardless of what you did or didn't do. And here he is going off on the children. Now I've got to call CPS in too. You better avoid him until they finish their investigation and even then, you know it is never safe."

   a. What three mistakes did the worker make?

   b. What assumptions led to these mistakes?

   c. What alternative assumptions might be applied to this case?

   d. What is the first point in this case where this alternative theory would create a change? What would this change be?

The School Worker

3. A school-based social worker was assigned to meet with children having behavior problems in school. A young Hispanic boy (10 years old) was referred for fighting. When she met with him, he appeared resistant and often responded, "I don't know" to her questions about why he was fighting. With some persistence on her part, she got him to agree that he needed to stop fighting and that he didn't like being in trouble. He became teary and blurted out that "They treat me like I am stupid so I have to hit them." She responded that she could see he needed to get control. She then explored things that he liked. He talked about McDonald's and his Beanie Baby collection. At the end, she told him that she would develop a behavior chart that would be monitored by his teacher. She would come to his classroom every Friday to review the chart with the teacher. If there were no fights, she would either give him a Beanie Baby or take him to McDonald's for lunch.

    a. What were three mistakes made by this worker?

    b. What assumptions contributed to these mistakes?

    c. What would a set of assumptions be for this child?

    d. How would the new assumptions make a difference?

The Family Support Worker

    4. This worker has been working with a church-based family support program with families going through separation or divorce. In meeting with an 8-year-old girl, the worker began with his regular set of questions beginning with "Do you know why your mother brought you here?" The child became sullen and tears welled up in her eyes. He then responded, "I know that there have been some changes in your family. . . ." At this point, the child began to cry. The worker continued, "You need to understand that divorce is a grown-up problem and children are never responsible for parental breakups." The child continued to cry, so the worker pulled in the mother and explained, "Your child feels very responsible for the marital breakup. I think you and your husband both need to come in here to meet with me so we can help your child feel better about the separation."

    a. What were three mistakes made by this worker?

    b. What were the assumptions underlying the mistakes?

    c. What would a better assumption or interpretation be for this client?

    d. What differences would this make in worker response?

Critical Chapter Themes

1. Workers must be able to think in order to apply the knowledge and theory base to practice situations.
2. Logical thinking helps workers develop linear linkages such as cause and effect, problem parameters, and developing the goals/objectives from the understanding of the situation.
3. Reflective thinking helps workers maintain their sense of purpose, identify their assumptions, and incorporate feedback into their approach with clients.
4. Critical thinking keeps workers skeptical and always learning new and better ways to perform their professional functions.
5. Correlational thinking abilities help workers identify patterns and relationships within the client situation.
6. Predictive thinking abilities help workers identify how clients may respond to interventions and different challenges that may occur in the client situation.
7. Mistakes in working with clients most often come from the assumptions and thinking that the worker has about the situation. Consequently, thinking and self-awareness work together to help avoid making serious mistakes with clients.

RECOMMENDED READINGS

Browne, N. M., & Keeley, S. M. (1994). *Asking the right questions: A guide to critical thinking* (4th ed.). Englewood Cliffs, NJ: Prentice-Hall.

Gambrill, E. (1997). *Social work practice: A critical thinker's guide.* New York: Oxford University Press.

Gibbs, L. E. (1991). *Scientific reasoning for social workers.* New York: Macmillan.

Gibbs, L. E. (1994). Teaching clinical reasoning. *The Behavior Therapist, 17,* 1–6.

Gibbs, L. E., & Gambrill, E. (1999). *Critical thinking for social workers—Exercises for the helping profession.* Thousand Oaks, CA: Pine Forge Press.

Kassierer, J. P., & Kopelman, R. I. (1991). *Learning clinical reasoning.* Baltimore: Williams & Wilkins.

PART TWO

Toward Developing the Helping Relationship

This part focuses on the second set of core skills. These skills build on the self-awareness, self-control, and thinking skills developed in the first part. In this part, readers will learn how to build upon their professional use of self-skills to establish an emotional connection to clients and engage them in service.

The chapters focus on two important skills. First, the reader will be introduced to tuning in skills. These skills help workers to become empathic with the client. Readers will learn how to tune into client experiences and into the dynamics of larger client systems.

Readers will develop abilities to identify the processing and action systems as they evolve as clients enter service, interact with the worker, and interact with other people. From such identification, readers will be guided in how this knowledge can help engage clients in service and in the helping relationship.

Written material and exercises will help students establish a firm skill base for empathically responding to clients. Such responding has long been considered a necessary ingredient in the helping professions.

CHAPTER

5

Tuning In to the Client

After developing knowledge, thinking, awareness, and control skills, workers must learn to build a helping relationship with clients. The development of the helping relationship is the second core skill set. This skill set involves two important skills, empathic tuning in and engaging clients. This chapter will focus on the first skill for developing the helping relationship—tuning in to the client experience. Some authors refer to the skill as tuning in, empathy, or empathic attunement (Egan, 1998; Rowe & MacIsaac, 1989; Shulman, 1999).

Empathy is the ability to accurately understand the client's experience within each of the response systems (affect, thinking, action, and interaction). Empathy requires the worker to mentally construct the client's experience through the careful use of awareness and thinking skills. High levels of empathy are one of the critical worker traits, separating highly effective from less effective workers (Lafferty, Beutler, & Crago, 1989; Ridgway & Sharpley, 1990).

Tuning in is the term coined by Lawrence Shulman (1999) to describe the mental processes that result in empathy. Empathy, consequently, is the end product of the internal process of tuning in. As the means to such an end product, tuning in to the client situation serves to sensitize the worker before meeting the client and in responding to client disclosures.

Tuning in to the client situation is contingent on the thinking skills discussed in the previous chapter. It is also highly contingent on self-awareness. If workers are not tuned in to themselves and how they react to different situations, it is unlikely they can fully extend themselves to understand the reactions of other people. Given that this skill builds on the previous two skills, and considering that thinking and self-awareness are ongoing processes, tuning in is always a skill in development. This means workers must always be working on this skill by expanding their knowledge/thinking, monitoring themselves, and extending these growing skill sets to better understand client experiences.

Tuning in and empathy are critical in the development of effective service (Shulman, 1999). Less effective workers tend to approach clients in a more intellectual fashion and lack empathy for the client experience (Bozarth, 1997; Lafferty, Beutler, & Crago, 1989). There are two levels of tuning in, preliminary and interactive. Each level of tuning in is important for understanding the client experience (Miller, 1999).

Preliminary tuning in starts before the client enters treatment. This level involves the worker taking time to understand the client experience of entering service. The empathy resulting from this level of tuning in allows the worker to more fully understand and respond to the client as they first meet (Miller, 1999; Shulman, 1999). The preliminary empathy consequently sets the tone for the working relationship by helping the client feel welcome, understood, and comfortable (Satterfield & Lyddon, 1998).

Interactive tuning in occurs after the client has entered service as the worker tunes in to the unspoken concerns and questions of the client (Shulman, 1999). Effective workers are able to understand how the client is experiencing the service and respond to the client's feelings (Najavits & Strupp, 1994). The client consequently begins to feel understood and thus is more willing to engage in the service being provided.

PRELIMINARY TUNING IN

Preliminary tuning in occurs before the client officially begins service with the worker. As the client starts service, the worker gleans information to begin tuning in to the client experience of entering service. Prior to the first face-to-face contact between worker and client, preliminary tuning in is used to begin the worker–client relationship (Miller, 1999; Shulman, 1999).

The Elements of Preliminary Tuning In

There are five areas of consideration in preliminary tuning in. Although these tend to occur simultaneously for many workers, they will be discussed separately to provide the fullest possible exploration. The five elements are:

- reflective thinking about the client situation
- reflective thinking about potential worker blocks
- reflective thinking about helping situation blocks
- identifying problem perspectives
- identifying concerns and questions

Reflective Thinking about the Client Situation.   In preparing to meet with the client, the first step is to review all possible information about the client to begin to understand the client's experience of coming into service (Miller, 1999). Possible elements to consider include:

- *Precipitating events.* What caused the client to seek service at this time (voluntary, involuntary, and type of motivation)? The worker reviews the file to understand how the referral was initiated and the history of the presenting request. If others are involved, what are their roles in the family and in the referral decision? If the worker is able to explore the referral with the client on the phone, information about the decision to enter service can be solicited directly from the client. The worker seeks to understand the client experience of entering service through the following types of questions:
  - "In this situation, would I really want this service or would I feel pressured to come here?"
  - "In this situation, what would I really want to have happen by coming here?"

- "How vulnerable would I feel coming here under these conditions?"
- "What strengths are indicated through the client entering service at this time?"

- *Current stresses.* What are the current stresses in the client's life (personal, family, community, economic, and social)? The worker reviews the current request and other information to understand the client's life situation. This might involve file reviews and gathering information about the community. For example, have there been any losses or trauma in the client community? Have there been economic stresses (e.g., layoffs)? The worker reviews the available information and considers:
  - "If I were living this life and experiencing these stresses, how would I cope?"
  - "In this kind of community, how would others be responding to this situation?"
  - "What would the supports and additional stressors be in the life space? How would I feel about them if I had the same history as the client?"
  - "Given the history and community, how would I feel coming into this service?"
  - "What strengths has the client used to survive to this point?"

- *Presenting request(s).* What is the client overtly and covertly asking for (client description of the problem, third-party issues such as getting someone else to respond differently, side-taking issues, wanting a report)? The worker considers the whole situation from the client's point of view and life circumstance to understand the client's motivation involved in seeking help at this time. In thinking about the situation, the worker asks:
  - "In this situation, what would I really want to have happen?"
  - "In this situation, how would I want the service to involve others?"
  - "In this situation, what are the normal and natural things for people to want?"
  - "What are the client's cognitive and emotional strengths displayed in making this request for service?"
  - "How can these client strengths be used to move toward the outcomes the client seems to want?"

- *Past experience with helping systems.* What history with helping systems might influence the client experience of coming in for help at this time (past involvement with this agency, past or present involvement with other agencies, past functioning)? The worker reviews the available information (and gathers additional information) to understand the client's social history and social situation. Often this involves soliciting reports from other services (with signed releases of information) to gain the fullest possible array of information. In reading the available information, the worker mentally extends him- or herself into the client situation asking questions like:
  - "What would it be like if others had written that information about me and I knew people were reading it?"
  - "How would it be for me to have lived this life?"
  - "If I had lived this life, what would it be like coming to this service?"
  - "If I were in this family and this person made the referral, how would I experience the person who referred me; how would I experience the decision?"
  - "If I were in this situation, what in the history or current situation might be influencing my decision to come into service at this time (anniversaries, losses, abuses, third-party interventions)?"

- "Throughout this history, what client strengths contributed to the client's ability to survive?"
- "How can those strengths be used in this service?"

- *Cultural and demographic trends.* What cultural and demographic traits seem important as the client enters service at this time (gender, culture, race, socioeconomic status)? Given the available information, what is the potential influence of culture and demographics on the client experience? The individual experiences of people entering service will vary according gender, economics, race, and cultural groups. Consider any potential problems that might interfere if left unattended. Such sensitization allows workers to monitor for potential problems with an open, rather than defensive, attitude. In considering the potentialities, workers need to ask:
    - "Given the history between helping systems and this group, race, or culture, how would I feel coming in to meet someone like me?"
    - "Knowing what I know about this group of clients, what is the meaning of receiving help?"
    - "What are the natural sources of help that are often used by this group?"
    - "What might the meaning be if this client is approaching the agency rather than these other sources of help (e.g., do they know about the natural sources)?"
    - "Is the client networked isolated or in the community ? (Might the client want privacy from the community?)"
    - "Is there a possible stigma associated with coming to this agency that might be complicated by the demographic grouping?"
    - "What are potential strengths in this demographic grouping that can be used to help the client situation?"

Reflective Thinking about Potential Worker Blocks.   The second area of reflective thinking in tuning in is the potential for worker traits to interfere with the client's ability to fully engage with the helping system. Such tuning in requires workers to reflect on the client's potential reactions to them when entering service. Workers also need to reflect on how they might respond to their clients. In such reflection, workers consider both their clients' and their own traits simultaneously. This often involves reflecting on similarities and differences existing between the worker and the client situation.

- *Life experiences and models of understanding.* In Chapter 1, students were guided through reflection on life history and inherited patterns of belief and behavior. It is important to consider how these models might appear to clients as they come into service. How would one's processing and action systems be experienced by the client? The worker needs to use the self-awareness skills to consider the following:
    - "Given my life situation and the client situation, what in my experiences, values, and beliefs might cause discomfort for the client and me?"
    - "How will this look to the client?"
    - "If I were this client, what would I notice about me?"
    - "How can I make sure that I am able to concentrate on the client story?"
    - "If I were this client, what would I notice if concentration started to slip?"

- "How can I achieve full self-control of my possible hot spots, cold spots, and blind spots with this client situation?"
- "What reactions would I see in me if I were this client?"
- "If I were avoiding or closing myself off from this client, what might the client's reactions be that could tell me that I am not understanding?"
- "What are the motivating themes in my life that I might inject into this client situation? How will the client see this?"
- "What in my action and processing systems might be different from this client's? How might this interfere with the helping relationship?"
- "What are my patterns/preferences of thinking, feeling, and acting that are similar to this client's? How might this influence the working relationship?"
- "How might my approach to life (time orientation to past, present, future, and locus of control) present challenges to my openness with this client situation?"

- *Demographic or cultural differences* (age, gender, race, dress, grooming, education, socioeconomic status). The demographic attributes and general presentation style of the worker is one of the first elements observed by the client as he or she enters service. Consider how the worker's looks might influence the client's first impression. Workers need to consider the client situation and answer the following:
  - "Given my age and the ages of people in the client situation, might the client have some questions about my ability to relate or be of help?"
  - "Given my gender and what I know about the client situation, could the client experience any concerns about me when we meet?"
  - "Given my ethnic background, might this client experience any concerns that I might not be able to understand him or her?"
  - "Given the struggles or lack of struggles in my life, might this client have doubts that I will be able to understand or be of help?"
  - "Given my general presentation style (e.g., weight, attractiveness, dress code, tidiness), could the client have concerns about my ability to relate or be of help?"

Reflective Thinking about the Helping Situation.

Aside from the client situation and how the worker appears to the client, there is another element warranting consideration while tuning in to the client situation. The client experience of the agency setting is a critical influence on the client experience. Many clients feel powerless as they come in for assistance (Green, Lee, Mentzer, Punnell, & Niles, 1998). Concurrently, agencies have reputations, procedures, attributes, or functions that influence the client experience. Such elements precede the worker's first contact with the client and are already influencing the relationship with the worker. A worker would be remiss to ignore these elements of service. In tuning in to this aspect of the client situation, the worker can reflect on the following elements.

- *Barriers to accessing service.* Agencies can inadvertently interfere with the client's ability to access and use service through their choices in setting, protocols, and services. As clients try to access service, they may feel unfairly scrutinized or inconvenienced. For example, some agencies serving economically oppressed clients house their services far away from their clients and send out lengthy questionnaires to complete before service is arranged. These experiences can engender resentment or distrust of the agency. It is important for workers to understand the experiences of the clients as they access service. This can allow for empathy at the service level as well as the client situation level. In reflecting on the barriers to service, workers often consider the following questions.

- "If I were this client with this problem, how would I feel getting to this setting and getting around in this building?"
- "If I were this client with this problem, what additional supports might be helpful as I come into service (child care, help completing forms)?"
- "If I were this client with this problem, how would I feel about completing the protocols from first contact to finally meeting with the worker?"
- "If I were this client with this problem, how would I feel having to tell my story in this office or room?"
- "If I were this client with this problem, how would I feel about the people who greet me and take my information?"
- "If I were this client with this problem, how would I experience the way my information is gathered and shared among the people in the agency?"

- *Perceived agency role and function in the community.* Agencies do not exist in a vacuum. Often clients know someone previously served by the agency or have otherwise heard about the agency. Sometimes client perceptions are influenced by the agency's role in the community or its reputation. If the perceptions are good, clients will approach the helping situation with optimism. However, if the agency has a bad reputation, clients may approach services with a negative expectation. Consider the reputation of the agency for similar clients to reflect on how the client might experience coming to the agency. For example, child protective services often are resisted because people fear they will lose their children. This reputation has remained influential despite most child protection agencies providing supports for keeping the child in the home. Clients will not be open to supports until their concerns about losing their children are resolved. In reflecting on the influence of reputation, workers might consider the following questions.

- "Given the nature of the client's request and the typical role of this agency, what might the client's experience be?"
- "Given this client's experiences with past agencies and past workers, what concerns might the client have coming into service at this agency?"
- "What press releases and articles might the client have read concerning this agency and how might this influence what the client believes about service?"
- "Given this client's life situation, what might the client believe about this agency and how we might be of help?"
- "What might this client fear (e.g., losing a child, being judged, being talked about, or being blamed) when coming to this agency?"

- *The visual impact of the agency.* The way agencies appear as clients enter the door influences their experience of service. For example, agencies housed in shabby settings might appear inferior to some clients. Conversely, opulent agencies might create an elitist impression. The agency impression is in part contingent on the way the agency is decorated relative to the life situation of the client. Tuning in to the client's experience thus requires workers to consider both the agency and the client. Workers need to consider the following questions.

- "Given the client's background and concerns, will the client feel comfortable in the helping environment (e.g., privacy, shabbiness/opulence, interpersonal atmosphere)?"
- "Given the client's background and concerns, will the client feel comfortable coming into the community (socioeconomics, turf, history)?"
- "Given the client's background and concerns, will there be others in the environment that might create discomfort (e.g., authority figures)?"
- "Given the client's background and concerns, are there agency linkages to funding sources or other agencies that need to be clarified for this client (e.g., Employee Assistance Plan, government contracts, limitations of service, limitations of rights)?"
- "Given the client's background and concerns, are there culturally inappropriate agency features (e.g., decoration, assessment protocols)?"

Considering the Problem Perspective in Preliminary Tuning In

When clients feel there are problems in their own lives, they are motivated to come into the helping relationship to explore and solve the problems (Stein, 1995). The feelings that motivate the referral are primarily internal to the person making the decision to seek service. When such clients enter service, defining the problem is a simple act of exploring the client's understanding, given there is a single perspective. However, when there are several people in the situation, the worker often must consider different perspectives on the situation.

With clients in complex situations, there are at least two problem perspectives affecting their motivations as they enter a helping relationship. It is important to tune in to the client's perspective in preparation for the first meeting. To guide this tuning in process, the worker must understand whose feelings are motivating the service. The worker must also understand that others might experience service differently. The perspectives on the problem are tremendously important when approaching larger client systems, as there will be several perspectives on any problem situation, with every person having his or her own unique perspective.

The Primary Felt Perspective.   In considering the various perspectives, the worker begins by trying to understand the feelings of the person initiating service. There is always one person whose feelings cause the referral for service. Because this person's feelings motivate the client to contact the agency, this person's definition or experience of the problem is called the *primary felt perspective.* The perspective is "primary" because the person's feelings came first and "felt" because the person's feelings motivated the referral.

For example, the client might be struggling with depression triggered by a relationship breakup. In such a situation, the client wants to enter the helping relationship to gain increased control over the internal reactions to the situation. The worker engages with the client and typically maintains a singular focus. If the client situation requires an expansion of services, the singular focus is maintained but the relationship adopts case-management functions (coordinating multiple relationships) concurrent with the primary-care function of helping the client.

The Secondary Felt Perspective.

When people are not the same person whose feelings precipitated the referral, they will have *secondary felt perspectives*. The perspective is "secondary" because the client's perspective is second to the person whose feelings prompted service and "felt" because they will have a very different feeling than the person insisting on service. One can expect that everyone in the problem situation will have a separate secondary perspective that is different from the person with the primary perspective. Effective workers are able to tune in to the secondary perspective on the situation concurrent with the primary position to allow for the fullest understanding of the client system.

Secondary perspectives are common with children referred by a parent for treatment. The child does not have the primary felt problem. The parent has the primary felt problem and the child's problem occurs when the parent attempts to correct the child. Coming into service, the child's experience of the problem will be influenced by the parent's interactions about the behavior and the parental expectations of different behavior.

For example, a parent is angry because his child never does what he is told and refers the child for service. The motivating feeling of anger is primarily the parent's. However, the child has a secondary felt problem stemming from the arguing and fighting with the parent. The child may even want to retain the freedom associated with the current situation. It is important to understand that there are two problems in this situation, not just one. It is also important to tune in to the position of each person in the client system because each experience is different.

The Externalized Primary Perspective.

Similar to the parent–child situation just described, there are times when nobody in the client system has the motivating feelings (primary perspective). In such situations, all people in the client system experience secondary felt perspectives. When client systems are motivated to enter service due to an externalized primary perspective, it can be complex because people in the client system are not emotionally invested in the initial problem. Instead, they experience one or more secondary felt problems.

For example, when a teacher is having difficulty with a child, it is common for the teacher to contact the parent. In such situations, the teacher has the felt problem and the parent develops the secondary problem. For the parent, the secondary perspective may be to improve the relationship between the child and teacher. However, the child becomes the recipient of service even though he or she is well removed from the primary felt problem. The child might have another secondary perspective with the teacher (e.g., stop her from yelling at me in class). The child may also have a secondary perspective with the parent (e.g., stop the parent from chastising me about my school behavior).

EXERCISE 5.1

Preliminary Tuning In

1. You are a worker in a shelter for abused women and their children. The shelter is in the city center and serves a wide variety of women and their children. You are preparing to meet a new woman being admitted to the shelter. This woman is coming into service because she has been badly beaten by her male partner after attending a social function. Her two small children, who were present during the violence, accompany the woman. A neighbor called the police, but the man left before they could take him away. The police consequently brought her into the shelter for her own protection. This woman is financially well off. She is an executive in a local company and her husband is a lawyer. She is well known to the shelter because she has donated her used clothes for the residents. Tune into this woman's experience in her personal life as she enters service and determine:

    a. What in the precipitating events are likely to influence her experience?

    b. Who has the primary felt problem (the primary perspective bringing them in)?

    c. What is the secondary felt perspective that might be occurring for the woman about her children?

    d. What might be the children's experience as they enter service?

    e. What in yourself might need to be monitored and controlled to assure that your traits don't interfere with service?

    f. What in the setting might influence the woman's experience as she enters service?

2. You are a new graduate hired to work with families receiving welfare. You were hired on a grant funding a pilot project. Although you don't know all the details of the grant, you know the basic premise is that children living in poor, single-parent families are at a higher risk for abuse and adjustment problems. The project is run through the local Department of Social Services. The agency is located on the edge of town where the buses do not run in the evenings. Consequently, you had many phone contacts with the women who will be attending the program to arrange rides. You are teamed up with a child protection worker who is also a member of your graduating class. The program involves a ten-week psychoeducational program focusing on helping the mothers to better understand and attend to their children's emotional needs. The program includes presentations and lectures. You are preparing to meet your first group of women. You watched them come into the building and noticed many looked older and appeared to have had difficult lives. As you prepare to meet with this group, tune in to the clients.

    a. In this situation, who has the primary felt problem?

    b. What secondary perspectives might occur given the nature of the primary felt problem and the premises of the group?

    c. How might the women experience you? What is your anxiety?

    d. How might the women experience your partner?

    e. How might the way the program is structured interfere with the women's experiences?

    f. What in the setting might interfere with the experiences of the women?

INTERACTIONAL TUNING IN:
THE FOUNDATION FOR EMPATHY

Identifying Unspoken Client Questions

From the empathy developed through tuning in, workers are challenged to identify the critical, unspoken questions and concerns in the client experience. The following types of questions are common when clients are entering the helping relationship.

Unspoken Client Questions about Themselves.   As clients enter the helping relationship, they are in a vulnerable position (Greene et al., 1998). This vulnerability can engender questions about their adequacy and/or sanity as they approach someone else (or are required to approach someone else) for assistance. Typical questions include such things as:

- "Is there something wrong with me?"
- "Did I do something wrong?"
- "Am I crazy?"
- "Am I hopeless?"

Unspoken Client Questions about the Helping Process.   Clients consistently have questions about what might happen as a result of entering service (Shulman, 1999). Clients seek to find hope and relief, but at the same time fear that neither will happen or they may fail. Some of the internal questions include:

- "What will be expected of me?"
- "Will they make me feel bad?"
- "What is going to happen?"
- "What will they do for me?"
- "Will this even help?"

Unspoken Client Questions about the Worker.   Typically, the client does not know the worker. Consequently, there will be anxiety about how the worker will respond to the client (Shulman, 1999). The answers to worker-based questions shape the working alliance between the client and the worker (Beutler & Clarkin, 1990). Clients experience the normal anxiety of meeting another person compounded by anxiety about their vulnerability in the helping situation. The resolution of these concerns is often seen as dependent on the ability and traits of this unknown person, the worker. Typical questions of this type include:

- "Will this person be able to understand me?"
- "Can this person help me?"
- "What will this person think of me?"

- "Will this person fix things for me?"
- "How will this person make me feel?"

Responding to Unspoken Client Questions

When working with unspoken client questions, it is helpful to address client concerns as they emerge (Shulman, 1999). However, many questions are asked in a disguised or indirect manner. Effective workers are able to hear the questions and respond to them or put the concern into words for the client (Shulman, 1999). The decision to be direct or indirect is usually based on the potential impact of addressing the question with the client. For example, if the client is worried about being crazy, many workers will indirectly address the unspoken question by using a response that normalizes people entering service.

Example of an Indirect Response.   A worker in a family service agency was conducting her first interview with a new client. The client presented initial concerns about relationship problems with her husband. There appeared to be some anxiety in the client, who began asking about the type of people usually coming in for service at this agency. She seemed most interested in the types of problems that people came into service to address. The worker felt the questions either reflected anxiety about the seriousness of her problems or anxiety about whether or not she was okay. Given two possibilities, the worker chose the following indirect response:

> This agency serves many people with many different types of concerns. Often these concerns are very normal concerns about situations that are outside of people's control. For example, people like yourself come in due to pretty normal frustrations that occur in relationships. Relationships can be so frustrating because much of what concerns you is outside of your control. Usually exploring what is controllable in life is very helpful for these types of people.

Example of a Direct Response.   A young worker was providing supportive services to elderly men and women in a nursing home setting. She noticed that many of her clients made comments about her age and compared her to their children. She felt these comments might indicate concern about her ability to understand elderly people. She thought about how to address the concern and selected the following response:

> I notice you refer to me as a "nice young lady" and once you even called me a "child." This stayed with me and I began to wonder if you might be concerned that I may not understand what you are going through because of my young age. Do you find that this is a concern for you?

In reviewing both types of responses, it is clear that the indirect response attempts to address the concern without any exploration with the client. Such responses are most useful if addressing a concern with a direct response might shift the focus away from the work, or when the concern is not clear and the worker wants to address more than one possibility. The direct response is useful when the worker feels the concern needs to be addressed in order for the work to proceed.

EXERCISE 5.2

Identification of Client Concerns

Read the following client statements and identify the unspoken questions within each statement.

1. A poor client is coming into an office that is very nicely decorated. He looks around and says, "Wow! This is a very nice office. I have never been in a place this nice before."

   a. What is the probable question about service that the client is experiencing?

   b. Write a response that can speak to the unspoken question.

2. A client booking the first appointment says, "I have been to workers before and it was never too helpful."

   a. What is the question about you that the client is probably experiencing?

   b. Write a response that can speak to the unspoken question.

3. An older client with a younger worker asks, "How many kids do you have?"

   a. What is the question about you the client is probably experiencing?

   b. Write a response that can speak to the unspoken question.

4. A woman coming in to see a male counselor says, "What kind of work do you usually do? Do you often see people like me?"

   a. What is the question about you that the client is probably experiencing?

   b. Write a response that can speak to the unspoken question.

5. A client coming into service for the first time says, "I have never been to a place like this before. What kind of things do you do here? I bet you hear some pretty crazy things."

   a. What is the question the client is probably experiencing?

   b. Write a response that can speak to the unspoken question.

Critical Chapter Themes

1. Effective workers establish an empathic relationship with their clients. Tuning in is the mental process that workers engage in to accomplish empathy. As workers are able to tune in to the client experience and reflect back client realities, the client can relax and become comfortable in the helping relationship.
2. Preliminary tuning in occurs before the client enters service when the worker uses information to understand the client experience of entering service. This helps identify fears, concerns, and vulnerabilities. Workers must also tune in to themselves and the helping situation to truly understand what it is like for clients to be entering the relationship. Clients will have concerns about the worker, services, and about themselves as they enter service. Tune in to all of their concerns.
3. An important element of preliminary tuning in is the problem perspectives. The person whose feelings caused the client to enter service has a primary perspective given that it is those feelings that are primary to the referral. This person would define the problem based on his or her perspective and feelings. Others, however, may not share the definition. Other people often have secondary perspectives that are influenced by their reactions to both the person whose feelings cause the referral and their experiences of the situation considered problematic. Workers must also tune in to these secondary per-

spectives. Clients may have a primary or secondary perspective depending on how the referral occurred.

4. Interactional tuning in involves identifying the underlying content, interactions, affect, and beliefs in the client statements. After these elements are identified, the worker can respond with empathy to the client. This style of responding can be developed through a formula but eventually should become second nature.

RECOMMENDED READINGS

Bozarth, J. D. (1997). Empathy from the framework of client-centered theory and the Rogerian hypothesis. In A. C. Bohart & L. S. Greenberg (Eds.), *Empathy reconsidered: New directions in psychotherapy* (pp. 81–102). Washington, DC: American Psychological Association.

Broome, B. J. (1991). Building shared meaning: Implications of a relational approach to empathy for teaching intercultural communication. *Communication Education, 40,* 235–249.

Ridgway, I. R., & Sharpley, C. F. (1990). Multiple measures for the prediction of counsellor trainee effectiveness. *Canadian Journal of Counselling, 24,* 165–177.

Satterfield, W. A., & Lyddon, W. J. (1998). Client attachment and the working alliance. *Counselling Psychology Quarterly, 11,* 407–415.

6

Engaging the Client and Focusing Work

Tuning-in skills are important in helping workers develop sensitivity and understanding of the client experience. These outcomes of tuning in are used to engage the client in service. Engagement is the process through which clients begin to feel comfortable with workers and focus on their goals. Through engagement, clients begin to feel more hopeful about service outcomes and take an active role in working toward their goals.

The critical outcome of engagement is the development of a collaborative working relationship between the worker and client (Gelso & Hayes, 1998; Ridgway & Sharpley, 1990; Walborn, 1996). As a collaborative and open relationship develops, the client is more receptive to intervention (Mallinckrodt, 1993; Reandeau & Wampold, 1991). The ability to engage clients in the helping relationship distinguishes effective from less effective workers (Gaston, 1990; Jennings & Skovholt, 1999; Najavitz & Strupp, 1994; Pritchard, Cotton, Bowen, & Williams, 1998). Engagement must not be confused with confronting or telling clients what to do. Such behaviors interfere with engagement (Bischoff & Tracey, 1995; Miller, Benefield, & Tonigan, 1993; Patterson & Forgatch, 1985).

The engagement process is not a static event but rather dynamic and changing over time (Gaston, 1990; Gelso & Hayes, 1998). As depicted in Figure 6.1, engagement progresses through three stages. Initially the client meets the worker and decides to engage in service. There is little depth to this stage as the decision lacks information about the full nature of the work. However, the client eventually does make an informed decision to either continue with service or leave. The decision to stay is referred to as *preliminary engagement*.

After making the decision to stay in service, the client decides how to engage with the worker. This decision, called *interactive engagement*, controls the levels of honesty,

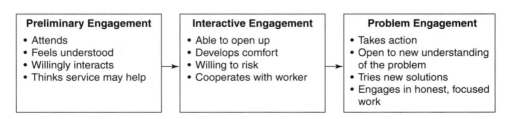

Preliminary Engagement	**Interactive Engagement**	**Problem Engagement**
• Attends	• Able to open up	• Takes action
• Feels understood	• Develops comfort	• Open to new understanding of the problem
• Willingly interacts	• Willing to risk	• Tries new solutions
• Thinks service may help	• Cooperates with worker	• Engages in honest, focused work

FIGURE 6.1   Levels of Engagement

cooperation, and openness in the working relationship. After deciding to open up (or interact), the client must decide how much change is reasonable in the particular problem situation. This level of engagement is called *problem engagement.*

PRELIMINARY ENGAGEMENT

When clients first make contact with the helping system, they are vulnerable and confused about the roles and requirements of service (Greene, Lee, Mentzer, Pinnell, & Niles, 1998). Clients consequently are very ambivalent about service and will be tentative about whether they want to participate. Until they get some sense of the service system and the worker, they cannot relax and begin to work toward their goals.

Preliminary engagement is achieved when the client has answered enough of the early concerns and basic questions and can make an emotional decision to continue coming in for service. If preliminary engagement does not occur, clients are not likely to continue (McKay, Nudelman, McCadam, & Bonzales, 1996; Samstag, Batchelder, Muran, Satran, & Winston, 1998). There are three elements of preliminary engagement that move from the basic to specific questions about the worker and service (Miller, 1999). These are introductions, orientation, and the opening statement.

Introductions to Service

The first thing clients want to know when coming in for service is who will be helping them. Most clients sense they will be working with someone but know nothing about that person. Consequently, the worker must first respond to these basic questions through facilitating introductions. Typically this occurs over three steps:

1. worker introductions
2. reciprocal introductions by the client
3. introductions to the helping environment

Worker Introductions.   When the worker meets the client, they usually shake hands and exchange names. This simple act of introduction often occurs outside of the room where the work will occur (e.g., in a waiting room, in a foyer outside of a meeting room, etc.). Depending on the situation and the cultures of the people involved, this act will either be formal (e.g., "Hello, Mr. Smith, I am Mr. Ragg and I will be meeting with you today.") or informal (e.g., "Hi, Mr. Smith, I'm Mark and I will be meeting with you today.") In choosing the level of formality, consider the cultural and subcultural aspects of the client. Some cultures prefer formality; others will not trust someone who is too formal.

Reciprocal Introductions by the Client.   In making introductions it is important to determine how the client would like to be addressed. Sometimes the name in the file is different from the preferred name. Effective workers ask clients to clarify how they would like to be addressed. This may sound something like "Hello, Mr. Smith, I'm Mr. Ragg. Would you like me to call you Mr. Smith or is there another name you feel more comfortable with?" This allows the client to have control over how he or she is addressed, which begins the process of empowerment by giving the client some power over the helping situation.

Introduction to the Helping Environment.   The last introductory element is the introduction to the helping environment. Clients are typically brought into an office or room where the service will occur. They are invited to seat themselves and become comfortable. Some settings also offer refreshments. All of these actions introduce clients to the setting in which work will occur. It is important to make sure the setting is client friendly. The clients can then relax and work toward their goals. Achieving a comfortable work space requires tuning into the client group. If working with children, then pictures, furniture arrangement, and accents should be child oriented. If working with professional or community groups, an orderly and efficient layout is probably more desirable.

Orientation to Service

After the "who" and "where" questions are answered, the clients are often concerned with the "what" questions (e.g., What will happen to me as I come into service?). Clients need to understand expectations, limitations, and parameters of the service (Miller, 1999). There are three common aspects to the orientation to service.

- orientation to the immediate events
- orientation to the agency
- orientation to the service/program

Orientation to the Immediate Events.   Most clients enter the helping situation wondering what will occur. It is useful to let them know what will be happening to them during the initial visit and how the first meeting will set the tone for future work. This decreases their anxiety of the unknown and opens the door for asking questions about procedures. Effective workers usually begin this discussion as they are getting settled into the room where the work will occur. For example, "Why don't you sit over there and I'll sit here. We will probably spend about one hour today exploring the events in your life that brought you to our agency. After that, we will discuss how the agency might best help you."

Orientation to the Agency.   Just as clients know little about the worker, many clients will know little about the agency. It is useful to share information with clients in order for them to understand what the agency does for people. Workers should avoid an overwhelming discourse about the history, mission, organizational structure, and other such boring details. Instead clients need to understand what kind of philosophy the agency has about service and what services are available. Some clients may also want to know the relationship between the organization and other organizations especially if they are connected to several agencies or have confidentiality concerns.

Orientation to the Service/Program.   The final aspect of orientation is an orientation to the services clients will receive. Such orientation includes a discussion about the expectations of service for the client (e.g., payment, paperwork, etc.), the limitations inherent in service (e.g., appointment limits, limits on service options, limits to confidentiality with duties to report), and the type of service provided.

Making the Opening Statement

Some of the most important client questions are the "how" questions. Such questions focus on how the client will be treated, understood, responded to, and respected. The answers to such questions are critical to answer and promote full engagement in the service. These questions are often the most awkward to explore, as they often focus on the worker.

It is important that the opening statement answer such questions (Shulman, 1999). This statement marks the transition from the service concerns to the relationship concerns, making it a very important element in engagement. If the worker builds an opening statement from their tuning in to the client, the worker will be able to address the critical concerns of the client early in the helping relationship. This will set the tone for the helping relationship with a focused and empathic reflection of the client's experience of entering service. Such sharing helps clients experience the worker as an understanding and potentially helpful person.

Typically, the opening statement occurs during that awkward moment when both client and worker are sitting down and they have to move from the safe conversations (agency, program, introductions) to the real reason why the client has entered service. At this point, the worker has a brief opportunity to make a statement prior to asking the client to share his or her story. When the worker builds on tuning in to address potential concerns, questions, and desires, feelings of being understood are promoted in the client. Given that one of the most common client concerns is the ability of the worker to understand the client's situation, sharing and understanding can dissipate such anxiety.

The Critical Components of the Opening Statement. Some workers avoid making an opening statement and ask a simple question to start the client speaking (e.g., "How can I help you?"). This is not the best start to the relationship, especially if the client's concerns about the worker are not answered. A more effective use of the transitional moment is to make a brief statement that can help the client feel understood and comfortable. The opening statement accomplishes this goal through four elements.

1. *Affirmation of the client experience.* The worker builds on his or her tuning in to affirm the client situation and request for help. In this element of the opening statement, the worker addresses anticipated concerns associated with the client's entry into the helping situation.
2. *Speak to and normalize client feelings.* The worker gives permission and normalizes the feelings likely be experienced by the client. This builds on the affirmation of the client situation.
3. *Instill hope.* Clients need to believe service can help achieve the changes they desire. The worker must integrate hope into the statement and make sure the expressions of hope are realistic. This requires workers to avoid patronizing and idealistic statements.

4. *Invite a response.* An effective opening statement will have captured the client request, addressed unspoken concerns, and introduced direction or hope about what can be expected through service. After making the opening statement, it is important to solicit feedback from the client. This often involves some sort of question or probe to determine whether the worker is moving in the right direction.

■ *Case Example.*   The following example is taken from a family-based program associated with Child Protection Services. The worker, meeting the clients at an office, completed the introductions and told them about the home-based approach to service. The family is sitting, and there is an awkward moment of silence. The worker starts her opening statement.

> I am glad that both of you came in today . . . on the phone you mentioned that the two of you do not agree on disciplining Johnny. It is sometimes hard to openly discuss such hot topics with a third person, especially when Child Protective Services has forced you to come here. You might feel that I am going to judge you or try to help them take away your children. Many people feel like that when we first meet and want to hold back until they get to know me. I want to assure you that it is not my job to take away kids. I am paid to try to help families work better together so they can keep living with each other. I have seen many families become strong and united in parenting . . . in fact so strong that they are still doing well without agencies telling them what to do. I would like to see that happen with you guys. I believe you want this too, or you wouldn't be here. Before we start talking about your parenting differences, are there any concerns you have about coming here today?

In the example, the worker tuned in to a potential concern about the agency's connection to Child Protective Services (CPS). In response, the worker ensured this concern was put on the table for the client. The worker also validated and normalized any feelings they may have about this before instilling hope. The worker then opened it up for the parents to discuss their concerns before proceeding with an exploration of the situation.

EXERCISE 6.1

Preliminary Engagement Exercises

The following client situations are the same situations used in Chapter 5 to practice tuning in. Build on your tuning in to practice engagement responses.

1. You are a worker in a shelter for abused women. The shelter is in the city center serving a wide variety of women and their children. This woman entered service because she was beaten by her male partner after a social function. Her two children witnessed the assault and were admitted with the mother. A neighbor called the police, but the man left before they arrived. The police brought her into the shelter for her own protection. The

woman is wealthy. She works as an executive in a local company and her husband is a lawyer. The woman is well known to shelter staff for donating her old clothes to the shelter.

    a. Write what you would say to introduce yourself to this woman as she comes into the shelter.

    b. Write the opening statement you would use to begin work with this client.

2. You are a new graduate hired to work with single-parent welfare families as part of a grant-funded pilot project. The basic premise of the program is that children from poor, single-parent families are at high risk for abuse and adjustment problems. The project is being run through the Department of Social Services. The agency is located on the edge of town where the bus service does not run in the evenings. Consequently, you made many phone calls arranging rides for the women. You work with a child protective worker who is also a member of your graduating class. The ten-week psychoeducation program attempts to teach parents how to understand and respond to their children's emotional needs. The program includes presentations and lectures. You are are about to meet your first group of women. When they came into the building, you noticed many of the women were in their late forties and appeared as if they had lived difficult lives.

    a. As these clients come into group, what might their concerns about you, your co-leader, and the agency be?

    b. Write what you would say as you introduce yourself to this client group.

    c. Write the opening statement you would use when beginning work with this client group.

INTERACTIVE ENGAGEMENT

As the client begins to respond to the worker, engagement should deepen through the frequent exchanges between the two. The client must feel the worker understands and cares about what the client is saying. If worker responses promote this experience, the client will begin to trust the worker with the details of his or her life story. Understanding and caring workers are most often workers who are skilled in the art of listening (Goldin & Doyle, 1991) and empathic responding.

Empathic Responding: The First Element of Interactive Engagement

Empathic responding combines the thinking and tuning in skills to provide a foundation for empathic worker responses. One also uses the response system framework to target the listening and observation. The elements involved in empathic responding are:

1. *Client disclosure.* The worker listens, hears, and observes a client disclosure, question, or reaction about some event, situation, or person.
2. *Identification of action elements.* The worker listens to the elements of the client statement and identifies what people are doing or saying that contributes to the disclosure feeling.
3. *Identification of processing elements.* While listening and observing, the worker reflects on the client statement and mentally labels the important thinking and feeling themes in the statement.
4. *Tabling the core concern.* From the action and processing elements of the client statement, the worker identifies which elements appear to be most important to the client.
5. *Validation and exploration.* When a worker has tuned in to the concerns and questions that might be evident for the client, the challenge is to get the concern out in the open and address it.

Communication skills are important to state the client concern in a way that can be validated by the client. Given that the worker and client must share an understanding of the situation and that this understanding must, at least in part, result from the worker's processing of the situation, it is important to involve the client in validating or shaping the meaning of the apparent concern (Broome, 1991). This is particularly important when there are cultural differences that may influence the client responses to the situation (Broome, 1991). Effective workers provide an opportunity for the client to validate or alter the understanding of the client concern. From the client response, the worker and client can then explore the concern.

The Process of Empathic Responding.   The five elements of empathic responding basically serve as a formula for developing skills. Such formulas are useful when first learning a skill to remember each of the elements. Over time, you will develop your own response style and will let go of the step-by-step awkwardness of the formula. For the purposes of this chapter, continue to use the formula. After completing the different exercises, experiment slightly with the formula to see how you can choose different words to make the response more consistent with your personality. The five elements result in the following formula.

1. *Expression.* What did the client say?
2. *Action elements.* What are the things that people are doing and saying?
3. *Processing elements.* What are the beliefs, thoughts, and feelings that seem important?
4. *Tabling.* What are the critical concerns? Put them into a response.
5. *Validation/Exploration.* How can I validate this concern? Where will I take this to explore the experience of the client?

In the steps of empathic responding, the first three steps are internal to the worker. The fourth step is critical because it is the response to the client statement that puts their concern on the table. When first learning empathic responding, it is helpful to use a formula that begins with a phrase such as "It sounds like . . . ," "It seems like . . . ," "I get the sense that . . ." Such phrases provide a springboard into the response. Many workers begin with such springboards to set the stage for the response.

The fifth step actually seeks a response from the client, and attempts to elicit client validation and exploration. This sequence of hearing, tuning in, and responding to the client sets the stage for an empathic relationship between the worker and client. As workers become practiced at using empathic responding, the need for a formula decreases. To better understand the formula, see how it is applied to this first-time client's statement.

> **CLIENT:** I don't know why I am here. People told me I should come and talk to you to see if it will help. I don't even know what to do. Every one tells me something different. What's the use? You can't help me either. I shouldn't even be bothering you.

In this statement, the worker can use the formula to capture the critical elements in the following manner.

1. *Expression.* He doesn't know if he wants to be here.
2. *Action.* People are telling him different things and he fears that this might not work.
3. *Processing.* There is confusion, fear, and ambivalence about whether he can do this.
4. *Tabling.* "It sounds like things are getting confusing with many people telling you what to do. This can make you feel like giving up on doing anything about a problem."
5. *Exploration.* "Do you feel a little like that today?"

EXERCISE 6.2

Empathic Responding

Use the empathic responding formula to respond to the following client situations.

1. An adolescent girl talking with a counselor says, "It is so hard in this family. People are down on you when you mess up but nobody cares when you are doing well. I worked hard at school to bring my grades up and was so happy when I got six As. I brought my report card home excited. When Dad read it, he didn't even look up at me. He just grunted and said, 'They must have given you the wrong report card.' I couldn't believe it. After hard work, all I got was a grunt and crap like that. But if I got six Ds, you know darn well he would spend time on it. I don't know why I even try to do well. I don't even know why I try at all."

    a. Expression:

    b. Action elements:

    c. Processing elements:

    d. Tabling response:

    e. Where would you try to guide the exploration?

2. You are a worker in the Department of Social Services talking with a single mother. This mother says, "Sometimes I just don't know if I can manage. It is the beginning of the month and the mailman just brings me pressure and pain. Bills, bills, and more bills. On top of that, I have to take care of my kids. They always want more things. Snacks, sneakers, school trips . . . it just gets impossible. Now you are telling me I have to work twenty hours every week just to get my benefits. The store wants me to work in the evening. That is when I need to be home with my kids. I feel like I can't win."

    a. Expression:

b. Action elements:

c. Processing elements:

d. Tabling response:

e. Where would you try to guide the exploration?

Active Listening: The Second Element of Interactive Engagement

Everybody listens; however, few people actively listen. Most people drift in and out of conversations frequently disengaging or changing subjects. Active listening refers to a state in which one is totally attending to what another person is saying. Active listening will be explored in fuller detail in Chapter 8; however, because the basic elements of active listening are important to achieve interactive engagement, the five behaviors that promote interactive listening are described here.

Attending Behaviors. Attending behaviors include verbal and nonverbal behaviors that communicate that the worker is listening and the client should continue talking. Some nonverbal behaviors include nodding, eye contact, gestures, and body position used to indicate a full interest in the client's disclosures. Verbal behaviors include "uh-huhs" and other short verbalizations that show listening. Effective workers use attending behaviors to encourage the client to talk. When clients feel the worker wants them to share and indicate interest, they are more likely to fully engage in the helping relationship.

Perception Checking. Effective workers also check their understandings of what the client is saying (Wubbolding, 1996). This involves asking for clarification or restating the understanding so the client can correct or validate it. This is an important element in all communication with the client. Many workers start perception checking with statements such as "So, are you saying . . . ?" or "So, are you telling me . . . ?" Be careful about always starting with the same word such as *so*, as it may cause the client to feel on the spot. Try the preceding two statements without the word *so*. Notice how a more straightforward approach can work well.

Pacing the Client's Speech.   When a person talks, there is a rhythm or pace to the speech. One can identify the pace through the person's breathing patterns and flow of talking. Effective workers are able to pace themselves with the client and use their own breathing and interactive pacing to help clients relax and relate more fully in the helping relationship (Angell, 1995; Bandler & Grinder, 1975; de Luynes, 1995). Part of pacing includes using the client's informational processing language (e.g., feeling, cognitive, visual, auditory, and kinesthetic words). For example, clients who tend to be visual will say things like, "Do you see what I mean?" whereas clients who are auditory might say something like, "Do you hear me?" It is helpful to use the same type of language when speaking to clients because it helps them feel understood.

Using Door Openers.   Effective workers encourage disclosure through noticing and using door openers (Baenninger-Huber & Widmer, 1999). Door openers are when something in the client's statement suggests there is more to be said. Door openers may be verbal or nonverbal indicators that are embedded in the statement causing one to think there is more to the story than meets the eye. Exploration can be initiated by the worker or picked up on when initiated by the client. Worker-initiated door openers occur when the worker:

1. *Observes something* in the client's current state and behavior (e.g., depressed).
2. *Shares the observation* with the client (e.g., "You look down today.").
3. *Waits for the client to respond.* Sometimes the waiting for a response yields an awkward moment if the client does not respond. In such situations, the worker can point out the lack of response and follow up more directly (e.g., "You didn't say anything when I said you look down. What does that mean about how you are feeling?").

Client-initiated door openers occur when clients make statements that contain a hint that they have something more to tell. Most people are aware of these types of statements in personal relationships. People sometimes call such statements *loaded* and work hard to avoid opening up the discussion. In the helping relationship, the worker needs to actively help clients to express what is difficult.

Exploring Disguised Content.   Very often clients will talk about subjects in a manner that does not readily identify themselves in the issue of concern (Shulman, 1999). Many clients will present issues parallel to their own to test the worker's response before discussing their concern. Most people have had friends talk about someone they know and then later discover the friend was really talking about his or her own situation. When clients present disguised issues, the worker needs to help them get the issue on the table for exploration. This often occurs through the following four steps.

1. *Identifying content* that is diffused or generalized. For example, a client says that a friend is thinking about moving in with a couple of friends.
2. *Matching content to themes* in the client situation. For example, "It is interesting that your friend is thinking about moving in with a group of other people. Last week

you were talking about friends of yours, and it seemed that you might be thinking about a move like that yourself."

3. *Ask the client if the parallel fits* for them. For example, "Is this a theme in your life
as well?"

4. *Invite the client to explore* the subject further. For example, "What kind of plans
have you thought about with your friends?"

EXERCISE 6.3

Client-Pacing Exercise

For each of the client situations, identify the processing style of the client and write a response using that style. If you notice a door opener, keep in mind the different steps in
responding.

1. A poor client coming into a professionally decorated office for counseling says,
"Wow, this is a very nice office. I have never been in a place this nice before. Look at
how well matched everything is."

    a. What type of processing is this client using?

    b. Write a response to the client that uses the same type of processing and ad-
dresses the client's unspoken concerns.

2. A client booking the first appointment says, "I have been to workers before and
it was never too helpful. Things just didn't go right and got sour pretty fast. But things
are spinning right now, and I felt that I should give it another shot."

    a. What type of processing is the client using?

    b. Write a response that uses this same type of processing and that can speak to
the unspoken questions of the client.

3. You are working in a family service agency. A couple comes in and the wife states,
"I don't think he loves me anymore. He comes home and lies on the couch to watch TV.
When I talk to him, he doesn't even look up. I don't see what else I can do." The husband
responds, "I don't know how you can say I don't love you. I come home and the first thing

out of my mouth is 'Hi dear, how was your day?' and the last thing out of my mouth every day is 'I love you, have a good sleep.' I really don't know how else to tell you that I care."

   a. What is the woman's processing language?

   b. What is her husband's processing language?

   c. What might be occurring to cause the problem?

   d. Write an empathic response using the same types of processing as the woman.

PROBLEM-BASED ENGAGEMENT

As the client becomes comfortable in service, it is important to focus the work on resolving the problems identified (Vallis, Shaw, & McCabe, 1989). However, the worker must also assure that the working relationship is never overshadowed by the desire to make the changes (Bischoff & Tracey, 1996; Ridgway & Sharpley, 1991). There are two common methods for engaging clients in the work. These include using problem perspectives to engage members of the client system and framing the problem definition to allow for hope. These methods allow people to focus on the situation while feeling understood. They also develop hope about problem resolution.

Using Problem Perspectives to Engage All Members of the Client System

As the client begins to discuss the problems he or she would like to address in the helping relationship, it is important to explore how the problem is affecting the client. Depending on how problems are experienced, clients will come into the relationship with different levels of motivation and different perspectives on what they would like to change.

    Three types of problem perspective were discussed in Chapter 5 (primary, secondary, and external). Although these are initially difficult concepts to grasp, they are important in engaging people into service. These perspectives affect client motivation as they enter a helping relationship. In order to engage each client within the client system, it is important to use the perspectives experienced by each client. As you read the descriptions of the problem types, you will discover increasing challenges to engagement as the problem situations increase in complexity.

■ *The primary felt problem.* This problem perspective refers to a situation in which the client's feelings motivate the entry into service. When the person with the primary perspective enters service, engagement is easy due to the personally felt motivation to explore and solve the problem.

■ *The secondary felt problem.* This problem perspective occurs when someone else in the client's life experiences the feelings that motivate service. Engaging such people requires exploration of the primary person's motivation concurrent with the secondary perspectives.

Often the person with the primary perspective wants service to change the person with the secondary problem (i.e., the client). Ineffective workers often meet with the client and try to engage the client in changing the behavior identified by the person with the primary perspective. However, the client (secondary perspective) will not engage easily because there is no investment in the primary feelings generating the referral.

For example, a teenage boy referred by his mother because he is not helping around the home will not easily work on this problem. However, he may have a secondary felt problem (e.g., tired of mother nagging him and expecting too much) that he might want to work on. Engagement will be enhanced through engaging people according to their *own* perspective on the problem. With parents and children, the parents may be engaged on lessening their frustration (the actual felt problem) and the child may be engaged on trying to create less hassle in the home (his feeling in the secondary felt problem).

■ *The externalized felt problem.* When the person with the primary felt problem is not part of the client's immediate system, engagement difficulties arise due to the person's external position. This is common when teachers or other professionals pressure people to enter service. Ideally, the person with the primary perspective can be engaged in the helping relationship. Alternatively, workers may have to adopt some mediation role in these situations in order to access the felt problem of the external person.

For example, if a teacher insists that a child get service, the teacher has the primary felt perspective because his or her feelings precipitate the referral. However, it is the mother and/or child coming in for service. If the worker cannot find some reason for the mother and child to continue (through their secondary perspectives), they will not engage. Ideally, the worker could meet with the family and the teacher to address the full range of perspectives, but this may not be possible. Consequently, the worker must find some feelings in the clients who are entering the service that can provide initial motivation to engage. It is unlikely that the teacher's frustration will suffice. However, if the family is frustrated by the teacher (secondary felt perspectives), there may be some hope for engagement.

Reframing the Problem for a Workable Definition

As the clients, with their various perspectives, come into service and begin to tell their stories, they often describe the problem in a way that maintains the problem or somehow prevents solutions from being effective (Buttny, 1996; Ivey & Ivey, 1998; Patalano, 1997). The following is a partial list of common definitions of initial frames that maintain problems rather than promote solutions.

- *Single perspective definition.* The definition of the problem caters to one person's perspective and ignores or diminishes the secondary perspectives.
- *Historical definition.* The definition of the problem is embedded in the history of the problem and this history prevents solutions from being applied.
- *Fatalistic definition.* The definition of the problem is couched as hopelessly embedded in the personality of one person and the trait is presented as permanent.
- *Solution-bound definition.* The definition of the problem excludes (yet the problem is associated with) elements of solutions to other problems that appear to be working just fine.
- *Total expenditure definition.* The definition of the problem includes a statement that there is nothing left that can be done.
- *Moral imperative definition.* The definition of the problem includes some moral imperatives that limit the possible solutions or inadvertently promote the problem.
- *Amorphous definition.* The definition of the problem seems to change possibly because a single definition is used for more than one problem or the real problem has not been discussed.
- *Totally externalized definition.* The definition or locus of the problem is totally controlled by someone outside of the system entering service.

Setting the New Problem Frame.   When faced with such definitions, effective workers seek to alter the frame so different experiences and perspectives can coexist within the definition. To set a more hopeful frame (or definition of the problem) the worker often uses the following four-step process.

1. *Listen to and understand the client's definition of the problem.* In such listening, the worker tracks the themes inherent in the situation. For example, an aging woman who appears depressed says, "I don't know what to do. I get so tired. Tom had a stroke last year and doesn't remember well. I send him up to put on his pajamas and he comes down in a suit. I can't go out anymore because he gets so confused. I sometimes find I don't even like him anymore. This is my retirement and all I seem to do is work."

2. *Identify the elements of the current understanding that interfere with solving the problem.* For example, in the woman's description, there are themes of her having to provide for her partner with little opportunity to replenish.

3. *Identify the important themes, constructs, and language that the client identifies with the problem.* For example, the woman seems to operate in the feeling mode, but there are also themes of cognitive confusion. The feeling themes are exhaustion and burnout. However, she is also externalized. The problem is defined as inherent in the partner. The health of the partner cannot change, so the frame of the problem is quite hopeless.

4. *Create an alternative definition.* Use the important themes and constructs to formulate a different definition of the problem that is close enough to the original definition but different enough to be hopeful. For example, "It sounds like you are very tired of having to always put out energy for your partner, and you don't get a chance to refill your energy. You used to be able to have a fully functioning partner and a life outside the home, but things seem to have changed. It seems that we need to explore ways you can start replenishing yourself. What do you think?"

When thinking about how to set the problem frame, the worker needs to make sure the client can experience some hopefulness about the solution and also needs to position the problem definition in a manner that is safe for the clients. Consider alternative definitions of the problem that fit the problem behavior patterns but avoid the traps inherent in the current definitions. In making the new definition, it is useful to maintain a positive or a strength focus to the definition. Table 6.1 contains several problem frames that are often presented by clients when they come into service.

EXERCISE 6.4

Problem Identification and Joining

Review the following case situations and then explore how you might start to engage the clients in service. The first case was used in Exercise 6.2 about empathetic responding.

1. The family of an adolescent girl was referred for service after she attempted suicide. The family consists of the girl, a father, and a stepmother. At the beginning of the session the girl reports, "It is so hard in this family. People are down on you when you mess up but nobody cares when you are doing well. I worked hard at school to bring my grades up and was so happy when I got six As this term. I brought my report card home excited. When Dad read it, he didn't even look up at me. He just grunted and said, They must have given you the wrong report card. I couldn't believe it. After all that work, all I get is a grunt and crap like that. But if I got six Ds, you know darn well he would spend time on it. I don't know why I even try to do well. I don't even know why I try at all." In response to this statement, the stepmother states: "I don't know why you always blame us. We just can't keep you happy. We are busy and have to rest after work. We can't give you all of our attention, we need some for ourselves." The father then touched the stepmother's arm and said: "I don't know why you always have to fight with her. Just relax and it will get better."

    a. Based on the types of problems (primary felt, secondary felt), label and describe the problem experienced by each family member.

    b. What would be a problem definition (frame) that might capture all of the (primary/secondary felt) problems in this family?

    c. Write the statement you would make to introduce the problem definition (set the frame).

TABLE 6.1   Problem Frames and Possible Alternatives

Problematic Definition	Promising Alternative Frame
Single perspective	In the frame, assure a definition includes conceptualizations that allow for all (primary and secondary) perspectives to coexist. For example, if a mother refers a child for noncompliance, use the frame of constant hassles because it includes the child's experience as well.
Historical	Explore the history to find alternative causal elements from the historical period and use these to change the causal links within the history. For example, if there was a trauma that set the problem in motion, explore this and then broaden the historical elements to include the family members' reactions to the trauma.
Fatalistic	Explore the situation in a way that includes the identified unchangeable person as well as the others in the environment. In setting the frame, include the reactions or interactions of the others so the problem becomes interactive (e.g., he is driving you nuts when he does that) rather than internal to one individual.
Solution bound	Explore the original problem and troublesome solution to determine what options might be possible. In setting the frame, include the solution in the current problem definition.
Total expenditure	Explore the felt exhaustion of possible solutions and search for some frame that can change the meaning of the problem slightly so a new batch of solutions might be undertaken. For example, with an argumentative couple, move from a definition that they need to get closer and stop fighting to one that they are fighting because they feel too close and need to achieve balance in the relationship.
Moral imperative	Explore the moral underpinnings that contribute to the problem. In exploration, explore a fuller range of morals to try to find a hierarchy of morals. In the frame, try to use the strength of high-priority morals to free up the ability of the client to act. For example, parents who do not discipline their child because they feel parents need to love the child might yield a frame where discipline is defined as an act of love.
Amorphous	Explore the problem definition and various aspects of the problem to try to identify the problems that are converging in the current definition. In setting the frame, identify the different problems or separate the situation so each problem can be addressed separately.
Totally externalized	Find some internalized felt problem for people within the system that might allow some energy to be applied to the presenting problem. In setting the frame, make sure the internalized problem is reflected in the definition.

2. You are a worker in a parent drop-in center talking with a single mother and her child. The mother says, "I always felt John could be stubborn, but he always does what he is supposed to if you just leave him. But maybe I'm wrong. His teacher called me in to talk with her and said that he was disruptive because he doesn't do what she tells him. I try to get him to change what he does, but then he gets mad at me running to his room and crying. I just want to do the right thing."

    a. What are the primary and secondary felt problems in this case?

    b. Who would you include in service?

    c. What would the definition of the problem be to include all of the problem perspectives?

    d. Write the statement you would make to the mother.

MAINTAINING ENGAGEMENT WITH THE CLIENT

Signs of Disengagement

One of the worker-related risks in the helping relationship is the worker drifting away from the client concerns (Allen, Gabbard, Newsom, & Coyne, 1990; Elkind, 1992; Patalano, 1997). Workers' minds can drift in many directions and often they do not even notice that they have broken their active engagement. When workers disengage from the client, they tend to move their mental energy into either their action systems or their processing systems. Worker self-awareness is important in identifying disengagement in order to reconnect with the client. Signs of disengagement are provided here to help workers tune into their patterns of disengagement.

Signs of Thinking-Based Disengagement. The following situations are examples of cognitive-focused disengagement. When workers engage in the following types of reflection, they often have disengaged into their own thoughts and are shifting the focus away from the client story.

■ *Moralizing about good and bad.* Workers can slip into thoughts or discussions of good and bad. This often is an attempt to influence clients to avoid or adopt behaviors that the worker feels strongly about. For example, when a client talks about her anger toward her child, rather than exploring the issues, a worker might lapse into a discussion of good and bad parenting. As another example, when a client has made a mistake, workers are tempted to engage in themes of "I told you so" or "What did that teach you?" This method of disengagement creates feelings of guilt or pressure in the client. These feelings will eventually erode trust and openness in the worker–client relationship.

■ *Evaluating/judging/approving.* Sometimes workers feel they want to make the client feel better. This can be identified when workers are tempted to respond to clients by assuring them they are good, or otherwise trying to help them feel better by providing a judgment about them (e.g., "You are a good parent, you just need to learn more problem-solving skills"). This approach often makes clients feel inadequate and can promote dependency on worker approval. Such dynamics disengage the worker from empowering the client or using client strengths because the worker has moved into a position of judging, which elevates the worker position.

■ *Logical argument.* Another form of disengagement from the client involves the worker lapsing into correcting or arguing points with the client. Statements such as "You need to understand," "Let's look at this logically," or simple corrections move the focus of the relationship from client disclosures to worker thoughts of what the client should be saying. This form of disengagement provokes counterargument and highlights differences rather than collaboration.

■ *Diagnosing.* Many workers disengage from the relationship by moving into a position of informing the client about what is wrong with him or her (e.g., "See, because of your history you just can't help yourself. This is called learned helplessness"). Again, there is elevation of the worker, who disengages into the expert mode and retreats into thinking. Clients may feel threatened by such judgments or believe the worker can see right through them. With feelings of threat, clients may disengage to protect themselves.

Signs of Affect-Based Disengagement.   A similar process can occur on the level of worker feelings and affective expression. As the worker listens to the client situation, the intensity of the work may cause escape from feelings by diverting the focus. The following are examples of this type of disengagement.

■ *Distracting from the emotion.* Workers may try to break the tension through the use of humor or other methods of diverting the client's attention. This can make clients feel the worker doesn't respect them or care about the situation.

■ *Consoling.* Many people try to console people when they are upset or otherwise talk them out of their feelings. Almost everyone has been sad or hurt and had someone say such things as "There, there, it's OK," "It's all for the best," or "You'll feel better soon." These are disengaging comments that basically ask the other person to stop feeling what he or she is feeling. Such responses make clients feel that the worker doesn't understand or care.

■ *Sharing own stories.* One of the subtle forms of disengagement is for the worker to share his or her own story with the client. Often workers state they are doing this to make the client know they can understand. However, there is no good evidence that clients feel understood when workers change the subject and begin having the client listen to their stories.

■ *Focusing on situational elements.* At times workers will disengage from the client's story by asking the client about other people or elements of the story (e.g., "What do you think they felt when this happened?" or "What exactly did they say back to you?"). This disengagement strategy makes clients feel unsupported.

■ *Chastising/admonishing.* One of the most damaging (to the helping relationship) disengagement moves by workers is chastising the client. For example, when a client tells the worker of a mistake, the worker might say "Whatever were you thinking when you made that decision?" Such statements make clients feel judged and disempowered.

Signs of Action-Based Disengagement.   There are times when the worker feels a pressure to act immediately to make the client situation better. This involves disengagement as the worker tunes into his or her own solutions and moves toward action rather than empowering the client to act on his or her own behalf. The following are some forms of disengagement through retreating into the action mode.

■ *Immediate advocacy.* At times workers tend to act quickly rather than engaging clients to act on their own behalf or negotiating the worker role in action (e.g., "I'll just call him right now and straighten this out"). This form of disengagement disempowers the client by creating dependency.

■ *Immediate engagement of other systems.* At times workers hear something in client stories that makes them want to act immediately to relieve the situation. This pressure indicates disengagement as the worker immediately begins formulating the services to put in place to take care of the situation. The response to the client disclosure feels like a runaround rather than an engaged response.

■ *Rescuing.* Sometimes workers react by immediately starting some action, such as planning to go with the client to perform a task. For example, a client was talking about difficulties with his lawyer and the worker responded with, "Well! We will see about that . . ." asking for the lawyer's phone number to book an appointment for both of them. Although attending appointments with clients can be an appropriate intervention, the worker needs a client to request such action.

■ *Showing the client what to do.* Some workers disengage through their impatience. They take action and expect the client to copy their behavior. This implies the client should be just like the worker. The worker disengages from the client through creating a message that the client is inadequate when compared to the worker.

■ *Inaction to force a response.* Sometimes workers will do nothing at all, even though they know the client needs support. Often this is rationalized by thoughts that the inaction is for the client's best good. For example, a worker was helping a client re-engage in school. Therefore, the worker refused to meet with her until she had attended a full day. The worker stopped all contact and refused phone calls from the client. At this point, the worker is more responsive to her own feelings than the client's needs.

Signs of Interaction-Based Disengagement.   When a worker disengages into the action systems, it is often expressed through the things said to the client. In such situations, the worker often feels pressure to say something. Although tuned into the pressure to speak, the worker disengages from the client. Some of the common verbal indicators of disengagement at this level include:

■ *Offering solutions.* When a worker really wants to help, there is an internalized pressure to provide a solution. With more difficult situations, the pressure increases. This disengages the worker because the solution is based on the worker's conjectures about the client situation. Offering solutions disempowers the client by having the client depend on the worker for solutions. The client is no longer engaged in trying to find creative solutions to the problems.

■ *Warning the client about what might happen.* Often workers hearing a client story with an element of risk jump to a conclusion and begin warning the client what might happen. This moves the focus away from the client and into the worker's conjecture. Given the disengagement, the worker and client are no longer partners in the story. At times the client may test the conjecture by engaging in the behavior to prove the worker wrong.

■ *Scrutinizing/third degree.* Sometimes when a client is telling a story, a worker will change the focus and begin finding blame around specific elements of the story. These moments often involve "why" questions with the worker trying to pursue the rationale around specific elements of the story (e.g., "Why did you do that?" "Why do you think he . . ."). This disengagement is often based on the values of the worker guiding the questions toward making a moral point. With this type of disengagement, clients tend to feel guilty or defensive. They will become less open with workers because they begin to feel the workers are gathering information on them and trying to control them.

■ *Ordering the client to act.* Sometimes workers become impatient for client action and use the relationship as leverage to force the client to act. For example, some workers refuse to see the client again until some action has been completed. This totally disempowers the client, who may feel humiliated and resentful at the implied rejection by the worker.

Methods of Re-Engagement

When a worker has disengaged from a client, an important skill is rapid identification and re-engagement. Workers need to be acutely aware when they stop listening. Once a worker has tuned quickly into the disengagement, it is important to re-engage as quickly as possible. There are four common methods of re-engaging.

Using Recall.   The simplest form of re-engaging is to mentally reconstruct the conversation to bring oneself back to the client situation. This works best if the disengagement is brief and has not yet resulted in a loss of focus in the discussion. For example, a worker notices he is starting to offer suggestions and responds, "Oh . . . sorry . . . I am getting ahead of myself here. You were mentioning your partner is sometimes challenging."

Re-Orienting to the Client Story.   Another simple system for re-engaging is to first notice the disengagement and then begin listening intently. If the worker can immediately recall the central themes of the story and little time has elapsed, the worker can re-engage without saying anything. This can be dangerous as the worker might have missed content that the client feels is important. Consequently, this strategy should be used with care.

Re-Engaging through Feelings.   Many workers re-engage by reconnecting with the feeling state using their own emotional reactions. This begins with the worker noting where he or she is during the disengagement. For example, a worker finds he is trying to change the subject to get away from emotionally heavy material. This can be used to re-engage by saying something like, "When you were talking I found myself wanting to change the subject to avoid facing the pain in your life. Do you find things overwhelming at times?"

Creating a Bridge Back to the Client.   If the worker has moved too far away from the client's story, the worker often has to create a bridge back to the earlier discussion. This involves self-awareness about where the worker was attempting to take the process. Then the worker can make a clear statement of where he or she is trying to go and ultimately make a connection to the point of departure from the client's story. For example, a worker was listening to a mother complain about her son's behavior. The worker offers suggestions for solutions that are rejected by the mother. He becomes aware that he is moving in a nonfruitful direction (has disengaged). The response is "A while back you were talking about your frustration and I seem to have jumped into trying to solve things, but I am not sure I truly understand what you were trying to tell me. You were talking about how you get so angry. Can you tell me more about the things that get you most angry?"

The engagement skills outlined in this chapter build on the tuning in skills discussed in Chapter 5. Readers will find that practice in these areas is critical to developing the helping relationship. The easiest stage of engagement is the introductions and orientation. Often workers develop a standard pattern of beginning with clients that flows from introductions through orientation. The engagement component most often ignored is the opening statement. This will require practice because it coincides with an awkward moment in the first meeting. Readers are encouraged to practice this aspect of preliminary engagement. Interactive and problem engagement is an ongoing process. Workers must remain focused to achieve these levels of engagement. These are also the levels of engagement most prone to worker disengagement.

Critical Chapter Themes

1. Workers must work to engage clients in the working relationship. This involves three levels of engagement.
2. Preliminary engagement involves introducing oneself with reciprocating introductions from the client, orienting the client to what will happen, and making an opening statement.
3. The opening statement is critical in assuring smooth engagement because it builds on tuning in to ensure client concerns are addressed, feelings are validated, and hope is instilled.
4. Interactive engagement builds on active listening and interactive tuning in to assure that clients feel the worker is listening and understanding what is being expressed.
5. Problem-based engagement begins work toward client goals. It requires the worker to tune in to the problem perspectives and develop a frame for the problem definition that will promote people wanting to engage in solving the problem.
6. Workers often disengage from the client during interaction. Disengagement often involves workers tuning in to their own response systems. Workers must become skilled at noticing their disengagement and then reconnecting to the client. Frequent disengagement can be damaging to the helping relationship.

RECOMMENDED READINGS

Buttny, R. (1996). Clients' and therapist's joint construction of the clients' problems. *Research on Language and Social Interaction, 29,* 125–153.

Ivey, A. E., & Ivey, M. B. (1998). Reframing DSM-IV: Positive strategies from developmental counseling and therapy. *Journal of Counseling and Development, 76,* 334–350.

Miller, R. (1999). The first session with a new client: Five stages. In R. Bor & M. Watts (Eds.), *The trainee handbook: A guide for counselling and psychotherapy* (pp. 146–167). London: Sage.

Pritchard, C., Cotton, A., Bowen, D., & Williams, R. (1998). A consumer study of young people's views on their educational social worker: Engagement as a measure of an effective relationship. *British Journal of Social Work, 28,* 915–938.

Samstag, L. W., Batchelder, S. T., Muran, J. C., Safran, J. D., & Winston, A. (1998). Early identification of treatment failures in short-term psychotherapy: An assessment of therapeutic alliance and interpersonal behavior. *Journal of Psychotherapy Practice & Research, 7,* 126–143.

Tokar, D. M., Hardin, S. I., Adams, E. M., & Brandel, I. W. (1996). Clients' expectations about counseling and perceptions of the working alliance. *Journal of College Student Psychotherapy, 11,* 9–26.

7 Tuning In and Engaging Larger Systems

When working with groups, families, organizations, and communities the complexity of the systems can make tuning in and engagement seem overwhelming. Consequently, social work programs have several courses working with different sized systems. This chapter cannot provide everything you must know about complex systems, but some basic strategies of tuning in and engagement with larger systems are discussed.

When reading this chapter, mentally apply the premises of tuning in and engagement from previous chapters to working with larger systems. Such application requires the use of thinking skills as the relationship-building concepts are adapted to larger client systems. As you begin to understand how the basic premises can be adapted, there will be an expansion of current skills. Such expansion provides a foundation for the information that will be provided in future classes.

One of the complexities inherent in more complex systems is the combination of individual and systemic elements. There are additional steps involved in tuning in because the worker must attend to dynamics at the individual and systems levels. Tuning in at the individual level must include some understanding of how the individuals and their concerns fit with the larger system. Conversely, aspects of the larger system influence individual concerns.

To truly understand the more complex client systems, the worker must be able to tune in and engage at both the individual and system levels. This chapter focuses on tuning in and engagement challenges with groups, families, and organizations. The same principles translate easily to communities; comments will be made but there will be limited examples of community practice.

When workers tune in to larger systems, the simultaneous attention to both the individual dynamics and the larger system dynamics is difficult because most humans tend to either focus on one or the other rather than consider both at the same time. When workers focus on both, they quickly find that the traits of each affect the other. For example, the dynamics of the individuals within the system influence how the system operates, and how the system functions also impacts how the individuals respond to situations.

When a worker struggles to engage larger systems into service, failure to engage often occurs because the worker has neglected the perspective of an individual in the system. The individual members can be very influential in causing systems to discount service or otherwise negate a worker's best efforts to involve the larger system in service. Consequently, one must be concerned about the individuals and how they influence the system functioning. This concern requires workers to be able to tune in at the individual level while trying to get larger systems involved in service. There are four critical elements associated with the individuals that will influence the tuning in and engagement of larger systems: issues of diversity/difference, issues of commonality, role/position within the system, and the individual's history in the system.

TUNING IN TO INDIVIDUAL DIVERSITY IN THE LARGER SYSTEM

Issues of diversity are a critical feature with larger systems. With groups, one must consider how individual differences affect the larger system when inviting members to join the group. In families, there are often differences in how situations are experienced and perceived that affect how the problems are defined. In organizations, there are many levels of diversity that often affect how people within the system relate to each other and how problems are defined (Daley, Wong, & Applewhite, 1992; Gummer, 1994; Nixon & Spearmon, 1991).

Workers must think about the experiences of the individuals as attempts are made to engage system members into service. This work occurs before the initial contact with the larger system. In this tuning in, the worker must consider the diversity among the system members. The following seven categories illustrate some of the tuning in required to understand system members on the individual level.

■ *Demographic features.* Differences in race, gender, age, and economic status lead members to have vastly different life experiences. The array of these different experiences and demographic profiles all contribute to the way the system operates. If most of the members are from a single demographic group with only one or two from another group, tensions often arise as the majority exerts a stronger influence on the group. The individual members of the minority group might feel the others won't understand them and will not feel free to engage fully in the system.

■ *Functioning levels.* Emotional, intellectual, psychological, physical, communicative, and other elements of performance may influence the individual's functioning within the system. If one member (or more) has traits that interfere with his or her ability to help the system achieve its goals, the system will have to adapt to compensate for individual levels of ability. Such dynamics can alter both how the system experiences the member and how the member experiences the system. This is common when organizations adapt to barely adequate employees and families adapt to having an alcoholic member.

■ *Life/work situation.* If a group is expecting investment from members in a system, it is important to tune into the life situations of the various members. Some members (e.g., single parents, shift workers) will be less able to invest additional time or may have to change their commitments. In systems where there are diverse life situations influencing investment in system goals, there is often dissension among members of the system about who is "truly committed" and who is "not committed" to organizational goals.

■ *Coping methods.* The patterns of processing stress can be a concern when bringing members of larger systems together. Too much difference or similarity can be problematic to the system. Also, if there are extremes in the way people in the system cope, the method of service delivery might need adjustment. This is especially important when there is violence to ensure the safety for all members of the client system.

■ *Problem perspective.* In the larger system, the problem perspectives are critical for understanding and engaging the individual members. Although this was discussed in Chapter 5, the concepts are abstract and warrant some repetition. In thinking about the problem perspectives, identify the person who first "put the problem on the table." This is the person who experienced feelings that led to entering service. This person has the primary felt perspective (note this person may not be a client system member). All of the other people in the system have secondary felt perspectives. Tune in to how they might experience the situation differently from the first person. Identify how they would describe the problem to determine each person's secondary felt perspective. With groups, there is often a different person with a primary perspective for each member.

■ *History.* The personal histories of individuals and length of time in the system provides unique perspectives for individuals. People with long histories in a system have special influence in their ability to guide less senior members of the system (e.g., "We tried that before and it didn't work"). Sometimes people with longevity in the system may also have some investment in the problem (e.g., they were on the committee that recommended the procedure that is now a problem).

■ *System roles.* People within larger systems often occupy roles or positions within the system that influence how they respond to events. Roles are often associated with decision-making hierarchies or functions performed in the system (Collins, 1995; Moosbruker, 1983; Paulson et al., 1999). The influence of the roles on the system is often conceptualized into three categories (Cartwright & Zander, 1968):

  ■ *Task roles* further the goal accomplishment of the system (e.g., leadership, promoter of ideas, decision maker).
  ■ *Maintenance roles* keep people in the system working together effectively and collaboratively (e.g., harmonizer, gate keeper, loyal opposition).
  ■ *Destructive roles* interfere with the other two role categories and obstruct work and cooperation (e.g., distracter, obstructer, attacker).

In many systems, roles are selected based on ability and traits, but in more formal systems they may come through job descriptions or positions.

The following example illustrates how the differences associated with history, coping, life situation, and problem perspectives influenced a larger systemic issue. In reading the example, you can begin to see how the individual diversities in the system help to influence the perspectives on the common problems. You can also identify the role of history in the diverse positions taken by the two teams and the subsequent actions.

■ ***Case Example.***   A family service agency during a time of expansion organized staff into an intake/assessment team and a long-term counseling team (*history*). After the reorganization, the agency developed a long waiting list and tremendous pressure for people to come into service. The intake team complained about the pressure, which resulted in an expansion of the team (*coping*). In the expansion, the intake team was able to take on some specialized functions and assessments and began providing services in the hospital as well as at the agency (*change in work situation*). The expansion of the team size and functions did not relieve the pressure of the waiting list. This was often raised by the intake team as a concern in staff meetings (*primary felt perspective*).

Every time the problem of the waiting list was raised, the intake workers argued that people who already received service should be quickly closed, so new clients could be moved onto caseloads. The ongoing counselors did not experience the same problem. Rather, they were acutely aware of the needs of clients already in service (*secondary felt perspective based on different roles and situations*). Whenever the problem was discussed at an organizational level, the intake workers tended to voice the problem from their position and the caseworkers would in turn discuss the problems at their position. There was no common ground for the two teams to work together because the perspectives were limited by the organizational roles.

TUNING IN TO THE COMMONALITY AMONG INDIVIDUALS IN THE LARGER SYSTEM

After considering differences and diversity, a crucial step in tuning in and engaging larger system members is tuning in to the commonalities among the people who make up the system. Understanding common understandings, experiences, and beliefs among members is important in helping the worker find a way to reframe the situation so different people will engage in the service.

There are many areas of commonality in larger systems. Regardless of diverse member perceptions, the worker must use the common ground to move members of the system toward engagement. This demands the ability to tune in and identify potential themes and concerns that can provide the common ground for the members. There are two basic areas of possible commonality that provide opportunities for identifying common ground: the experiences associated with service and the systemic processes.

Finding Common Ground in the Experience of Entering Service

When larger systems approach service providers there are two important areas that one needs to consider. First, like with individuals, there are concerns associated with entering service. Such concerns include the normal anxiety and apprehension accompanying the unknown. The second element providing potential common ground is the overlap between individual perspectives and experiences of the problem.

Tuning In to the Experience of Entering Service.   When people from larger systems enter service, there are often predictable initial concerns and feelings. When workers tune into these experiences, they often can identify overlapping or common concerns as potential common ground. The most common overlapping concerns about service include:

- *Assuring acceptance.* Members coming into service will have normal anxiety about how they will be treated by the other members and by the worker while in service.
- *Assessing expectations.* Members will want to know what is expected of them (what will they have to do) as part of receiving service.
- *Establishing interaction.* Members will have concerns about whether people will listen to them and value their input.
- *Establishing the purpose.* Members will want to have a clear understanding of what will be accomplished as a result of service.
- *Establishing influence.* Members will be concerned about who will have influence over the outcomes of the service and how much influence they have.

Workers can use these common concerns to create initial engagement. By highlighting these concerns in the opening statement, workers communicate that they understand the experiences of the system members. This can promote a willingness to open up and engage in service.

Tuning In to Problem Overlaps. In the section on diversity, readers explored the primary and secondary perspectives of the different members in the client system. In the problem definitions generated by each member or constituency in the system, there are overlaps providing common ground for engagement. Workers track the themes of the members to identify possible overlaps in what people want.

This tuning-in process involves listening to the people or groups in the situation to identify how different positions can be combined into collaborative action. The worker identifies the many messages and themes in each position and then the possible common ground in overlapping themes.

Table 7.1 illustrates the process of identifying common ground. The situation is based on an earlier example of conflict between an intake team upset that clients were languishing on the waiting list and the ongoing counselors. The ongoing team of counselors argued that people in service should not be ushered out the back door to make room for people on the waiting list. Although two constituencies appear most active in the example, there are really four when one considers management and clients. Table 7.1 portrays the possible positions of each constituency along with themes and overlaps to illustrate how different positions can lead to common ground.

Based on the themes common to the different constituencies, one can identify two possible themes to use for common ground. The first is the desire to provide good service to clients and the second is to engage others in collaboration. Either of these themes can be used to highlight common ground in trying to engage the different constituencies.

Tuning In to the Systemic Processes

With larger, more complex systems, tuning in can be challenging because there are many interactions occuring simultaneously. These interactions, actions, and interpretations of situations operate at a level beyond the individuals in the system. This is referred to as the *systemic level.* This term basically shifts focus from individual members to the operations of the family, group, organization, or community as a unit.

TABLE 7.1 Identifying Overlapping Themes from Different Constituencies

	Expressed Concerns	Themes	Overlapping Themes
Intake Team	• Feeling pressured • Concerned that people not being served • Feel ongoing counselors hang onto clients too long • Want faster flow of clients	• Wanting best treatment for clients • Wanting others to engage in assuring best treatment • Wanting less pressure • Wanting others to change	• Wanting the best for clients • Wanting others to engage and cooperate
Counseling Team	• Feeling blamed for pressures • Concerned that people being shortchanged • Feeling that intake team only interested in themselves • Arguing that the clients in service deserve the best possible service	• Wanting others to change • Wanting best service for agency clients • Wanting others to engage in making sure treatment is the best	• Wanting the best for clients • Wanting others to engage and cooperate
Management Team	• Wanting to make sure people get service • Wanting to make sure service is high quality • Not pleased with in-fighting among teams	• Wanting the best services for clients • Wanting teams to cooperate in service provision	• Wanting the best for clients • Wanting others to engage and cooperate
Clients	• Wanting to get service • Wanting to make sure service is accessible • Wanting to make sure service is good	• Wanting service when it is needed • Wanting service to be appropriate and responsive • Wanting professionals to collaborate	• Wanting the best for clients • Wanting others to engage and cooperate

At the systemic level, there are response systems, as there are with individuals. These response systems still break down into action systems and processing systems. To understand how response systems generate an understanding of systemic dynamics, the typical larger system processes are discussed. As with previous chapters, the discussion will focus on the action and processing components of tuning in and engaging the systems.

The Action Systems of Larger Client Systems.   Like individuals, the larger systems have action systems that influence how the system acts and interacts. However, because the system is more complex, one must tune in to more structures and processes to understand how the system influences the behaviors and interactions of people in the system.

Families, groups, organizations, and communities have processes governing how the action systems operate. It is useful to understand these processes because they provide a guide for tuning in to the larger system. Although you will learn much more about these processes in future courses, this discussion will provide some brief descriptions of four action system processes useful in understanding how to tune in to more complex systems. These processes are the decision-making/authority structures, control mechanisms, boundaries, and patterns of affiliation/interaction. Workers can learn important information about complex systems through these four areas of process.

Decision-Making/Authority Structures.   All larger systems have systems of making decisions and establishing direction (Anderson, 1997; Godwin & Scanzoni, 1989; Harvey, 1988; Minuchin, 1974; Rusbult, Johnson, & Morrow, 1986). Every organized system has levels of decision making and freedom influencing how the system operates (Boverie, 1991; Greenblatt, 1986; Robbins, 1993; Tjosvold, Andrews, & Struthers, 1991). In complex systems, such as organizations and communities, there are formal systems of decision making (e.g., parliamentary procedure, protocols). Similar processes occur in families and groups. In larger systems, there are also informal processes seeking to influence the decisions (e.g., lobbying).

It is important to identify how decisions are made in the system to understand the power structures and procedures used within the system. When engaging the system, workers need to attend to these structures to make sure the system is fully engaged in the work. Common mechanisms of decision making include bureaucratic, indigenous, and politicized systems. When tuning in, it is useful to identify which type of decision making is used in the system.

■ *Bureaucratic.* The criteria and power to make decisions are based on the position that people occupy in the system; for example, parents make family decisions; management makes all important organizational decisions. Such systems often have many rules and procedures about how people will act in certain situations. Energy is invested in making sure there are enough rules and structures in place to govern the responses of the system members.

■ *Indigenous leadership.* Decisions and leadership evolve from the authority and skills inherent in members. Leadership emerges in response to the situation. People do not know who will take leadership roles because people within the system emerge to take leadership when it is required. In such systems, the structure tends to be very flexible, allowing people to respond. Energy is invested in making sure people work well together so the whole system can move quickly when needed.

■ *Politicized.* The criterion for decisions rests in subsystem goals or the goals of powerful people operating within the illusion of achieving system goals. People within the system often use the system goals as a rationale, but then integrate their own goals into the solutions. Often the people most invested in the outcomes are very active in leadership roles, allowing them to influence goal directions. Leadership is often vested in select individuals regardless of the bureaucratic positions or roles.

For example, a new worker in a community health center had noticed that the coordinator of the center was very strongly networked with the doctors and important committees in the community. In many meetings, he reported on different community group activities. Several people had deferred to this person in making decisions. When the worker wanted to start a new group for community parents with learning disabled children, she first began by "bouncing" ideas off the coordinator. She later shared a position paper on the program and integrated suggestions. The coordinator became enthusiastic about the program and became very helpful in promoting the program and ensuring success in the community.

In this example, the worker identified that the coordinator was central to community decision making. The worker felt that this was a politicized system of decision making and sought to engage this individual person early in the process. The engagement of the coordinator paved the path to engaging others in the community.

Control Mechanisms.   Control mechanisms refer to the methods the system uses to control the behavior of members (Sabourin, 1990; Shaw, 1971). Control mechanisms are central to the action system because they reinforce desirable behavior and/or dissuade problem behaviors in the system. It is important that the mechanisms be consistently applied with a rationale endorsed by most people within the system (Lansberg, 1988; Smith, Kamistein, & Makadok, 1995).

Some systems have no control mechanisms. Member behaviors are expressed without systemic attempts to influence or limit the members. Such systems often become the focus of external scrutiny and control attempts to assure that the lack of limits do not impinge on other systems. There are many systems of control, but four particularly are worth considering: coercion-based, relational-based, reward-based, and outcome/goal-based systems of control.

■ *Coercion-based systems.* Powerful individuals within the system control the actions of others through punishment and threats. Punishment may include such things as physical harm, withdrawal of privileges, creation of discomfort, and banishment. The power that underlies this control system is the fear of what might happen if one diverges from the wishes of the powerful individuals.

■ *Relational-based systems.* People control themselves within the system because they do not want to disappoint other people in the system. People within such systems tend to be open about their thoughts and plans and seek input before taking action. The power that motivates the self-control is inherent in the respect that people hold for each other within the system.

■ *Reward-based systems.* Powerful individuals within the system give prestige, privilege, and concrete rewards (e.g., money, time off, special events) to people who perform up to their expectations. The rewards are public and efforts are made to motivate all members to engage in similar behavior. The power inherent in this method of control is the power of self-interest.

■ *Outcome/goal-based systems.* The sole purpose of this system is to achieve some outcome or goal (e.g., teams and task groups). The reason for system membership is to accomplish an outcome. The system retains members that contribute to the outcome. If members do not contribute to the goal, they become expendable and are removed from the system.

Boundaries. Boundaries are evident in all of the larger client systems (Boverie, 1991; McKay & Lashutka, 1983). Boundaries refer to the structures that separate a system from its environment (Bowen, 1978; Minuchin, 1974). Information and resources needed by the system are brought across the boundary to keep the system functioning. There are also boundaries between the different parts of the system. Typically, there are boundaries between different levels of decision making and positions of power within the system.

When tuning into complex systems, workers often want to understand the permeability of the boundaries. If people outside a system (or subsystem) can too easily cross boundaries, it is often a sign of problems. For example, when children begin assuming parental functions, it is often a sign that the parents are not functioning well. Similarly, front-line workers in an organization should not be making management decisions. Boundaries are influenced by culture; consequently, workers must consider the cultural context of families, groups, and organizations as they tune into how boundaries maintain separation between systems (subsystems).

Patterns of Affiliation and Interaction. Patterns of affiliation focus on the web of relationships within the system. Communication among members promotes cooperation (Webb & Wheeler, 1998). Often members become closely aligned with those with whom they tend to interact, those whom they support and who support them; those with whom they share perspectives, and/or those with whom they share positive affection (Allcorn & Diamond, 1997; Biringen, 1990; Boverie, 1991; Hare, 1982; Ray, Upson, & Henderson, 1977; Wheelan et al., 1994). On the other hand, there are patterns of negative affiliation when some members dislike other members. This sets up factions within the system. When tuning into larger systems, it is important to consider the affiliation dynamics (McPherson, Popielarz, & Drobonic, 1992). Such dynamics include:

■ *Patterns of interaction.* Who talks to whom and who is left out of interactions can indicate alliances and affiliations.
■ *Frequency of interaction.* The frequency of different members speaking to each other in the system often indicates affiliation.

- *Content of interaction.* Along with frequency, workers need to consider the content of member disclosures because it indicates important information about the relationship.
- *Balance of interaction.* What is the positive, neutral, or negative affect expressed in the interaction.

The Processing Systems of Larger Client Systems.

Similar to individual clients, larger systems have processing systems that justify the action systems and processes that occur within the system. These processing systems govern how events and situations are interpreted. Such processes in turn shape the action responses. The processing of larger systems maintain the affective and cognitive elements with affect focusing on system-wide emotional dynamics and cognitions focusing on interpretation frameworks. There are three common processing mechanisms found in larger client systems: the system purpose (mission), systemic affect, and belief/meaning transmission systems.

Systemic Purpose/Mission, or Function.   Larger systems usually have a purpose or mission. With families, the purpose is often the raising and socialization of children (Bowen, 1978, Minuchin, 1974). Groups often have a purpose or task to accomplish. Organizations are usually incepted to achieve some outcome (Dunn & Ginsberg, 1986). In social services, this is often outlined in legislation. The purpose provides ample common ground that can be used to engage the individual members of the system.

For example, a worker in a shelter for homeless families found staff ignored client needs by shifting work onto other people and teams. All of the teams were very overworked trying to respond to the increasing needs of the clients. This created stress, and people would try to ease their stress by sending clients to the others for service even though they could respond themselves. At a staff meeting, the worker wanted to raise this pattern as a problem but needed to overcome the diversity problems associated with self-interest and team stresses to engage people in solutions. The worker used the purpose of the agency "to serve homeless families" to frame the issue saying, "I think many consumers are upset and feel we are not providing the service we are promising. Many consumers have said that we have become bureaucratic and give them the runaround. I wonder if we can look at how we handle client requests."

Systemic Affect.   In larger systems, there is often shared emotion or affect. The shared affective experiences influence how situations are experienced by the system. Communication and openness in the system is influenced by the shared affect occurring at the system level (Allcorn, 1995; Forgatch, 1989; Robbins, 1993). Two types of affect are commonly discussed: atmosphere/morale and cohesion.

- *Atmosphere/Morale* (Alissi, 1980; Shaw, 1971). In larger systems, atmosphere refers to the nonverbal emotion that seems to be in the air at a given time. The atmosphere can be quite influential over the openness that people have to situations.
- *Cohesion* (Anderson, 1997; Hare, 1982). Cohesion refers to the sense of "we-ness" and the intermember bonds in the system. When people within the system develop

this sense of togetherness and common purpose, there is unity in interpretations and understandings of various situations.

Belief/Meaning Systems.   Complex systems possess mechanisms for transmitting values and beliefs to the members (Bagarozzi & Anderson, 1989). Such systems often involve repetitive messages that contain themes of how members should respond to situations. Such themes may indicate positive examples for the members or themes of how not to respond.

Typically, the transmission systems involve verbal sharing to induce members into the proper beliefs. Repeated stories, themes, or comments are often indicators of transmission systems. By tuning into such exchanges, workers can identify the important beliefs and meaning systems inherent in the stories and themes (Byng-Hall, 1988).

One of the transmittal systems of belief and meaning is the sharing of stories among the members. It is important to listen to the themes and focus of stories to tune in to the underlying beliefs that seem to govern the system. With complex systems, it is also important to tune in to who is sharing the stories. When only one person is sharing a story, there is often an attempt to manage people's opinions about the person telling the story (Byng-Hall, 1988). When many people in a system share the same stories, there is a broader attempt to transmit information or influence others.

For example, a residential center for developmentally disabled adults operated a group home for many years. When a second group home started, there was a shift in staff with some going to the new home and new staff taking their place. When the new staff were hired, the minimum requirements were raised to include a bachelor's degree in human services.

The older staff members were already cohesive when the new staff were hired and began inducting the staff into the system. Initially the cohesion of the old staff was expressed by inside jokes and the exclusion of new staff members during informal conversation. Over time, they began to share increased amounts of information with the new staff. Consistent themes in the stories included how the director (with an MSW) could not be trusted and examples of great work done by the "nondegree" staff members because they were experienced. The newer staff members were included, provided they supported these themes.

Some of the new staff members challenged the decisions and strategies supported by older staff arguing that some of the approaches they learned in school should be tried. The older staff members argued against such changes and began telling stories about the "incompetence" of the most vocal new staff. Over time the older group developed inside jokes about some of the new staff. The new staff began to find it hard to do their jobs with people watching them for mistakes. It became common to scrutinize and criticize the individuals that were targeted by the older staff members. The new staff, who felt targeted, approached the director who raised the concern. Older staff used the supervisory support as an illustration of how the director could not be trusted.

In this situation, it is clear how the preexisting system used value-transmission processes to shape the new system. Interaction/affiliation patterns were used to form cohesive groupings and the influence of atmosphere on system functioning.

EXERCISE 7.1

The First Day in the Mental Health Center

You have just been hired into a position in a community mental health center. Your job is to work with clients in transitional housing. On your first day at work, you arrived early and the director of day treatment, Dr. Hook, greeted you when you came in the door. He took you around the main building and showed you some of the interviewing and treatment rooms.

After the tour, Dr. Hook suggested that if you wanted to learn real therapy skills, you should look for an opening on one of his teams. He stated you would probably learn some useful information about the community on your current job but you will probably want to switch later to continue your clinical growth. As he began to explain the expertise of his teams, one of his workers came up and asked for advice on a case. He introduced you and suggested that you wait in a chair until your supervisor came in. He joked that your supervisor should be in sometime before noon, and then he and the other worker disappeared into his office.

After about three minutes, your supervisor, Damien, came out of a meeting with another worker and welcomed you. He asked if you wanted coffee and showed you the staff room explaining where to get cups and how people tended to look after their own mess. He then added, "at least people are supposed to, but somehow there is always some mystery mess that occurs." Damien brought you to your office and warned that it might be a "wind tunnel" for the first day, due to being passed up and down the "food chain" meeting people and learning procedures. He said you would not be able to recall everything you learned in the first few days and booked a meeting with you in the middle and the end of the week to ensure you had a chance to ask questions.

As Damien left to attend a meeting, he gave you a large binder of policies and procedures to read. He told you other people were likely to try to influence your beliefs about the agency. He stated, "One of the reasons you have this job is that you showed an ability to think. All I ask is that you form your own opinions. You can ask me any questions you want to help with that." You settled into an office to review the binder but were constantly interrupted by coworkers wanting to welcome you to the agency. As they introduced themselves, they told you things about the agency.

Typically the workers stated the agency was a pretty good place to work, but then would talk about other workers to be wary of. As staff members came and went, you noticed some trends. It seemed that people from one team talked of how they did the therapy in the agency and made comments about how many of the other interventions didn't really seem to be useful for clients. Members of the other teams tended to warn you about the day-treatment workers. They suggested that Dr. Hook's teams often got preferential treatment but did not really do better work, "They just brag a lot and get their own way." The day-treatment workers did not come to your office, but they were in the staff room when you took a break. As you sat at the table with them, they implied the reason that they were busy is because people knew the fine work they were doing.

You only met one other person from your program, Bob, who smiled and commented about all the traffic in and out of your office. He suggested there was politics in the agency with managers having two different professional backgrounds, presentation styles, and approaches to work. You mentioned you noticed some dress code differences, and he suggested that is one of the ways to tell team membership. Bob suggested these differences were just the tip of the iceberg and the two managers did not get along.

1. What affiliation patterns do you notice?

2. What appears to be the competing authority systems in the agency?

3. Describe the organizational atmosphere/morale and how it seems to be affecting cooperation.

ENGAGEMENT WITH LARGER CLIENT SYSTEMS

Just as with smaller client systems, the more complex systems require the worker to use interactional tuning in and engagement skills. Workers must interact with the individuals while attending to the system as a whole. One of the critical differences with larger systems is the need to engage the individuals within the system in some form of combined effort to accomplish goals (Cameron & Wren, 1999; Shulman, 1985/6). The different types of systems one approaches will have slightly different needs when one works toward deepening the engagement.

The need to engage more than one person requires the worker to adopt multiple perspectives when in interaction with the client system. Often, two positions become important in this interaction. The worker consequently tunes in to each person and then is challenged to decipher the differences and commonalties in their interaction. This follows the same general pattern outlined in Chapter 6.

Expression
- The worker listens to each person or constituency tuning in to what each person is expressing from his or her unique position in the system.
- The worker tracks the themes in the individual positions identifying commonalities for potential common ground.

Processing Elements
- The worker tunes in to the systemic processing systems to identify potential common ground at the system level.
- The worker mentally tries to identify how the various individual systems of processing complement and/or interfere with each other in the system.

Action Elements
- The worker identifies systemic action systems that contribute to the problems.
- The worker considers how the systemic action systems complement or are interfered with by the individual systems of processing.

Tabling Response
- The worker mentally combines the preceding aspects of the situation to formulate an understanding of how each person is affected by, and is affecting, the others within the situation.
- The worker states this understanding in a way that stresses and builds on the common ground among the system members.

When formulating the response, workers must ensure they attend to issues of diversity and commonality. This allows the worker to minimize the potential problems associated with diverse positions in the system, while concurrently maximizing commonalities.

Maximizing Commonalities and Collaboration

In framing the response to the members of the client system, workers will want to select observations and frames that build on shared experiences and goals among the system members. Such worker statements affirm the position of the different members and promote collaboration toward goals. Some of the methods used to maximize commonalities include:

- *Frame the situation as enhancing shared purpose.* Collaboration toward change works best when there is a fit with the goals of everybody within the system.
- *Create win-win situations.* Try to create situations in which all involved come out looking good or get some benefit from the collaboration.
- *Identify partners.* Try to identify other people (or systems) who are interested in the change, will benefit from the change, or are willing to work toward the change.
- *Use shared experiences to provide examples.* When talking to people in a larger system, try to use examples they already know. They will feel affirmed by such examples.

Minimizing Opposition Associated with Diversity

A second consideration in framing the response is to make sure people with diverse traits, roles, or positions will not oppose the direction of change in the system. This is important because it only takes one system member to undermine change efforts. Accurate tuning in and sensitive framing of the situation promote engagement. Some of the methods of minimizing the oppositional forces include:

- *Neutralize informal pockets of resistance.* Try to think of people who might be negatively impacted and mitigate the impact before taking action.

- *Form partnerships with the people who will have to implement the action.* It is useful to first work out the details at the level that will have to implement the change strategy before introducing the idea at the system level.
- *Attend to the roles and hierarchies in the system* (Greenblatt, 1986). When promoting systemic change, be aware of the hierarchies that sanction change, and try to work through them to avoid setting up conflicts.
- *Follow the principle of minimal systemic disruption.* When requesting changes, understand that changing a system is like pushing a rope uphill. Do not push too hard or expect large changes. Try to tailor requests to something that might actually occur.

TUNING IN TO LARGER SYSTEMS: SOME EXAMPLES

This chapter has made larger system interactional engagement sound very complex. This is because it is broken down into small steps. In the actual situation, it happens very quickly by tuning in to the package each person puts on the table. To show how this works, the following exchange is taken from a treatment sequence between a mother and her 14-year-old son. The son was referred to a children's mental health center because he was breaking his curfew when he went out with his friends. The mother had tried to exert control by grounding him, but he was not responding. Arguments were frequent. The problems were confined to the home situation and the son was doing well in sports and school.

> **MOTHER:** (directed at the worker) I don't know what to do. I tell him to be in at a certain time but he does what he pleases. Last night I said to be in at ten and he came in at eleven-thirty. How can I raise a child right if he won't let me?
>
> **SON:** You don't understand. I am the only one who has to be in at ten. All of my friends have to be in at eleven-thirty. When they went home, I went home. You treat me like I am some sort of criminal or something. We are not bad, we're just teenagers.
>
> **MOTHER:** I didn't say you were a criminal. Why do you always do that to me? I am your mother and you should do what I tell you. I only want the best for you.
>
> **SON:** You don't know what is best for me. I am not a kid anymore. You just better get used to it.

Through the exchange, the worker was working feverishly in his mind to tune into the positions of the two family members to make a useful engagement response. The formula used by the worker is shown in Table 7.2. When reviewing this table, notice how the worker must consider both people in the system to engage the dyad in service. In the engagement response, the worker very quickly sees what each person is putting on the table and finds the areas of commonality and difference that appear important. By minimizing differences and maximizing commonalities, the worker was able to respond in a way that affirmed both people while promoting the changes that the family wanted to achieve.

TABLE 7.2   Interactional Engagement of the Dyad

	Mother	Son
Expression	This mother feels she is trying to do her best but it is not working. Her son is moving away from her influence and defying her. This may be normal family development based on the transition to adolescent children.	This son is stating that he is a normal teenage kid and wants to be treated like his friends. This might be a normal stage of development.
Processing Elements	The mother wants to be a good mother. She believes this requires setting rules and structure for the son. When he disobeys her, she feels powerless and inadequate in her role and begins to fear that he might turn out badly. To overcome these feelings, she increases her attempts to gain control of the son.	The son is feeling frustrated. He wants to be normal (like his friends) but can't do that without disobeying his mother, who then makes him feel bad. The son seems to believe that the mother thinks he is bad and does not see that he is normal. He fears the structure will take him out of the norms of his friends.
Action Elements	The son's move toward autonomy and shift to the peer group seems to have diminished the feedback system that the mother used to feel she was doing well in her role (following structure).	The son needs acceptance from his friends to feel normal and is willing to sacrifice the relationship with his mother to achieve this.

Engagement Response

"When I listen to the two of you, I am struck by how normal you are. Mom, you have done well in raising your son. He is doing very well in school and sports. I see that you have done this by maintaining rules and expectations for him and you are worried that he might be going astray by fighting those rules at this time in his life. John, I see that you have benefited by the rules that your mom has had for you, but as you become more independent as a teenager, you also are finding that your friends have rules and expectations of you. It is difficult when their rules and your mother's rules don't fit together easily. As I listen to you, I get the sense that both of you just want to be normal and successful. You as a mother and you as a teen . . . I think that the two of you are struggling with the need to balance Mom's rules, friends' rules, and growing up. This growing up is challenging for everyone in a family. Even though you are the one that is a teenager, John, your mom also has growing pains from time to time. Let's try to slow down and see what is getting in the way . . ."

The same system of interactional engagement works with organizations. The next example is taken from a situation in which a worker has noticed client needs that might be best met through interorganizational collaboration. Notice how the worker uses strategies for minimizing differences and maximizing commonalities to engage the director.

WORKER: I have been noticing some client needs I would like to tell you about. I know you have been busy planning and thought this information may be useful. I think I might have an idea that could help with the problem of the long waiting list. (*Finding a shared situation or concern*)

DIRECTOR: What kinds of things have you been noticing?

WORKER: Well, there are a lot of kids who are in violent homes coming into service. I talked with all of the children's team and they indicated that about 20 percent of their caseloads were children from violent homes. There seems to be enough to use a group-work approach. I was reading in the journals that this seems to be a better way to proceed with these children, and it would free up the caseworkers to see other children. (*Highlighting impact on organizational mission, identifying caseworkers as partners, using an example that affirms many positions.*)

DIRECTOR: I don't see how it would free up the caseworkers because you need to have a caseworker to be in the group. (*Dealing with a historical process, potential mine field if the work is doubled by having two workers for every child in group.*)

WORKER: I am not sure why the children would need a caseworker to be in the group. Would it be possible to just have a group worker? (*Engaging around the history.*)

DIRECTOR: We need someone to be responsible for the family contacts, paperwork, and administration of the case. That has always been the job of the caseworker. (*Determining the history.*)

WORKER: In other jobs I have had, group workers fulfilled those functions for people in their group. Could I look into how the group system worked in those agencies and develop a plan? Maybe we could try it here and see if it might work. It would enable many more children to be seen and give the agency some options that might work well for the children from violent homes. (*Trying to develop a partnership with director.*)

DIRECTOR: Why don't you get more information about how we can make sure that all the case functions can be met and get back to me. We can talk about how we might try it out then. (*Successful engagement.*)

EXERCISE 7.2

Tuning In and Engaging Families

You are working in a family service agency seeing a child referred by the Child Protective Service Agency. The family was reported for suspected abuse after the school saw bruises on the child's arm. The abuse was not substantiated, but there were high levels of conflict in the family. The parent and child admitted to frequent arguments and the bruises were a result of the child trying to run away as the parent was bringing the child home (after breaking curfew). This worker wanted the family to enter service to learn better parenting skills.

The family consists of a 26-year-old mother, a 28-year-old father, and an 11-year-old son. Apparently, the mother had difficulty gaining compliance from the child but did not consider it a problem. The father reports no problems between him and the child. The father has used physical punishment with the boy in the past and credits this for the son's compliance. The father has stated the mother is too soft on the child; that is why he doesn't take her seriously.

The family described some background during the telephone intake that was supplemented by the child protection worker. Apparently, the father had been involved with child protection as a child. His parents had been very severe in their discipline. At one time, he was removed from the home and placed in foster care. He continued to run away to return to his family. He had learning disabilities and dropped out of school after grade 8. He and the mother were in elementary school together and started dating in junior high school. She lived in a sexually abusive home that never came to the attention of the Child Protection Agency. She left home at a very young age to move in with her husband, became pregnant, and dropped out of school.

The family is living in a poor section of town. Both parents work several odd jobs to pay the bills. The mother works as a cleaning lady for families in the area, and the father works part-time for a salvage company and does car repairs in various garages around town. Both work long hours and are seldom home.

1. Using the framework of primary and secondary problems, identify and describe the problem perspective for each family member.

   a. Mother:

   b. Father:

   c. Child:

2. Within this framework of understanding, tune in to the experience of the family members as they enter treatment (be sure to include the elements for individual members listed in the earlier sections of the chapter).

   a. Mother:

   b. Father:

    c. Child:

3. What would be a problem definition that would overlap the three perspectives?

EXERCISE 7.3

Tuning In with Organizational Systems

You are working in a child protection agency as an intake worker. Your job is to investigate complaints of abuse, document your findings, and prepare for the apprehension of children at risk of continued abuse. Early in your job, you notice some problems between your supervisor and the supervisor of another team. Your supervisor, Bob, is a 40-year-old Caucasian male with a long employment history at the agency. He repeatedly points out problems in how one of the other managers, an African American woman, follows procedures.

The other manager, Kenyata, has been at the agency much longer than your supervisor and was one of the managers that interviewed him for his current position. Kenyata is very popular and has a very easy way of working. She encourages critical thinking among her staff and tries to promote creative responses to help the families make the changes needed to stabilize the families at risk of losing their children.

Bob, your supervisor, is always impeccably dressed and very well spoken. He insists you dress professionally and follow all procedures. He watches over people on the team to make sure they are following procedures and provides weekly reports on the entire team to the executive director. The director, an elderly Caucasian male, appears to appreciate the written reports and attention to detail and is constantly commending the intake team for their proficiency at staff meetings.

Recently, the negativity has become worse than usual. Team members from the intake team have been watching members from the other team and reporting any breaches of procedure to Bob. He in turn has been documenting potential problems and forwarding them to the executive director, pointing out it is important for all of the managers to be consistent in following policies and procedures. Kenyata has not engaged in any watching behaviors but has been very vocal about the need for people to respond to client needs and to be creative in their ability to respond.

In considering the individuals in this situation, use the information provided to answer the following questions.

1. What possible issues of diversity might be contributing to the situation?

2. How might the organizational roles of the two teams contribute to the organizational problems?

3. What in the history between the two managers might contribute to possible competitiveness?

4. Your manager has the primary felt perspective on the problem; what would his definition of the problem be?

5. The other manager has a secondary felt perspective on the problem. What does her perspective appear to be?

6. What is your secondary felt perspective on this organizational problem?

EXERCISE 7.4

Tuning In and Engagement with Group Members

You are a worker in a shelter that serves battered women and their children. You are beginning a group for children who have witnessed their mothers being beaten. The group includes the following children:

■ Mary is a 9-year-old Caucasian female. She and her mother are new in the shelter. Her mother was badly beaten by her father about one week ago and the police brought them in. The fight started when the father began yelling at Mary about her report card. The mother argued to protect Mary and the fight escalated. He was going for his gun to kill the mother when the police arrived. He is currently under arrest.

■ Katy is an 11-year-old Caucasian female. She has been living in the shelter for the past month. A boyfriend had abused her mother. They were staying at the boyfriend's home and are planning to move into a new apartment at the beginning of the next month. Since coming to the shelter and deciding to make the separation permanent, the boyfriend has been threatening to kill the mother.

■ Tonja is an 8-year-old African American female. She and her mother have been in the shelter for about two weeks. Tonja and her mother came to this shelter from a city about one hour away. Apparently, her mother's boyfriend has threatened to kill them, and they moved into this shelter to be safe.

■ Tony is a 7-year-old African American male. He came into the shelter with his mother about one week ago. Reportedly, his father is quite dangerous and is prone to threatening his wife with weapons. Tony was hurt during the last incident because he tried to protect his mother.

■ Maria is an 8-year-old Caucasian female. She came to the shelter with her mother last week after witnessing her mother's boyfriend trying to stab her mother during an argument. This is not Maria's first time in this shelter. She has been here in the past; each time things settled down and her mother returned to her boyfriend.

■ Jayme is an 8-year-old Caucasian female. She was picked up from school by her mother and brought to the shelter because the mother's ex-boyfriend had threatened her mother. Apparently, they have been separated for about one month, and the boyfriend had been drinking heavily. He has tried to kill the mother in the past, and it was felt that the shelter might be the safest place until things settle down.

1. Focus on diversity issues and identify three people in this group that might be feeling differently from others in the group.

2. Using preliminary tuning in skills, identify two areas of commonality for the children.

In the first group meeting, you had asked what the group members wanted to get out of the group meetings. In response to this, Mary began crying and said, "I don't want to get anything out of this. I don't even know why I am in this group. I didn't do nothing. I came here with my mother and now people are telling me what to do. I don't have my own room anymore and every time I turn around, people are asking me questions."

3. What are the individual processing elements in this expression?

4. What are the action elements that contribute to the expression/feeling/meaning?

   a. Actions/interactions of others:

b. Own behavior and statements:

5. What are some commonalities that can be developed from this statement (e.g., what content can be pulled out that can highlight things members have in common)?

6. Write a response that can capture the personal meaning/feelings and also capture the commonality among the members of the group.

Critical Chapter Themes

1. With larger systems, workers have additional challenges with tuning in and engagement because they must attend to both the system and the individuals within the system.
2. When engaging individuals workers must first tune in to the diversity among the members. There are many sources of diversity.
3. When engaging, the worker must find methods of traversing the diversity so that all members of the system can find some common ground.
4. When building common ground, workers must consider the experience of coming into service,
5. Larger system responses are also influenced by response systems. Workers can tune in to action (decision making, control, boundaries) and processing (purpose, beliefs, atmosphere) systems that can be used to focus work and engage the system.
6. In engagement, the worker seeks to minimize the impact of diversity while maximizing the commonalities among the system members.

RECOMMENDED READINGS

Boverie, P. E. (1991). Human systems consultant: Using family therapy in organizations. *Family Therapy, 18,* 61–71.

Bowen, M. (1978). *Family therapy in clinical practice.* New York: Jason Aronson.

Smith, K. K., Kamistein, D. S., & Makadok, R. J. (1995). The health of the corporate body: Illness and organizational dynamics. *Journal of Applied Behavioral Science, 31,* 328–351.

Wheelan, S. A., McKeage, R. L., Verdi, A. F., Abraham, M., Krasick, C., & Johnston, F. (1994). Communication and developmental patterns in a system of interacting groups. In L. R. Frey (Ed.), *Group communication in context: Studies of natural groups* (pp. 153–178). Hillsdale, NJ: Lawrence Erlbaum.

PART THREE

Toward Developing an Accurate Understanding

In the first part, readers developed a sense of self-awareness and professional conduct. The second part used the self-awareness, knowledge, and professional control to establish an open and collaborative relationship with the client. The following set of chapters builds on these skills to provide an understanding of the client situation. Throughout the next few chapters, readers will apply their thinking and relating skills to explore client situations. Exploration and thinking yields accurate assessments and a direction for service.

The ensuing chapters will highlight and provide practice of specific skills needed to explore client situations through the helping relationship. Exploration strategies will include observation, questioning, and reflecting skills through which workers help clients to explore and better understand their situations. By the end of this part, readers should be able to skillfully use exploratory strategies with clients. At the same time, readers should be able to combine the information gleaned from clients with their own knowledge to understand the situation and develop a direction for service.

8

Listening and Observing Skills

After engaging the client in the helping relationship, the worker collects information about the client situation. This is central to conducting the assessment and developing a plan of service. Collecting information requires the skilled use of the worker's senses. Data gathering and building an assessment incorporates self-control, self-awareness, thinking, observation, and questioning to promote an accurate understanding of the client and the client's environment. Although people often state that they listen and observe as part of their regular life, professional use of these skills requires significant sharpening and focusing.

PROMOTING EXPLORATORY COMMUNICATION

The first aspect of professional communication requiring development is how workers attend to the different levels of client communication. All of the response systems are represented in any verbal statement. Action and interaction information as well as client processing themes are found in the content of the statement. Effective workers are able to pick up on all four of the response systems in communication with their clients. This occurs through an ongoing interpretive sequence in which each person makes an interpretation between receiving a message and responding (see Figure 8.1).

In the interaction between the worker and client, the action, interaction, affect, and thinking themes develop depth and are transformed as each player interprets and responds to the communication of the other. Most often the processing systems are construed from the nonverbal communication of the other. This presents challenges to understanding because there is room in the communication for distortion as the worker may construct meanings that are not intended in the client communication. Likewise, the client may misconstrue the worker. This occurs through a cycle of statements and resulting responses (see Figure 8.2).

In reviewing the communication cycles depicted in Figures 8.1 and 8.2, note that communication and interpretation is an ongoing process. This process occurs on verbal and nonverbal levels. Often the action and interaction themes rely on verbal presentation. The emotional investment and meaning often occur behind the words, demanding that workers be effective in taking in information on both the verbal and the nonverbal levels (Watzlawick, Beavin, & Jackson, 1967).

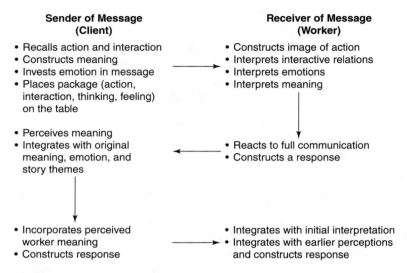

FIGURE 8.1   The Interactional Process

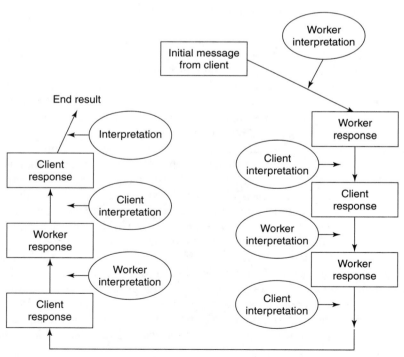

FIGURE 8.2   The Interpretation-Response Cycle

In communication, the workers engage clients in exploratory interactions while using their senses to take in information from the clients. There are two senses that most commonly help the worker gather information, auditory and visual. Workers use their auditory sense to hear the client story and track verbal/nonverbal themes as the client talks. This requires active listening skills. Additional nonverbal elements of communication are collected through visual observational skills and subsequent exploration of the observations.

Effective workers respond to clients in a way that encourages the client to continue sharing his or her story (Okun, 1997). This involves the development of active listening skills. Active listening involves the worker responding to the client in ways that maximize the client's comfort and desire to continue talking. Active listening also suggests that the worker is able to tune into the important elements of the client disclosures. To use these skills effectively, workers use nonverbal and verbal responses to promote continued disclosure and exploration with the client.

Nonverbal Skills for Promoting Client Communication

There are two helpful types of nonverbal responses used by workers when listening to and observing clients, pacing and attending. When clients experience these responses, they feel the worker is listening and understanding. Such feelings encourage further disclosure and comfort in the helping relationship.

Pacing Skills.   Pacing skills involve the worker's ability to talk and phrase discussion at the same pace as the client (Bandler & Grinder, 1975). Breathing, speaking, and phrasing sentences become consistent with the client patterns of discussing the situation. When a worker loses pace with the client, the interaction becomes strained or awkward. In achieving a good pace, the worker needs to:

1. *Be aware of the client's pace.* The worker should take note of the speed at which the client breathes and talks. If the client is anxious, the pace is likely to be quick and uneven. If a client is depressed, it is likely to be very slow.
2. *Match the pace.* Effective workers tend to respond initially at the same pace as the client. If the client is slow, the worker will tend to use the same pattern of breathing, forming, and inflecting the statements.
3. *Tune into the impact of the pace.* Effective workers are able to identify feelings associated with the pace. They then monitor for other indicators of the feeling states in the client.

Workers often must restrain their impulse to alter the client pacing and allow clients to process their situation at their own pace. Consequently, workers must often wait for their clients to speak and think without finishing sentences or otherwise pressuring them to hurry.

Nonverbal Attending Skills.   Attending skills refer to the worker validation of the client disclosure so the client feels the worker is listening and understanding what is said.

Attending behaviors do not repeat content back but rather validate the expression of the client. There are two common attending behaviors used by workers.

- *Nonverbal supportive behaviors.* The worker uses physical posturing and expressiveness to validate the client communications. These expressions include such things as nodding, maintaining eye contact, facing the client, leaning forward toward the client, and facial grimaces reflecting emotional content.
- *Paraverbal supportive behaviors.* The worker makes guttural noises that validate the client system communication but do not involve statements or clear verbal content. These behaviors include such sounds as *uh-huhs*, groans that parallel client emotion, exclamations, and other short indicators of understanding.

Verbal Skills for Promoting Client Communication

Effective workers support client disclosures through several verbal strategies. There are four types of verbal responding strategies that promote, clarify, and support client disclosures. Through using these skills, workers help clients continue their disclosures and assure that interpretations between disclosures are accurate. The five strategies are language matching, prompting, checking understandings, probing, and summarizing.

Language Matching.   Bandler and Grinder (1975) in their work on neurolinguistic programming found that people tend to process information in different ways. Inherent in the differences among people are preferences for different types of sensory processes (Hoenderdos & van Romunde, 1995). Each type of processing has a distinctive vocabulary. Table 8.1 provides comparable alternatives in visual, auditory, and sensory language. In observation with highly effective workers, it was found that strong workers tend to match the client's preferred processing language (Bandler and Grinder, 1975). The typical types of processing are:

- *Cognitive.* Clients tend to use words that reflect cognitive functions and process information through rational capacities (e.g., "Things just don't *make sense*").
- *Visual.* Clients tend to use their visual observations to interpret situations and express their understandings through visual language (e.g., "I don't *see* what the problem is").
- *Auditory.* Clients tend to use their hearing and talking capacities to sort out situations. When talking, they will often frame things in verbal terms (e.g., "It's like *talking* to a brick wall").
- *Kinesthetic.* Clients tend to be somewhat intuitive in making sense of situations and will use sensory or action-focused language (e.g., "Something just doesn't *seem* right but I can't *put my finger on it*").
- *Gustatory.* Clients tends to use smelling and tasting metaphors in their use of language (e.g., "This really *stinks*").

Neurolinguist practitioners also noted eye movements indicating the type of sensory processing used by the client (Angell, 1996; Hoenderdos & van Romunde, 1995). Effective workers observe the direction of eye movements and are able to identify processing

TABLE 8.1   **Language Alternatives for Different Expressions**

Visual Language	Auditory Language	Sensory Language
I see . . .	I hear . . .	I feel . . . , I sense . . . ,
It looks like . . .	It sounds like . . .	It seems like . . .
Your expression seems . . .	Your tone seems . . .	My gut tells me . . .
I noticed . . .	I heard . . .	I sensed . . .
Let's look at this . . .	Let's talk about this . . .	Let's explore this . . .
Let's see what is going on . . .	Let's talk about what is going on . . .	Let's find out what is going on . . .

preferences from the direction of eye movement. Figure 8.3 illustrates some of the common directions of pupil movement and the types of processing they might indicate.

As with pacing, the worker engages in two steps while using this skill. First, the worker observes the client to note the type of processing language he or she tends to use. Second, the worker frames the sentences directed at the client using this type of language. When working with several clients in larger client systems, different people can be addressed using different types of language.

Prompting for Further Elaboration.   The second verbal strategy for promoting communication is prompting. A prompt is a short question or statement designed to encourage further elaboration (Murphy & Dillon, 1998). There are two types of prompts frequently used by workers, the question and request prompt. The two types of prompts can be used interchangeably, promoting further client disclosure.

■ *The Question Prompt.*   Question prompts are very quick questions, often no longer than a sentence fragment. The function of the question is to encourage the client to continue the disclosure. The worker does not shift focus from the client and seeks only to prompt more disclosure. For example, a worker might say, "and then what happened?" or "and then you said?"

Looking up is a sign of visual processing.

Looking down is a sign of tactile processing.

Looking to the left side is a sign of auditory recall processing.

Looking to the right side is a sign of auditory construction processing.

FIGURE 8.3   **Eye Directional Cues and Processing Preferences**
Source: Bandler & Grinder, 1975; House, 1994.

In using brief question prompts, there is no need to set up the question because the question is based in the client response to the initial question. However, there may be times when the worker wants to validate the initial disclosure with a brief statement and then immediately provide the prompt (e.g., "You sound upset. What's going on?").

■ *The Request Prompt.* Request prompts are statements used to further the client elaboration by asking the client to continue. Request prompts are sometimes referred to as commands or demands because they very clearly tell the client to act in a certain way. Given this book's grounding in strength-based approaches to service, there is reticence to use words like demand or command to describe a behavior that should be respectful and empowering.

When making a request, the worker says very little aside from the request for further clarification or disclosure. For example, the worker might say, "Tell me more about that," or "Describe what you want to say." The worker may briefly validate the client disclosure but immediately continue with a prompt for the client to continue talking (e.g., "That sounds interesting . . . tell me more").

Checking Understandings.   Checking skills involve the worker clarifying client disclosures that might be misunderstood or misinterpreted. This is an interaction occurring before the final interpretation of the observed communication. This is most important when there are inconsistencies in what the client is saying or between what the client is stating and the accompanying nonverbal behaviors. Checking can be as simple as pointing out that one does not fully understand a statement. For example, the worker might say, "What do you mean by that?" "Can you explain what you mean?" or "Are you telling me . . . ?" Checking can also be in a statement, such as "I'm confused."

Exploratory Probing.   Probes involve the use of pointed questions, statements, or prompts that guide the client in specific areas of exploration. Probing influences the direction of the client's elaboration, typically focusing on one of two directions. At times, the worker wants the client to incorporate other elements of the situation in the exploration. To accomplish this, workers use generalizing probes. At other times, the worker wants the client to focus on what is occurring internally. Workers in such situations use personalizing probes. The function of the probe is to set the stage for productive work and exploration with the client.

Generalizing Probes.   To help clients expand their understanding or to shift the focus away from them, generalizing probes seek to incorporate broader elements or understandings into the client's current understanding. Three common generalizing probes are:

■ *Expanding scope.* This strategy involves the worker asking the client to consider other elements of the situation. For example, a batterer may say, "I don't know what to do; my wife left and charged me with assault. I have tried to call her like I usually do, but she seems to mean it this time. I don't know what is happening." In response, a worker may want to expand the man's scope of understanding because he is tuned solely into himself. Consequently, the worker might say, "What do you think has been happening that makes her take things seriously this time?" Such expansion of scope guides the client to elaborate more on this aspect of the situation.

■ *Logical conclusions.* Logical conclusions move the discussion toward conclusions that may logically follow the client disclosure. In such a strategy, the worker might combine what the client has described and expressed to help focus the situation. In the preceding example, this might occur in the following response, "From what you have been telling me, it seems like you need to make some changes. What changes does this situation seem to be demanding of you?"

■ *Highlight themes.* Highlighting themes involve generalizing through identifying and building on commonalities in the patterns of the client's stories or disclosures. For example, this strategy might involve the following statement, "You mentioned that your partner has left you in the past. What did those times have in common with her leaving this time?"

Personalizing Probes. Personalizing probes shift the focus of work in the opposite direction of the generalizing probes. In using this type of probe, the worker tries to help the client apply the material to him- or herself. These types of probes seek to promote insight or challenge currently held interpretations of the situation. Three common types of personalizing probes are:

■ *Personal implication probes* These probes seek to help the client construct meaning in an event or series of events and apply the meaning. By asking the client to interpret the events and apply the meaning, the client must take ownership for the meaning that he or she construes. The worker can then help the client take the new meaning and work with it toward accomplishing client goals. In the preceding example, this strategy might look like the following statement, "Your wife has left you and had you charged for assault. What do you think her message about you might be?"

■ *Integrating the ignored probes.* This strategy highlights the elements of the situation that are currently being excluded from the client interpretation. The worker uses known or strongly suspected elements in the situation that can help the client gain insight or understanding. These elements, however, are not currently used in the interpretation. The following statement would be an example of this strategy, "Just for a minute, think back before the last fight. What clues has she given you in the past that she is not happy with the way you treat her?"

■ *Reinforcing ownership.* This type of probe reinforces the unacknowledged information already evident with the client. This is useful when a client seems to have made decisions or insights but is not incorporating them into the current interpretation of the situation. For example, "I think that deep down inside of you, you have already decided what action you need to take. Can you talk to me about what you have already decided and we can see how I can help you get there."

Summarizing Skills. When clients talk about their situation, they move from one element of the situation to another, often losing their train of thought or becoming confused. One of the verbal responding strategies is to summarize what has been said at different points in the discussion to reinforce that the worker is listening and allowing an opportunity to clarify misunderstandings.

The worker leaves out interpretations of what might be occurring and simply summarizes the content. The summary should not be a long discourse by the worker but a brief summary of client disclosures. Workers often use summarizing when the train of thought seems to be getting lost. Workers also summarize at transitional and ending points in order to organize and carry forward the content of the meeting.

Maximizing Active Listening through Monitoring Themes

In active listening, the worker listens intently to all levels of verbal and nonverbal communication. In such listening, the worker tracks the themes to promote an understanding of the client situation. The themes heard in the client communication shape the direction of exploration to achieve deeper understanding. Four types of content themes are common when exploring the client situation: response system, word choice, content, and mystery themes.

Response System Themes.   In exploring client situations, the worker explores all response systems to develop an understanding of the client situation. Workers also track client use of the different systems to identify preferences or tendencies in the client among the different response systems. If clients tend to overuse one system (e.g., feeling) and underuse another (e.g., thinking), this provides important information for understanding the client experience. Workers must develop skills to identify the different response system themes.

- *Action themes* are usually contained in the content when it tends to focus on events, people, or things in the client's life. Clients will consequently tell you what they were doing, who they were with, and describe important scenes.
- *Interaction themes* emerge from the client descriptions of what was said, providing a sense of the interactions and relations with others in the story.
- *Affect themes* include the feelings that are associated with the content. In the emotional component, one often finds the power that the situation holds over the client. Workers will hear this in the nonverbal aspects of the client's voice.
- *Meaning themes* are communicated through client expressions of their beliefs, interpretations of events, values, and rules for living.

Client Wording Themes.   The wording chosen by the client provides clues to the affective components in the statement. Often emotionally laden words operate on polarity. Some of the most common polarities include:

- *Negative versus positive wording.* Some clients will tend to tune into the negative elements or interpretations of a situation even when there are positive alternatives. This choice of wording often is associated with frustrating situations (e.g.,

"I don't know what to do about his *bad behavior*" versus "I am trying to help him *learn to get along* with other children").

■ *Absolute versus tentative wording.* Some clients will use words suggesting there is never an exception to the problem situation. This is often associated with feeling that the situation is hopeless or outside of the client's control (e.g., "He *never* listens" versus "When he is watching TV, he doesn't pay attention").

■ *Internal versus external wording.* Often clients who feel out of control of their own situations choose words that indicate the control is outside of themselves (e.g., "*Things just keep going wrong* no matter what I try" versus "I can't figure out how to tackle this problem").

■ I *statements versus* you *statements.* When working with larger systems or relationships, clients often choose words indicating the other person is responsible for their feelings, rather than taking ownership of their own feelings. This is often associated with feelings of hopelessness about their ability to influence the relationship (e.g., "*I feel* upset when . . ." versus "*You make me* feel . . .").

When the words selected by the client reflect only one pole on any dimension, this can often indicate clues about the affective component of the client statement. Workers listen for repeated or stressed word choices and explore situations containing polarized word themes.

Content Themes. Often as clients tell their stories, workers find recurring themes and patterns emerging (Murphy & Dillon, 1998). These recurring themes and patterns often indicate important issues in the client's life. Effective workers quickly identify themes as the client tells a story. Particularly powerful themes in client stories include:

■ *Loss.* Individual clients and even larger client systems often have themes of loss in their stories. At the individual level, this might include such events as divorce, abandonment, death, and geographic moves. At the organizational or community levels, events such as multiple deaths in a community/organization, changes in leadership, business or community leader relocations, high turnover, and layoffs can indicate themes of loss.

■ *Disempowerment.* Client stories often include themes in which people and systems have negatively interfered in their lives with little to no accountability to the client system for the impact. At the individual level, this might include intrusions by others, controlling authority figures, exploitation, and backgrounds of being controlled. At the larger system levels, events such as oppressive management systems, takeovers, coups, business ultimatums/power plays, and oppression can indicate disempowerment.

■ *Powerlessness.* Often events described by the client system depict situations in which the client system has little to no power, and other people or systems have much higher levels of power. When several such events or situations are described, a theme of powerlessness might be inferred.

■ *Rejection.* Sometimes clients describe situations in which they are emotionally rejected. At times, these themes involve them reaching out and having their overtures rejected.

At other times, the rejecting body is more proactive through actively excluding the client system. Events that can cluster into themes of rejection include exclusions of the client system, secrets that don't include the client, denial of requests/overtures, ignoring of the client system, and neglect of obvious needs.

■ *Victimization*. At times, client stories will include descriptions of events in which the client system has experienced itself as a victim in the themes inherent in the story. In such situations, the worker will identify a clear oppressor in each described event concurrent with a clear identification of the client system as a victim.

Effective workers are able to identify themes in the client stories and use them in understanding the client situation. Client system responses are best understood through the emerging themes and patterns because all response systems tend to be used as clients adapt to life themes and events.

Mystery Themes. There are times when the themes in the client communication indicate that there are unspoken issues that are important for understanding the situation. This is the most difficult type of theme for monitoring and responding. Mystery themes are inferred from observations and hunches rather than open disclosures. Some of the indicators of mystery themes include:

■ *Gaps in congruity*. Effective workers scan client contact for consistency across time, situation, and response systems. If client statements are internally consistent, a worker can infer a stable pattern of responding across time and place. However, when there is a lack of congruity, there may be some indication of additional meaning in how the client interprets the situation (Watzlawick, Beavin, & Jackson, 1967). For example, if a client is sad because of some life event, such as a relationship ending, and begins smiling as she talks, there is a lack of congruity between her interaction (what she says) and action (what she does) systems. This is a clue that the client's processing of the event is mixed. Effective workers pick up on the lack of congruity to explore the possible unexpressed meaning or feelings that may underlie the lack of congruity.

■ *Door Openers*. Often statements of unclear meaning are made during client interaction. Often these are sort of trial balloons sent out by the client to see how the worker will respond, or may indicate a subject that has emotional energy for the client. It is important to respond to these veiled communications (Baenninger-Huber & Widmer, 1999). There are three skills commonly used in this work to ensure clear communication.
  ■ Identify unclear or disguised statements that require interpretation or assumption.
  ■ Query the meaning ("Do you mean to say . . . ," "Sounds like you mean . . .").
  ■ Clarify one's understanding ("Okay . . . so you are finding that . . .").

■ *Disguised content*. Often clients will avoid open disclosures of powerful themes by expressing themselves through metaphors or analogies. This is similar to someone saying, "I feel like I was hit by a truck." Effective workers pick up and explore analogies that appear important.

For example, a worker was meeting with an adolescent boy in legal trouble who said, "I feel like I am sitting in a bubble with a pin in my hand and the bubble keeps shrinking . . . getting closer to the pin." The worker asked, "What happens when the bubble touches the pin?" The boy replied, "I die."

Notice in the example how easy it would be to ignore the analogy shared by the youth. The suicidal ideation was well hidden, but the drama between the bubble and the pin indicated some power in the situation causing the worker to explore the analogy. The worker was then able to develop a safety plan and increase contact until the youth became more hopeful about his situation.

USING OBSERVATIONAL SKILLS IN CLIENT COMMUNICATION

Along with developing skills in exploring content, workers develop skills in understanding nonverbal communication. Important information can be observed through the nonverbal communication of a client (Watzlawick, Beavin, & Jackson, 1967). Effective workers develop keen abilities to draw information from behavior and inflections. Everybody interprets nonverbal information as part of daily living. Most people can often tell a friend's emotional state before the friend says anything, just by the way the friend enters the room.

Observation allows the worker to glean information from how clients act and interact with others. Effective workers become highly skilled in gathering information on client action systems through:

1. *Observing interactional processes.* The worker observes the client's patterns of interaction with other people.

2. *Observing behavioral responses.* The worker observes behavior and action patterns produced by the client.

For observed information to be useful in exploring the client situation, workers must be able to put the observation on the table for further exploration. Consequently, a critical skill is promoting exploration through sharing observations.

Observing Interactional Processes

When working with larger client systems, the worker has the opportunity to observe interactional processes when two client system members interact with each other. In such observation, the worker observes multiple perspectives in the interactive sequences. Recall from the interactional cycles and sequences in Figures 8.1 and 8.2 that the potential for miscommunication occurs when the receiver of a message interprets. With multiple receivers, the potential for miscommunication expands. The interactional process is similar in that more people provide for more opportunity to misinterpret content. Consequently, workers often focus less on the content of interaction and more on nonverbal and interactive processes.

Observing Interactional Processes.   In observing interaction among members of larger client systems, the worker builds on the tuning in skills discussed in Chapter 7 to track and understand the interactional processes. Table 8.2 provides some observable indicators of

TABLE 8.2   Larger System Process Indicators

Process Area	Content and Noncontent Indicators of the Process
	Action System Processes
Decision Making	1. Deference patterns to one person when decisions are being made 2. People taking over the discussion while decisions are made 3. Participation levels of the different people 4. Activities that lead to the decision 5. Nature (content) of the decision that is made 6. Effectiveness of the decision in implementation 7. Benefits to constituencies in the final decision
Role Structures	1. Leadership and following patterns 2. Formal authority structures 3. Patterns of approval seeking and checking in 4. People who attend to the tasks that need to be done 5. People who attend to the emotion of the system 6. Patterns that obstruct the work of the system 7. Patterns of self interest and self promotion
Control Mechanisms	1. Patterns of threats and sanctions 2. Formal rule structures 3. Formal consequence structures 4. Patterns of secrecy and avoidance of specific people 5. Overt pressures on people to conform 6. Acceptance/rejection/ostracization patterns 7. Patterns of celebration and reinforcement
Boundaries	1. Frequent talk of people outside of the system 2. Including opinions of outsiders in decision making 3. Frequent absences of members from the system 4. Frequent intrusions of outsiders into the system 5. Indiscriminate sharing of information outside the system 6. Secrecy expectations for those inside the system 7. Refusal to let outsiders or outside information into the system
Authority Structures	1. Level of bureaucracy and protocol involved in achieving tasks 2. Level of limitation on members' autonomy 3. Level of ritualization and procedures for daily operations 4. Level of expected conformity across situations and time 5. Level of centralization in decision making 6. Level of energy invested in monitoring and sanctioning members 7. Patterns of requesting input by system members
Norms	1. Repeated interactional or activity themes 2. Repeated attending to situations, events, or statement themes 3. Repeated ignoring of situations, events, or statement themes

Process Area	Content and Noncontent Indicators of the Process
	Action System Processes (continued)
	4. Repeated valuing statements (support, celebration) around the same content or interactional themes
	5. Repeated devaluing statements (put downs, make fun of) around the same content or interactional themes
	6. Repeated encouragement of new members to behave in certain ways
	7. Repeated chastizement for different or variant behaviors or interactions or themes
	Processing System Processes
Patterns of Affiliation	**1.** Who talks to whom?
	2. Who ignores whom?
	3. Who tries to sit together or apart from whom?
	4. Who supports whom in interaction?
	5. Who challenges whom?
	6. Who says what to whom?
	7. Who speaks how often to whom?
Atmosphere	**1.** Restlessness among people in the system
	2. Giggling
	3. Sudden changes of topic
	4. Silences
	5. Levels of eye contact
	6. Levels of verbal interactions
	7. Intensity of nonverbal communications
Tension Management	**1.** Who gets the group to laugh during tense moments
	2. Who changes the subject with all members following suit
	3. Who is able to get the members to be quiet and listen
	4. Who is able to motivate others in the system
	5. Who draws people's anger toward him- or herself when tension is high
	6. Who do people turn to when they need reprieve
	7. Who do people turn to when something needs to be done
Cohesion	**1.** Frequency of statements containing the word "we" or "us"
	2. Frequency of statements containing words or themes such as *them* or *they*
	3. Sharing of feelings that those within the system are somehow special
	4. Follow-up questions on past disclosures to follow members' stories across time
	5. Ease in reaching consensual decisions and direction
	6. Celebration of accomplishments of the members
	7. Low levels of talking about others while they are absent

the different interactional processes. Although indicators are not finite, the table provides seven common indicators to help develop some initial skills in observing various processes. Effective workers are able to tune into these interactional process indicators in assessing and intervening with larger system problems.

Communication Pace.   The speed that people talk can provide clues about their affective condition. For example, someone talking very slowly might have something on his or her mind that is drawing his or her attention away from the current topic (de Luynes, 1995; Murphy & Dillon, 1998). Slow speech might also indicate depression or excessive concern about some issue. People who talk quickly and do not allow others to enter into the conversation may feel driven to get their point across. This might indicate anxiety or concern. When tracking the pace of talking, remember pace can be culturally determined. Workers must be careful when interpreting pace as emotional, until culture has been considered.

Communication Flow.   In addition to the speed of discussion, take note of the rhythm or flow of what is being said by the client (Angell, 1996). If sentences tend to drift off or there is hesitancy in client responses, there may be some indication that emotions are underlying the discussion. Hesitancy might indicate depression or anxiety. Drifting off might signal life events that are overwhelming the client. Similarly, if the flow is forced and seems pressured, the client might be trying to convince the worker of something. This might lead to exploration of client concerns about the helping relationship or the client's expectations of service.

Communication Tone.   The vocal tone of client statements can provide a clue about the affective state of the client. Low-pitched sound quality can indicate sadness or preoccupation. Higher pitches are often associated with nervousness and anxiety. Effective workers tune into these tonal qualities and take note.

Communication Volume.   The volume of client statements is an important indicator of the affective responses. Quiet statements are often interpreted as indicating sadness or shyness on the part of the speaker. Higher volume can indicate anger, frustration, or some other emotional pressure in what is being said. Higher volume also increases the tension in the room and indicates that the speaker is attempting to control others through the escalation of tension.

Communication Focus.   The recipient or focus of client statements can indicate affect through patterns of inclusion or exclusion. If one person never addresses the other person, this can indicate some negative affect about the other person or even a lack of affective investment. Similarly, if all communication tends to be focused on one person, this might indicate significant affective investment in the person. For example, in a staff meeting, one team directed all of their positive or neutral comments to the director or another team with a shared supervisor. No positive or neutral interaction was directed at teams that were supervised by other supervisors. This team tended to feel superior to the other teams. The processing systems were very transparent in the focus of their conversations.

EXERCISE 8.1

The Client Disclosure

A client is meeting with you for the first time. In the first meeting, this woman makes the following statement. "*(Sigh)* I am not sure what is happening to me *(looks down and avoids eye contact)*. I feel like things are slipping through my fingers. I have worked at the brake plant for twenty years and I just heard they are closing down. It is just rumors right now, but it is eating away at me. I feel frozen and unable to do anything. I come home and my husband is on me to do things for him, and all I can do is keep this sick feeling from bursting out all over the place. Then I go back to work and the rumors greet me at the door, and we go round and round again. It is getting so I can't sleep at night and I don't want to have anything to do with my family *(looks straight at you)*. I just want to crawl in a hole and pull the world in on top of me."

1. What is the woman's processing language?

2. What themes are evident in her choice of words that might lead you to think she is in a distraught emotional state?

3. Identify a mystery theme about her emotional state that would need to be checked to assess her emotional situation.

4. What would you share as observations (list three things) in checking the meaning of her statement about crawling into a hole?

5. Write exactly what you would say to her in sharing the observation and checking the meaning of her "crawl in the hole" statement.

6. Write a brief (ten-word) summary statement of what she was saying to you.

Observing Behavioral Responses

Very often, clients produce behaviors and traits that provide the worker with clues about their emotions and meaning while telling their stories. These clues involve many nonverbal manifestations that provide the worker with information. Effective workers are able to tune into the behaviors and actions and identify the meaning associated with the nonverbal communication.

Observing Behavior.   Effective workers are keen observers of client behavior. Often client behavior provides information on how clients are responding to their situations. Specific indicators include:

- *Posture.* How clients hold their bodies (e.g., slumped over, rigid, relaxed).
- *Position.* How clients position or angle their bodies (e.g., facing away, leaning toward, arms crossed on chest, etc.).
- *Gestures.* How clients move their hands while speaking (e.g., punching movements, pointing, open palms, etc.).
- *Movement.* How clients shuffle or fidget while talking or listening.
- *Eye contact.* How clients make, maintain, or avoid eye contact with workers.
- *Eye movement.* How clients shift their gaze while talking or responding. Breaking off gaze or patterns of eye movement can indicate different meanings. Some theorists often feel that certain eye movements indicate that the client is accessing different types of information (House, 1994). See Figure 8.3 (page 153) for a review of how eye movement indicates processing preferences. First, eyes cast down will typically indicate that the client is feeling some affect. Second, eyes moving to the side will indicate that the client is either recalling spoken words or thinking what to say. Finally, eyes looking up typically means they recall something they have seen.
- *Mouth movement.* Grimacing and moving the mouth muscles (e.g., clenching teeth, pursing lips) can indicate some emotion.
- *Facial expressions.* Movement of the face and different facial expressions can indicate mood or affect (e.g., eyebrows up may indicate surprise).

Observing Nonverbal Mismatched Behavior.   When a client is talking, the nonverbal behaviors just described may at times be incongruent with the spoken content. Effective workers pay close attention to the way nonverbal behavior of clients fits with the form and content of what they are saying. Specific areas of focus include:

- *Congruence with language.* Is the nonverbal behavior consistent with the words they use to express themselves?
- *Congruence with feelings expressed.* Is the nonverbal behavior consistent with the feelings expressed, or is it invalidating the communication?
- *Congruence with action.* Is the nonverbal behavior consistent with what the client is doing?
- *Congruence with context.* Is the nonverbal behavior consistent with the situation and context of the client?

Observing the General Presentation Style.   The client's style of presenting him- or herself to the world can indicate issues or problems. Presentation style might indicate affective components like depression, frustration, and disruptions in functional behavior. For example, people who are suffering from depression may wear the same clothes repeatedly. However, presentation style might also provide information about environmental circumstances. For example, people who work with their hands for a living often have dirt on their hands and their clothes. When considering presentation style, it is important to treat the observations as indicating possible directions for further inquiry, rather than a clear statement about the client. In considering presentation, workers often observe how the client dresses, maintains personal hygiene, moves about, and breathes.

Observing Physical Manifestations.   Physical manifestations can indicate information about the client's current situation. People's bodies often portray part of the story through visual manifestations of injury, bodily functioning, and current state of the body. Some indicators include:

■ *Skin tone/coloring.* Often when one is experiencing either an emotional or physical state, the blood flowing to the skin is impacted and changes. Malnutrition or physical illness often yields pale skin tone, whereas someone rested and healthy might have increased color in his or her skin.

■ *Flushed.* If someone is experiencing a temporary condition, such as overexertion or embarrassment, the skin tone may temporarily change and become flushed.

■ *Labored functioning.* When one aspect of a person is overworked, often other systems tend to compensate for the functioning. For example, people may develop a limp, begin to sweat, or use one body part more than others. In organizations or communities, similar manifestations occur when one segment of the system takes on more than it can handle. This subsystem will develop visible reactions to the labored functioning (e.g., complaining, underperformance).

■ *Marks/lesions.* When damage has occurred, the client system will display evident marks or lesions. For example, abused children will have bruises or scars. In organizations and communities, situations such as abandoned housing, high turnover, and other manifestations can indicate damaged portions of the community or organization.

EXERCISE 8.2

Observing Client Wording and Presentation

You are a worker placed in a drop-in support service for parents of children receiving financial assistance. Your job is to listen to parents and help them develop solutions to their parenting problems. A parent has just approached you to talk. She comes to where you are sitting. As you look at her, you notice she has dark skin but her ethnic origin is not immediately clear. She is wearing older style clothes that are clean but appear worn and faded. As she walks toward you, she glances up, but then her eyes appear to focus on your mouth as she begins to talk. It is hard to really tell much about her eye contact as she is wearing dark glasses, but the angle of her head suggests she is looking down. You notice there are some dark marks around her neck; the rest of her skin is very smooth and clear. She is soft-spoken, appearing monotonic when speaking.

The woman begins, "I really don't know what to do with Mike. I try to do what's right with my son, but he doesn't want to listen to me. He just does what he wants. I tell his father and just get crap about how I'm an unfit mother. Then he watches TV or goes out and plays ball with Mike. They just leave me there (*sighs quietly and stops for a pause*). I try to get my husband to back me up and he just gets mad. It's like it's them against me and I'm always on my own."

1. In this exchange, focus on the spoken aspects of the meeting and identify content and noncontent indicators that help you interpret what the client is saying. Read the case situation again and find indicators that help you identify (a) the emotion felt by the client and (b) the meaning that the story appears to have for the client. Complete the following grid.

	Words/Phrases	Themes	Nonverbal Behavior	Presentation
Emotion				
Meaning				

2. Based on these indicators, what appears to be the primary felt emotion(s) for this woman (try to avoid simple guesses, such as sad, and focus on what the indicators tell you).

3. What in the presentation, content, and noncontent aspects of the client story lead you to hypothesizing that there might be more going on in this family? Complete the following grid.

	Words/Phrases	Themes	Nonverbal Behavior	Presentation
Indicators of Potential Problems				

Promoting Exploration through Sharing Observations

In conjunction with observing client systems, effective workers have strong communication skills (Goldin & Doyle, 1991). When using observed information, a critical skill is placing the observation on the table for exploration with the client. This requires workers to be able to objectively describe what they observe and allow the client to respond and begin exploration.

The Skill of Describing the Observation. The skill of describing observations involves the worker's ability to summarize his or her observations of the client and share them directly with the client. This skill is used in describing simple observations (e.g., "I notice your face is flushed today.") as well as more complex interactional processes (e.g., "I notice that whenever you say 'no,' your child throws his toy"). Any observation is available to be described.

When describing observations, workers must first practice sharing observations rather than conclusions. "I notice your face is flushed today." is qualitatively different from, "You look flushed." In the first statement, the worker is sharing an observation with the client so the latter can respond. In the second, the worker is sharing a conclusion.

Although the distinction between conclusions and observations may seem insignificant when talking about looking flushed, it is an important distinction when describing indicators of emotional processing. Most readers will have had experiences in which someone has said, "You look angry." and been either wrong or unwelcome. However, if the person had said, "I notice that your fists are clenched and your voice seems louder than normal. Is something going on?" a change might occur in the response.

The usefulness in describing observations to get someone to open up seems to come from two elements. First, the worker is only describing an observation. There is no statement or judgment about the client that may make the client defensive. Second, the technique is descriptive, which tends to provide a picture for the client to reflect upon. Visual images tend to be experienced holistically by clients and are less prone to logic-based defenses.

When using a description of an observation, the worker wants to get something on the table so it can be explored with the client. As such, this is very much a tabling technique engaging the client in further disclosure. Describing observations is a three-step process.

1. *Make the observation.* The worker observes processes or indicators suggesting something important may be occurring with the client. The worker reviews the purpose of the helping relationship and decides the observation will further the service goals.

2. *Formulate a description.* The worker describes the observation. This is a description rather than a judgment or interpretation (conclusion) of what the worker believes is occurring. To protect against sharing conclusions, it is helpful to begin the sentence with the word *I* rather than *you.* *I* statements keep the focus on what was observed, whereas a *you* statement tends to be a conclusion about the client.

3. *Invite the client to explore.* The purpose of the description is to get the observation on the table for exploration. Given that the statement made to the client is descriptive, the client needs to be invited to comment. Often this is a simple probe or question such as "Is something happening that we need to talk about?"

The ability to share observations with clients is critical in promoting further disclosures. The strength of using described observations is inherent in the visual nature of the interactions. When the worker describes an observation, the client tends to reflect on him- or herself in a visual manner. For example, if a worker says, "Your face seems drawn and you look a little down today. Is everything okay?" the client mentally reflects on his or her presentation and then considers the question. The mental reflection is more visual in nature than the simple task of answering the question. As a result, the client is less apt to resort to the automatic responses that people use when someone says "Is everything okay?"

For example, a worker was seeing an adolescent who tended to hold feelings in and deny that things were bothering him. He would later become volatile, yelling at people over little things. The youth had entered service to work on this pattern. One day he came in to meet with the worker. In this meeting, the youth was silent and avoided eye contact, giving one-word answers to questions. The worker had a hunch that things were building up but was not able to engage the client. The worker consequently said, "Tom, when you came in today, you were looking down at the floor and tended to push away my attempts to talk about things (*sharing the observation*). I know that when you are upset about things, you often don't talk about them and then you blow up. This is something we are trying to get a handle on. I can't help but wonder if things might be building up again (*sharing the hunch*). What do you think?" (*invitation to elaborate*). The client responded that there was no problem so the worker stated, "Well, if everything is going well, I don't know what I am seeing. If anything comes to mind, just let me know and we can talk about it." The client nodded and began talking about things that were upsetting him.

EXERCISE 8.3

Sharing Observations

You are working in a drop-in center for at-risk families. Your program is in the center of a medium-sized city. You are watching a mother and her 8-year-old daughter interacting when you notice the mother constantly correcting the child's behavior. In less than three minutes, she identified seven things the child should do differently. Whenever the mother made a correction, the child would stiffen and ignore her mother. The mother kept talking at the child until the child threw down a game and swore at the mother. You moved closer to make sure things did not escalate. The mother turned to you and said, "She is impossible. I try to help her but she has such a temper. What would you do?"

1. Identify the interactions you observed that might be useful to explore to help the mother understand the situation.

2. What would be a positive frame (interpretation) to put on the observations so the mother would be willing to engage with you?

3. Write what you would say to the mother (describing your observations) to get the situation on the table. You want to explore the processing that underlies her constant correcting of the daughter.

4. Write a question or probe you could use to help the mother begin to explore the situation.

Critical Chapter Themes

1. Workers explore the client situation through attending to the verbal and nonverbal communication of the client. This requires active listening and observation skills.
2. Verbal communication with clients is easy to misconstrue and requires active listening skills to make sure the worker understands the client story.
3. With active listening skills the worker promotes client disclosure and communication through nonverbal promotion (pacing and attending) and verbal techniques (language matching, prompting, clarifying, probing, etc.).
4. In the communication, the worker monitors the verbal themes in the client disclosures (response systems, wording choices, content themes, and mystery themes).
5. When observing the client the worker observes the nonverbal communication (pace, tone, volume, etc.), the action systems (behaviors, presentations, and physical manifestations), and client interactions with others (interactions and interpersonal processes).
6. Effective workers share observations in descriptive form to get observations on the table to be explored with the client.

RECOMMENDED READINGS

Angell, G. B. (1996). Neurolinguistic programming theory and social work treatment. In F. J. Turner (Ed.), *Social work treatment: Interlocking theoretical approaches* (4th ed., pp. 480–502). New York: The Free Press.

Bandler, R., & Grinder, J. (1975). *The structure of magic I: A book about language and therapy.* Palo Alto, CA: Science and Behavior Books.

Goldin, E., & Doyle, R. E. (1991). Counselor predicate usage and communication proficiency on ratings of counselor empathic understanding. *Counselor Education and Supervision, 30,* 212–224.

Hoenderdos, H. T. W., & van Romunde, L. K. J. (1995). Information exchange between client and the outside world from the NLP perspective. *Communication and Cognition, 28,* 343–350.

Murphy, B. C., & Dillon, C. (1998). *Interviewing in action: Process and practice.* Pacific Grove, CA: Brooks/Cole.

Watzlawick, P., Beavin, J. H., & Jackson, D. D. (1967). *Pragmatics of human communication: A study of interactional patterns, pathologies, and paradoxes.* New York: W. W. Norton.

9

Exploratory Questioning Skills

One of the most important skills for gathering information is questioning. Questions solicit information about the client, the client situation, and the problems influencing the client. Effective workers select questions based on their thinking about the client situation and the goals of service. Every question used by the worker should be based on his or her current knowledge and designed to expand or confirm the understanding of the situation.

Most people believe they know how to ask questions. One cannot get through a day without using questions. Without asking, one would not receive information or other desired outcomes. However, the use of questions in the professional relationship is much more purposeful and cognitively consistent than regular questions. This chapter will explore some questioning formats to effectively help clients disclose and elaborate on their stories. However, first it is important to review some of the questioning habits a worker must break because they interfere with the helping relationship.

QUESTIONING FORMATS TO AVOID

There are several types of questions that are counterproductive in the helping relationship. Although these types of questions are common in personal relationships, they are not helpful with clients. Consequently, many of the question types that follow will represent habits that readers will need to break. It is important to avoid these questions with clients, because many of the questions limit the information that is gleaned and often disrupt the helping relationship. Problematic questioning formats include:

- closed-ended questions
- multiple questions
- vague questions
- why questions
- leading questions

Closed-Ended Questions

Closed-ended questions are somewhat useful when a worker needs to either confirm or rule out a specific possibility. The questioning style is only useful when there are two possible answers (e.g., "Did you phone your probation officer?"). However, when there are more than two possible responses, the question style is problematic because it closes off any free disclosures (Evans, Hearn, Uhlemann, & Ivey, 1998; Murphy & Dillon, 1998). If closed questions are used in situations beyond two possible answers, the worker must follow up with additional questions to glean a full understanding. This generates exchanges of several questions that can feel like a third degree or inquisition. For example, a female client was talking about her fiancé. She was very ambivalent about remaining in the relationship. The worker picked up on this and the following sequence of questions occurred rather than an open-ended question:

WORKER: Do you want to leave him? *(closed)*

WOMAN: (pause) Well yes, but . . .

WORKER: Do you want to stay? *(closed)*

WOMAN: Well . . . no, but you know he is sometimes so sweet and I am not sure that I will ever find someone who loves me as much as he does.

WORKER: Does he make you feel loved? *(closed)*

WOMAN: I guess so.

WORKER: Do you love him? *(closed)*

WOMAN: I don't know.

WORKER: What do you mean? *(open)*

WOMAN: Well, we have been together since high school. I loved him so much then and was so happy when he asked me out. But that was five years ago and I am not sure I have been able to really get to know who I am. . . .

In this example, see how closed-ended questions boxed the woman into choosing between two possible answers, neither of which really captured her situation. The worker then had to follow up with additional questions to elicit more information. However, when the worker asked an open-ended question, the woman was able to open up about her feelings. Whenever possible, use an open-ended format so clients can volunteer as much information as possible.

Multiple Questions

Multiple questions occur when a worker is not quite clear on the question. Multiple questions commonly occur when:

- there are several possibilities.
- the worker thinks the client misunderstood the first question.
- one question leads to additional thoughts while asking.

Clients often become frustrated and confused with multiple questions because they start thinking about one question, and just as they begin formulating an answer, additional questions are asked. Consequently, the client chooses one question to answer and the rest remain unanswered (Murphy & Dillon, 1998; Patton, 1980). If the worker does not receive the information he or she wants from the question the client selects, the worker must ask additional questions that might invalidate the initial client response.

For example, in this excerpt, the worker is checking in with a client at the beginning of a meeting. The client is a homeless man who, in the previous meeting, decided to approach a church to see if they could give him relief money. He hoped to use the money as a deposit on a room above a hotel. As it turns out, the church needed a custodian and the man was able to get some temporary work. However, as a result of multiple questioning the worker made it hard for him to share this information at the beginning of the meeting.

> **WORKER:**   So how did it go? Did they give you money or were you turned down again? Have you checked into the hotel? *(multiple closed questions)*
>
> **MAN:**   (selecting the most recent question) No, I didn't check into the hotel yet.
>
> **WORKER:**   That's too bad. I really thought that they would come through for you. Do you want me to phone them? *(closed)*
>
> **MAN:**   No, don't phone them.
>
> **WORKER:**   Well, I really want to make sure you are okay. I want to do something for you.
>
> **MAN:**   You don't need to do anything. I am fine.
>
> **WORKER:**   How can you be fine if they turned you down? *(open)*
>
> **MAN:**   Well, when I went to the church some guy had gone home sick and they really needed someone to clean up the hall. There was going to be a supper that night and the reverend asked me if I wanted to earn some money . . .

Notice how the multiple questions forced the client to choose one question to answer. It is not unusual for the client to choose the last question because it is the easiest to remember. If the worker had stopped with the first question "How did it go?" she would have provided an open-ended question (albeit somewhat vague). Quite likely the open-ended question would solicit the information the worker wanted rather than having to go through a long questioning process. When a worker has several questions in mind, it is best to formulate a strategy to systematically solicit the information through one well-phrased question with follow-up questions based on the client's answer.

Vague Questions

Often, when workers have not fully formulated what they need to know, questions are asked in a very vague manner lacking clear and understandable content. When this style of question is used, clients become confused and do not know how to answer (Patton, 1980). They will answer what they believe the question to be, often taking the discussion offtrack. Workers must then try to find ways to re-orient the discussion.

For example, a worker in a battered women's shelter was talking with a woman about an argument with her partner. The worker wanted to help the woman understand how verbal abuse was undermining her feelings of competence. However, the way she formed the question was so vague that the focus was lost.

> WOMAN: I couldn't believe it. All I said was how was your day and he was off on me. He said all I did was sit on my ass all day and think of ways to make him feel bad when he came home. I had his supper cooked for him and was trying to be good to him. He said I was the worst wife in the world and that I needed to learn to greet a man when he comes home.
>
> WORKER: (Tuning into how he was able to make her second guess herself.) When you were talking it seemed that . . . well, I was wondering, what did you think about when he said that?
>
> WOMAN: I thought . . . hey, I have been working my ass off all day long here. I don't sit on it . . . I work it bone thin. How can he say that crap to me? *(she took the question concretely)*
>
> WORKER: (Since the client ended with a question, the worker must follow.) He just doesn't know what goes on when he's not home. How do you respond when he says those things?
>
> WOMAN: I can't respond. He will beat me.

In this example, it is clear how the opportunity to explore the cognitive processing of the woman was lost because of the vague question. The woman picked up on part of the question and answered what she thought was the question. This took the discussion in a different direction. If the worker had been more specific, the direction may have gone as planned. For example, "When he said that you needed to learn to greet him, what did that cause you to believe about yourself?"

Why Questions

Although workers often want to know why a client is engaging in a certain behavior, it is important to resist the impulse to voice this underlying stream of consciousness. Why questions are difficult for several reasons:

- They presume a cause-and-effect relationship. In this presumption, the client is assumed to have all the important information about the cause and effects. This presumption requires the client to go beyond his or her range of competency to construct an answer to the question (Patton, 1980).
- They limit the potential response because they assume there is a single cause to the behavior. Consequently, answering the why question leaves all of the other partial reasons for the behavior undisclosed. Later the client is held responsible for the disclosure and often feels trapped (Patton, 1980).
- They disempower the client as they create the need for the client to explain him- or herself (Patton, 1980). This can lead to resentment and disrupt the helping relationship.

For example, a worker was talking with a teen runaway in a street program. The teen was talking about a problem he had with his girlfriend that led to them breaking up.

TEEN: I was really messed up. She was talking with John and I got jealous. I asked her nicely to stay away from him but she kept saying they were just friends. I started to get pissed. She wouldn't do one simple thing for me. You'd think she would if she really loved me. I loved her and I didn't flirt around with other girls, but she wouldn't do that one thing. I thought if John is more important than me then have him. So I told her to go f_ _k herself.

WORKER: If they were just friends, why would you break off with her and tell her to f_ _k herself? *(note that this is both a multiple and a why question)*

TEEN: When a man and a woman are together, they should be together.

WORKER: But he was just a friend, why dump her? *(another why question)*

TEEN: Cause she was my woman—not his.

WORKER: I still don't understand.

TEEN: That's just it man, nobody understands.

In this example, the youth was very open and talking freely before the question was asked. After the question, the youth seemed to get defensive and defend his decision rather than explore the situation. As the worker persisted with the why questions, the youth shut down and the relationship with the worker seemed to be in jeopardy because the client felt the worker did not understand him.

Leading Questions

With leading questions, the worker usually has a hypothesis about what has happened. This hypothesis guides the questions so they are framed to confirm what the worker already believes rather than allowing multiple possible answers. In the desire to confirm the hypothesis, the framing is set so the client becomes backed into the confirmation rather than actually sharing the true story. This limits the client's ability to disclose his or her own information. For example, the worker suspects that a child has been sexually abused because of something observed in her drawing. The worker also has been told that others in the family have been molested and is convinced that the child is a victim. The worker wants to have the child admit to the abuse.

WORKER: I was looking at your picture and it tells me that there is something going on in your family, right? *(leading question and so vague that she must say right.)*

CHILD: Yeah.

WORKER: This kind of thing has happened before, hasn't it? *(again, vague and leading.)*

CHILD: What kind of thing?

WORKER: Well, I know that your sisters were taken away for good reasons, right? *(vague and leading.)*

CHILD: Well yeah.

WORKER: And now the same thing is happening to you, isn't that true? *(leading)*

CHILD: No.

WORKER: It's okay, tell me how are you being abused? *(leading)*

In this example, notice the pressure being placed on the child because the worker has already predetermined answers to the questions. The child is being boxed into responding in certain ways. With the pressure and the boxing, the child may respond positively just to make the worker stop. This would be most unfortunate, for even if there were abuse going on, a lawyer could get the perpetrator off because of the questioning techniques.

USING QUESTIONS TO EXPLORE CLIENT SITUATIONS

Knowing the questioning strategies to avoid is one part of questioning. Workers must also develop strong skills in asking appropriate questions. Questioning focuses on gathering information about the client situation through systematic inquiry. This style of inquiry is typified by:

- having a clear purpose for asking questions.
- using the purpose to order questions so the answer to one question leads to the focus of the next question.
- covering one area of questioning thoroughly before proceeding to the next area of questioning.

To accurately understand the client situation, questions cannot be asked in a random fashion; they must occur systematically. Systematic inquiry is the cornerstone of assessing any client situation. Whether the client system is an individual, family, group, organization, or community, the worker begins by asking questions to reach an understanding of the situation. This requires systematically developing the content area. There are five critical elements of inquiry into the problem situation:

- *Who.* Clients have many people in their life space; workers must explore which people are involved in the problem situation. When considering the who, also consider issues of culture, economic vulnerability, oppression, and other factors that influence identity and responses to situations. In the exploration of the people involved in the situation, workers will want to explore the perspective of each person and his or her experience of the problem (primary and secondary perspectives).
- *What.* In the complex life of the client, what area of life appears to be experiencing difficulties and what exactly is occurring? In exploring the what of the situation, workers try to determine the action and interaction sequences occurring.

- *When.* The worker tries to determine if a time pattern appears to influence the problem (e.g., Does it occur at certain times of the day, on certain days of the week/month, during recurring events? When did the system decide that the problem was important enough to enter service?).
- *Where.* Is there a pattern inherent in the setting in which the problem situation occurs (e.g., inside/outside, in public/private, specific settings or places of activity)? Often the where indicates environmental factors that must be considered in addressing the situation.
- *How.* The worker attempts to understand how the client and others behave as the problem unfolds (e.g., Who does what first, what follows that, and who becomes involved? One also must determine how people are processing the situation?).

Each of these elements explores the response systems of people involved in the problem situation (action systems and processing systems). While exploring each element of inquiry, it is important to understand the client's thinking, feelings, interactions, and actions. In this exploration, the worker needs to be aware of the interplay between the action and processing response systems. Both areas of response are associated with the evolution and maintenance of the problem.

In exploring the client situation several types of questions are used. The following sections explore many questioning formats that can promote systematic inquiry. Questions for exploring situation parameters, action systems, and processing systems are provided. It is unlikely you will remember every format. However, you can gain an appreciation that there are many options to use when exploring client situations.

QUESTIONS TO EXPLORE
THE SITUATION PARAMETERS

Parameter questions attempt to explore the who, when, what, where, and how of the client situation to begin to understand the basic structure and flow of the situation that has brought the client system into service. There are two basic types of questions that help the worker develop the parameters: background questions and problem identification/scope questions (Patton, 1980).

Background Questions

Background questions seek information about the general client situation. Such questions generally focus on the client life space and history and try to establish the general linkages to the problem situation. Specific styles of questioning include:

- *Client situation questions.* These questions ask the client about his or her current life situation (roles, family situation, community, etc.) so the worker can begin to construct the setting in which the problems tend to occur. For example, "Where are you when John tends to be most disobedient?" The worker also attempts to determine the history of what has been done about the problem situation and what brought the client to the point where service became an option.

■ *Knowledge questions* (Patton, 1980). Knowledge questions solicit information on the range of knowledge that the client system brings into the problem situation. For example, "Are you aware that the school system has testing for children like John?" Especially with people of different cultures and life situations, workers cannot expect their clients to have the same knowledge about situations.

■ *Background demographic questions* (Patton, 1980). Background questions seek information on a client's history or current circumstance in the broader social systems. Often these need to be grouped according to demographic categories (economic, cultural, neighborhood, family background) and asked in some order to provide a comprehensive set of questions. For example, "What is the last year of school you completed? Where did you attend school?" In the four-cell exercise in Chapter 1, there were many background questions asked of you in the environment cell.

Problem Identification and Scope Questions

Identification and scope questions are central to inquiry because they seek to determine the nature of the problem. Understanding the extent of the problem and situational elements can be solicited through this type of question. Specific styles of questioning include:

■ *Descriptive situational questions.* This style of questioning involves asking the client to describe the events within a situation. These questions involve a client describing the immediate past or current circumstances associated with the problem situation. For example, "What was happening for you that made you think this agency might help?"

■ *Future projective questions.* These questions shift the focus of inquiry by asking the client to think about the future and describe what might occur. For example, "What do you hope will happen for you as a result of coming to our agency?" "What are you afraid might happen if you don't change this situation?"

■ *Classification questions* (Patton, 1980; Palazzoli-Selvini, Boscolo, Cecchin, & Prata, 1980). Classification questions create order in understanding the situation by organizing events or people into roles or groups influencing the problem. For example, "When you are angry at John, who is supportive to you?"

■ *Scaling questions* (Miller, 1994; Shilts & Gordon, 1996). Scaling questions inquire about the different experiences between people, at different times or places. In using this type of question, the worker asks the client to rate the severity or impact of a problem or problem element. For example, "On a scale of one to ten, how awful would it be for you if John doesn't go to bed on time?" This also can be used comparatively. For example, "Mom's anger scores a three on the Richter Scale, where would your dad score?" This type of question is very important when trying to make service goals measurable.

QUESTIONS TO EXPLORE CLIENT RESPONSE SYSTEMS

Along with the general parameters of the problem, workers want to be able to explore how clients (or client systems) are responding to the situation. Often the problematic aspects of the situation may be embedded in the client processing or action responses to the situation. The following sections describe some questioning options for exploring the action and processing systems of clients.

Action System Questions

Often workers want to gain clear information about how people are behaving in the problem situation. Workers tend to use specific types of questions to explore the action systems of people's responses to the situation. There are two types of questions common to this type of exploration. First, there are straightforward questions asking about behaviors. Second, there are questions used when asking about difficult or embarrassing actions. These questions allow the worker to attend to the feelings of the client while still exploring the client's action system.

Action system questions glean information about the sequences and patterns associated with the problem behaviors or events. The goal of this type of questioning strategy is to provide the clearest possible picture of the problem situation in an almost frame-by-frame format.

Direct Questioning Formats. The following seven types of questions are commonly used to seek information about behavioral and interactive response systems. They are direct questions that are designed to explore behavior and interaction.

- *Simple behavioral description.* Simple behavioral questions ask clients to describe exactly what they did. Ideally, workers ask for the details so the clients do not provide general categories of behavior but rather a full description of what actions they took in the situations. For example, "Please describe for me exactly what actions you took after you decided it was time to put John to bed."

- *Outcome questions* (Miller, 1994). Sometimes the worker wants to stress or highlight the outcomes of a client system's action system. This is common when the action system responses are implemented to solve a problem, but somehow they inadvertently contribute to the problem situation. In such situations, the worker wants to include the action system as an element of the problem. After exploring the problem sequence, the worker asks about the outcomes of different actions. For example, "When you yell at John, does it make him go to bed right away or does it seem to make things worse?"

- *Sensory-focused descriptive questions* (Patton, 1980). When people might have different processing preferences, workers often want to focus on different sensory experiences of people within the system. In focusing on the description of events, the worker asks about what is experienced within the different sensory systems (seen, heard, tasted, touched, and smelled by the client). For example, "When you ask your son to go to bed, what do you actually see him do, what are his actions? When he does these things, what look do you see on his face?"

■ *External perspective descriptive questions* (Miller, 1994). Sometimes workers wish to have clients describe their action systems from a new perspective. This alters the processing systems associated with the actions by having the client assume the position of a third party. In this way, the worker can solicit information that would be observable if the worker were in the situation with the client. This type of question can be combined with pattern sequencing and sensory questions, if the worker wishes to focus the questioning. For example, "If I were at the dinner table with your family, what would I see happening at the beginning of the meal?"

■ *Verbal quote questions.* Verbal quote questions ask the client to repeat exactly what he or she said to another person. It is desirable that the client give an exact quotation to understand the full situation. In asking the question, the worker must ensure the vocal tones, pacing, volume, and general delivery of the answer are consistent with the behavior in the situation. For example, "Please say to me exactly what you said to John. Make sure it is the same words, volume, and delivery as you used when arguing with him." Very often the worker must follow up with probes to make sure the volume and nonverbal communication is the same as the original.

■ *Auditory reception questions.* Auditory reception questions ask the client what he or she heard in the verbal response of another person. Again, it is important to assure that the nonverbal communication is the same as the original communication made toward the client. For example, "Using the same vocal tone and volume, say to me exactly what John said to you."

■ *Interactive pattern questioning* (Penn, 1982). This type of questioning actually uses several verbal quote and auditory reception questions asked in tandem to develop the pattern of events within a problem situation. Typically, the sequencing begins before the problem occurs. In interactive pattern questioning, the worker requests step-by-step information of people's actions and interactions. This style of questioning seeks to find the details of the interactional sequences depicted in Chapter 8. An example of this sequencing might be:

WORKER: When you asked John to go to bed, what was he doing?

FATHER: He was watching TV.

WORKER: Was the show on or did you catch him during a commercial?

FATHER: It was during a commercial.

WORKER: Were you in the same room?

FATHER: No, I was in the kitchen, but it is attached to the family room.

WORKER: What exactly did you say to him to get him started to bed?

FATHER: I said, "John . . . bedtime."

WORKER: What was his immediate response when you said this?

FATHER: He ignored me.

WORKER: When he responded this way, what did you say next?

FATHER: I said, "John . . . I said bedtime."

WORKER: You sound calm right now, were you that calm at the time?

FATHER: No, I was getting angry.

WORKER: Say it again as you said it that night.

FATHER: (loud) "John . . . I said bedtime!"

WORKER: What was his response?

FATHER: He threw down the remote and stomped off to bed.

WORKER: When this happened, what did you do?

Although this type of questioning is tedious, as the questions evolve, the worker re-constructs the event step-by-step to the point of conclusion. In this questioning, the worker needs to make sure that tone, actions, and other people are included by asking questions like, "How did you sound when you said that?" or "Did you do anything when you said this?" This allows the worker to gain the clearest possible picture of how problematic actions unfold in the situation. It is useful to map this out in the circular format outlined in Figure 9.1. This allows tracking of the sequence in a step-by-step system. From the schematic, the pattern is clear and it is easy to identify areas conducive to intervention. There is also space for taking notes about processing systems on the same diagram.

Questioning Formats for Hard-to-Disclose Behaviors.   Often workers want to ex-plore sensitive behaviors where questions might arouse emotional reactions or avoidance. It is difficult to glean information about these behaviors with simple questioning formats because they do not attend to the client feelings when asking the question. Sensitive-behavior questions attend to the client's feelings in setting a frame for the question. This makes it easier for the client to share information without undue embarrassment or avoid-ance. There are four types of sensitive-behavior questions.

■ *Presupposition questions* (Patton, 1980). Presupposition questions are useful when inquiring about information that might be somewhat sensitive. These questions are framed so the client does not have to disclose the behavior first. Instead, the client can talk about the dynamics of the behavior. If the behavior does not exist, clients inevitably will respond by correcting the worker about the supposition; however, if the behavior does exist, the client is freed from the difficult task of having to openly disclose the existence of the behavior.

Given the assumption inherent in this type of questioning, the worker must only ask this type of question when there is a strong likelihood that the behavior exists. For exam-ple, if a worker knows there is fighting in a family but wants to know about the extent of parental fighting, the following question can help solicit the information: "John, when your mom and dad fight, how often does the arguing lead to them screaming at each other?"

■ *Neutrally balanced questions* (Patton, 1980). Neutrally balanced questions attend to the client's feelings about the behavior by disclosing a full range of values potentially

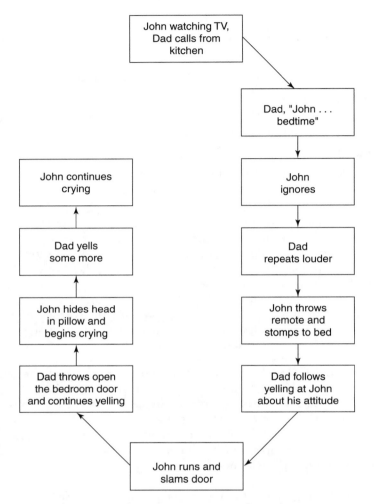

FIGURE 9.1   Tracking the Interaction Sequence

associated with the behavior. This acknowledges feelings the client may have about the behavior before the feelings emerge. In this questioning strategy, the worker balances the positive and negative values attached to the behavior before presenting the question. For example, "John, we know arguing is both growth enhancing and at times disruptive in families. How often are people in your family arguing?"

■ *Illustrative example questions* (Patton, 1980). When attempting to elicit the disclosure of very difficult information, it is useful to frame questions in a way that communicates the worker has heard it all before, and thus will not be shocked at the disclosure. Workers consequently provide an illustration highlighting tolerance when introducing the question. In this strategy, the client's fears of what the worker might think are answered before they are aroused by the question. For example, if a worker wanted to solicit information about violence, the following question might be used: "I know that all couples disagree with each other and have conflict. In some families, conflict leads to behaviors like swearing and plates flying around the room. In other families, conflict is resolved though calm and quiet discussion. In your relationship, how would you say you deal with conflict?"

■ *Exaggerated extremes questions* (Patton, 1980). When workers want to assure that clients will not be embarrassed by the question, they often want to use illustrations that are worse than the client behaviors. In such situations a worker may want to exaggerate the extremes that are illustrated providing a much broader range of acceptance for the client. This is particularly useful when a worker thinks the client may be more embarrassed than the behavior warrants or when a worker does not know the extent of the client behavior. In using this strategy, the worker balances out the extremes of the polarized possibilities rather than providing different illustrations. For example, "John, sometimes when families fight they feel good afterward . . . like clearing the air . . . and sometimes when families fight, it feels like the sky before a thunderstorm. What is it like after people in your family fight with each other?"

Processing System Questions

To fully understand the client situation, workers often must explore processing systems as well as action themes. The exploration of processing systems uses slightly different questions because the worker gleans information on internal processes. Processing system questions seek information about the feelings, beliefs, interpretations, and thinking underlying the problem situation. These questions are based on an assumption that all behaviors are supported and justified through internal processes.

There are two categories of questions used to draw out processing. First, workers tend to use direct questioning strategies. Such questions are undisguised and clear about their content. The second questioning strategy is indirect and complex in framing questions.

Direct Questioning Strategies. Direct questioning uses straightforward questions to ask about beliefs or feelings. Belief questions seek to determine how clients value, interpret, and understand situations. In the belief cell of the four-cell exercise in Chapter 1, readers answered direct questions about beliefs and values. There are six direct questioning strategies commonly used by workers. In reading these strategies, notice how the later strategies are direct almost to the point of confrontation. When using highly direct strategies, workers must be sure the working relationship is strong enough to avoid clients feeling pressured by the worker.

■ *Opinion and value questions* (Patton, 1980). Opinion and value questions try to understand the cognitive value set used by the client in processing situations. Often beliefs and values support the behavior that contributes to the problem situation. For example, in the struggle about the bedtime routine, a worker might ask, "What is so important about having John go to bed by 8:00?"

■ *Feeling questions* (Patton, 1980). Feeling questions try to understand the emotional responses to cognition or actions. Workers often use these questions when looking for adjectives related to an event ("Do you feel nervous, happy, sad, angry, anxious when you tell John it is bedtime?"). In forming such questions, workers often have to set the stage. For example, "Remember when you were in the kitchen and about to tell John it was bedtime, just before you told him to go to bed, what was the feeling you experienced?" In using feeling questions, avoid disguised opinion questions such as, "How do you feel about that?" Such questions really solicit opinions, not feelings.

■ *Primary/secondary emotion questions.* There are two levels of feeling in many situations. One level is the primary feeling (e.g., inadequacy, hopelessness, and joy) operating on a visceral level. As such, there is a blend of affect and body sensation. The secondary feeling level tends to be a blend of emotional and cognitive processes. There is often a hierarchy, with the primary feeling being deeply felt and fueling the reaction. The secondary emotion is reactive to the primary feeling. Anger is an excellent example of how this reaction system works, because anger is typically secondary to a precipitating feeling. Most often workers find feelings like powerlessness, inadequacy, hopelessness, or futility below the anger. Questions to get at these feeling levels are quite simple. The worker first identifies the secondary emotion and then asks what feelings were going on underneath the emotion. For example, "You mentioned you were getting angry when John ignored you; what feelings can you identify underneath the anger?"

■ *Identification of underlying belief systems.* Workers often want to understand the beliefs associated with different behavior sequences. As the astute reader noted in Chapter 8, the processing in interactive sequences is important. To solicit processing information underlying interactive sequences, the worker can identify each step of the interaction (see Figure 9.1) and then ask clients to identify the processing associated with each step. As the client elaborates on the beliefs and thinking behind each step in the pattern, the worker develops a very clear picture of the situation. For example, at the first step one might ask, "When you tell John that it is bedtime, what are the thoughts going through your mind?" At the second step, the worker might focus on the mother's thoughts, "When John ignores your statement that it is bedtime, what do you think this means?" Each step of the interaction will have an accompanying belief.

■ *Inner should questions.* Inner should questions ask about the injunctions and internalized rules that a person holds. Often beliefs governing client behavior have accompanying feelings of threat if the injunction is not followed. For example, the father struggling with the bedtime routine may feel he has to get John to bed on time in order to be a good father. To get at such information a worker might ask, "When you decided it was time for bed, what were the thoughts going through your head?" An alternative question might be, "What are some of the reasons people should get their children to bed on time?"

■ *So what questions.* Beliefs that generate strong emotions are particularly powerful and require workers to strip away rationalizations and layers of belief to get at the feelings. So what questions attempt to ladder down to the personalized meaning and feelings associated with problematic processing. In using so what questions, workers ask the client to justify or explain his or her conclusions in a sequential way with each answer yielding another "so what" response by the worker. Through challenging the rationale at each level, the questions try to promote a deeper analysis of the meaning for the client. Such questions require a positive relationship because they are confrontive and can yield defensive reactions. For example, in exploring the bedtime problem the worker might engage in the following type of so what questioning:

> **WORKER:**   What is the problem if John does not go to bed on time? *(version of so what)*
>
> **FATHER:**   Kids need to get a good night's sleep.
>
> **WORKER:**   How is it a problem for you if he does not get a good night's sleep? *(variation on so what)*
>
> **FATHER:**   If he doesn't get a good night's sleep, then I am not doing my job.
>
> **WORKER:**   What is so bad about not doing your job? *(another variation on so what)*
>
> **FATHER:**   Then you are not a good father.
>
> **WORKER:**   And if you are not a good father, what is so bad about that for you? *(another variation on so what)*
>
> **FATHER:**   Then I am no good.

In this example, it is clear how each successive question leads the father deeper into his beliefs trying to uncover the personalized beliefs. Notice how the questions are worded differently to disguise the "so what." Some of the questions are general and some focus directly on the attributed meaning of the father. Changing of the wording allows the worker to focus the exploration without appearing repetitive.

Indirect/Complex Questioning Strategies.   The indirect or complex types of questions use client responses to situations or scenarios to bring out values and beliefs. Such questions generate illustration and application of client beliefs and interpretations. This type of questioning involves planning and thought in forming the question. Readers will want to become comfortable with direct questioning strategies before practicing the more complex forms of questioning. There are four strategies of indirect/complex questioning focused on processing systems.

■ *Comparative questions* (Penn, 1982). Comparative questions try to determine client beliefs about specific elements of the problem situation by comparing events or situations. In using this type of question, the worker focuses on one person to explore how the client believes that person performs across situations. For example, "How does John's arguing about bedtime compare to his arguing about curfew?" or "How is Dad's anger expressed in public compare to his anger when nobody is watching?"

■ *Normative comparisons* (Patton, 1980; Penn, 1982). Normative comparisons are comparative questions in which the worker asks people to share their beliefs about the normal functioning of people and groups involved in the problem situation. The comparative element of the question occurs when the worker asks the client to compare how different people in the situation perform various functions in relation to each other.

For example, "How do the white police treat you differently from the Native American police officers?" or "Who in the family would normally be supportive to John and who would push for punishment?"

■ *Simulation questions* (Patton, 1980). Simulation questions ask the clients to comment on a simulated event or situation. This puts clients in the role of an expert. Often such questions allow clients to view their own situation more objectively and may outline aspects of the problem they are less willing to explore using direct questioning. For example, if a worker wanted to tease out some of the father's thinking about bedtime routines, he could ask, "If a family was being very lax about bedtimes with their young child, what would your advice be to them?"

■ *Interpretive or explanation questions* (Penn, 1982). Interpretive questions ask the client to interpret the behavior or statements of another person in the problem situation. Workers often use such questions to seek information about values or belief conflicts among the people in the client situation. Often people's negative beliefs about the other will be embedded in their answers. This brings out any distorted beliefs or miscommunications in the situation. For example, the question, "What do you think John is trying to say to you when he ignores you?" might get at information important to understanding the father's next reaction.

EXERCISE 9.1

Exploratory Questioning Exercise

1. You are doing your student placement in a nursing home. One of your jobs is to meet with people entering the home for the first time. You are sitting down with an elderly woman who is struggling with the need to go into a nursing home. In your discussion with her she says, "I have always taken care of myself. I still remember the Great Depression and have always felt it was important to do things for myself. Now they tell me I can't. My son says I have to come in here and let you take care of me. He just out and tells me. I don't know what to do." You want to explore the situation with the woman. Devise questions to explore the situation based on the following criteria.

   a. Devise a question to find out more about the exchange when the son told her about coming into the home.

   b. This woman has pride about her independence. Devise a question to explore some of the things she used to do for herself (her accomplishments).

c. You don't know what activities she is struggling with that caused people to tell her she needs to come into the home. Devise a question to identify what areas of care she might need.

d. You hear in her voice some beliefs about what it means to be independent. Devise a question to get at her beliefs about doing things for herself.

e. You hear some emotion and confusion in her voice. Ask a question to find out more about her feelings.

2. You are a student doing your placement at a Child Protective Service agency. You are meeting with a family already assessed and receiving services. The family has had problems with spousal and child abuse in the past. They just came in to meet with you and reported that it was a rough week. You are concerned there has been some form of violence. Use a general type of exploratory question to begin finding out how the week has been, and then follow up their responses with a question that can help get at hard-to-disclose behaviors.

a. General question:

b. Their responses:

c. Question for hard-to-disclose behavior:

d. You now want to explore some of the thinking behind their behaviors. Develop a question to determine the underlying beliefs contributing to the problems.

3. You are meeting with a mother and a child experiencing escalating arguments. You want to track the behavior patterns of the arguments. Compose a series of action system questions to track the pattern.

a. Question 1:

   Answer:

b. Question 2:

   Answer:

c. Question 3:

   Answer:

QUESTIONS TO EXPLORE LARGER
CLIENT SYSTEMS

Most of the questions discussed are used with individuals. Although one can use them with members of larger systems, there are important types of questions specifically designed for exploring larger system processes. For example, a worker can not only ask clients about themselves and their experiences, but about how others in the system experience each other. Larger system questioning can yield information about relationships and systemic response systems concurrent with individual response systems.

The common term used for exploratory, systemic questions is *circular questions* (Tomm, 1988). This term is used because the questioning allows for the information from the question to provide feedback to the system (Palazzoli-Selvini et al., 1980). Such questions not only yield valuable information, but also enhance the working alliance (Adams, 1997; Dozier, Micks, Cornille, & Peterson, 1998).

Setting Up Systemic-Based Questions

The questions designed for larger systems have largely come from the group and family intervention fields. These schools of intervention use questions to explore and create change in both individuals and systems (Freedman & Combs, 1993). In using systemic questions, workers must carefully set up the questions (Adams, 1997; Brown 1997b). The setup of large-system questions follows five basic steps:

1. *The context.* The worker sets the stage for the question by setting a different context for the system to hear the question. For example, in working with a family struggling with decisions about a disabled child, a worker might try to shift the context of family thinking through the following question introduction. "If Johnny were suddenly better and put himself to bed every single night, . . . " Such a setup guides the family's thinking in a different direction from the current context.

2. *The response system target.* To frame the question, the worker focuses on one of the response systems. In the initial question, this decision is based on the thinking skills of the worker. In most other questions, the target response system evolves from the client response on the table. The worker will target whatever system appears to be the most important system in the client statement. This skill will be discussed in detail in the later discussion on transitional questioning.

3. *The focal member(s) of the system.* Within the new context developed in the setup, the worker usually tries to focus the implication of the new context on the system member(s) most affected by the old context. In the preceding example, the person most affected might be the mother. Consequently, the worker may want to either ask the mother the question or ask another member of the family about the mother.

4. *The question.* Often the worker wants the system to engage in specific types of reflection. Consequently, the worker follows up questions with probes directing the focus. This might include something like, "If Johnny were suddenly better and put himself to bed every night, how would this change your life? You spend about two hours per day in this struggle, what would you do with your time?"

5. *The follow-up.* After the question has been asked, effective workers follow up the question with further exploration. In follow-up, the worker will either use other exploratory questions or resort to prompts and probes.

Larger-System Questioning Strategies

In working with system members, it is important to glean an understanding of the relationships that exist among the members. The web of relationships can be very complex and viewed differently from the various positions in the system. Larger-system questions have people in different positions in the system reflect and report on the other members. The content produced through reflection on the different members, interactions, and individuals provides valuable information for understanding the relationship structures. The following types of questions have proven useful in gleaning relational information.

■ *Triadic reports* (Palazzoli-Selvini et al., 1980). Triadic reporting allows the worker to gather relational information by having one system member report on the relationship between two other members. Triadic questions focus the question on one person, but targets information on the relationship between people in the system. When the person answers, the worker gleans information about the others in the system concurrent with information about how the reporter views the others. Often workers will use this type of questioning with more than one member of the system in sequence. For example, if gathering information on member side taking with power struggles, the following questions might be used, "Samantha, when the manager of the Casework Team wants to change the program, but the manager of the Assessment Team does not, who tends to get her own way? Mary, from where you sit in this organization, who tends to get her own way when the Casework Team wants to do something and the Assessment Team does not?"

■ *Process identification questions* (Yalom, 1985). Often workers notice interpersonal processes in the family they want to highlight with the system. By bringing these processes to light, the worker can identify aspects of the system that may have some influence on the problems. Process identification questions follow four steps.

- The worker notices a pattern of interaction or reaction among one or more members.
- The worker decides whether the process is likely to be associated with the work that has been contracted.
- If the process seems to be important, the worker asks a system member to reflect on the flow of interaction.
- The worker expands the focus to further explore the situation.

For example, in a family working on difficult parent–child interactions, the following question might be used to highlight the maternal role in the conflict, "Mary, do you notice that whenever you say 'I don't know,' your mother rolls her eyes back in her head? Tell me, what does this mean?"

■ *Coalition questions* (Penn, 1982). In larger client systems, often coalitions exist in which two or more members consistently take sides against others. Workers are often challenged to determine who has taken whose side in the system. Coalition questions ask members to reflect on the consistent side-taking actions of system members. For example, in a family in which the children are becoming involved in parental problems, a worker may address the children with the following question, "Mary, sometimes family members have special relationships where they kind of take each others' sides no matter what is going on. Who in the family always takes Mom's side? Who in the family tends to take your father's side?"

■ *Agreement/disagreement questions* (Penn, 1982). Similar to coalition exploration, workers want to know who agrees with whom on specific issues within the system. This is different from stable coalitions because in issue-specific alliances, the side taking shifts with the topics being addressed. Agreement/disagreement questions ask for focused reflection. The worker asks family members to first consider an issue, then consider the alliances that exist on the specific issue. For example, "When it comes to wanting to have later bedtimes, who agrees with you that you go to bed too early?"

EXERCISE 9.2

Exploration with Larger Systems

1. You are a worker in an adult mental health program. You are meeting with a family consisting of a mother, father, and two children. The mother has been diagnosed with a bipolar disorder. She has been manic, which is interfering with other family members' abilities to function. You think the mother may be experiencing some new stresses that interfere with her stability. You want to explore who in the family might create these stresses and who might mediate the stresses. Use a triadic question to find out who supports the mother when she is upset.

   a. Who would you select to answer the question?

   b. Write exactly what you would say to this person (specify the setup and delivery of the question).

2. You are working in a family service agency in which two teams have been arguing about case management procedures. One team states the other does not care about clients on the waiting list because they are keeping clients in service too long. This makes it hard to move clients from the waiting list into service. The other team argues the first team does not understand the complexities of long-term service. You notice whenever someone from either of the teams makes a statement, the other team does not respond or engage in the discussion. Instead, they just make an unrelated statement supporting their own position. You believe the lack of engagement keeps the two teams from understanding each other. Use a process identification question to begin an exploration of the communication problems between the two teams.

3. You are a group leader working with youth at risk to drop out of school. You notice that two members always sit together, support each other, and are becoming too separate from the rest of the group. You want to explore this risk with the group. Use a coalition type of question to begin this exploration.

Critical Chapter Themes

1. Questioning is one of the primary skills for gathering information from clients. Effective workers use questions as part of systematic inquiry into the client situation. Such inquiry provides the information necessary for assessment and understanding.
2. There are five types of questions a worker should avoid using: closed-ended questions, multiple questions, why questions, vague questions, and leading questions. These questions can interfere with information gathering and the working relationship.
3. There are several categories of questions: situational questions for exploring the problem situation, questions for exploring client response systems, and questions for exploring larger client systems.
4. Situational questions explore problem parameters and background to determine the history, background, and environmental factors as well as the perspectives and experiences that people have about the problem situation.
5. Response system questions focus either on action responses or processing responses in the client situation. Action system questions include straightforward questions and questions for hard to disclose behaviors. Processing system questions include direct and indirect questioning strategies.
6. Questioning strategies for larger client systems require more setup and focus than individual-focused questions. Questioning strategies include triadic, process-focused, coalition, and agreement questions.

RECOMMENDED READINGS

Adams, J. F. (1997). Questions as interventions in therapeutic conversation. *Journal of Family Psychotherapy, 8,* 17–35.

Brown, J. E. (1997). The question cube: A model for developing question repertoire in training couple and family therapists. *Journal of Marital and Family Therapy, 23,* 27–40.

Penn, P. (1982). Circular questioning. *Family Process, 21,* 267–280.

Tomm, K. (1988). Interventive interviewing: III. Intending to ask lineal, circular, strategic, or reflexive questions? *Family Process, 27,* 1–15.

CHAPTER

10

Reflective Responding Skills

Reflective responding refers to the ability to identify, and communicate back to the client, an accurate understanding of the client situation. Along with questioning, reflecting is one of the most commonly used practice skills. In professional communication, reflecting back an accurate understanding helps the client feel understood (Evans et al., 1998; Murphy & Dillon, 1998). This outcome helps deepen the helping relationship by putting the client experience into words.

THE OUTCOMES OF REFLECTION

Reflection is a skill that can greatly enhance service delivery for the client. The reflection of empathic understanding is associated with effective workers (Lafferty et al., 1989). Reflection strategies are associated with a stronger working relationship with the client (Chang, 1994). Understandably, the use of reflection tends to yield more favorable client responses (Uhlemann, Lee, & Martin, 1994).

There are many potential outcomes of reflection. It promotes engagement, insight, cognitive changes, and work—depending on how the reflection is used. The use of reflection tends to change over time. Early in the relationship, reflection helps the relationship form because without feeling understood, the client will not open up and work. Reflection of the content of what clients are saying is most useful when the worker is gathering information for assessment purposes. Later in service, reflections are used more for promoting insight and goal achievement. Some of the most common applications of reflection include:

- *Deepening the working relationship.* Early in service, clients need to feel that their workers understand them (Shulman, 1999). If clients feel understood, they are more likely to invest in the helping relationship. Conversely, when clients do not feel their workers understand them, they are likely to distance themselves from the relationship or withdraw their investment and active involvement.
- *Affirming understandings* (Murphy & Dillon, 1998). Similar to developing the relationship, workers often wish to ensure their understandings of their clients are accurate. Reflective responses are used to check the understanding. This is vital

early in the helping relationship when the worker is exploring the situation for assessment and goal setting. Such reflection typically includes questions for client feedback.

■ *Transition into work.* Often when a client is first entering the relationship or the session, social exchanges and explorations of life events occurring between contacts. Many workers use reflection techniques to transition from general discussion to more focused work. Reflections can be used to highlight themes in the general conversation that are consistent with the goals or other elements of service. When the similarity is reflected, the transition into work is facilitated.

■ *Promoting further disclosures* (Murphy & Dillon, 1998). Sometimes the worker wants the client to continue telling his or her story. Reflective responses are used to summarize and focus what the client has said. In response, the client can continue disclosing and elaborating on what was said. This is most useful when a client is unfocused.

■ *Promoting discussion* (Evans et al., 1998). When a worker wishes to encourage specific areas of exploration, reflection is used to highlight issues for further exploration.

■ *Promoting insight* (Murphy & Dillon, 1998). Sometimes a worker wants to stimulate client thinking about the situation. Reflection is used to promote client reflection on the situation. This is most common when the worker reflects meaning or affect back to the client. Often the worker does not use follow-up questions to avoid distracting the client from hearing the reflection.

■ *Promoting thinking changes* (Evans et al., 1998). When workers want to challenge a style of thinking, they often use reflection. Reflection of discrepancies and strengths are common reflective strategies to challenge previously held beliefs or promote new avenues of thinking. Like the promotion of insight, this use of reflection often allows the client to reflect on the communication.

THE ELEMENTS OF REFLECTION

There are three basic elements to reflection: identification of a critical component of the client disclosure, communication of the critical component back to the client, and receiving feedback on one's understanding of the critical components.

Identifying the Critical Components of the Client Disclosure

The identification process relies heavily on tuning in skills discussed in Chapter 5. In using these skills, workers consider their observations of the client and their hunches to identify the important elements for reflection (Rober, 1999). Through tuning in, workers identify critical content themes, feelings, meanings, or strengths in what clients disclose. Effective workers also reflect back client strengths and communication discrepancies that can promote client goals. The following is a description of some of the common elements that are reflected.

Identification of Response System Components.   Many authors distinguish between reflecting content and affect (Murphy & Dillon, 1998). This creates several types of reflection to remember. It is simpler to use the response system framework to identify the area that one wishes to reflect. The worker listens to the client and identifies the action, interaction, meaning, or feeling themes that appear to be most important to the client. Once identified, the worker tracks selected themes from one disclosure to the next identifying important elements for the client. For example, a common theme for adolescents is to resist parental (and authority figure) control. This theme might become present in discussions about parents, teachers, and even the worker. Recurring trends are important to identify.

Identification of Client Strengths.   The worker tracks instances in which the client has exhibited mastery and ability within the problem situation. Often this involves comparing knowledge of the client's past to the present disclosure (Saleebey, 1997). For example, the teen mentioned previously might discuss a school situation in which he felt controlled but, rather than lashing out (as done previously), he took another form of action. Even if the other form of action was not highly successful, strength is indicated through the attempts to gain mastery.

Identification of Discrepancies.   The worker listens to the client disclosure and identifies discrepancies among feelings, thinking, interactions, and actions that appear to be significant in maintaining the problem situation (Evans et al., 1998). The worker believes identification and exploration can promote goal achievement.

Communicating the Critical Components to the Client

The actual reflective act involves communicating the identified components back to the client. Given that communication involves verbal and nonverbal actions, it is useful to consider that both verbal and nonverbal reflection can be used. Content is usually reflected verbally; affect can be reflected verbally and nonverbally. There are six very common methods of reflecting critical components back to the client.

- restatement
- paraphrasing
- stating observations
- reflective challenges
- metaphoric reflection
- nonverbal reflection

Restatement.   The simplest reflective response is to restate what the client has said (Murphy & Dillon, 1998). Commonly, a single word or a phrase can communicate the important components back to the client. For example, when a client states his or her week has been a "week from hell," the worker might respond "from hell?" This short response conveys both a reflection of meaning and implies a need for more information. Such responses are a punctuation type of reflection, briefly supporting the client's initial disclosure while shifting focus back to the client for additional disclosures. Frequent use is not recommended, given that the parrot-like or mimicking-type of response does not display understanding or depth.

Paraphrasing.   Paraphrasing communications provide clients with a summary of their words and phrases pulling together the critical content or themes in the client disclosures (Murphy & Dillon, 1998). With the emphasis on words and descriptions of events, this is often an important skill in working with the client action systems. Paraphrasing highlights important themes and helps organize the client's thinking. For example, going back to the teen, the worker might say, "At school you say teachers are telling you what to do and at home you say you parents are telling you what to do. Now you are here and I am telling you what to do. It seems everywhere you go people are trying to tell you what to do."

Stating Observations.   In reflecting discrepancies and strengths, sometimes it is useful to share observations. This type of reflection tends to be descriptive. By describing what has been observed, clients are less likely to dismiss the reflection, because it is based on observable information rather than values or impressions. There are four types of observation common in this type of reflection.

■ *Simple observation.* Reflecting on an observation is most useful with the processing systems when critical themes in the client communication are apt to be nonverbal. In simple observation, the worker shares the observations that apply to the critical components in the disclosure. An example of simple observation of a discrepancy might be, "Even though you said you didn't care, you looked sad that they didn't ask you what you thought." A simple observation of strength might be, "You have told me you lose it when people criticize you. Just a minute ago, I told you how your behavior was making it hard to get focused; you were polite and responded well. We got focused immediately and did some good work. Maybe you have more control than you give yourself credit for." A simple observation of feeling might be, "When you talked about the yelling in your home, your eyes looked watery and sad."

■ *Process comments* (Yalom, 1985). The interaction in larger systems allows the worker to reflect on interpersonal processes. Such reflections are powerful interventions with all members of the interpersonal process. Process comments increase the awareness of the interpersonal processes creating changes in the interaction. For example, in a team meeting, a supervisor complained about chronic difficulties staffing the food bank and staff members having to cover shifts for volunteers. In response to this common theme, the director sometimes committed resources to hire temporary staff to relieve the pressure. Consequently, a worker suggested bringing in the director. The team leader resisted, so the worker used the following process comment, "Every year we have these meetings because people get stressed, and every year nothing changes until Robert attends the meeting and offers to hire people to relieve the stress. It makes sense to involve him now because nothing happens without his resources."

■ *Normalizing observations.* Sometimes a worker wants to reflect both on what the client is stating and on normal reactions to similar situations. This is important when workers want to reassure clients they are having normal and natural responses to their situations. This type of reflection promotes client reflection on their own behaviors, as well as a comparison of the reaction to an external standard. With reflecting on a discrepancy, a worker might say, "You know Tom, you glanced down and your face tightened when you told me you did not care. Often people tighten up and look down like that when they do care." With feeling themes, a worker might use a reflection such as, "When you talked about having to go into the nursing home, you sounded sad. I guess there is not much else to feel when dealing with such a difficult move."

Reflective Challenges. In a reflective challenge, the worker contrasts the client response to a normal reaction to the situation. Typically, the worker follows the reflections with a question or probe. Through the challenge, clients reflect on their situations and assess aspects or alternative interpretations. For example, "Wow, you are probably the only person I have talked to that didn't care when his girlfriend broke up with him. Most people are flooded with different feelings. How is it that you don't care?" Be careful using this type of observation, because it can seem argumentative. Such reflection requires a solid helping relationship providing a context and history of support.

For example, a family service worker was working with a mother to find other ways of expressing anger. When the mother came in for her appointment, the worker asked, "How was your week?" The woman looked down and spoke in flat affect when she stated, "Oh . . . it was all right." The worker reflected, "From the look on your face and the tone in your voice, I think there is more to the story than you are telling me. What happened last week?" This reflective challenge led to the woman to disclose that she had lost her temper and slapped her children in the past week.

Metaphoric Reflection. Sometimes metaphors or analogies can be used to reflect the feelings or meaning of the client through an image (Kopp, 1995). This allows the client to experience the reflective communication in a different way. The reflection often is processed through different brain mechanisms, yielding a different effect than a more logical or verbal approach to reflection. For example, when a client says she is are overwhelmed, the worker might try the following response. "When you talk about working all day and then doing the housework, I picture you with a heavy backpack full of everyone else's belongings that they don't want to carry for themselves."

Nonverbal Reflection. Nonverbal support and reflection of affective meaning is achieved through the following nonverbal methods. Many positive client responses are related to the nonverbal expressions by the worker (Wiseman & Rice, 1989).

- *Touch* can convey support, caring, playfulness, and many other messages (Durana, 1998). However, a worker must be careful when using touch in the helping relationship. Many clients have had difficult experiences with unwanted touch and may not be able to discuss their discomfort with their workers (Durana, 1998; Horton, 1997). Before touching a client, use the following precautions.
  - Make sure the client is not touch defensive and does not have a history of victimization by authority figures.

- Make sure the touch cannot be interpreted as aggression or sexual advances.
- Move from the distal areas of the body (e.g., hands) to the proximal areas closer to the torso.
- When touching the torso, touch the back rather than the frontal areas.
- Make sure the client is always in control of the touching (Horton, 1997).
- *Body position*, posture, and movement can reflect an understanding of the emotional state of a client. For example, moving forward or leaning toward the client can convey that the worker understands how important the disclosure is to the client.
- *Gesturing* can convey both support and understanding. Use of hand gestures, facial gestures (e.g., wincing), and body gestures (e.g., shrugging) are easy methods of conveying support and meaning without stopping the client's disclosure.
- *Moaning*, *groaning*, or an exclamatory word in response to a client's disclosure can convey an understanding of the emotional impact of the disclosure. Like the other nonverbal methods, this does little to disrupt the disclosure of the client.

The types of reflection are often used for setting up questions or probes. The worker also finds that the different types of reflection are used in rapid succession. The following example illustrates different reflective strategies interspersed during conversation.

■ *Case Example.*   A fourteen-year-old girl is in care because she and her mother frequently have physical fights. The mother was an alcoholic and the youth raised herself. The mother sobered up one year ago and decided to implement rules. The daughter resisted the rules, leading to ongoing power struggles in the home. After six months in care, the daughter is about to return home. As the worker informs her of the return, the following exchange occurs.

WORKER: So, you are going home soon, how does that feel?

YOUTH: Not bad.

WORKER: Not bad! *(restatement)*

YOUTH: Yeah . . . I don't care one way or the other.

WORKER: You know, I have worked with thousands of kids in care and you are the only one that has said that to me. *(reflective challenge)*

YOUTH: Well . . . I just don't know. For years things were okay, then she comes on like some tyrant with rules for this and that. She doesn't have a right to tell me what to do. Not after what I've been through.

WORKER: Sounds like things were rough for a while. *(reflection of meaning)*

YOUTH: Yeah . . . She would be passed out and I would have to do everything for myself. She wasn't the mother, I was. I took care of her. Now she stops drinking and thinks she can pick up as if nothing happened.

WORKER: After raising yourself and giving up on her it almost seems too-little-too-late. That would make any kid mad. *(reflection of feeling with normalizing observation)*

YOUTH: Well, it sure made me mad.

WORKER: (makes sneer face) Uh huh . . . *(nonverbal reflection of feeling)*

YOUTH: . . . and when she tries to lay down rules it all comes out..

WORKER: So things have been bottled up for so long that when she tries to open it up, it goes off on her. *(metaphoric reflection)*

YOUTH: Yeah.

WORKER: Have you talked to her about how you feel?

YOUTH: Yeah, whenever she pisses me off, I tell her.

WORKER: You only express your feelings when you are angry. *(paraphrasing)*

YOUTH: No. I can express myself other times, but it seems to come out that way.

WORKER: Would it help if I sat down with you and your mom before you went home to get some of this out on the table?

YOUTH: Maybe . . .

EXERCISE 10.1

Reflective Identification and Responding Exercise

You are a worker in a women's shelter. You are meeting with a young mother of a 5-year-old son and a 3-year-old daughter. The family came in due to severe violence. In the most recent violent incident, the son tried to protect his mother by getting into the middle of the fighting. He was knocked to the ground bruising his head and causing brief unconsciousness. Even after injuring the child, the husband continued hitting and yelling at the woman for making him hurt the son. The woman is talking with you and says, "I just couldn't believe it. It is bad enough he hits me all the time, but he didn't even stop when John got hurt. I kept trying to get to John hoping he would stop, but he kept hitting me and yelling that I was a bad mother. He feels it was my fault because I didn't mind him. That just doesn't seem right. I was trying to get to my son like a good mother. I can't put up with this crap anymore. I just gotta do something."

1. What are the critical content elements in the woman's statement for the action and interaction systems?

    a. Action:

    b. Interaction:

2. Write a response that reflects the action/interaction elements to the woman (*Hint*: Most workers start the statement with "Looks like . . . ," "Sounds like . . . ," "Seems like . . . ," "Feels like . . . ," depending on client processing).

3. What is the feeling conveyed in the woman's statement?

4. What in the statement helped you identify the feeling?

5. Write a reflective response capturing the feeling. (*Hint*: Many beginning workers start these statements with, "Based on *mention the elements* . . ." or "From your statements *mention the elements* . . ."

6. What is the meaning (belief systems) conveyed in this story? What aspects of the story lead you to this meaning?

7. Write a reflective response indicating that you understand the meaning of what this woman has said.

8. What do you see as the strengths of this woman?

9. Write a reflective comment you could make to help this woman see these strengths.

Soliciting Feedback on the Worker Understanding

After the reflection, it is important that the worker gains some indication that the reflection is accurate (Broome, 1991; Omer, 1997). Consequently, after reflecting back to the client, the worker needs to be highly attentive to make sure the understanding or expression is consistent with the client's experience. This uses observational skills to detect looks and other indications of affirmation. If the client appears puzzled, the worker needs to question whether or not the reflection fits the client's experience. This allows the client to correct the worker's misunderstandings of the situation.

EXERCISE 10.2

Reflecting Responding Exercise

You are working in a vocational program for people with developmental disabilities. Your client is a young woman with Down's syndrome. This woman is 19 years old and operates at a moderate to mild level of disability. You have been working with her to increase her assertive social skills in preparation for a work placement. She has been unassertive in many social situations and the team wants her to increase her skills. She is talking to you about her boyfriend. This is the first you have heard about her boyfriend, and you want to understand the nature of her relationship, but you know she will stop talking if you ask too many questions. Consequently, you need to be reflective to encourage her talking. She begins the conversation by saying, "I have a boyfriend named Tom. He goes to my school with me. He is not in my classroom. He goes down the hall where the big machines are (machine shop). He doesn't come by my class much because he doesn't like people seeing us together. I think we might be getting married after school ends. I like him a lot and we go to his car and kiss during our lunch hour (she giggles and looks down and says softly): I like him, that is important. (She then adds quickly), He is almost 20 you know, I am getting to be pretty grown up. Mom doesn't know that, but I am."

First, consider that you want to get her to expand her story by reflecting action themes.

1. What are the critical elements (what sections of the client statement) you would use in reflecting back the action themes?

2. Write down exactly what you would say to reflect back the content to this client.

3. What would you say (e.g., what questions would you ask) to the client to prompt her to give you feedback about the action theme you reflected?

4. Identify how you would promote client goals with this reflection (and the ensuing discussion).

Second, consider you want to get her to expand on her affect through reflecting her feelings.

5. What are the critical elements you would use in reflecting her feelings?

6. Write down exactly what you would say to reflect back the feelings to this client.

7. What would you say to the client to prompt her to give you feedback on the feelings you reflected?

8. Identify how you would promote client goals with this reflection (and the ensuing discussion).

Third, consider you want to get her to explore what this relationship means to her.

9. What are the critical elements you would use in reflecting the meaning in her statement?

10. Write down exactly what you would say to reflect back the meaning to this client.

11. What would you say to her to prompt her to give you feedback about the accuracy of the meaning?

12. Identify how you would promote client goals with this reflection (and the ensuing discussion).

Fourth, consider you want to use this opportunity to highlight her strengths.

13. Identify indications of her strengths you would use to reflect her strengths.

14. Write exactly what you would say to reflect back the strengths to the client.

15. What would you say to prompt feedback and integration of the strengths?

16. Identify how you would promote client goals with this reflection (and the ensuing discussion).

Fifth, consider that you want to highlight discrepancies in the client statement.

17. What elements of the client statement would you select to reflect discrepancies?

18. Write exactly what you would say to reflect the discrepancies to the client.

19. What would you say in follow-up to promote feedback and discussion?

20. How would you use this reflection and the ensuing discussion in your goals with this client?

Critical Chapter Themes

1. Reflective responding involves communicating important aspects of the client's disclosure back to the client. This skill is instrumental in deepening the relationship, promoting insight, assuring an accurate understanding, and continuing the exploration.
2. In the reflective response, the worker (1) identifies the critical component in the client disclosure, (2) communicates the critical component back to the client, and (3) monitors feedback about the accuracy of the reflection.

3. In identifying critical components, workers monitor response systems (action, interaction, belief, and affective) to select the themes that appear to be most important given the client's disclosure and service goals.
4. There are several methods of communicating the critical components back to the client. These include verbal (paraphrasing, sharing observations, etc.) and nonverbal (touch, sounds) reflections.
5. Receiving feedback on the reflection is important to assure that the worker is aligned with the client.

RECOMMENDED READINGS

Bozarth, J. D. (1997). Empathy from the framework of client-centered theory and the Rogerian hypothesis. In A. C. Bohart & L. S. Greenberg (Eds.), *Empathy reconsidered: New directions in psychotherapy* (pp. 81–102). Washington DC: American Psychological Association.

Broome, B. J. (1991). Building shared meaning: Implications of a relational approach to empathy for teaching intercultural communication. *Communication Education, 40,* 235–249.

Chang, P. (1994). Effects of interviewer questions and response type on compliance: An analogue study. *Journal of Counseling Psychology, 41,* 74–82.

Rober, P. (1999). The therapist's inner conversation in family therapy practice: Some ideas about the self of the therapist, therapeutic impasse, and the process of reflection. *Family Process, 38,* 209–228.

Uhlemann, M. R., Lee, D. Y., & Martin, J. (1994). Client cognitive responses as a function of quality of counselor verbal responses. *Journal of Counseling & Development, 73,* 198–203.

Transitional
Responding to Deepen
the Exploration

The probing, prompting, questioning, and reflecting skills explored in previous chapters all explore the client situation. In the exploration, there is a back-and-forth exchange between the client and the worker in which the worker first focuses the meeting and then begins the exchange of information with the client. The worker responds to each client disclosure in a way to further the exploration.

This back-and-forth exchange is often awkward for workers. Some awkwardness emerges when a worker asks a series of questions and eventually finds he or she does not know what to ask next. Inexperienced workers then disengage and go into their own thinking to determine what to do. This can be problematic, as it may take the worker further away from the client, rather than help to explore the situation through the client's experience.

For example, the worker may *think* that something is occurring and begin asking questions related to some thought, rather than to what the client is saying. Such questions take the client by surprise, because they are connected to the worker's thoughts rather than the client's statement. At best, interaction becomes stilted, creating discomfort for both client and worker.

▪ *Case Example.*　　A client, meeting with her child protection worker says, "I feel so overwhelmed by all the pressure in my family. I am carrying the load for everyone and nobody seems to even care. I don't think I can take it anymore." The worker assumes that the husband was probably not helping out with family tasks and asks, "What is your husband doing to help out?" The client responds that he is helping out all he can but is working overtime. The worker does not know where to go because the question in her mind has been answered. Therefore, she shifts the focus asking, "How are the kids doing in school?" The client answers, completing the shift to the children. Throughout the session, this shifting of focus is frequent. Eventually the mother arrives at a discussion of her sick mother moving into the home and discloses how this is creating stress for her.

In this example, the worker initially disengaged from the client by asking about the husband instead of linking the question to what the client had placed on the table. Given that the question was linked to the worker's thoughts, there was no direction to move after the client indicated her hypothesis was wrong. The worker consequently changed the subject to the children. Much later, the pressures experienced by the client resurfaced as an issue. Workers need skills in responding to what is put on the table. In the response, the worker needs to continue exploring important client themes while concurrently shifting the discussion to explore worker hypotheses.

These challenges and the need to develop an exploratory direction underscore the importance of combining active listening with purposeful responding. Such skill allows the worker to transition from one client disclosure to the next with clear engagement and direction. Transitional responding can deepen the exploration while still attending to goals and preventing awkward disengagement. This chapter introduces this skill of transitional responding first through a formula and then through identified linkages to client response systems.

THE MECHANICS
OF TRANSITIONAL RESPONDING

When exploring client situations, strategies for ordering and linking the exchange between worker and client are needed to keep the flow of interaction smooth. Transitional responses solicit information that is based on the package of information most recently placed on the table by the client. The metaphor of dealing with what is placed on the table is used to describe the transitional process as a user-friendly picture capturing the spirit of the transitional response.

In the preceding example, the client had put a package of information on the table. The client outlined themes of action (she is working hard to take care of family needs), interaction (others are not helping), thinking (others don't care) and affect (she is overwhelmed and can't take it). A first transitional response would pick up on one of these themes to begin exploring the situation. For example, "It sounds like you are near the end of your rope. Whose load seems to put the most pressure on you?" This response allows the client to continue with her feelings and begin to move deeper into the situation. When the next package is put on the table, the worker asks another question that considers the client's new statement and the direction of exploration. This might progress something like:

> **CLIENT:**   I feel so overwhelmed by all the pressure in my family. I feel like I am carrying the load for everyone and nobody seems to care. I just don't think I can take it anymore.
>
> **WORKER:**   It sounds like you are near the end of your rope. Whose load seems to put the most pressure on you?
>
> **CLIENT:**   All of them . . . I work, I cook, I clean up, and nobody lifts a finger to help me.
>
> **WORKER:**   If someone would lift a finger, who would you want it to be?
>
> **CLIENT:**   John, my husband . . . but he can't. He goes off to work and with the overtime he can't help with the kids because I have already put them to bed when he gets home. That leaves it all to me, and with my mother living with us there is so much to do.
>
> **WORKER:**   Your mother sounds like a new addition. When did she move in?
>
> **CLIENT:**   She just had surgery and moved in with us to recuperate.

WORKER: Are you providing all of her care as well?

CLIENT: Yes. She does not have good insurance and I have to do it all. I don't mean to complain but it is just so much work.

In this example, the worker linked each response to the package placed on the table by the client. In the responses, the worker takes what is on the table and then uses reflection, questioning, or probing to encourage further exploration. This is a two-part response with the worker first validating what is on the table and then using exploratory skills to move the discussion to a deeper level. This is where the tuning in and thinking skills shape the work.

Moving toward Deeper Exploration with Clients

The focused movement toward depth in exploring client situations is very important. Anyone can listen to shallow descriptions of a problem situation. Many friends, bartenders, and hairdressers operate at this level of problem exploration. Professionals must achieve deeper levels of exploration, helping the client move from the description of the problem to an exploration of the action and processing themes within the situation. Such exploration tends to follow the pattern in which exploration at one level leads to a deeper level. Figure 11.1 shows how transitional responding can take both worker and client deeper into the client's understandings of the situation.

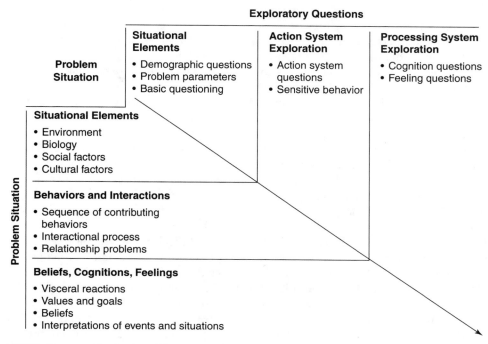

FIGURE 11.1 Exploring Client Situations

In Figure 11.1, the issues are listed down the left side of the diagram. This list illustrates the elements that may be in the problem situation. They begin with situational elements and extend to interpretations or feelings that may contribute to the problem. Across the top of the diagram, the types of questions explored in this chapter are listed. The large arrow sloping down depicts the path of transitional exploration. Transitional responses bring the exploration to the deepest possible levels one step at a time. In considering these aspects of the situation, the worker can see how the transitional depth can inform the assessment model outlined in Chapter 3.

The Transitional Process

In client–worker interaction, transitional responses move the content of the interaction step-by-step to the next level. This occurs in a way that does not cut off client concerns, but rather helps the client expand on his or her concerns while still answering the questions in the mind of the worker. The skill in using transitional responses is in the linkages to the response systems. Remember in the previous chapters, all elements of the response systems are contained in the verbal communications (action, interaction, thinking, and feeling). In transitional responding, the worker picks up one of these elements from the table and deepens the exploration in that area of client responding.

In using transitional questions, the worker identifies and forms questions based on the response systems through a four-step process.

1. The worker listens to the client expression identifying the critical action and processing themes (doing, saying, thinking, or feeling) in the package of information placed on the table by the client.
2. Based on perceived importance of the different themes, the worker selects one aspect of the package on the table to explore deeper.
3. Based on the client disclosure, knowledge, and goals, the worker identifies a direction for deeper exploration.
4. The worker links a response (question, reflection, probe, or prompt) to the themes on the table that can take the exploration deeper.

Basically, effective workers link each of their verbal responses (question, reflection, probe, or prompt) to one of the response system themes whenever responding to the client communication. To help understand how this four-step process works in practice, techniques for linking to each response system are explored in this section.

Through reading how linkages occur with each response system and examining the examples, readers can understand how workers track and link the transitional responses. In reading and practicing this skill, readers may find it difficult at first. This is because few people listen as actively as this skill requires. Over time, this skill becomes second nature as readers develop their personal style. To enhance this adaptation, practice monitoring themes when listening to a conversation. Initially, just identify the themes in what people say. The faster one becomes at identification, the smoother the skill becomes. After developing identification skills, explore questions, probes, reflections, or prompts for each response system. Anyone can do this while listening to conversations. Identifying responses requires one to be able to link one's responses to the different response systems. The following sections highlight methods for linking the responses to client response systems.

Linking to Action Themes.   When the action content of the client disclosure provides the best possible movement, the worker asks a question or responds to elaborate the action aspects of the client story. This most often occurs when the worker does not understand some aspect of the client's life that might be important in providing service. For example, if a client discloses something seemingly important about the past, the worker will pick an action theme from the table to take the exploration to the next level. Through a series of small exploratory questions, probes, or reflections about the content, the worker can move the exploration to the client's history.

■ ***Case Example.***   The following example is of an exchange between a child protection/prevention worker and a mother. In the first statement, there are strong feeling themes (anger), interaction themes (she wouldn't do anything), and action themes (wanting to shake her). There is also an inherent thinking theme associated with the mother's interpretation of the daughter's refusal to do what she is told. The worker selected the action theme for follow-up and exploration. If you think about possible questions for the other themes, you can identify how they would take the discussion in a different direction. The worker selected the action theme because she wanted to reinforce the mother's restraint.

> **CLIENT:**   I got so mad at her last week . . . she wouldn't do anything she was told. I just wanted to shake her.
>
> **WORKER:**   (first wanting to affirm her display of strength) I am glad you were able to keep your cool. From the emotion I hear in your voice, that must have been hard at times. How did you keep your control? *(action theme question)*
>
> **CLIENT:**   Well you know, she just blew me off . . . no matter what I said to her, she just would not respond. I felt myself getting tense and told myself to take a walk.
>
> **WORKER:**   How long did you have to walk to cool down the anger? *(continue with action theme)*
>
> **CLIENT:**   About five minutes, I went and wandered through the garden.
>
> **WORKER:**   Five minutes . . . that is shorter than many of your arguments. You not only kept your cool, you also trimmed time. When you calmed down what did you do? *(continue with action theme)*
>
> **CLIENT:**   Well, I went in the house, turned off the TV and sat down with her and said we have to work this thing out. I remembered about what we said about consequences and told her if she didn't do her part, I was going to take the power cord out of the TV for the rest of the day.
>
> **WORKER:**   Did that work? *(continue with action theme)*
>
> **CLIENT:**   Definitely.

Linking to Interaction Themes.   In some communication, there is an unmistakable inference about relationship and interaction. Similar to the action themes, the interaction themes describe a story line; however, there is a relationship context because there are at least two people involved in the story. If the relationship context appears more important than the action sequences, workers will begin linking the questions to the interactive and relational themes.

■ *Case Example.*   This example involves a worker from a battered woman's shelter and a woman. The woman is angry about her partner's abusiveness and discloses information about past relationships that the worker feels might be important. Again, there are other themes that could be pursued. There is a strong action theme ("I am going to stop taking this"), a strong feeling theme ("I'm fed up with being abused"), a strong thinking theme ("Others believe I will keep putting up with this"), and the interaction theme ("Others have abused me too"). This worker selected the interaction theme rather than the other themes.

> CLIENT: I have had enough of this abuse. All my life I put up with people dumping on me and if anyone thinks I am going to keep putting up with this crap, they have another thing coming.
>
> WORKER: (Begins to wonder if the client has a history of victimization that might need to be overcome.) So your husband is not the first one to treat you this way? *(interaction theme)*
>
> CLIENT: No, almost everyone in my life has dumped on me.
>
> WORKER: (Wants to move gently and explore supports as well so strengths can be maintained concurrent with exploring potential problem areas.) You say almost everyone . . . was there someone in your life you felt was supportive to you? *(stays with interaction)*
>
> CLIENT: Yes. I had an aunt I used to go to.
>
> WORKER: What kinds of things would you go to her for? *(stays with interaction)*
>
> CLIENT: Oh . . . when things were not good at home she would always be there for me.
>
> WORKER: It sounds like she was an important refuge for you. What kinds of things would happen at home to make you want to see your aunt? *(switch to action)*
>
> CLIENT: We used to fight a lot.

Linking to Affective Themes.   There are times when the worker hears or observes powerful emotion in the client disclosure. As the worker tunes into this level of feeling, he or she often decides to elaborate on the feeling to promote deeper understanding. The worker consequently links his or her response to the feeling themes on the table. When working with feelings, it is important to maintain the purpose of the client service to avoid distracting from client work.

■ *Case Example.*   A woman approaches a worker in a homeless prevention program and hesitates to make a request. There are strong action themes in her statement (can't afford to pay utilities), a strong interaction theme (getting evicted), and a strong feeling theme (hesitant to ask for help). The thinking theme is subtle with the woman seeming to believe she doesn't have a right to ask. The worker elects to follow up on the hesitation (the feeling component). Once again, note how following up on any of the other themes would take the conversation in a totally different direction. Notice in this example how the worker switches back and forth between the different elements as the discussion continues.

CLIENT: I don't know if I can even ask for money from you, but we cannot pay for our heat and are probably going to get evicted.

WORKER: (puzzled) Our service is available for all people. What makes you worry about asking for our help? *(feeling theme)*

CLIENT: Well, I don't know if we really need it, my husband might not like it.

WORKER: It sounds like your husband might have strong opinions about your situation. Are his opinions the same as yours? *(move to interaction)*

CLIENT: No. He doesn't want to ask anyone for help. He thinks we should be able to make it on our own, but I don't see how we can make it without some sort of help.

WORKER: I get the sense the two of you have talked about this before and your differences are still in the way. Tell me what is important to your husband and what is important to you about making things work out. *(move to thinking)*

CLIENT: My husband wants to be successful and sees it as his job to keep a roof over our heads. I think he feels like he is failing. I just want to stay in our apartment.

WORKER: Is it receiving handouts that creates the disagreement between you and your husband? *(back to interaction)*

CLIENT: Yes.

WORKER: You know there are some programs that can help without making you take handouts. Some programs are work related and some are like loans. Would you like me to give you some information on these programs? *(move to action)*

CLIENT: Yes, please.

WORKER: When you take these home, will your husband feel you are going behind his back? *(back to interaction)*

CLIENT: No. If I came home with money from you he would feel that way, but I told him I was coming here anyway. He might feel relieved I didn't come home with money.

WORKER: Here is my card and the material on the programs. If he seems interested, I recommend the two of you come in so I can explain the programs and what would be expected. That way, both of you will be able to hear about them, and I can help you two make a decision that will work for both of you.

Linking to Thinking Themes.   Just like finding emotional investment in the client statement, workers often find there is implied meaning in an exchange or situation. When there is power or emotional investment concurrent with the situation, one often finds an associated meaning. As such, this meaning underlies the emotional investment. Upon finding a convergence of situation/emotionality/meaning, effective workers often move through the exploration of feelings and continue exploring the meaning systems that fuel the emotional investment.

■ *Case Example.*   A child protection worker is talking with a mother. In this meeting, the mother is struggling with her feelings. In her statement there are strong themes associated with each of the response systems. There is a strong action theme ("I lose control of my feelings"), and interaction theme ("She takes control"), and emotion theme ("I am powerless"), and a thinking theme ("Others are controlling me"). Because the themes seem to thread together around a thinking distortion, the worker decides to pursue the thinking theme.

CLIENT: I don't know how she gets control of my feelings. I don't know what to do.

WORKER: Do you think she takes control or do you think that somehow through feeling ignored, you let the control slip through your fingers? *(thinking question)*

CLIENT: I don't know . . . (a few seconds of silence). How would it slip through my fingers?

WORKER: Earlier you said something about . . . if you don't matter to your children what good are you? *(switch to feeling)*

CLIENT: Yes . . . (again some silence) well what good are you as a mother if your kids don't care about you?

WORKER: This sounds like a tough rule to live by. Tell me, in your experience, is this rule kind of like "one must matter to their kids in order to be a good parent"? *(back to thinking)*

CLIENT: Yes.

WORKER: In this rule, who has the power? *(switch to action)*

CLIENT: Parents have the power because they are parents.

WORKER: But in this rule, who has the power to say the parents are any good? *(back to thinking)*

CLIENT: . . . well . . . I guess it is the child.

WORKER: I agree with both of the things you have said lately. I agree that the parents should have the power because they are parents. I also agree that in this rule, the power is given to the child. Do you think this rule causes you to give your power away? *(continue with thinking)*

Using the Transitional Responses.

Throughout the preceding discussion and examples, it is clear that the transitional responses can be any type of question, reflection, probe, or prompt and can focus on the past, present, or future. Also the flow of the conversation moves from response system to response system as the worker explores the situation. This is because one response system often seems more important given the package on the table and goals of intervention.

Worker thinking skills are critical in selecting the transitional component to pursue. The preceding examples show how selecting one component takes the discussion in a particular area. It is the worker's thinking and tuning in skills that help select the area. Workers who are not thinking about client goals or who are unaware of themselves will often select directions that are not fruitful. The worker must actively think and listen throughout the entire exploratory process.

■ ***Case Examples.*** To illustrate the interplay between the different types of responses, the following example of transitional reflection and questioning is taken from a session with a woman upset that at his daughter's Christmas concert, her partner threatened to leave her. The woman had been coming to meetings with the social worker for about three months while living with her abusive partner. The woman had one son and her partner had two daughters all residing in the home. There was often friction between the woman and the youngest daughter leading to fights about parenting standards. During times of tension, the man would threaten to leave and would often become violent. The woman came into this meeting after attending the Christmas concert.

CLIENT: I was so angry, he has always treated me bad, but to tell me he was leaving at his daughter's Christmas concert was the worst thing he could do.

WORKER: *(suspecting there was some additional meaning)* You told me about many of the things he has done. This must have been horrible to be considered the worst. *(setting up the question)* What was it about telling you at the concert that made this worse than all of the other abuses you have suffered?

CLIENT: It was just so humiliating.

WORKER: *(again reflecting the meaning)* Humiliating often means someone feels vulnerable and on display. *(setting up the next question)* Was there someone watching?

CLIENT: Yeah, Colleen's (the daughter's) teacher. She is always taking Colleen's side against me. Tom talks to her about Colleen's needs and the two of them are forever ganging up on me.

WORKER: *(worker thinks she feels put down so pursues the meaning by reflecting the content to set up a probe about personalized meaning)* So it often feels as though they are against you. When this happens, what does this say about you as a mother?

CLIENT: It says I am no f_ _ _ing good, that is what it says . . . but they just don't know what it is like. They always take her side.

WORKER: *(suspects there is more to it so reflects the content and changes direction)* You said they think you are not a good mother, but somehow there seems to be more to it . . . something to do with Colleen. How does she seem to benefit when they make these kinds of judgments about you?

CLIENT: She wins. She always wins by making me look bad. No matter how much I try to get her to tow the line, she connives and gets her dad on her side and then I lose every time.

WORKER: *(still unsure of where the personalized meaning might be, chooses a general reflection of meaning)* So it sounds like you are always the one who loses. *(suspecting there is a history to the theme, the probe is also general)* Can you think of a time in your life when you felt like you were the winner?

CLIENT: Never, first it was my sister setting me up and now it's Colleen.

WORKER: *(wants to underscore the parallel so reflects content)* Someone has always beaten you out, first your sister and now Colleen. *(still wants to get at the personalized meaning)* When they beat you out and you lose, what do they win?

CLIENT: Love, respect . . . nobody ever treats me right. They always set me up so I don't get the love.

WORKER: *(reflecting the meaning)* So when you get set up by your sister or Colleen, it robs you of the love and respect you feel you deserve. *(providing a probe to tie in the current situation)* How were you robbed today at the concert?

CLIENT: He told Colleen before the concert, and I know they told the teacher. Now I can't even get her respect. No matter what I do, I just can't seem to win.

WORKER: *(reflecting the feeling to begin transitioning into an exploration of the ongoing patterns)* It seems that all your life you have wanted love and respect but have felt powerless. It seems that somehow people are robbing you of your power over yourself and your feelings. Are you willing to explore how people rob your power so we can help you keep control?

In the example, the reflection validates one aspect of the package while setting up a question to further the exploration. In reading the comments accompanying the example, one can identify the thinking and exploratory direction of the worker. One can also see how the two elements of responding (reflection and question) can be used differentially to change direction in the exploration.

EXERCISE 11.1

Transitional Responding Exercise

1. You are meeting with a child as part of your placement at child protective services. You know there has been parental violence that has produced high levels of anxiety in the child. The child has been seeing you for a couple of months, and you know each other quite well. She comes in for a meeting today and you notice she is not making eye contact and seems down. You open the meeting by asking her, "How was your week?" She responds, "I don't really know how the week has been. There have been good days and bad days and . . . it has just been one of those weeks. I do all I can to get through and not rock the boat. I don't know if I want to talk about it."

   a. What is the action theme?

b. Write a transitional question based on this theme.

c. What is the interaction theme?

d. Write a transitional question based on this theme.

e. What is the thinking theme?

f. Write a transitional response based on this theme.

g. What is the feeling theme?

h. Write a transitional response based on this theme.

i. Which of the response systems would you select to explore?

j. What is your reason for selecting this system?

2. You are working in a battered women's shelter. You are meeting with a woman who has just come into the shelter with her three children. She is visibly upset and has been badly beaten. One of her eyes is swollen shut, and there are numerous welts and bruises on her face. You ask her, "What happened?" She responds, "I should know better than to confront him when he has been drinking, but he drinks so often nowadays I can't help it. He blew his entire paycheck at the track and now we have no money to eat with. I just couldn't help it. I know he is sorry now that he is sober, but I just hate it when he is so damn irresponsible and I have to tell him. Then all hell breaks loose."

a. What is the action theme?

b. Write a transitional response based on this theme.

c. What is the interaction theme?

d. Write a transitional response based on this theme.

e. What is the thinking theme?

f. Write a transitional response based on this theme.

g. What is the feeling theme?

h. Write a transitional response based on this theme.

i. Which response system would you select to explore in this situation?

j. What is your reason for selecting this system?

3. You are working in a transitional program for people who have a developmental disability. Your job is to work with clients ready to go into competitive work assignments. You are meeting with a woman about to go into a factory work placement. She has been in a sheltered workshop for several years, and this is her first venture into a more competitive environment. She asks, "What am I supposed to

do when I get there? People tell me it is really scary and hard to do things right. I want the money but I don't know what to do when I get there."

a. What is the action theme?

b. Write a transitional response based on this theme.

c. What is the interaction theme?

d. Write a transitional response based on this theme.

e. What is the thinking theme?

f. Write a transitional response based on this theme.

g. What is the feeling theme?

h. Write a transitional response based on this theme.

i. Which response system would you select to explore?

j. What is your rationale for selecting this system?

Critical Chapter Themes

1. In conducting an exploration of the client situation, there is a risk that workers will either run out of things to explore or disengage when one line of exploration seems to end. This is disruptive and often takes the exploration off track.
2. Workers must be able to respond to client disclosures in a way that both validates the disclosure and helps move exploration to increased depth.
3. Transitional responding links worker responses to the package that the client has placed on the table. Workers link their responses to the action, interaction, thinking, or affective themes in the client's last statement.
4. In moving toward increased depth, workers build on one of the response system themes in asking their next question or making their next response.
5. Questions, reflections, probes, and prompts can all be used as transitional responses in moving the discussion in a direction without disengagement.

RECOMMENDED READINGS

Chang, P. (1994). Effects of interviewer questions and response type on compliance: An analogue study. *Journal of Counseling Psychology, 41*, 74–82.

Palazzoli-Selvini, M., Boscolo, L., Cecchin, G., & Prata, G. (1980). Hypothesizing-circularity-neutrality: Three guidelines for the conductor of the session. *Family Process, 19*, 3–12.

Patton, M. Q. (1980). *Qualitative evaluation methods.* Beverly Hills, CA: Sage.

Uhlemann, M. R., Lee, D. Y., & Martin, J. (1994). Client cognitive responses as a function of quality of counselor verbal responses. *Journal of Counseling & Development, 73*, 198–203.

Wubbolding, R. E. (1997). Professional issues: The use of questions in reality therapy. *Journal of Reality Therapy, 16*, 122–127.

PART FOUR

Toward Focused and Helpful Responding

The previous parts helped the reader develop skills in using themselves, forming the relationship, and exploring the client situation. At this point in the book, most readers will have proficiency in knowing what clients need to resolve their situations. This part focuses on the last core skill, helping the client to focus and work toward his or her goals. This skill builds on all of the previous parts. The worker consciously uses him- or herself to motivate and focus the relationship. The motivation draws heavily on the conscious use of the self and the relationship that is formed with the client. The focus evolves from the purpose and direction associated with the worker's thinking.

In this part, readers will learn how to identify and use client's motivating feelings. Readers will further learn how to confront challenges and renegotiate the working alliance in response to the inevitable problems in the helping relationship. Client, worker, and relationship problems that might interfere with the working relationship are explored along with strategies for re-orienting the relationship toward client goals. Finally, readers will explore how to end the helping relationship so client gains can be continued into the future.

CHAPTER

12

Change Facilitating and Interventive Questions

The previous set of chapters discussed how to explore the client situation so an understanding and assessment could be developed. After the assessment, workers must alter their responses from exploration to establishing a direction of service. Focus and direction lay the foundation for change-focused intervention strategies that will be covered in future courses. This chapter explores the adaptations to questioning skills important in setting a focus for change.

The questioning skills and techniques of Chapter 9 focused on exploring the client situation. In Chapter 11 readers learned how to use the questions as part of transitional responding. In this chapter, these skills will be used in conjunction with change-focused questions for moving client systems toward goal achievement. Change-focused questions put specific material on the table so that the exploration can help set the stage for change. In the exploration that results from such questions, the groundwork for change tends to evolve from the client answers (Freedman & Combs, 1993; Tomm, 1987).

Change-focused questions are often referred to as reflexive because they cause members of the client system to reflect differently on the situation (Greene et al., 1998; Tomm, 1988). Change-focused questions come from the family intervention and solution-focused literature. These two groups of professionals have become very influential in recent years. In later courses, you will be exposed to intervention models like narrative, solution-focused, and constructivist. The skills in this chapter come from these three schools of thought.

The change-focused questions have been used with great excitement in the helping professions with many adaptations and variations on questioning strategies. This type of question tends to build strong working alliances while quickly focusing the change effort (Adams, 1997; Dozier et al., 1998). The assumption of change-focused questions is that the clients tend to define the problem situation in terms that are too narrow or too broad (Brown, 1997b). The questions shift client understandings, resulting in insight, new meanings, and focus for change (Tomm, 1987).

USING CHANGE-FOCUSED QUESTIONING

The basic premise of change-focused question formats is that the introduction of information into the client system will cause people to consider a situation from different perspectives. The change in perspectives can then be used to promote change. Some questions focus on introducing information that might produce changes in the action system; others focus primarily on the processing systems.

It can be argued that questions in previous chapters can introduce information and promote systemic change through the creation of insight. Insight in turn can create change. However, the general goals of the earlier question strategies were to explore the client situation. Such questions are well suited to gleaning an understanding for assessment purposes. The questions in this chapter are different in that their sole purpose is to set the stage for change.

Formatting and Focusing the Question

In using questions to set up change with client systems one needs to formulate the question so the system is positioned to respond (Brown, 1997b). There are five critical areas to consider in formulating the question: targeting, focusing, setting up the question (making a statement that leads into the question), delivering the question, and following up the question with exploration.

Targeting the Question.   Like larger system questions, the change-focus questions target one of the response systems central to the problem. In larger client systems, the targeting also includes specific individuals or constituencies. The goal of the question is to promote a readiness for response change by the person or constituency targeted for change. For example, when working with a neglectful father, the worker would target his behavior for change.

Focusing the Question.   The change-focused question typically is asked of one member or subsystem of the client system even though the person may not be the target of change. This person is selected to answer the initial question based on the assumption that the person provides the best prognosis for mobilizing change. It is assumed that the responses from the person (people) can be best used to promote change with others in the client system. For example, a worker might select a child to comment on a situation with the intention that the child's answer may cause a parent to reconsider his or her actions.

Question Setup.   The worker makes a statement or shares some observation that prepares the client to hear and respond to the question. Some questions require the client to visualize situations, others simply want to direct the thinking of the client prior to delivering the question. For example, "I know that sometimes you get John to go to bed on time." The setup is critical to the success of change-focused questions. If a worker does not set the stage for the question, it will not likely have the desired impact.

Question Delivery.   The worker asks the question; for example, "When John does go straight to bed without argument, what is different from the times when he fights with you?" In the delivery of the question, the worker seeks to get something very specific on the table for exploration. In this example, the worker is attempting to direct the exploration toward situations in which the problem does not occur.

Follow-Up and Exploration. It is never enough to just ask a question and then change the subject. With follow-up and exploration, the worker explores specifics and dynamics that strengthen the potential for change. All of the exploratory skills already discussed are used. Without the exploration and follow-up, the power of the change-focused question will diminish (Santa-Rita, 1998; Shilts & Godon, 1996). In the preceding example, the worker may start with, "Is there anything different about how you approach John?" Based on the response, the worker will begin a full exploration using transitional and exploratory responding. In focusing the response, the worker may want to use the response systems as a targeting system to ensure that all areas are covered.

The five elements of the change-focused question are used differentially in different types of questions. Some types of questions require careful thinking during the setup, whereas others may require negotiation. To understand the functioning of the change-focused question, the following sections explore the different change-focused questioning strategies for action and processing systems.

TYPES OF CHANGE-FOCUSED QUESTIONING STRATEGIES

Questions to Promote Change in Action Systems

To create the potential for change in the action system, questions must help people to clearly identify the changes they want to make. This strategy is inherent in many of the solution-focused questions that force members of the system to conceptualize the end product of change. Inherently, such questions help the client system clearly see the details of the necessary changes.

The initial question introduces global vision of change, and the exploration helps members of the system actively describe what they must do differently. These descriptions provide an image or blueprint of the desired changes in the action systems. In this way, system members begin to envision themselves without the problem. Based on this vision, members can begin to adjust their behaviors according to the image. Visualization strategies must include exploratory and transitional questions because the vision is crystallized through exploration. The following questioning strategies are common examples of helping clients visualize the change.

Exceptional Situation Questions. The exceptional situation question focuses on client strengths by assuming clients sometimes demonstrate mastery in the problem situation (DeJong & Berg, 1998; Hillyer, 1996). These questions attempt to explore the exceptions to the problem. Workers shift focus away from problem discussions by instructing their clients to reflect on times when they responded without a problem.

As the exceptional situation is explored, the worker helps the client assess the critical differences between times when the problem does and does not occur. After the exploration, the client is helped to draw solutions from their illustrated strengths and optimal functioning. For example, "Ms. Jones, there must be times you've asked John to do things and he is obedient. Can you describe exactly what you say during these times?"

Exceptional situation questions consist of the following five steps:

1. *Targeting.* The worker wants people to identify a time when the problem could have occurred but did not occur. This needs to be placed on the table for exploration.
2. *Focusing.* The question can be asked to anyone associated with the problem situation. With larger systems, the worker may want to ask the question to the whole group to maximize the potential to identify an exception. When focusing on the larger group, try to avoid arguments about whether or not something is an exception.
3. *Setup.* The worker helps the client identify the exceptional situation. By asking about times when the client had the same thoughts, feelings, or stresses but was able to respond without the problematic elements, the worker introduces hope for change. Concurrently, the worker introduces the notion that the client already controls the situation. For example, the worker might ask, "Ms. Jones, think about a time when you wanted John to go to bed and he went without argument."
4. *Delivery.* After the set-up statement, the worker asks or requests the client to describe the exception. With the setup used in step 3, the worker might say something like, "Tell me about one of those times." In making this request, the worker may need to probe and prompt the client into seeing that there have been positive outcomes. Once the client begins to identify times when the problem did not occur, the stage is set for exploratory questioning about the exceptional situation.
5. *Exploration of the exception.* Using the exploratory skills, the worker helps the client identify the contextual and response system factors that contribute to the exceptional situation. In this exploration, workers use transitional responding skills with a clear focus on the elements that might help contribute to client success in the situation. For example, "When he went straight to bed that night, what was different about the activities family members were doing?" Often this exploration first involves a contextual exploration (e.g., "Who was there?" "What were they doing?" "What was going to happen in the next while?" "What did John appear to want?"). The exploration will then shift focus to the action systems (e.g., "What exactly were you doing when you asked John?") and the processing systems (e.g., "When John got up, what did you think?").

After the exploration, the worker wants to get the client to think about how to apply what he or she already knows. This should involve reflective types of questioning (rather than telling the client) so the client can identify parallels between the problem and exceptional situations. Again, this uses the exploratory and transitional questions to explore how the current situation might allow the client to apply the same skills already demonstrated to ovecome the problem. For example, the worker might ask, "What in the times when things worked well might be tried in the current situation?" or "What have you learned about handling these problems?"

Miracle Questions.   The miracle question is similar to the exceptional situation question in that clients identify the details of a solution. The main difference in the miracle question is that the worker asks the client system to visualize the differences without using past experiences as a model (DeJong & Berg, 1998; Hillyer, 1996). Instead, the members of the client system are asked to conjure up mental images of what it might be like without the problem situation. This occurs through careful setup and delivery of the question. The miracle question consists of the following five steps:

1. *Targeting.* The worker seeks to have clients describe the details of how people would act, interact, think, and feel if the problem ceased to exist. Consequently, the worker is targeting a different way of perceiving the situation.

2. *Focusing.* Typically the worker will want to focus the question on someone who is invested in solving the problem but seemingly open to adopting a different position. The worker needs someone to assume leadership in beginning a more positive set of interactions.

3. *Setup.* First the worker describes a normal situation, such as sleeping or waking. By prompting the client to think about something he or she might frequently do, the stage is set for making the change believable.

For example, the worker might say, "I want you to imagine yourself going home tonight and having a very deep sleep." After setting a normal stage, the worker introduces the miracle. The miracle is typically done with little ceremony because it is not the miraculous event that is important, but rather the client's observation of how the changes might look. Consequently, the miracle is a simple statement of the problem being magically solved. For example, "Imagine for a minute you woke up tomorrow, and through some miracle . . . the problem was solved while you were sleeping, but of course, you would not immediately know the problem is gone. It would not be until you notice that things are different that you suspect the problem is solved."

4. *Delivery.* From the introduction of the miracle, the worker has clients begin to explore what they would need to notice to recognize the miracle had happened. This exploration focuses the observations on what would be different with whom. The worker has the member mentally observe others in the environment to describe the actions that would be different. At this point, the worker must be careful to prompt clients to move beyond statements of nonbehavior (e.g., we wouldn't be fighting) and help them describe the actual behaviors indicating the absence of the problem. This often uses a series of sensory and transitional questions to help the client develop the scene. For example, "I want you to imagine yourself waking up and leaving your room. What would you notice that would make you think that maybe the problem was no longer part of your family?"

5. *Explore differences at the client level.* In the exploration, workers use transitional questions and probes to glean what each member would be doing differently after the miracle. This allows each member to mentally observe him- or herself in interaction with the others. The worker helps the clients visualize exactly how they would be behaving differently. Exploratory techniques develop the fullest possible description of behavioral and processing changes that could solve the problem. The final task is to explore with system members how they might take some of the behavior into the current situation. Promoting discussion about what it would be like to have the change motivates them to take some changes back into the situation. For example, "Ms. Jones, what would you see your husband doing differently that would tell you the problem is no longer in your family? Mr. Jones what would you find yourself doing differently? What would you notice your wife doing differently?"

Using the miracle question is at times challenging for new workers because it is so easy to move back into problem exploration rather than exploring what the miracle would look like. Workers will need to use many prompts and probes to redirect clients into describing the positive observations rather than the old negative exchanges.

Embedded Suggestion Questions.   Sometimes workers want to introduce a suggestion to the family in a way that will not be filtered out or resisted. One way to accomplish such influence is to embed suggestions in a question (Tomm, 1987). As the family members hear the question, they prepare to answer by attending to the content of the question. Mentally, they are in a responsive mood, as compared to the potentially resistant mood that may accompany an open suggestion. Embedding allows the suggestion to remain somewhat hidden from the logical screening systems applied to suggestions. As such, family members are more likely to hear the suggestion.

For example, a worker might ask, "How does your mom stop herself from punishing you when you fight with each other, even though you both know you deserve to be punished?" This question asks the child to report on mother's methods of avoiding discipline. However, the question also acknowledges that the children need to be punished, but the mother takes no action. With this question, the mother, although not involved in the exchange, is targeted for change as the members agree she should discipline the children. Embedded suggestion questions employ the following five steps:

1. *Targeting.* The worker focuses on an action that needs to be promoted or challenged with one of the system members. Often a worker wants to promote a behavior to help decrease the problem or decrease a behavior that maintains the problem. In developing the focus, the worker selects the person whose behavior is the target of change as the subject of the question. In the previous example, it would be the mother.

2. *Focusing.* In larger systems, the worker selects a member involved in the problem who is not the target of change. By selecting someone involved in the problem pattern, the worker legitimizes the suggestion through association with an actor in the problem. Concurrently, by selecting someone other than the target of change, the target is allowed to remain a passive or indirect participant in the intervention. This is similar to eavesdropping when someone is talking about you, you can hear but not argue. With individuals, the worker asks the client to reflect on his or her own behavior.

3. *Setup.* The setup is fairly minimal with this type of question. The worker asks the member to reflect on the problem situation and introduces the suggestion.

4. *Delivery.* The question causes reflection about the situation but does not directly make the suggestion. In the example, the member was asked to comment on how the mother stopped herself from taking disciplinary action. The question focused on the restraining forces in the situation to promote increasing the suggested behavior (discipline). If working with just the mother, the worker might ask, "You know you need to shape the children's behavior, how is it that you talk yourself out of taking action?" Again, when the client answers the question, the suggestion is supported. In the preceding example, the worker focused the question on the member requiring punishment to legitimize the suggestion.

5. *Exploration.* After the client responds to the question, the worker uses transitional questions to help the client explore the situation and move closer to a decision to alter the behaviors. In the exploration, the worker will need to explore the processing systems to neutralize thoughts or feelings that might maintain the problem behaviors.

Opposite Focus Questions.   Opposite focus questions interfere with negative interaction patterns by disallowing one focus and stressing the opposite (Tomm, 1987). The worker shifts focus to the opposite of whatever is traditional for the client system. This type of questioning is useful when clients appear stuck in patterns of relating. By shifting focus to the opposite, the worker helps the client system develop new patterns of interaction or processing that can be used to overcome the problems.

For example, a family developed a habit of coming into sessions with a complaint about their daughter. Week after week, the family would come in and present a problem. The worker responded by engaging the family in problem solving. The family would leave and return the following week with a new problem. Wanting to block this pattern, the worker informed the family that the old system of working was not helpful. The worker negotiated a change of focus to positive behaviors by the daughter. There would be no negative story telling in the presence of the daughter. Every meeting consequently began with the question, "So what is Brenda doing well this week?" If the parents became negative, the meeting ended and the worker booked a parental session without the daughter. This shift in focus lead to dramatic improvements in the behavior of the child. The opposite focus question consists of the following five steps:

1. *Targeting.* The worker identifies a clear pattern associated with the problem. In the preceding example, the negative talk was consistent and appeared to maintain the problem by reinforcing negative perceptions of the child. The worker felt this reinforcement maintained the misbehavior on two levels. First, the child continued to hear only the things she was doing wrong. Second, the family appeared to feel as if they needed a problem for the worker to solve.

2. *Focusing.* The worker typically focuses on all members of the system participating in service.

3. *Setup.* The worker negotiates the change with the family to switch focus to the opposite of the problem. In the example, it was the child's positive behavior. Such a switch interrupts the existing pattern, breaking any systems of rumination and habitual behavior. This switch also engages the system in new behaviors, thus promoting change. In this example, the change was behavioral with the parents but perceptual with the child because she would hear increased positive messages. The worker negotiated the system so the parents could also meet any needs associated with the old pattern in an alternative form—a separate meeting. This assured the worker did not disconfirm the family.

4. *Delivery.* Given that this type of questioning is a shift in procedure, delivery is ongoing. Typically, the worker begins meetings with a question such as, "Tell me, what went right for you last week?"

5. *Exploration.* The exploration is inherent in this strategy because the change in focus limits only one aspect of the work (the focus). As such, the exploratory questions and transitional responses are heavily used to validate the new behaviors and perceptions that evolve with the changed focus. In this example, the session length remained the same, so there was significant exploration of positive behaviors and accomplishments.

EXERCISE 12.1

Change-Focused Questions: The Action System

This exercise guides you in thinking through critical areas for different types of questions.

1. You are meeting with a parent having difficulty negotiating services with the school system. She has a 9-year-old son with learning disabilities and feels the school is not open to providing services. You know she has been negotiating with the system for a long time and has at times been successful in gaining positive outcomes for her child. Apply the exceptional situation questioning technique to this situation.

   a. What would you say to introduce the question?

   b. What would the exact wording of your question be?

   c. What would you explore with your follow-up questions?

2. You are beginning work with a family struggling with parenting difficulties that result in escalating arguments between the oldest child and the father. You want to use the miracle question technique to help them visualize what the changes would look like.

   a. What would you say to introduce the question?

   b. What would the exact wording of your question be?

    c. What would you explore with your follow-up questions?

3. You are working in a welfare department with single mothers. One of your clients is a young woman with three children. In talking with this woman, you notice she is conspicuously intelligent and insightful. However, this woman dropped out of high school when she became pregnant. You want to encourage her to develop the obvious mental strengths, but do not want to tell her what to do. Embed the suggestion you would like to make in a question.

    a. What would you say to introduce the question?

    b. What would the exact wording of your question be?

    c. What would you explore with your follow-up questions?

4. You are working with a team of social workers very negative about a hard-to-serve family. This negativity seems to interfere with their ability to see the strengths in the family. They do not like that the mother is fiercely loyal to her children and fights hard to protect them from the teachers at school. You want to shift the focus of the team to consider the strengths in the family. Using the opposite focus questioning strategy, address the following:

    a. What would you say to introduce the question?

    b. What would the exact wording of your question be?

    c. What would you explore with your follow-up questions?

Questions to Promote Change in Processing Systems

The second type of change-focused questioning seeks to challenge cognitions or interpretive frameworks used by the client in problem situations. Challenging understandings helps set the stage for behavioral change. A critical assumption is that behavior is grounded in one's understanding of the situation. The following types of questions focus on altering the cognitive frameworks of client systems while concurrently exploring the situation.

Perspective-Taking Questions.   Perspective-taking questions cause members of the client system to view situations from the position of other members (e.g., have mom view herself from the perspective of her child) (Tomm, 1987). This provides informative client perceptions of others and of how the client believes others perceive him or her. One member can also take the perspective of another member and report on a third party (an adaptation of triadic reporting). For example, the mother might take the position of the father and report on the son's relation with the mother. Perspective-taking questions employ the following five steps:

1. *Targeting.* The worker targets a specified situation in which other perspectives may help the client consider alternative interpretations. Unlimited reflection is not desirable. Most often it is best to limit the situation so the member observes within a specific interaction or situation. This focuses the insights and challenges that might be gleaned from this type of questioning.

2. *Focusing.* The worker picks a member who might offer helpful insights or use the question to table misunderstandings for further exploration. When there is more than one person in the meeting, the worker must be active in limiting the interference of others. Often others will experience an impulse to correct, react, or answer the perceptions expressed by the member. Workers need to actively dissuade interference, ensuring opportunities for insight rather than conflict.

3. *Setup.* The worker reinforces the member for taking the perspective of another. If insights are demonstrated, the worker also reinforces that the person has strong insights into him- or herself and the perceptions of others.

4. *Delivery.* The worker asks the member to think about and comment from the perspective of a different member.

5. *Exploration.* As with the other questioning strategies, exploratory and transitional questioning must occur to ensure that the perspective of the member and ensuing reactions are explored. With the processing focused questioning, the worker wants to explore the thinking and affective components rather than the details of behavior. As processing is highlighted, the worker explores the insights and perspectives with others in the system. This provides an opportunity to integrate insights into the system and for others to share their insights and reactions.

There are many variations on perspective-taking questions. Although they all follow the same basic format, the variations are helpful in exploring how the strategy can be differentially applied. The following are examples of perspective-taking questioning.

- *Thought guessing.* Thought guessing involves asking one system member to guess the thoughts of another member. For example, "John, when your dad told me how hard he works, your mother became silent. What do you think she is thinking right now?" Once the thoughts are identified and the person is reinforced for guessing, the members can explore the insights about family members' relationships to each other.
- *Identifying reactions.* Similar to thought guessing, the worker has a member reflect on another member's reactions to a situation. For example, "Ms. Jones, we know that you and your husband fight when you talk to other men. We also know he hates dancing and the two of you are going to a wedding next week. What do you think might happen because . . . you love to dance and he won't dance with you?"
- *Identifying attitudes.* Often people have preconceived notions of what others might think of them. As they act on these notions, behavior patterns emerge and are maintained. Often a worker can bring the preconceived notions out into the open by asking one member to describe him- or herself from the other's perspective. In the description, the preconceptions are apt to become evident.

With individual clients, the perspective-taking questions often take a hypothetical tone with the worker by asking the individual to respond as another person in the situation. For example, when exploring a client who often engages in defensive behavior, the worker may ask how another would describe his or her motives.

Double Bound Questions. At times, the worker wants to disrupt the processing systems in the client system by putting two incompatible messages in the question (Tomm, 1987). The coexistence of the incompatible thoughts in one question creates dissonance that can confuse the client's processing of the situation. In the confusion, clients often become open to new ways of understanding the situation. However, double bound questions can be tricky. Consequently, it is important to have the strategy well thought through before beginning the question. Double bound questions are implemented through the following five steps:

1. *Targeting.* The worker targets an alternative thinking or interpretation that may help the client alter his or her approach to understanding the situation. The new frame for understanding should promote changing the patterns if adopted by the client.

2. *Focusing.* The worker generally focuses the question on the member of the system who appears to be in the best position to reinforce the new frame. It is wise to avoid system members who are heavily invested in the problem patterns. In larger systems, it is often best to target the more open member to work with the new frame while others observe. With individuals, it may be necessary to adjust the frame depending on how invested the individual is in the problem situation.

3. *Setup.* Setting up this type of question is very involved. First, the worker establishes a positive frame for asking the question. It is important to introduce double bound questions in a positive manner, to begin to shift the system understandings from a negative position.

For example, a parent who never disciplined her child because she wanted to "love him" came into service because her child was "out of control" at day care. The worker wanted to promote discipline, but the mother tended to view indulgence as loving behavior and punishment as the opposite. The worker consequently wanted to build a positive frame for the new understanding. This began with setting a positive frame for the mother. "Ms. Farmer, I know that you work very hard as a loving parent and want the best for your child, as all loving parents do."

The setup is further developed as the worker grounds the positive frame in observable reality. The frame should be consistent with the ongoing patterns of behavior in the system; this way, the statement will not likely be challenged or dismissed. In this example, the grounding of the frame was developed through the following phrase, ". . . and as a loving parent. I know that you provide the nurturing and guidance that are so important for child development. I can tell that your child is healthy and from the puzzles he was doing in the waiting room, he seems very bright."

After grounding the statement, the worker finishes the setup by reinforcing the positive frame in a way that sets the stage for a new understanding. This time, the positive frame is less general and provides an element on which one can double bind the old understanding. The final element of the setup in the example was "As the parent of a bright child, you have exceptional joys and responsibilities when your child is noticed by others. I think you kind of like it when people notice how bright Shane is." This frame put the child's brightness and the mother's investment into the same framework as being a loving parent.

4. *Delivery.* The worker asks a question that combines the new frame with the elements of the old processing. The two frames are put together in such a way that elements of the old understanding must change for the two to coexist. The wording of the question builds on the positive frame. When the question is answered, the client must accept the new understanding as an element of the positive frame. This acceptance makes it hard for them to maintain status quo. The question in the example continued, "The challenge with bright children is they demand the toughest act of love, discipline. The problem is they are hard to shape because they are bright. Can you tell me what kinds of discipline tend to be hard to implement with Shane?" In this question, the positive frame (bright child with a loving mother) sets the platform for the need to discipline (an act of love necessary for bright children).

5. *Exploration.* The worker follows up on the response with an exploration based on the answer to the double bound question. In larger systems, other system members generally affirm the content of the client answer, which strengthens the new frame for understanding. With individuals, workers use the exploratory and transitional responding strategies to develop the thinking in the new frame. In the example, the mother began describing her desire to discipline Shane along with exploring strategies that did not seem to work with her bright child.

Care must be taken when using this style of question because it can appear gimmicky. In the example, the worker had to build on positive elements in the mother to bring her on board. Also, the worker targeted a simple change in her beliefs about discipline.

Maintaining Status Quo Questions.   Many times, members of the client system are heavily invested in maintaining the status quo, even when they verbalize a desire to change. Investment in the status quo is commonly associated with fear of the unknown, inherent payoffs in the problem, or other reasons. In using status quo questions, workers must explore how members are invested in maintaining the problem. Workers can diminish the power of restraining forces, by asking questions about how and who is invested in keeping things the same. As members answer status quo questions, the concurrent pressures to change and not change become acknowledged. This allows system members to explore what they might need to give up in order to achieve changes (Tomm, 1987).

For example, a worker was conducting family work with a mother and an out-of-control teen. Even though the mother wanted the child to change, she often undermined the child's success. The worker used a status quo question asking, "Mary, if you were to suddenly follow all of the rules, what would be most difficult for your mother to accept?" Mary replied, "Mom won't be able to get sympathy from her family anymore." This led to a discussion about the mother reaching out to her family when frustrated with the daughter. This was a pattern whenever the mother became frustrated. The daughter also noted that these stressful times were the rare times her mother received support from her family. After exploring what the mother might have to give up, the worker shifted focus to explore what the daughter might have to give up. In the latter conversation, the mother identified how the daughter was able to escape responsibility. Status quo questions employ the following five steps:

1. *Targeting.* The worker notices members of the system (or the client) appearing ambivalent about changing the situation (e.g., not following through on tasks or agreements). The worker targets the ambivalence for change.

2. *Focusing.* The worker focuses on a member not ambivalent about change, but involved in the problem sequences. With individuals, the worker asks the client to reflect on his or her own behavior.

3. *Setup.* The worker introduces how problems often yield some benefits for people. This must be introduced in a neutral tone so the client does not feel judged or blamed for the problem. The setup should be tentative and stated almost as a normalized probe. For example, "Maxine, I know it is very difficult to have a husband who is never around. But I also know that sometimes when husbands aren't around, people find things to fill their time. These things sometimes become hidden benefits even thought they are not initially wanted. What are the hidden benefits that you find?"

4. *Delivery.* The actual presentation of the question builds on the setup but is very quickly delivered. In the preceding example, the small finishing sentence linked to the setup statement causes the client to reflect on the situation.

5. *Exploration.* The worker moves to exploratory and transitional questions in order to explore the beliefs and payoffs for different members. This permits full exploration of the forces in the situation potentially restraining members from change.

Relative Influence Questions.   Relative influence questions (White, 1988) challenge the perception that clients have no influence over their problems. Many clients come into service feeling victimized by the situation. This strategy begins with the client experience and expands exploration, highlighting the possibility that clients are unaware of the power they possess in the problem situation. The relative influence strategy is a two-part questioning technique. The worker has clients describe the problem from two perspectives, which requires careful setup and delivery. The relative influence questioning strategy is implemented through the following five steps:

1. *Targeting.* The questioning highlights the client influences over the problem situation.

2. *Focusing.* The worker selects any member of the client system that seems to be affected by the problem. With larger systems, the worker may want to make this a general statement and allow exploration.

3. *Setup question.* The worker asks the client (or system member) to describe the influence the problem has on his or her life. The wording of this question is important. When phrasing the question the focus must remain on the problem influence on the client (client system).

4. *Delivery.* The worker shifts focus, asking clients to describe the influence that they have on the problem. This strategy juxtaposes the externalized and internalized position forcing the client(s) to consider both influences simultaneously.

5. *Exploration.* The worker has the system members explore times when they had influence over the problem. The unique outcomes or exceptions are highlighted to illustrate client influences over the problem. In exploring client influences, the worker asks for several examples, helping clients identify their influence on the problem. At the end of the exploration, scaling questions can be used to determine which influences are greater.

For example, a man charged with assaulting his wife was being assessed for entry into the violence abatement group. The worker asked the man, "It sounds like this problem of violence has created some problems for you; what is the influence this problem has on your life?" The man responded that the problem was making his life miserable. He claimed that his wife was impossible to live with and treated him so badly that he had to resort to violence because of her consistent disrespect. The worker responded with the following change-focused question, "What are the influences that you have over the problem?" The man initially claimed to have no influence but the worker prompted him with, "Surely you sometimes do things that make the problem better or worse at times." The man disclosed that when he was miserable he often came home late. He also identified other behaviors that made his wife upset. The worker used this to explore the different actions and interactions that he used to create difficulties with his partner. These were then linked to the violence.

Embedded Hypothesis Questions.   Workers often want to introduce a new way of thinking that can alter the client perception of the situation. However, workers must avoid trying to force interpretations onto the client. Consequently, workers incorporate hypotheses or new ways of thinking into a question (Tomm, 1987). When such hypotheses are reasonable to the situation, the new cognition/belief can generate new ways of thinking about the situation. Embedded hypotheses work similarly to the embedded suggestion questions.

For example, a worker was providing services to a family with a learning-disabled young adult living in the home. This young man was not working, although there were several past attempts to help him work and become independent. Each time the man had failed and returned home. The mother brought the young man back home each time responding to his problems in a nurturing manner. A belief evolved that he was not able to take care of himself. The worker wanted to introduce a different hypothesis through the following question: "We know that children sacrifice their freedom all the time to make sure that mothers are not lonely, what are the sacrifices you see John making to keep your life feeling full?" The embedded hypothesis question consists of the following five steps:

1. *Targeting.* The worker reflects on the client situation and generates a hypothesis about what processes might be maintaining the problem. In the example, the worker hypothesized that the son's behavior was instrumental in keeping the mother engaged and feeling connected. The worker assumed that adoption of this new thinking (child's behavior is a sacrifice) would promote change in the problem situation through different interpretations of events.

2. *Focusing.* The worker selects one member as the focus of the question. The selection is based on the person's potential to confirm the hypothesis by answering the question. The answer becomes information to challenge the processing of the other members. In the example, the worker selected the mother to challenge the son.

3. *Setup.* The setup for a hypothesis-embedded question is the delivery of hypothesis. This is presented in a tentative form but captures the patterns of the situation. This is shared with the client (or members of the system).

4. *Delivery.* The worker asks a question of the focal person (mother) causing the person to either confirm or disconfirm the hypothesis in his or her response. The question is asked in a way that presupposes the hypothesis is true. Note the wording in the example is very similar to the presupposition questions described in Chapter 9.

5. *Exploration.* The worker follows up on the delivery with exploratory and transitional questions expanding and highlighting the indicators of the hypothesis.

Success Over Adversity Questions.   Success-focused questions are associated with the strengths approach to practice. Such questions are used when workers want to reinforce the strengths in different members of the client system (DeJong & Miller, 1995; Saleebey, 1997). One way of stressing people's strengths is to ask people to describe challenges they have successfully mastered. Exploring past successes makes the skills and strengths needed for the current challenge become evident.

During the exploration phase, the worker highlights themes and examples of strengths that can be used in the current situation (although not on a blatant level) to allow the system members to identify how they can use the skills. For example, "Ms. Jones, you mentioned John was very sick last year, but earlier I heard you say he had a B average in school. Tell me, how did he manage to maintain such a good average at school after being sick? Many children would have to repeat their year."

In discussing the answers to the question, the worker can use exploratory questioning to explore the strengths of the individual along with the strengths of the system supporting success. Similar to other types of questioning, the strength-focused question re-orients thinking away from a problem focus. Success over adversity questions are employed through the following five steps:

1. *Targeting.* The worker highlights client strengths, examples of mastery, and past successes over parallel situations.

2. *Focusing.* The worker focuses on people who may identify positive outcomes. People feeling overwhelmed or hopeless should be avoided.

3. *Setup.* The worker often asks a general question having the client(s) describe times of past adversity.

4. *Delivery.* The worker asks the system members to describe a time when they were able to achieve success over an adverse situation.

5. *Exploration.* The worker explores the attributes that allowed the system to achieve the past success. Using exploratory and transitional questioning skills, the worker explores how the system approached the situation, how they supported each other, and how they found the internal resources to overcome the situation.

EXERCISE 12.2

Change-Focused Questions: The Processing System

This exercise guides you in thinking through critical areas for processing system questions.

1. You are working with a woman deciding whether or not to stay with an abusive partner. During your discussion, it becomes evident that the woman doubted her ability to take charge of her life. You want to change this belief to help her see she has more capacity than she is willing to admit. You know she has put up with a lot of difficult situations in the past. Use this knowledge to establish a success over adversity question to highlight her strengths.

    a. What would you say to introduce the question?

    b. What would the exact wording of your question be?

    c. What would you explore in your follow-up questioning?

2. You are working with a parent and child each caught up in their version of problems between them. The mother complains the child does not listen to her. The child levies the same complaint. You believe they don't understand each other's positions and want to help them explore their misunderstandings. At the beginning of a meeting, the child comes in and complains that the teachers at school are picking on him and no one seems to care. You want to use this statement to help the two explore their beliefs about each other. Use a relative influence questioning strategy to explore the situation.

   a. What would you say to introduce the question?

   b. What would the exact wording of your question be?

   c. What would you explore in your follow-up questioning?

3. You are working with a team of social workers planning a parenting program for economically vulnerable parents at risk of abusing their children. Some of the team members are planning an educational program with readings, handouts, homework, and heavy use of positive reinforcement. You know many of the parents had difficulty in school and have no money. You are concerned the parents might not take well to this type of program. Use a perspective-taking questioning strategy to help the other team members be more sensitive to the perspective of these clients.

   a. What would you say to introduce the question?

   b. What would the exact wording of your question be?

   c. What would you explore in your follow-up questioning?

4. You are working with a young male having difficulty controlling his anger. He has been fighting with many authority figures in his life and consistently feels unjustly criticized by them. You want to help this young man understand that his reactions may contribute to the problems. You know he often reacts badly to teacher feedback.

You want to use this pattern in a question that requires him to look at how he interprets teacher feedback. Use an embedded hypothesis questioning strategy to explore the situation.

    a. What would you say to introduce the question?

    b. What would the exact wording of your question be?

    c. What would you explore in your follow-up questioning?

5. You are working with a defiant adolescent living with his mother. You believe the adolescent is using fights and oppositional behavior to create his identity (e.g., I am the opposite of what my mother wants me to be). You are concerned this might put him at risk for problems because his mother wants the best for him. You want to stress the paradox (dependence on mother being used to form an independent identity) so he might explore other ways to form his identity. You have decided to ask him a question forcing him to deal with this paradox. Use a double bound questioning strategy to explore the situation.

    a. What would you say to introduce the question?

    b. What would the exact wording of your question be?

    c. What would you explore in your follow-up questioning?

6. You are working in a community health clinic always discussing the need to change intake procedures to make them more responsive to clients. However, nothing seems to happen. You think some of the intake workers feel comfortable with keeping things the same. You don't think this resistance is malicious, but rather a tendency to avoid change. You are at a staff meeting and want to highlight this normal resistance to change. Use a status quo type of questioning strategy to explore the situation.

    a. What would you say to introduce the question?

b. What would the exact wording of your question be?

c. What would you explore in your follow-up questioning?

7. You are working with an adolescent runaway. He reportedly ran away because of a heated power struggle with his parents. The youth is now scared about living on the streets, and you think his pride is keeping him from contacting his parents to come home. Use an embedded hypothesis question to explore the situation.

   a. What would you say to introduce the question?

   b. What would the exact wording of your question be?

   c. What would you explore in your follow-up questioning?

Critical Chapter Themes

1. Workers must use their skills to help clients achieve their goals. This requires adaptation and application of the interpersonal skills already learned. An adaptation of questioning is the change-focused question that emerged from the family therapy, strength-based, and solution-focused approaches to helping.
2. Change-focused questions have five elements, (1) targeting, (2) focusing, (3) setup, (4) delivery, and (5) exploration. These elements vary according to the change-focused question strategy but are evident in all questions.
3. There are two common categories of change-focused questions; questions that try to change the action systems (behavior and interactions) and questions that try to alter processing systems (thinking and feeling).
4. Action system questions include exceptional situation questions, miracle questions, embedded suggestion questions, and opposite focus questions.
5. Processing system questions include perspective-taking questions, double bound questions, status quo questions, relative influence questions, embedded hypothesis questions, and success over adversity questions.

RECOMMENDED READINGS

Adams, J. F. (1997). Questions as interventions in therapeutic conversation. *Journal of Family Psychotherapy, 8,* 17–35.

DeJong, P., & Miller, S. D. (1995). How to interview for client strengths. *Social Work, 40,* 729–736.

Freedman, J., & Combs, G. (1993). Invitations to new stories: Using questions to explore alternative possibilities. In S. G. Gilligan & R. Price (Eds.), *Therapeutic conversations* (pp. 291–308). New York: W. W. Norton.

Santa Rita, E., Jr. (1998). What do you do after asking the miracle question in solution-focused therapy? *Family Therapy, 25,* 189–195.

Shilts, L., & Gordon, A. B. (1996). What to do after the miracle occurs. *Journal of Family Psychotherapy, 7,* 15–22.

Tomm, K. (1987). Interventive interviewing: Part II. Reflexive questioning as a means to enable self-healing. *Family Process, 26,* 167–184.

CHAPTER
13

Supporting and Developing a Working Alliance

In the last chapter, readers explored applications of questioning to set the tone for change. As the worker and client focus on achieving goals, the helping relationship becomes a working alliance. In the working alliance, the worker and client collaborate with each other in a very intense, but goal-focused relationship. This chapter will explore applications of other skills that focus and enhance the working alliance with clients.

The working alliance is critical for successful service. Success is based on three outcomes of the alliance. First, without the establishment of a working alliance, many clients withdraw from service (Samstag et al., 1998). Second, a working relationship is associated with intervention receptivity and a commitment to work (Gaston, Marmar, Thompson, & Gallagher, 1988; Reandeau & Wampold, 1991). Finally, the working alliance predicts positive service outcomes and goal achievement (Gaston, 1990; Mallinckrodt, 1993).

The engagement explored in Chapter 6 provides a foundation for the working alliance. Workers build on this foundation as service progresses through focusing the interaction and decisions on client goals. Inherent in this focus, the relationship must change from an authority relationship to an egalitarian partnership (Crits-Christoph, Demorest, & Connolly, 1990). The change in authority underscores the need to attend closely to the relationship, while still focusing on the work. One cannot rely on the authority of the worker, changes occur through the strength of the working alliance (Gelso & Hayes, 1998).

There are three critical types of worker activity that help focus and maintain the working relationship over the course of service: motivating the working alliance, nurturing the working alliance, and focusing the client work. In each of these areas, the worker must combine thinking, awareness, observing, listening, questioning, and reflection skills into responses to promote client goal achievement. This chapter explores responses that focus and promote goal achievement with clients.

ENHANCING MOTIVATION IN THE WORKING ALLIANCE

When helping clients achieve their goals, the worker adjusts the relationship according to client motivations. This requires a balance of attending to the relationship and to the goals of service (Ridgway & Sharpley, 1991). This is a tenuous balance because too much focus on goals and tasks may result in relationship problems (Vallis, Shaw, & McCabe, 1988). Conversely, too little focus on goals will result in interactions that fail to achieve results.

Dimensions of Motivation in the Working Alliance

Most clients are motivated by their feelings when entering service (Stein, 1995). It is their feelings that create the "felt problem perspectives" described in Chapters 5 through 7. The initial motivating affect is an important consideration because it is central to engaging clients and establishing focus. As the helping relationship progresses, the need for the initial motivating affect is ideally replaced by the working alliance. To build this alliance workers use motivating feelings to help their clients work toward their goals.

There are two dimensions inherent in the initial motivation. The first dimension is the internal/external dimension. Sometimes the motivating feeling is based on feelings internal to the client. Alternative, the client feels controlled by external people or events. The second dimension is stability. Some motivating feelings are consistent; others shift or diminish rapidly. These two dimensions can be understood through the four-cell model in Table 13.1. The table illustrates how two dimensions form different foundations for building an alliance.

Stable/Internal Motivating Affect: Allying with the Motivated Client.   When the affect is both stable and internal, the client usually highly motivated rather than relying on others to motivate. Such people often desire assistance to improve their situations. There are two common types of motivation found in this type of client.

■ *Self-growth motivation.* Although it is rare, some clients enter service wanting to optimize their situation and capitalize on their growth potential. New parents taking a parenting course are a common example of this. With organizations and communities, this type of motivation occurs in prevention and revitalization programming. Clients with internal/stable motivation are typically ready to work as soon as they engage and maintain motivation throughout service.

■ *Compensation motivation.* Similar to growth motivation, some clients come into service wanting to compensate for perceived problems associated with past events. Such

TABLE 13.1   Affective Dimensions in Client Motivation

Stable/Internal	Stable/External
• Self-growth motivation • Compensation motivation	• Status quo motivation • Externalized goal motivation
Unstable/Internal	**Unstable/External**
• Pain motivation • Stress-release motivation	• Coerced motivation • Secondary perspective motivation

clients often want to improve their life situations by adjusting past adaptive responses. For example, a sexually abused client may come into service to increase his or her ability to trust. The motivation tends to provide a solid base and focus for a helping alliance.

Unstable/Internal Motivating Affect: Allying with the Client in Crisis. Internal and unstable motivating affects are most often transient and will shift and disappear rapidly. Such motivation is not long lasting, therefore workers must consciously (and quickly) engage the client and build a solid working alliance. This provides a relational motivation when the affect decreases. There are two common types of motivation that reflect internal and unstable affect.

- *Pain motivation.* There are times when clients experience an event that creates pain or discomfort; for example, when couples are about to separate. In such situations, the goal is to decrease the level of pain. The client will feel the service is complete when the pain has subsided.

- *Stress-release motivation.* Similar to pain motivation, sometimes clients enter service because stress levels have exceeded the level of tolerance. Such clients are highly motivated to begin immediately. They can be quite demanding in their attempts to enter service. When stress subsides, the motivation may dissipate. Workers must engage such clients quickly to build a relationship that can carry the client through after the initial motivation subsides. A positive relationship can promote a continued working alliance (Harris, 1996; Sommers-Flanagan & Sommers-Flanagan, 1997).

For example, a parent under a lot of stress felt that she could not continue. She called the child protective services and complained about her child. The worker talked with her for an hour and told her that she would refer her to a child service agency. The worker then called the agency and made a crisis referral. The new agency phoned and talked with the woman for another hour. The mother was able to calm down and the worker booked an appointment for two days later. The mother never arrived for the appointment and resisted follow-up attempts to engage her in service.

In this example, the initial motivation subsided with the reduction in stress. With the reduction in motivation, the client no longer desired service. Even with follow-up efforts, there was no establishment of a working alliance. With such clients, timing is important to establish the relationship. The worker needs to quickly build the relationship and capitalize on the initial motivation.

Stable/Externalized Motivating Affect: Allying with the Uncertain Client. When the affect motivating the client is from an external source, the working alliance is difficult to develop. Difficulties arise because the motivating source is not accessible to the worker. When the client goal is to influence external events or people, the worker must personalize an element of the goal. Without an area of the situation the client can influence, the worker and client cannot establish realistic goals for service. Personalizing probes are instrumental in achieving ownership of the situation. Only after a sense of ownership is achieved, can a focused working relationship develop. There are two types of common motivating affects.

■ *Status quo motivation.* Often people enter service to stop something from occurring in their lives. Their motivation is to keep some element of the situation from changing. This is common when a member of a family might leave (e.g., divorce and child removal). In such situations, the worker helps the client identify elements over which he or she has influence. These elements are used to develop a focus for the working alliance. In negotiating the alliance, workers must assure that goal outcomes are within the client's potential control. The stability of affect in such situations is helpful because it allows time to develop the internalized elements around which the alliance can form.

For example, a man contacted a batterers treatment group asking to be placed on the priority list. He appeared distraught and in crisis. The worker met with him right away discovering that his wife had entered a shelter and was planning to leave him. Initially, the man wanted to save the relationship. The worker acknowledged this motivation and helped him outline the behaviors that were driving the wife away. The man was able to explore some of these behaviors and eventually formed goals to control these behaviors regardless of his wife's decision (to stay or leave him).

In this example, the externalized motivation was instrumental in bringing the man into service. However, it would have been unwise and unethical for the worker to ally himself with a goal of keeping a woman in an abusive relationship. The worker consequently moved quickly to bring him in and explore stable elements of the situation over which he had some control. The personal elements were instrumental in forming the working alliance and ongoing motivation.

■ *Externalized goal motivation.* There are times when clients enter service to achieve new goals and relationships. This was common when social work students went into treatment to gain a better self-understanding. Such entry into service was expected in many schools. Treatment was recommended so workers would control their responses when working with clients. Work and relationship goals are probably the most common externalized reasons for people to enter service (e.g., wanting to drop habits, develop new skills).

Unstable/External Motivating Affect: Allying with the Involuntary Client.
Many clients come into service against their wills. Court-referred clients are a common example of such motivation. However, there are others who enter service with milder forms of coercion. Children and youth are prime examples of people who often do not make a choice to enter service. Such clients are not eager to form an alliance with the worker. Although the problem perspectives explored in Chapters 5 and 6 help with engagement, the alliance requires finding a personal reason for the person to focus and work with the worker. There are two common types of involuntary motivation.

■ *Coerced motivation.* Many clients come into service because an authority figure has told them they must comply or suffer a punishment. In the experience of such clients, service is viewed as only slightly better than prison or another noxious punishment. This does not provide intrinsic motivation for building the working alliance. When forming an alliance with such clients, begin with the reality that their motivation is to avoid punishment. Within this acknowledgment, the worker can explore the actions guaranteed to bring on the punishment (Slonim-Nevo, 1996) and build an alliance to help gain control of those behaviors. Such exploration must occur early in service. If it is delayed, there is a risk of colluding with the client against the authority figure.

■ *Secondary problem motivation.* A very common externalized motivation is when the person insisting on service is not part of the client system. This is a common occurrence when professionals (e.g., teachers and medical doctors) recommend service. When the person enters service, the primary goal is to stop the external person from pressuring them about service. With such clients, it is important to explore the events that led to the recommendation. In this exploration, screen for elements of the situation in which the client has feelings that can be used for internal motivation and promotion of a working alliance.

For example, a man was referred to a substance abuse program due to persistent public drunkenness and driving under the influence. He came into the program to avoid doing time but initially did not want to attend. The worker resisted the temptation to use the legal mandate and instead began exploring why he had chosen the program over jail time. The man outlined a solid rationale, explaining that he had a job, a wife, and his own apartment. The worker explored these elements of his life and asked what might happen to these things if he were to go back to court. The man explained he would lose everything and would have to do time. The worker shifted exploration to the man's motivation to keep his marriage and possessions, things that drinking was putting at risk. From this motivation, the man was able to commit to working on his drinking behavior.

In this example, the worker stayed with the motivation presented by the client. He was able to expand the motivation to overlap with the goals and purpose of the program. Within this overlap, the worker was able to begin an alliance with the client motivation.

NURTURING THE WORKING ALLIANCE

Once established, the working alliance must be nurtured to retain its positive focus and goal direction. Because it is based on goals as well as a relationship, the alliance tends to shift and change over the course of service (Allen et al., 1990; Crits-Christoph et al., 1990). This demands the active attentiveness of the worker to monitor and adjust the working relationship throughout the delivery of service.

There are two basic responses workers use to deepen the working alliance: offering support/feedback and using self-disclosures. If used well, each of these response types can advance both the relationship and work toward client goals. The worker must be careful when nurturing the relationship to ensure the alliance also maintains the goal focus.

Strategies for nurturing the alliance require high levels of self-awareness and control by the worker. Most of our communication skills develop in our personal relationships where we freely share personal information. Such sharing deepens the relationship. With the working alliance, people must resist the impulse to rely on such well-developed methods by filtering relationship-nurturing interactions through the professional purpose of the relationship. This means the worker will have to limit disclosures and discussions based on the purpose and goals of the working relationship.

Providing Feedback and Support

In attending to the working alliance, effective workers attempt to maintain a positive relationship with the client (Chang 1994; Patterson & Forgatch, 1985). Positive relationship elements include providing support while empowering the client. Workers actively supporting, encouraging, and clarifying client positions tend to have collaborative working relationships, whereas those who teach and confront tend to decrease collaboration (Allen et al., 1996; Bischoff & Tracey, 1996; Miller et al., 1993; Najavits & Strupp, 1994; Patterson & Forgatch, 1985).

Another helpful element in maintaining a positive alliance is sharing perceptions of the relationship, client strengths, and quality of work being done (Chang, 1994; Henry, Schacht & Strupp, 1990). In the sharing of perceptions, it is important to be genuine. The client must be able to recognize him- or herself in the feedback to strengthen the working alliance (Omer, 1997). If worker feedback is inconsistent with client self-perceptions, the worker will be viewed as deceitful or manipulative.

Workers must be prepared to support negative and positive client responses. This includes possible negative feelings about worker performance. Such feelings and expressions must be heard and validated by the worker (Safran, Crocker, McMain, & Murray, 1990). This is often difficult because negative feelings create defensive reactions in the worker. High levels of self-awareness and control are needed to support clients during these moments of service.

In providing feedback to clients, workers go through a four-step process ensuring feedback is accurate and targeted on client goals. Most of the four steps occur internally as the worker reflectively thinks about the feedback and predicts potential impacts.

1. *Maintaining a nonjudgmental stance.* The first task is to ensure that the feedback is not a judgment of the client. Even positive judgments like praise are judgments that can disempower the client (Allen et al., 1996). Consequently, the worker needs to avoid evaluative words, such as *good*, that communicate a worker judgment. Enthusiasm should replace such expressions.
2. *Grounding the feedback in observations.* When sharing feedback, it is important to base the feedback on observations. Consequently, the worker must be able to identify specific actions or responses that illustrate some strength or competency to promote goal achievement.
3. *Describing the observation.* When workers describe their observations, it is easier for clients to see themselves in the feedback and visualize the situations.
4. *Reflecting the meaning of the observation.* The finishing touch on feedback is a reflection to highlight the meaning and potential strength in the observed responses. Such reflection builds on the observation while highlighting positive client traits.

For example, a woman came in to see a worker in a family drop-in center. The woman had been struggling with asserting herself with a new boyfriend. When describing events of the past week, the client reported, "I finally let him have it. He was sulking and expecting me to give in again so I said, 'Grow up . . . . You are a man now and need to deal with disappointments.' I then walked out and weeded the garden. He came out and apologized later." The worker replied, "When I hear you describe your stand it gives me goose bumps. I can hear the power in your voice when you talk. You are sounding so assertive . . . nobody is going to mess with you."

In this example, notice the enthusiasm of the worker as she responded to the client. When workers feel enthusiastic, they are at high risk for using words such as *good*. However, the worker used descriptive language to describe her reaction and observations. After the observation, the reflection remains positive for the client and focused on client goals.

Using Self-Disclosure

A second type of communication used to focus and maintain the helping relationship is worker self-disclosure. Workers are half of the helping relationship. To develop mutuality, this half of the relationship often needs some development. With careful sharing of self-information, the worker can enhance the working alliance (Hendrick, 1988; Tyron & Kane, 1991; Walborn, 1996). Such sharing, however, must be very carefully done to serve client goals and ensure a clear sense of purpose.

Self-disclosure is a very tricky type of communication that draws heavily on worker self-awareness and self-control. It is easy to disclose information that can move the relationship away from professionally focused work and into a friendship situation. Workers must be wary of this temptation at all times. The risk of moving toward a friendship relationship is associated with common patterns of relating. In friendships, shared information yields reciprocation by the other person. This model of relationship often makes the professional relationship awkward because disclosure is one-sided. Any disclosure by the worker must have a clear association with client goals.

In using self-disclosure, the worker follows five critical elements. The first three critical elements employ self-awareness and self-control skills. There is also a need for critical thinking to mentally work through the first three elements of self-disclosing. The final two elements make use of tuning in, engagement, and reflection skills.

1. *Awareness.* The worker becomes aware of an internal impulse to disclose some aspect of his or her life to the client (usually a story). For example, the client is upset that his girlfriend is breaking up with him and the worker is reminded of a story about a past breakup.

2. *Purpose.* The worker reflects on the purpose and goals of the helping relationship. If the disclosure does not clearly promote some service goal, the worker should abandon any thoughts of self-disclosure. For example, the worker thinks about the client goals of overcoming depression. The worker identifies the purpose of the story as instilling hope.

3. *Critical thinking.* The worker mentally reflects on the risks or misinterpretations that may evolve from the disclosure. If the worker does not identify aspects of the disclosure that might interfere, it is okay to proceed to the next step. If there is some risk, the urge to disclose should be abandoned. For example, the worker considers whether or not the story might be experienced as minimizing the pain or taking focus away from the client.

4. *Limited disclosure.* The worker communicates the information. In this communication the worker:

- first introduces the goal or aspect of the client work that triggered the urge to disclose,
- then describes the event or personal story that relates to the client situation,
- finally stops the story without further embellishment or personal disclosures.

For example, the worker says, "It can be so hard when a girlfriend breaks up with you. When you are in the middle of it you think the pain never ends. As I hear you talk about your pain, I remember feeling that way when my college girlfriend dumped me for another guy. I thought I would never be able to even think about smiling again."

5. *Transitional reflection.* The worker directs the discussion back to the client situation and client goals. For example, "When I listen to you, I think about all the new things I had to do to keep myself from dwelling on the pain. What have you been doing to deal with your pain?"

EXERCISE 13.1

Communicating Motivation

You are working in a mental health agency. You meet with a woman diagnosed with schizophrenia. When not on her medication, she hears voices talking to her and becomes paranoid. She has been working in a sheltered workshop and living in a group home for the past five years. This woman has not missed a day of work since entering the shelter. However, she has a pattern of doing well for a while, going off her medication, and then regressing. The woman wants to live in her own apartment and get married. Her boyfriend from the workshop entered competitive employment last year. The two of them are becoming serious about their relationship. They talk about marriage, but currently cannot afford to marry because she does not make much money in the workshop. The only thing standing in her way of living independently and getting married is her inability to take her medication consistently. She has been doing well and you want to keep her motivated.

1. What things in her life seem to have provided motivation for this woman in the past?

2. What are some of the anticipated rewards that might come with the ability to self-medicate?

3. What are three strengths evident in the woman that can help her succeed?

4. Using one of the sources of motivation, write exactly what you would say to encourage her to continue doing well.

5. What is your rationale for choosing that particular source of motivation?

FOCUSING THE CLIENT WORK

The professional working relationship requires both focus and purpose. When the focus of the relationship begins to stray away from the main purpose of service, the worker must refocus the relationship to proceed toward the goals. There are times when the need to re-focus occurs as part of the pattern of work (e.g., at the beginning of meetings). At other times, the need to focus the work occurs through the worker placing demands on the client.

Sessional Focusing of Work

At the beginning of each client meeting, workers must focus discussion toward achiev-ing client goals. Many events occur between meetings and workers typically must help clients' transition from the out-of-service aspects of their lives to the goals of service. This sessional focusing helps clients re-orient to the work and previous meetings. There are three very common strategies of sessional focusing: task follow-up, reflective ques-tions, and integrative focusing.

Task Follow-Up.   Task-centered focusing begins the session by following up on exer-cises used or assigned during the previous meeting. Workers who use homework as-signments or tasks often use a reporting system in which clients describe what they have done between meetings. This follow-up focuses the new session on the goal-focused work.

Reflective Question Focusing.   Reflective question focusing is less rigid or structured than tasks. Reflective questioning involves asking clients a question to produce an answer that begins the work. Solution-focused workers often ask questions such as, "What have you found yourself doing differently since our last meeting?" Such questions focus the clients while allowing them to set direction in how the work will proceed.

Integrative Focusing.   Integrative focusing is the least structured sessional focusing strategy. Integrative focusing uses a period of "catching up" on events between meetings to tie current events to goal-directed work. Based on client descriptions of events, the worker reflects on elements of the client's story that build on work from the last meeting.

Workers choose their level of structure based on many aspects of the work. First, the worker wants to consider the client and the client needs. When the client is hard to focus, a structured approach may be desirable. However, highly structured strategies limit the client's ability to table any new concerns. Second, the worker considers agency requirements. With managed care and decreased service availability, many workers must focus quickly to ensure that time is used expediently. In such situations, the reflective questioning and task-centered approaches are desirable.

Making Demands and Managing Tension in the Working Alliance

The second type of focusing is used when work is offtrack or when a worker must place demands on the client to work toward his or her goals. This type of focusing may increase stress in the relationship. Consequently, workers must be skilled in managing tension (Edwards & Bess, 1998). Some workers are hesitant to refocus clients because they fear tension may disrupt the working alliance. The maintenance of the positive working alliance does not preclude the demands for work or tension (Shulman, 1999). Clients know they are in the relationship to accomplish a goal. Workers must maintain their goal focus to remain credible with the client.

Focusing on goals must be balanced against becoming too demanding or directive. Directive workers tend to yield client noncompliance and poorer outcomes (Bischoff & Tracey, 1996; Vallis et al., 1988). Directive types of behavior, such as teaching and confronting, also tend to diminish collaboration and client outcomes (Patterson & Forgatch, 1983; Miller et al., 1993). Consequently, workers need to remain tentative in their approach, but still place expectations on the client (Baenninger-Huber & Widmer, 1999).

Dealing with the Tension Associated with Demands for Work.   Effective workers are skilled at balancing support with the demands for work. Support helps manage tension in the relationship. It is important to understand that tension is different from a rupture in the working alliance. Most people have noticed that tension is present during times of learning and personal growth. Most important relationships have periods of tension. There are four types of tension that may emerge as workers begin to increase the focus on change.

- *Tension from demanding client work* (Shulman, 1999). When the worker places a demand on the client to make changes, tension will increase in the relationship through the placement of demands. Consequently, the worker must support the moves to change. This requires attending to the relationship if any changes occur as a result of the demands (Allen et al., 1990).

- *Tension from expecting the client to assume responsibility* (Baenninger-Huber & Widmer, 1999). Part of supporting clients is allowing them to make decisions and do their own work. However, when assuming responsibility for making changes, tension is created. At times, tension occurs when clients want their workers to take over their problems rather than making their own changes. While this is tempting, effective workers coach clients to develop their own skills.

- *Tension from grappling with uncertainty.* People do not necessarily know what to expect when they are making changes. Even when a situation is difficult, it is familiar. Change, on the other hand, is unknown. When making demands for change, workers help clients deal with the anxiety associated with the unknown. As clients begin to trust their new skills in the situation, the ambivalence about change decreases.

- *Tension due to feeling inadequate.* Even when people know they must change, there are feelings of criticism or inadequacy when others promote the change. Such feelings can promote frustration when the client has difficulty mastering the change or would rather not change. This requires very active support by the worker and the ability to note and reflect small changes and outcomes.

In focusing the work with clients, workers use all of the supportive strategies described in the previous sections. Workers must maintain a focus on all four response systems because the changes promoted tend to be changes in action, interaction, and processing. But, the worker must concurrently support the feelings inherent in the situation. To accomplish a balanced approach to focusing the work, effective workers tend to combine their core skills to assure that the client simultaneously experiences the challenges and support of service.

Skill Combinations for Making Demands for Work. In refocusing clients, workers must often build on their motivating affects. The motivating feelings become critical as the workers use client desires to remind them of the goals of service. When the worker brings the client back to the reasons for working, the worker can promote focus and work through the following six-step process.

1. *Build on earlier discussions.* The worker reflects on earlier discussions, highlighting feelings, thoughts, and actions that symbolize the client motivation (painful feelings, desire for improved situation, self-feelings).
2. *Reinforce the client decision to work.* Using descriptive language, the worker describes the positive observations made during these earlier discussions about the client's desires to improve the situation. The worker will especially want to highlight positive client motivations.
3. *Express faith in the client to achieve the goals.* The worker shifts the focus from past to present by expressing his or her belief that the client wants to, and is able to, achieve the goals.
4. *Bring the commitment into the current challenges for action.* After the faith has been expressed, the worker focuses on what they need to do with this motivation. This shifts focus from the internal experience of the client to the work that must occur to achieve the goals.
5. *Reflect on the shared responsibilities.* The next shift is to reflect on the actions and changes in processing that must be tackled by each person in the alliance. This builds on the expression of faith and the worker's supportive position to partner with the client in accomplishing the goals.
6. *Engage the client in exploration.* The final step is to open up the discussion so the client can either recontract the initial expectations or begin to engage. Both possibilities need to be open for the client so the client can take the alliance in any direction that may be right for him or her in achieving the goals.

For example, a sheltered workshop worker was preparing a client diagnosed with a developmental disability for a work placement. The worker wanted to motivate him to acquire important skills. The worker began with the following statement, "Frank, when we first talked about getting a work placement, you were talking about what you would do with the money. You had some plans about getting into independent living and being able to go out with Betty. You seemed pretty determined to make it into the workplace. Do you remember? *(reference earlier decisions)* I thought you were working hard in a direction that you wanted to go. You really looked like you had a plan for yourself. *(reinforce the decision)* I believe that deep down you still want to get that money and start having more freedom. I believe you can do it if you work hard. *(expression of faith)* It is my job to help you get the skills to make this happen, do you know what I mean? In order for you to get that money, we are going to have to learn some safety skills. *(brought into current alliance)* These skills will be a bit of work for you, *(shift responsibility)* are you sure you are willing to do this work? *(opens it up)*"

In this example, the worker used many skills in the motivational exchange. He used tuning in to identify the important elements of earlier discussions. He used observational descriptions concurrent with reflecting and questioning to pull together the exchange.

EXERCISE 13.2

Making Demands for Work

You are working with homeless families in a program helping people to get their own homes. You have been working with a single mother and her two young children referred by a domestic violence shelter. She had been in the shelter for two months before coming into the homeless shelter associated with your program. She stated that she wanted to provide a stable environment for her children. She connected well with the other residents in the program and is well liked. You are finding she does not follow through on the homework assignments. She was supposed to search possible apartments in the paper and arrange to view apartments on several occasions but took no action. This is a change from when she first came into the program. You want to place some demands on her to assume responsibility for the work.

1. What earlier client statement can be used to build on?

2. Write a statement using this earlier statement to introduce the need for this woman to assume more work responsibility.

3. Write what you would say to reinforce/support this woman's motivation and express faith in her ability to accomplish the task (make sure you draw on the strengths you have observed).

4. Write what you would say to this woman to help motivate her commitment to accomplishing the goals of getting her own place.

5. Write what you would say to outline (1) the responsibilities you would assume in helping her and (2) the responsibilities she would need to assume.

6. Write the statement you would make to transition the discussion into negotiating the next moves that each would need to take to assure goal accomplishment.

Critical Chapter Themes

1. After clients have engaged, the worker must diligently attend to the working alliance to keep work focused on accomplishing client goals. This is accomplished by using combinations of the core skills discussed in previous chapters.
2. Attending to the working alliance requires motivating, nurturing, and focusing the working alliance to make sure the worker–client relationship remains positive and focused on accomplishing service outcomes.
3. There are two polarized affective dimensions of client motivation that can help workers keep clients working toward goals. These include internal/external and stable/unstable.
4. Nurturing the working alliance requires workers to provide active feedback and support to help clients identify their strengths and abilities for accomplishing their goals. Judicious use of self-disclosure can also help to nurture the alliance.
5. Focusing the work occurs at the beginning of each meeting in sessional focusing and also when keeping the alliance focused on accomplishing goals. Workers often must place demands for work, which requires them to manage tension in the alliance.

RECOMMENDED READINGS

Edwards, J. K., & Bess, J. M. C. (1998). Developing effectiveness in the therapeutic use of self. *Clinical Social Work Journal, 26,* 89–105.

Mallinckrodt, B. (1993). Session impact, working alliance, and therapeutic outcome in brief counseling. *Journal of Counseling Psychology, 40,* 25–32.

Rollnick, S., & Morgan, M. (1996). Motivational interviewing: Increasing readiness for change. In A. M. Washton (Ed.), *Psychotherapy and substance abuse: A practitioners' handbook* (pp. 179–191). New York: Guilford Press.

Slonim-Nevo, V. (1996). Clinical practice: Treating the non-voluntary client. *International Social Work, 39,* 117–129.

14

Managing Threats to the Working Alliance

Every worker will experience periodic threats to the working alliance. Some threats emerge in the client responses to the worker; whereas, others emerge through worker responses to the client (Elkind, 1992). Regardless of the origin of the threat, it is important to monitor and correct potential problems before the alliance is ruptured and service is prematurely ended.

THREATS TO THE WORKING ALLIANCE: A RELATIONAL VIEW OF RESISTANCE

Client-originated threats to the working alliance are often referred to as resistance. The term *resistance* is an old psychodynamic term that locates the problem within the client. Since the time when resistance was introduced, much thinking and research has been conducted. As a result of this thinking and research, resistance is now considered a problem in the working relationship rather than solely a client problem (Worrell, 1997). In a relational view of resistance, threats can originate with the client or worker or at the relationship level.

There are several indicators that the working alliance has been disrupted, some are logical and others counterintuitive. Knowing the indicators refines the worker's ability to tune into possible indicators that the working alliance has been ruptured. Some of the indicators are:

■ *Negative sentiments* (Safran et al., 1990). When a client confronts, complains about service, or indicates service is not helpful, there is a clear indication that the working relationship is in jeopardy. Although such expressions do the worker a favor by identifying concerns, the worker will experience awkward feelings when this occurs. Similar to clients harboring negative sentiments about the worker, when workers speak negatively about clients, there is also a rupture in the working alliance. A worker cannot speak negatively about clients and expect to maintain a positive alliance.

■ *Disagreement about the goals and tasks of therapy* (Safran et al., 1990). When a worker argues, disagrees, or pressures a client about the direction for service, the working alliance is in trouble. These behaviors are qualitatively different from negotiation. If the client is negotiating different aspects of the service, the alliance is being negotiated; however, impasses that cannot be resolved will damage the alliance.

■ *Unquestioning client compliance* (Safran et al., 1990). Compliance is a counterintuitive indicator of alliance problems. Although many consider compliance a good sign, compliance to avoid angering the worker, creating tension, disappointing others, or risking rejection indicate challenges to the working alliance. Such compliance is a sign of potential problems. Workers must monitor the compliance patterns of the client to ensure the client is actually agreeing rather than acquiescing.

■ *Avoidance* (Safran et al., 1990). Client absences, partial completion of tasks, and indecisiveness indicate problems in the working alliance. Often the understanding of the problem is incorrect, or they are forming an alliance around the wrong goals.

■ *Self-esteem enhancing (defensive) statements* (Safran et al., 1990). When clients feel judged by the worker or are concerned about worker perceptions, they make statements to protect their self-esteem. When clients stress their good points or attempt to build esteem, there may be a problem in the working alliance. This is common when the alliance has a negative focus and clients feel a need to protect their self-images rather than working toward goals.

■ *Nonresponsiveness to intervention* (Safran et al., 1990). When workers have invested time and energy but the situation does not improve, the working alliance may be weak. There are many possibilities in such situations. The lack of resolution may be due to the problem being too consistent with the client's self-image. At other times, it may be because the worker and client have not defined the problem accurately and are working in the wrong direction. Regardless, there is a problem inherent in the alliance. Exploration is important to determine necessary changes.

PROTECTING AND SALVAGING THE WORKING ALLIANCE

There are three types of threats to the working alliance. Some problems are a result of client traits or behaviors. Others are due to worker responses to the client situation, and still others are due to the way the worker and the client have formed the alliance. Each type of potential problem has its own nuances. It is useful to understand the challenges to the working alliance so one can respond appropriately to each type of threat.

Client-Related Challenges to the Working Alliance

When clients withdraw collaboration, it is often an indication that they need to redefine themselves in the working relationship (Worrell, 1997). A worker who notices such withdrawal must pause to address the potential problem in the alliance. The withdrawal of cooperation in effect puts the relationship on the table to be explored and rectified. As the relationship is renegotiated, the work may continue in the current direction or take a shift due to a new definition of client and worker roles.

When working with clients, strong tuning-in skills are needed to understand and to adjust the working alliance around the client's adaptations to the service. Some of the issues common to client withdrawal from the alliance include:

- *Focus on behaviors congruent with client self-image* (Dowd & Sanders, 1994). When clients come into service as a result of behaviors upon which they build their identity, it is difficult to change the behaviors without threatening client self-conceptions.
- *Focus on shame-promoting behaviors* (Carpenter & Treacher, 1989). When clients are referred due to behaviors that stigmatize or cause judgmental reactions, they will be reticent to open up.
- *Difficulty trusting the worker* (Elkind, 1992). Many clients have histories that preclude trusting relationships. In such situations, the alliance is always under scrutiny and tenuous.

When workers must confront a client issue interfering with the alliance, they must approach the issue with very skilled communication to avoid further threatening the alliance. There are two common communication strategies for accomplishing this task, communicating concern and confronting the situation.

Salvaging the Alliance through Communicating Concern.

At times, situations arise requiring immediate action to ensure the client's best interests are not compromised. For example, sometimes clients avoid situations hoping that the problems will go away if they don't address them. This is common when students get behind in their homework and it starts to feel overwhelming. At these times, workers often want to take control of the situation and tell the client what to do. Although such action helps the worker feel better about the situation, it does not help the client increase mastery. The worker must communicate urgency while still allowing the client to remain responsible for the situation.

Confrontation of Problems with the Client.

When a worker notices inconsistencies among client words, thoughts, feelings, or actions, it is important to communicate this back to the client to begin exploration. In addition, if the client has stopped working toward the goals of service, exploration is necessary. Such situations are an indication that the alliance is in jeopardy. It may be the client does not trust the worker, the worker is not in tune with the client, or perhaps the client situation has changed to the point at which the service is no longer aligned with the client's needs. Regardless of the reason, the worker must confront inconsistencies or behaviors that interfere with the working alliance. When confronting the client, use descriptive language in sharing observations that there may be a problem. Description grounds the confrontation in observable behavior rather than judgments. It is also important to encourage the client to respond so the situation can be explored.

Clusters of Skill for Navigating Client-Based Challenges.

Expressions of concern and confrontation require the careful use of the skills described in this book. A worker must be very self-aware and in control to ensure the client's best interests remain the focal concern. Concurrently, workers must be tuned into their clients to monitor how they are responding. Describing one's observations is important to avoid sounding judgmental. The combination of skills places the issue on the table for exploration. After the issue is tabled, the worker uses the transitional responding, exploratory questions, probing, and reflecting to determine the problem and move toward solution. There are four critical elements in this type of professional communication.

■ *Introduce the observation of discrepant conditions.* The worker communicates that he or she has noticed something. The statement indicates seriousness without condemning the client. Inherent in the introduction, the worker must be self-aware and in control of his or her feelings so the sharing reflects concern rather than anger or upset. For example, "I have been noticing something that I think we need to discuss. I feel it is important for achieving our goals." A worker who is confronting an inconsistency between the working agreement and client follow-through might say, "I can't help but notice a couple of things that don't seem to fit." Likewise, if a client was giving inconsistent messages (e.g., smiling while describing anger), the same introduction could work.

■ *Describe the behavior, thought, or feeling through sharing the observations.* For example, "For the past two meetings together, the tasks that needed to be done were not complete." With an inconsistency between verbal and nonverbal communication with the client the worker might say, "I noticed you were smiling but talking about how angry you felt."

■ *Describe the inconsistency between the understanding of the relationship and the observed behavior.* For example, "Even though we agree in the meetings to do things at home, the homework is not completed." In the example of the verbal/nonverbal inconsistency the worker might say, "It seems odd that you would smile when talking about how upset you are fighting with your daughter. I don't know what to pay attention to—your statements that you are upset or the smile on your face."

■ *Open up exploration of the observation.* After putting the observation on the table, the worker must explore the situation to determine the meaning for the working alliance. For example, "I am concerned that I may be out of step with you or may be expecting too much. Is there something going on?" In the inconsistency, one might say, "Sometimes people experience several emotions at once when stressful things occur. What kind of experiences are you going through?"

In the exploration following a confrontation, there may be attempts to sidetrack the discussion. This requires the worker to maintain focus throughout the exploration. By keeping the discrepancy focal in the confrontation, the worker can move the discussion toward some form of resolution. If the discussion gets sidetracked, this will not be possible. In some confrontations, maintaining the focus is hard if the client tries to put the worker on the defensive (e.g., states the worker doesn't care).

■ *Case Example.* When working with a batterer to stop his violence (verbal and physical), a worker noted a discrepancy between agreements in session and follow-through. Meetings explored stressful situations and how to resolve situations without escalating tension. However, the batterer never used the alternative solutions. The worker had met with the supervisor and decided to confront the situation with the batterer. The following exchange is an excerpt from the meeting.

> **WORKER:**   I need to talk to you about a concern I have. I am really concerned that our meetings are not helping you as much as we had hoped. We have been meeting for several months. In that time, we have come up with several plans. You decided to use time-out procedures, you developed a cueing system, you were going to use a stress-monitoring system and extra meetings to assure things were cool. I can think of about four other plans that we developed together. Do you remember each of those plans? *(introduces a concern, describes the observations, then validates the observations)*
>
> **BATTERER:**   Yes.
>
> **WORKER:**   You know . . . everytime we arrive at a plan we feel pretty hopeful. I see you get motivated and when you leave you seem like the plan might help. Yet none of the plans have been used when you are with your partner. I am concerned that even though we said we were going to change the violence at home, things are not changing. *(describes the behaviors and discrepancy with the goals)*
>
> **BATTERER:**   (looking angry) CHANGE . . . are you saying I am not good enough!
>
> **WORKER:**   I am not saying you are not good enough, I am saying we are not being true to our goals. The reason we keep meeting is to make these changes, right? *(maintains the focus on the discrepancy and avoids the bait to engage in defensive justification of the confrontation)*
>
> **BATTERER:**   No—I meet with you so you can make me feel better. That's your job, you are my counselor.
>
> **WORKER:**   I do want you to be happy, but I don't believe that is what we agreed on when we started meeting. My understanding is we want you to start being happier at home, not just in this office. To be happier at home, we need to get your violence under control. I cannot do that for you; it can only happen through the changes that you make. *(maintains position and focus on the discrepancy and tries not to invalidate the client)*
>
> **BATTERER:**   (becoming teary) Everyone tells me that I am not good enough and I have to change.
>
> **WORKER:**   I did not make this agreement on my own. Remember when we first met, you are the one that said you wanted to stop beating your partner. Has that changed? *(still avoiding sidetrack attempts and maintains focus on the discrepancy)*
>
> **BATTERER:**   I just want her to treat me better so I can be happy.
>
> **WORKER:**   It seems like you would prefer other people to change to make you happy, but we can't control what others do. We can only control what you do. I am concerned we are not making good use of the opportunities we have had to make that change. *(reflects the thinking themes in the discrepancy and grounds it in the discrepancy)*
>
> **BATTERER:**   So you're taking her side?

WORKER: No, I am taking your side. If you stop for a minute and look deep inside you, you know what you need to do. You knew the day we first met and I think you still know it. Just stop for a minute and check in with yourself (pause). Do you truly believe that everyone else has to change and not you? *(tries an expression of support to reach for motivation)*

BATTERER: No . . .

WORKER: I didn't think so. You are far too bright for that. *(still supportive)*

BATTERER: (mumbles something)

WORKER: Making changes in yourself can be a little uncomfortable can't it? *(note that this is a leading question—don't do it)*

BATTERER: Yeah.

WORKER: To meet your goals, you will need to do some things that are uncomfortable and new. Are you still wanting to try to make the changes that we agreed on when you first came in? *(opens up the possibility for recontracting the goals, still focuses on discrepancy)*

BATTERER: Well . . . I'll try.

EXERCISE 14.1

Navigating Client Challenges to the Alliance

You are working in a job-readiness program for families coming off welfare. You are meeting with a woman on state welfare coming to the program on the insistence of the welfare worker. You have worked with her on job interview skills and writing her resume and cover letters. Each week the client is assigned a task to complete but never brings back any indication that the task has been accomplished. Instead, the client tells you some reason she was not able to complete the homework. You feel you need to address the situation.

1. What observed behaviors would you use to focus the discussion?

2. Write exactly what you would say to introduce the discussion.

3. Write exactly what you would say in your descriptive statement to highlight the discrepancy between goals and behavior.

4. Write the probe you would use to open up the situation for discussion.

5. Where would you try to guide the discussion so the helping relationship might be renegotiated?

Worker-Related Threats to the Working Alliance

Throughout the book there have been multiple discussions of how workers need to be self-aware and in control of their response systems. This theme is important because most ruptures of the working alliance are worker-related. It is critical to understand how different behaviors and approaches disrupt the working alliance. In exploring some of the potential problems, you will discover that ethics and professional values described in Chapter 2 are important in maintaining the alliance. Most of the potential ruptures in the working alliance involve an overlooked value or ethical principle.

Common Worker-Related Threats to the Working Alliance.   Researchers and experts have been exploring the worker-related threats to the working alliance for many years. From the time of Freud, worker behaviors and approaches have been a central concern. In the ensuing years, several worker-related breaches of the alliance have been identified. These threats to the alliance are common and are related to workers forgetting to use their core skills. Workers may overlook professional values, forget to tune in, try to take shortcuts, and find themselves in situations in which the working alliance is threatened.

The threats listed here are painfully common in the field today. Most workers will find that they stumble into these threats at some point in their professional careers. When this occurs, they will have lots of company because every worker makes mistakes. The best workers are able to quickly recover from mistakes so the alliance is not seriously threatened. Effective workers are also very effective in understanding their mistakes and adjusting their methods.

Seven of the most common breaches are described here. When reading the breaches, picture yourself in the position of the person causing the breach. Imagine what it would be like and how you might know when you are engaging in the different behaviors that cause breaches. This will help identify when you are acting in a way that may threaten the alliance.

- *Proceeding as if one knows more than the client about the situation* (Allen et al., 1996; Elkind, 1992). This mistake occurs through worker disengagement into his or her own thinking. Based on this thinking, the worker feels he or she understands more about the situation than the client. When this occurs, the alliance is ruptured because the worker acts as an expert on the client's experience/situation rather than relying on the client.
- *Teaching the client/telling them what to do* (Bischoff & Tracey, 1996; Patterson & Forgatch, 1985; Vallis, Shaw, & McCabe, 1988). When the worker teaches and directs clients in what to do, a breach of the alliance occurs. Such teaching creates

an assumption that the worker has the answer. This type of breach is common in practice models that teach skills.

- *Breaches of empathy* (Elkind, 1992; Patalano, 1997). There are times when the worker fails to tune into the client or some aspect of the client situation. The worker response, consequently, will be off target and potentially upsetting to the client.
- *Frequent disengagement* (Omer, 1997; Patalano, 1997). Workers who frequently disengage from their clients (e.g., start thinking about details while the client is speaking) often have no accurate picture of what the client is expressing. Without a connection, the worker may create his or her own picture of the client experience out of theory and conjecture. Worker responses will be off target resulting in the client feeling disconnected.
- *Intrusions onto the client* (Smith & Fitzpatrick, 1996). Sometimes workers are intrusive, exploring areas of the client situation that are not part of the service contract. For example, some workers ask about clients' personal relationships or go uninvited into the clients' life space (e.g., going to their school, following them at the mall).
- *Overly confrontational* (Miller et al., 1993; Patterson & Forgatch, 1985). Although there are times when a worker must confront an issue, some workers go beyond issue-specific confrontations and become antagonistic in their approach to service. Service becomes an experience of badgering and probing. In such situations, there is no working alliance, but rather a relationship between a client and an inquisitor.

Dealing with Worker Mistakes.   Being human, workers will make mistakes. However, many workers believe they should not make mistakes. This belief creates problems by interfering with the worker's ability to deal with and learn from mistakes. Some of the most common worker mistakes come from wanting the best for clients. Another common source of mistakes is deriving feelings of competence from clients or measuring self-worth through client performance. Most mistakes involve the worker disengaging from the client and moving in a direction associated with worker, rather than client agendas. The best prevention for mistakes is to diligently maintain engagement with the client. Some of the most common sources of worker mistakes include:

- *Overinvesting in client outcomes.* Sometimes workers feel they must accomplish something with a client and end up pushing too hard for changes.
- *Expecting too much from the client.* At times, the goals that the worker envisions for clients are not the goals selected by the client. In such situations, the worker tends to promote decisions and actions that the client may not want.
- *Distancing oneself from the client.* There are times when the client evokes such strong reactions in the worker that the worker would prefer the client withdraw from service. Often this has some connection to client traits (e.g., poor hygiene, habits, and lifestyle) interacting with worker issues (e.g., beliefs about hygiene, etc.).
- *Siding with a single problem perspective.* Often, workers develop an affinity for one person and become biased in favor of that person. When this occurs, other members of the system are viewed as causing the problem rather than being equal partners in the problem.

It is useful to consider worker mistakes as part of learning. If dealt with properly, workers can learn from their mistakes. After all, one learns absolutely nothing from doing things perfectly. The trick to success is to be aware of mistakes, mitigate the potential damaging effects on the client, and understand what went into making the mistake. This process allows the worker to proceed differently next time. The only shame in making a mistake is not using it for learning and future development.

Renegotiating the Relationship after Making a Mistake.

Negotiating mistakes takes the utmost self-awareness and control because workers will tend to feel defensive and want to minimize the mistake. This response helps workers to feel better but places worker feelings as a higher priority than dealing with the mistake. Workers must tune into the impact on the client and assume responsibility for the situation. Finally, workers must engage the client in post-mistake exploration so the client can express his or her feelings and move back into the relationship.

Dealing with mistakes involves a four-step process to ensure that the mistake has minimal impact on the client. Workers should consider a fifth step—discussing the mistake with a supervisor so the learning from the mistake can be maximized.

1. *Identify that a mistake has been made.* The worker must tune into his or her impact on the client through watching nonverbal and verbal behavior suggesting the client is displeased with the worker's actions. In this tuning in, the worker listens to the words used by the client and attends to nonverbal communication to understand how the action has impacted the client system.
2. *Take full responsibility for the mistake.* The worker must control his or her anxiety and openly admit the mistake. This is a descriptive communication telling the clients what the worker did. After acknowledging the actions, the worker takes responsibility for the emotional impact on the client system.
3. *Explore the impact on the relationship.* After the clients have seen the worker take responsibility for the mistakes, they will be open to explore the situation. The worker must ask about client reactions to the mistake. Through such exploring, the worker can validate the client experience and ensure feelings have been expressed.
4. *Negotiate a reparatory response.* Through the exploration, the worker will glean information of client impact and whether the relationship is salvageable. Most mistakes can be overcome by taking full responsibility so the worker and client can negotiate a new system of working rather than finding a new worker. In this step, the worker identifies the nature of the mistake (most are well meaning) and explores better systems of working so similar mistakes can be avoided.

■ **Case Example.**   A worker was working with a family in which a stepmother was very upset with one of her husband's children. The worker wanted to help the family resolve the conflict and suggested a family meeting. In the meeting, the stepmother began verbally attacking the child. The attack was vicious, and it took several attempts to curb the barrage. Eventually, the worker said, "Betty . . . stop." The stepmother became upset and left the office. The worker explored the reactions of other family members and vowed to contact the stepmother the following day. This excerpt is taken from the ensuing phone call.

WORKER: Betty, I am sorry you became so upset during our meeting yesterday. I got you to open up about your feelings and then shut you down. I didn't want things to get out of hand and did not know what to do. It was not fair to shut you down like that. You must be very angry with me. (*identifies mistake and begins to assume responsibility*)

BETTY: Damn right I am angry.

WORKER: I know . . . I didn't mean to make you angry. When I saw how upset you were with Nancy (stepchild) I was worried you might say things you would regret later. I set up the meeting to make things better. I should have spent time understanding the power of your feelings before doing that. (*takes responsibility for setting up ill-fated meeting*)

BETTY: You shouldn't have told me to stop after getting me started.

WORKER: You're right. I shouldn't have even gotten you started unless I knew you and everyone else would be all right. (*reinforces responsibility*) It was my mistake. I am just really glad that you are willing to talk with me still. (*begins to explore impact on relationship*)

BETTY: Well . . . I wasn't going to. I was going to just stop everything and not bother trying to make things better.

WORKER: That would be very sad if you gave up on making things better because of my mistake. (*continued exploration on impact*)

BETTY: It certainly would.

WORKER: You know, I was trying to get you and Nancy to clear the air so fighting would stop. I almost set it up so you would continue to fight. I think I missed how upset you were. How can I tell when you are that upset? (*reinforces impact and begins negotiating*)

BETTY: I don't like to talk until I get really mad.

WORKER: Is there some way I can ask you, or try to get a feel for things, before making another mistake? (*continued negotiation*)

BETTY: Well, you could ask me.

WORKER: How would you respond?

BETTY: I would say that everything is okay.

WORKER: And would it be okay?

BETTY: Not really.

WORKER: So should I ask you if it is really okay or are you trying to avoid talking? (*continued negotiation*)

BETTY: That might work.

WORKER: I would like to do something different from what I did this time. (*reinforces responsibility*)

BETTY: Me too. (laughter)

WORKER: Can I make a promise to always check things out rather than moving too fast? (*finalizing negotiation*)

BETTY: You better.

WORKER: I promise I will check things out.

In this example, see how the worker started by voicing responsibility? If the worker started making excuses, the discussion would have become immediately counterproductive. After the impact had been established, the worker was able to re-engage the woman in the relationship. This point of transition can be seen by the rhythm of the exchanges with the worker talking less and the client making more contributions. After the re-engagement, the worker was able to explore and begin negotiating. If the woman did not re-engage, it would probably lead to a decision to help her find a new worker.

EXERCISE 14.2

Dealing with Worker-Related Problems

A worker in a long-term residential facility for the elderly helps new residents adjust after being placed in the residence. A new client (placed about one month ago) continually stated he was going home. The worker continually reminded him that he is permanently placed, yet the man could not remember due to past strokes. The man's wife visited once in a while, but visits ended with the man getting angry and swearing at her for not taking him home. The wife consequently refused to visit, creating feelings of abandonment in the man. The man became depressed and upset that his wife has abandoned him.

The worker met with the wife and found her to be negative about her husband. She spoke of many years of having to live with him but not loving him. There was a suggestion that the man had ruined her life. As she described their life, the worker began to feel badly for the male client. At one point the woman said, "You don't know what it was like living with him. It was horrible. I put up with him and his dementia for four years and it seems that he is still putting stress on me." The worker responded to the woman by stating, "You don't know what it's like being abandoned in a place like this. Your husband is hurting, and I don't see you caring one bit about his feelings."

1. What type of common mistake was made by this worker?

2. What seems to be the motivating feelings leading to the mistake?

3. Write exactly what you would say to this woman if you had made this mistake.

4. If you were going to try to re-engage this woman to help the man adjust, what feelings can you identify that might motivate her to re-engage with you?

5. Write exactly what you would say to try to negotiate with her so the two of you could work together?

Relationship-Related Threats to the Working Alliance

There are times when challenges to the working alliance evolve from the initial engagement and relationship rather than people's traits and behaviors. These are perhaps the hardest challenges to identify, but often the easiest to resolve. Identification of such challenges is difficult because each person tends to be content. However, there is little progress toward client goals or the alliance seems to be drifting apart.

Indicators of Relationship-Related Threats to the Working Alliance. There are five common relationship-related threats to the working alliance. Most often, relationship-related threats are a result of incomplete negotiation or mixed communication resulting in client and worker operating from different sets of assumptions. In such situations, worker and client work at cross-purposes. Common relationship-based challenges to the alliance include:

■ *Lack of consensus on who to include in service* (Carpenter & Treacher, 1989). There are times when the worker and the client differ on who to include in service. This is most common with larger systems in which the member in service may not have the primary felt problem. If one member is in service, and the worker is having difficulty engaging the person with the primary felt problem, the alliance will be difficult. Alternatively, there are times when the worker, based on a theoretical approach, attempts to engage more people than the client is willing to work with. Again, there is a strain on the working alliance.

■ *Ambivalence about the direction of service* (Carpenter & Treacher, 1989). There are times when clients don't feel comfortable with the direction of service and withdraw collaboration. This is a frequent cause of "resistance" (Rennie, 1994). When clients become hesitant, effective workers immediately engage them in exploration of the alliance to re-establish a direction for work.

■ *Refusal or failure to complete tasks and agreed assignments* (Carpenter & Treacher, 1989). When clients fail or refuse to engage in tasks decided in meetings, there is a clear indication of problems in the working relationship. Such events are a clue that the worker must explore the expectations and procedures involved in the work.

■ *Mismatched goals or expectations about what will occur in or through the service* (Elkind, 1992). Many challenges are a result of differing expectations of what will happen in service. This sets the stage for client and worker to operate at cross-purposes with each other.

■ *Stalemates as a result of worker–client collusion* (Elkind, 1992). There are times when the client and worker issues coincide. In such situations, critical issues may be overlooked or avoided. For example, if both the worker and the client avoid tension, this can create collusion that can interfere with outcomes for the client.

Common Relationship-Related Threats to the Working Alliance.
Workers often work harder than clients in achieving client goals. At these times, workers often experience pressure to accomplish the goals and notice the client is not working as hard. Often, this is because the worker and the client have different visions of service. These situations can produce worker frustration.

Effective workers tune into their frustrations as a possible sign that they have lost their pace with the client. Once the worker has identified a loss of pace, it is important to determine what is disrupting the working alliance so the relationship can be refocused. At this point, the worker can no longer trust the goals negotiated at the beginning of service. Instead, the worker must assess the working relationship to determine sources of confusion or interference.

Assessment requires very strong self-awareness, thinking and tuning-in skills. The worker must be attuned to what is occurring within him- or herself, the client, and the relationship. Through such tuning in the worker identifies patterns and indicators of problems. In assessing the working relationship, there are three very common patterns that emerge. The problems all tend to reflect situations in which the client was not clear or open about his or her desires when first entering service. The three common alliance outcomes are:

■ *Dealing with mismatched or unclear goals.* When clients enter service in crisis or in a confused state, they may not be clear about their goals. Consequently, the initial exploration and assessment may lead to mismatched (between client and worker) or unclear goals. As the client becomes clearer about what her or she wants from service, it may not be the same as the worker's understanding, producing different levels of commitment to the goals.

■ *Dealing with changes in goal parameters.* There are times when client motivation early in service is artificially high due to pain or crisis. This may cause the worker to overestimate the desired goals. When the initial motivating pressures diminish, clients may settle for goal achievement different from the stated goals. The worker, however, not knowing the shift in goals may continue working toward the initial goals.

■ *Dealing with hidden agendas.* There are times when a client comes into service with unarticulated expectations. This is common when the client has the secondary felt problem and the person with the primary felt problem is not part of service. In such situations, the worker observes the client engaging in activities counter to the agreed goals or failing to engage in activities reflecting work toward goals.

In making the assessment of the working alliance, workers first acknowledge a feeling that something is not right. Workers then track the potential threats retrospectively over three to four sessions to assure that the loss of pacing is accurate. The retrospective reflection attempts to determine when things veered offtrack. It is the patterns that carry across weeks that provide the most important information in identifying the nature of the problems.

Strategies for Resolving Relationship-Related Threats to the Alliance.   When client goals appear to shift from the identified parameters, clients often distance themselves from the working alliance, straining the client–worker relationship. In such situations, the worker should recognize there is some sort of change and explore the observations with the client. Resolving the potential problems in the alliance requires tuning in, observation, description, and exploration skills to get the possible problem on the table to be explored. After the potential problem has been explored, the worker must re-engage and recontract to assure the working alliance is adjusted. To accomplish such resolution the worker engages in a four-step communication process.

1. *Identify that the goals have changed for the client or pacing has been lost.* The worker notices he or she is working harder (or is more motivated) on the expressed goals than the client. For example, a woman in a shelter initially expresses that she wants to leave her abusive husband. Later, however, the worker finds that she is seeing him while out of the shelter, and they are talking about reconciling.
2. *Identify actions and interactions that indicate potential problems in the alliance.* The worker identifies the actions and interactions that have caused pacing to be lost. The actions and interactions are noted in a descriptive way so they can be described back to the client rather than expressed as a conclusion.
3. *Communicate the observations back to the client.* The worker describes first the goals and then the observations to the client. For example, "I recall that when you first came in you were talking about getting your own place, but lately you have been spending time with your husband.
4. *Open the discussion up for exploration and recontracting.* The worker opens up the conversation through a question or probe enabling the client to change the initial contract. For example, "Do we need to be rethinking the goal of you getting your own place and start exploring how to keep you safe when you go home?"

In the renegotiation, workers must be open to changing the goals and altering the working relationship. If the worker attempts to continue working toward the old goals or using the old system of work, the alliance may rupture. In some ways, this may feel like starting over. Renegotiation can require discussion with supervisors and altering paperwork in the agency.

In renegotiation, the worker must also be careful to avoid shifting goals every other week, moving into a crisis-prone or unfocused style of working. The assessment of what threatens the relationship is important in deciding direction. To shift goals too often may be a sign that the worker is unfocused with the client. Such situations will require discussions with a supervisor to determine what is occurring with the alliance that is not allowing a clear focus to emerge.

■ *Case Example.*   A woman in a shelter for domestic violence was meeting with a worker about her son. Initially, the woman wanted to increase the child's cooperation around chores, and some clear goals were established about what he should be doing to help around the home. After a period of progress, the woman seemed to become inconsistent with her son. Even though in meetings the worker and woman were focused on making the child perform all the chores, the mother let the child off the hook on an ongoing basis. This was beginning to frustrate the worker so the following conversation ensued.

> **WORKER:**   Fiona, we have been working on these goals for a couple of months and I have noticed Jean improve for a while and then slack off. When watching you, it seems you wanted him to help around dinner and other pressure times, but now you are comfortable with his behavior. Are you rethinking the goals we have been working on?
>
> **MOTHER:**   Well, sort of.
>
> **WORKER:**   Sounds like a little yes and a little no. What is the no part?
>
> **MOTHER:**   Well, I know I should make him do more but dinner and those other times are so busy for me. I just don't want the hassle of trying to make him set the table every night.
>
> **WORKER:**   So making him do the chores creates too much pressure?
>
> **MOTHER:**   Yeah. I got into this to decrease the pressure on myself and it seems stupid to put more on myself to make him do these things.
>
> **WORKER:**   Well, you have him tidying the public areas of the house when he makes a mess and putting his book bag away after school and what else?
>
> **MOTHER:**   He clears the table after meals.
>
> **WORKER:**   Is this enough to take pressure off of you?
>
> **MOTHER:**   It seems to be. I sometimes would like him to do more, but I don't want the battle. It seems like things are good enough right now.
>
> **WORKER:**   You know your own pressures. I think we may have met the goals you really had. What do you think?
>
> **MOTHER:**   I think so.
>
> **WORKER:**   Tell you what—why don't you try things just as they are for awhile and see if you still feel okay with him. If things feel right, then we will stop meeting about his behavior; if not, we will figure out what else will help. How does that sound?

In this example, see how the worker first made observations that the woman was not following through on agreements. When bringing this to the woman's attention, the worker first described observations about the goals of service and then described what she had been observing. This clearly places the issue on the table for exploration in a way that does not condemn the woman. Permission to renegotiate was communicated in the question about whether or not the woman was rethinking the goals. As the worker helped the woman explore the situation, it became clear that the woman had committed to goals that she was not currently willing to follow through on. Instead, she had achieved a point of comfort and was willing to remain at this level. Renegotiation adjusted the alliance so the woman could experience success through redefining her goals.

EXERCISE 14.3

Resolving Relationship-Based Challenges

You are working in a work training program. Your client has attended every meeting and is very open and eager when meeting with you. However, in the past four weeks, the client has not completed tasks agreed upon during the meetings. You have encouraged the client to prepare resumes, write letters of application, and to set up interviews, but the client never seems to follow through. The client is being funded to attend the training after being laid off from a long-term job. You think that he may be attending to collect the extra benefits associated with the training program. You are feeling that the client may have a hidden agenda of keeping income up rather than the expressed goals of trying to get a job. You want to get the issue on the table.

1. What specifically have you observed that indicates there might be a problem in the alliance?

2. Write exactly how you would describe the observations back to the client to get the issue on the table.

3. Write a question that you would ask to begin an exploration of the possible hidden agenda.

Critical Chapter Themes

1. *Resistance* is relational and must be interpreted as an indication that the worker and client are no longer in pace with each other.
2. Threats to the working alliance can be client, worker, or relationship-based with each requiring a different method of getting potential problems on the table for resolution.
3. Whenever the working alliance is threatened, it is important to get the issue on the table so potential problems can be explored and resolved.

4. When a client-related threat to the alliance is evident one must:
   - Balance support with demands so the client never feels judged or attacked.
   - Be descriptive when putting the issue on the table so the client feels supported.
   - Explore the situation so the client position can be validated and the goals of service can be pursued.
5. When a worker-related threat to the alliance is present one must:
   - Acknowledge and validate the impact on the client rather than avoid.
   - Take full responsibility for the problem rather than minimize.
   - Move toward resolution of the problem in a way that maintains the service alliance.
6. When a relationship-related threat to service is evident one must:
   - Identify a clearly describable pattern that indicates a loss of pacing.
   - Be descriptive when putting the potential problem on the table.
   - Explore the situation so that the alliance can be renegotiated.

RECOMMENDED READING

Bischoff, M. M., & Tracey, T. J. G. (1996). Client resistance as predicted by therapist behavior: A study of sequential dependence. *Journal of Counseling Psychology, 42,* 487–495.

Dowd, E. T., & Sanders, D. (1994). Resistance, reactance, and the difficult client. *Canadian Journal of Counselling, 28,* 13–24.

Elkind, S. N. (1992). *Resolving impasses in therapeutic relationships.* New York: Guilford Press.

Patterson, G. R., & Forgatch, M. S. (1985). Therapist behavior as a determinant for client noncompliance: A paradox for the behavior modifier. *Journal of Consulting and Clinical Psychology, 53,* 846–851.

Rennie, D. L. (1994). Clients' accounts of resistance in counselling: A qualitative analysis. *Canadian Journal of Counselling, 28,* 43–57.

Worrell, M. (1997). An existential-phenomenological perspective on the concept of resistance in counselling and psychotherapy. *Counselling Psychology Quarterly, 10,* 5–15.

Maintaining Gains While Ending the Helping Relationship

The experience of ending a relationship is troubling and powerful for most people (Leigh, 1998). Endings affect everybody and can give rise to strong emotions—as evidenced by the myriad songs, tributes, and tears about endings. In extreme situations, suicide, breakdowns, and avoidance are common reactions to ending, reinforcing the power inherent in ending any relationship (Boyer & Hoffman, 1993).

Deeper investment in the relationship is a major predictor of difficulty with ending (Hynan, 1990; Tyron & Kane, 1993). Such findings have direct implications for workers who often forge very strong and intense relationships with clients. This is exacerbated by workers ending the relationship just as the client's life situation improves. This is not an easy task for either the worker or the client.

This chapter explores the complex worker responses instrumental in helping clients separate from the helping relationship. There are several helpful strategies for minimizing the stress and maximizing service gains with clients. In this exploration, the discussion is limited to clients who forged a working alliance with the worker. Clients who dropped out or failed to engage are omitted because the alliance did not develop (Tyron & Kane, 1993). Although it would be ideal to engage such clients in an ending process (Quintana & Holahan, 1992), premature endings do not provide the opportunity to bring closure to the relationship.

CLIENT RESPONSES TO ENDING

People often try to avoid or deny endings when they arise. The following reactions are commonplace in both personal and professional relationships. Examples of personal reactions are provided to illustrate reactions with familiar examples.

- *Denial* (Garland, Jones, & Kolodny, 1976). As endings arise, people avoid the pain through denying or refusing to believe the ending is near. There are two common forms of denial. First, people often deny the upcoming ending by thinking that they will continue meeting (e.g., there are more appointments left). The second form of denial pretends there will be no loss and the relationship was not important. All readers recall friends who have had a relationship end but refused to admit the ending was real. In romantic relationships, this often occurs through statements such as "Let's be friends."

■ *Regression* (Garland et al., 1976). Often as endings become imminent, people regress or exhibit behavior similar to the referring concerns. Another form of regression is to create new symptoms so service might be prolonged. Although regression is not often conscious, it serves as a ploy to get the worker to extend service. Readers may know of someone who, during the ending of a relationship, regressed in their functioning for a period trying to maintain the relationship (e.g., returning to early dating behavior or threatening suicide).

■ *Fight* (Garland et al., 1976). If feelings are difficult, it is not unusual for anger and fighting to erupt around the time of ending. Fighting allows clients to avoid pain through making the ending abrupt while externalizing the feelings (e.g., blaming the other for any upset). Readers all know someone who ended a relationship by picking a fight with the other person. This is a common ploy with adolescent dating.

■ *Flight* (Courtright, Millar, Rogers, & Bagarozzi, 1990). Similar to the fight response, flight avoids feelings by making the ending abrupt while controlling the timing of the end. There are two common strategies of flight. First, members create reasons not to attend the final meeting(s). This allows them to avoid feelings. Second, clients distract from the feelings by planning a party or some other event on the last day. This preempts discussions of the feelings associated with ending. In personal relationships, the flight commonly occurs through people drifting away and not returning phone calls.

■ *Shifting focus* (Courtright et al., 1990). Often when endings are imminent, clients may focus their attention on events outside of service to increase the value of new experiences and decrease the value of the helping relationship. The amplified importance of the new experience diminishes the feelings of loss associated with ending. Readers will know someone who left a relationship by entering a new relationship prior to ending the first.

The experience of ending is influenced by past ending experiences and the client investment in the working alliance (Boyer & Hoffman, 1993). If clients are highly invested and are doing well in service, they are likely to experience a greater loss. Similarly, if the member has experienced past difficult endings, the feelings about the current ending are likely to elicit more severe reactions.

Endings affect all sized client systems including families, groups, and organizations. In Chapter 7, large system processes were discussed to aid tuning into the larger systems. These same processes can be used to tune into the effect of ending on the larger systems. Table 15.1 contains the dynamics associated with each type of process. A review of this table shows the different dynamics occurring as the working alliance is brought to a close.

Toward Facilitating the Ending of Service

With any sized system, workers tune into the dynamics of ending to prevent colluding with avoidance strategies. For endings to be helpful, workers must explore the feelings and thoughts associated with the ending experience. Such exploration affirms the helping alliance yet intervenes into the very difficult feelings associated with endings.

TABLE 15.1   Large System Responses to Ending

Process	Separation Dynamic
Decision making	• Often reverts to the worker as members become ambivalent about ending and withdraw emotionally. • Often avoids decisions so worker must take more active role.
Role structures	• Some rapid shifting of roles as members try on roles they haven't been able to explore while in service. • Tension around ending can cause members to re-occupy the roles they revert to under stress or when threatened with abandonment (e.g., scapegoating).
Control mechanisms	• Relationship control often decreases in influence given the impending loss of the relationships • Fight–flight reactions usually require worker to assumed increased functioning.
Boundaries	• Boundaries re-open with members starting to focus more on nonservice aspects of life. • Increased absenteeism as members re-orient to the outside.
Power–authority structures	• As service ends, the power structure begins to dismantle and reform. • Worker power elevates again as members turn to worker hoping to avoid the ending. • Worker needs to help group through the ending.
Norms	• Norms decrease in influence as the relationship endings are imminent. • Members revert to their own norms around endings as feelings associated with past endings are experienced and individual coping comes into play.
Interactional patterns	• Often patterns of avoidance occur with issues of ending. • Discussions again become somewhat shallow and focused on out-of-group events. • Patterns of denial around the ending (e.g., talking like the service will continue). • Increased sub-grouping as people form smaller groups for support.
Atmosphere	• Tense/avoidant as the members deal with feelings about the ending. • May experience some angry impulses from members who have had very difficult good-byes. • Often some emotional withdrawal to avoid feelings.
Tension-management cycles	• Tension once again becomes high. • Members who drew off tension earlier in service may revert to these roles. • Often the promotion of work and task accomplishment falls on worker.
Cohesion	• Cohesion becomes disrupted as alliance prepares to end. • Members want to retain the closeness and bonds and resist letting go or entertain fantasies of continuing. • Cohesive factions may form to resist the ending.

To begin facilitating termination, it is useful to introduce the concept of ending prior to the last session. Some shorter-term approaches to intervention (e.g., solution-focused) limit the number of sessions at the onset, thus introducing the ending in the first meeting. However, the ending will still require reinforcement as it approaches to prevent reactions.

In deciding when to introduce termination, the worker must consider the potential feelings the ending will create. If the issue is introduced too early it may distract from the work. If too late, it may prevent working through feelings associated with the ending. Generally, the worker needs to be sure that the ending is discussed at least two or three sessions before the final meeting to allow for people to respond and complete their work.

The same power that creates anxiety and avoidance in endings imputes a strong potential for positive growth (Anthony & Pagano, 1998). There are two potential outcomes that can be tremendously strength producing in clients:

- Many clients and client systems have had difficult endings in their lives and the feelings associated with such endings may be unresolved. Through experiencing the ending of the working alliance, old feelings are expressed, resolved, and replaced by a new ending experience.
- As clients leave service, they have a different experience of themselves. With careful planning and facilitation, this experience can be launched toward the future so service gains can be maintained.

Endings consequently present important challenges. First, workers are challenged to facilitate the ending of service without colluding with resistance or avoiding (Boyer & Hoffman, 1993). This is a difficult challenge because workers, like everyone else, have some anxiety about endings. This requires self-awareness and self-control in the worker.

The second major challenge for the worker is to facilitate the generalization of changes so clients maintain their mastery into the future. This requires tuning in and predictive thinking so the worker can guide clients toward the future. Carrying gains forward minimizes the risk of relapse as workers help clients identify risk factors and plan for client responses.

PAST, PRESENT, AND FUTURE: THE KEYS TO HEALTHY ENDINGS

The power associated with endings comes from the convergence of three times. Although the past, present, and future exist in every moment of life, people focus on one time to the exclusion of others. When we are planning something, we are future-focused, thinking little of the other times. When sad, people often dwell on the past, ignoring the future. This shifting of focus is common in the way people live.

When one deals with an ending, the pattern of focusing on a single time dimension breaks down because all three times have equal urgency. One cannot ignore any of the times because of feelings associated with each. To help clients process the ending of service, it is important to attend to the difficult feelings associated with each time.

Responding to Issues of the Past

Issues of the past focus on both individual histories and the history of the working alliance. The worker, consequently, must attend to multiple dimensions of ending service. The worker helps the client gain mastery of his or her individual responses to ending as the helping relationship terminates. In larger systems, the worker must also attend to the multiple relationships and how the ending impacts the web of interconnected relationships in the client's experience. Individuals will have different experiences associated with each relationship.

At the individual level, feelings associated with past good-byes are agitated as soon as the ending of service approaches. Clients with past rejections, losses, or other difficult partings experience difficult reactions. It is the worker's job to help the client(s) acknowledge and express these difficulties with endings. Through exploring the past good-byes concurrent with the emotional reactions to the current ending, a full range of experience can be explored (Anthony & Pagano, 1998).

At the working alliance level, the past is more contained and the history is shared. The shared history provides an opportunity to highlight the growth of each member during the time of service. Such exploration provides an opportunity to affirm clients and reflect on the service history (Garland et al., 1976). Affirmation includes exploring the gains and changes made by the client during service provision (Murphy & Dillon, 1998). Such exploration logically leads to an exploration of feelings that are associated with the ending of the working relationship.

Given the power inherent in people's historical experiences of endings, the worker uses a skill set attending to individual historical experiences as well as a review of service progress. The commonly used skills at this juncture include:

- *Tuning-in skills.* The worker tunes into the responses of the system members and uses past preliminary tuning in to understand each member's experience.
- *Thinking skills.* The worker uses his or her knowledge of each member's history, goals, and performance during service to understand responses to ending.
- *Engagement skills.* The worker leads system members in sharing their feelings about past endings. The worker also engages the system members in an exploration of the shared time together.
- *Reflecting skills.* The worker reflects on his or her own, and other people's, responses to endings so that meanings and feelings can be expressed and clarified.
- *Questioning skills.* The worker uses questioning to explore the impact of the past good-byes and memories of the shared history of the client system while in service.

Workers often use these skills in different combinations or response strategies. The following response strategies are frequently used to focus the exploration of past issues associated with endings.

Working with Personal Histories of Ending/Loss.   With the emotional power associated with people's histories of ending, workers need to attend to the different experiences of the members to move on with the current termination experience. Some of the more common strategies of dealing with the individual endings include:

- *Rotten good-byes.* Almost everyone has had difficult good-byes that still evoke emotion. It is easy for the worker to share his or her own feelings about good-byes with the client(s) to help them get focused. Through talking about how the worker hates good-byes and how many endings are really rotten experiences, the client engages in an exploration of his or her own ending experiences.

- *Exploring the rot.* Once feelings about endings are expressed, it is useful to move from the feelings to assess the elements making good-byes so difficult. Such discussion elicits common themes such as rejection, powerlessness over the ending, and loss of important people. In larger systems, such exploration can pull members closer as each has different experiences, but common feelings.

- *Possible "good" good-byes.* After exploring negative affect, it is sometimes useful to explore if there have been any good-byes that have been okay. Through exploring positive good-byes, the potential for a healthy good-bye is introduced and a model for the ending can be developed.

Working with the History of the Helping Relationship.   After exploration of personal histories of ending, the worker can shift focus to termination of the working alliance. As the focus shifts from the feelings within the client to the shared experiences of the helping relationship, progress and shared experiences are explored. The following strategies are commonly used to accomplish this focus.

- *Review.* To help clients focus on the current ending, it is useful to reflect back on the chronology of service provision so changes can be highlighted (Murphy & Dillon, 1998). A brief discussion of the historical highlights of service often yields some stories and affirmations for the client(s).
- *Reinforcement of progress.* In discussing the service history, it is important to point out progress in the client(s) (Murphy & Dillon, 1998). This affirms that they are doing well and that they have made important changes. Positive changes are often ignored during the day-to-day lives of the clients, and they may be unaware of their progress. In the ending, the worker can highlight and reinforce their growth.
- *Remember when's.* To help lighten the ending, humorous anecdotes about the worker, client, or events can be helpful. This is particularly useful with larger client systems in which there will be many shared experiences. Remembering lighter moments allows members to laugh a little and also take some positive memories away with them.

■ ***Case Example.***   As part of an internship, a student ran a social-skills group for developmentally disabled adults who were preparing for independent living. The group had become cohesive and the men had arranged to continue the group with another staff member after the student left. The group had also explored ways to raise money to fund social events. There were five men in the group. All were in their mid-twenties and operating in the mild range of mental retardation. They worked in a sheltered workshop with periodic placements in competitive employment settings. The men either lived with parents, in foster homes, or in group home settings. All of the men had also been placed in institutions as children. The men included:

Raulf

Raulf was a 25-year-old Egyptian male. He was not a highly active member of the group following the lead of the more dominant members such as Roberto, Anthony, and Dennis. He was bright and functioned well in his placements. He had a physical problem that resulted in a severe limp. He did not talk much. Raulf was placed in an institution at the age of 6. His parents visit him at Christmas but have little contact beyond special occasions.

Roberto

Roberto was a 27-year-old Hispanic male. He was very high functioning and often served as the group spokesperson due to his advanced verbal skills. Roberto was active in the community and lived in specialized foster care. He disliked having people tell him what to do. He was placed in an institution at the age of 4 and has not seen his parents since his placement. Roberto was first on the list for a supported independent-living apartment.

Anthony

Anthony was a 25-year-old African American male. He lived in an institution from the age of 3 until 22. He cannot remember his parents. He currently lives in a specialized foster home and is slated for a supported independent-living apartment.

Cleveland

Cleveland was a 26-year-old African American male. He was one of the lower functioning group members. He was placed in the institution at the age of 5 and remained there until 12, when his parents returned him to their home where he still lives. He was scheduled for competitive employment and was being considered for a supported independent-living placement.

Dennis

Dennis was a 24-year-old Caucasian male living in a group home. He was placed in an institution at birth and his parents never attempted to keep in contact. He was moved to a community placement at 12, when it was discovered that he was misdiagnosed. Apparently, most of his difficulty was a hearing impairment. He is fairly high functioning mentally and can now hear with hearing aids.

In the last official group meeting, the group leader had tuned into the past good-byes and wanted to be sure that the power in the ending did not create problems for the men. The worker was aware that frequent staff changes in the setting had jaded the men somewhat about how professionals would come and go. The worker consequently began the discussion of ending with the rotten good-byes technique.

WORKER: I hate good-byes. Most of them are not very good. Have you guys had any crappy good-byes? *(introduce the issue of ending)*

ROBERTO: Yeah . . . I had crappy good-byes. I never see my parents. They didn't want me because I had a disability.

DENNIS: Me too . . . I see my parents sometimes but when I was a kid, I was stuck at the state school.

CLEVELAND: Me too.

ANTHONY: (almost simultaneously with Cleveland) Me too.

WORKER: Raulf, these guys have had difficult good-byes, especially around the institution; what have your good-byes been like? *(making sure all are engaged)*

RAULF: Not good.

WORKER: What do you think makes good-byes so crappy? *(trying to engage in exploration)*

RAULF: They hurt inside.

ROBERTO: Yeah . . . and people leave because they don't want to be with you.

OTHERS: (mumbles) Uh huh.

WORKER: So it seems that most good-byes are painful and it seems like people are dumping you. *(reflecting meaning)*

ALL: Uh huh.

WORKER: Have there been any good endings that you can think of? *(trying to elicit exceptions)*

ROBERTO: There aren't any . . . people just leave and you stay. You never see them again.

WORKER: That is difficult because the group is ending. That is a difficult good-bye. I feel like I am leaving you guys in the middle of something—like the middle of a stream. *(introduce the group ending, reflecting emotion)*

ROBERTO: You are abandoning us in the middle of the stream. You are like one of them (staff) leaving us. We should get him.

DENNIS: Like how?

ROBERTO: Well . . . he is Canadian. We can have him deported back to Canada.

CLEVELAND: That will show him.

DENNIS: Yeah . . . let's plant some pot in his brief case and call the cops.

ROBERTO: And immigration.

ANTHONY: Yeah . . . call them both on him.

ROBERTO: That will fix him for leaving us.

WORKER: Sounds like you are angry with me for making you go through another good-bye *(reflecting meaning)*

ALL: We sure are.

WORKER: I bet, we have done a lot together. You guys don't even seem like the same guys who started this group five months ago. *(begin the review)*

DENNIS: What do you mean?

WORKER: Well, what do you remember from when we first got together? *(using questioning to continue the review)*

ROBERTO: I remember you were supposed to teach us cooking or something like that.

ANTHONY: Yeah, we got pretty good at cooking.

CLEVELAND: . . . and now we got a club.

ROBERTO: . . . and the club will keep going because it is ours.

DENNIS: As long as you don't start wearing diapers again.

ALL: (laughter)

WORKER: So Roberto has made some changes you like. *(reflecting meaning)* What other changes have you noticed? *(using questioning to continue the review)*

In the group exchange, see how difficult the good-byes are for these men. The history still evoked emotion as they spoke about past good-byes and about the current ending. With permission, the men were able to express feelings about the ending of the group. They were also able to use fantasy to try to feel they had some control over the ending. The worker became quiet during the expressive sections as the members were doing the work. Notice how the worker activity levels were much higher earlier as he tried to get the men engaged about the ending. Worker activity again increased when he tried to transition the group into reviewing the shared history.

EXERCISE 15.1

Responding to Issues of the Past

Based on the preceding example, think about the ending issues evident with this group.

1. What are the historical ending themes that will make this ending difficult for the group members?

   a. Raulf:

   b. Roberto:

   c. Cleveland:

    d. Anthony:

    e. Dennis:

2. Based on the histories of the group members, what do you think are the important themes to address in this ending?

3. What was the worker statement that actually engaged the group in the exploration of past issues? Why do you think this worked?

4. When Roberto made his statement about the worker abandoning the group and wanted to "get him," what reflective statement would you use to capture Roberto's processing?

5. When Raulf said that good-byes hurt, others agreed with him. Write a question that you might use to explore the group experiences with painful good-byes?

Responding to Issues of the Present

The past tends to bring feelings of loss into the ending process, but the feelings must be addressed in the present. Consequently, the worker focuses on how clients deal with their feelings in the here-and-now (Murphy & Dillon, 1998; Sells & Hays, 1997). After clients have expressed their feelings about the past, the worker re-orients them to their feelings about both the current ending and about the current relationship(s).

    Regardless of the client system size, the struggle to deal with feelings in the present is consistent. Even in organizations one finds avoidance strategies such as picking fights, phoning in sick, and taking vacations that ensure endings are avoided. For example, an agency providing adult mental health services had a ten-year history of fairly high turnover. Although many departing staff were dynamic and popular, they were never described as a loss to the agency. Instead, management would tarnish their reputations as soon as notice was given, so no feelings of loss were experienced by the time of ending.

    Workers must help members of the client system acknowledge and explore their feelings about the ending. Such feelings include loss (the ending of relationships) and feelings of anxiety (what will it be like without the relationship, can I make it). If clients cannot table these feelings for exploration, they are likely to be suppressed or acted out rather than used to build growth-focused experiences.

The second goal of responding is to create an ending experience that is qualitatively different from previous ending experiences. The worker tunes into the themes of the past endings and then engages the members to find ways to end without defensive responses or difficulty. This development of new experiences contains the potential benefit for changing clients' future ending experiences.

The worker uses a combination of skills to attend to the present-focused ending needs of clients. The most common skills used at this point in the ending include:

- *Self-awareness/control.* The worker builds on their self-awareness of ending responses to assure he or she does not avoid exploring the difficult feelings. This prevents colluding with client avoidance. Self-awareness also provides insights and feelings that can be shared with the clients to promote engagement and exploration.
- *Tuning-in skills.* The worker tunes into the avoidance and struggles that each member has about exploring difficult feelings.
- *Thinking skills.* The worker considers the different reactions and themes in the responses so they can be tabled for exploration.
- *Engagement skills.* The worker encourages members of the system to discuss their responses to the ending and find ways to make the ending different.
- *Reflection skills.* The worker uses reflecting skills to validate and express the different feelings associated with the ending.
- *Questioning skills.* The worker uses questioning to make sure that the system members explore the different issues associated with the present.

The worker uses these skills in activities to promote a thorough and healthy ending experience for the members of the client system. The following strategies are common when dealing with present-focused issues of ending.

- *Make it different.* After discussing past endings and how they have been difficult, the worker explores how the clients can make this ending different or somehow better than the other endings. This begins to put the clients in control of how feelings will be expressed or not expressed and shifts focus from the past to the present.

- *Cumulative good-bye effects.* Sometimes members are dealing with other good-byes at the same time they are ending service. The worker must be wary of a cumulative effect when there are several concurrent endings. In such situations, the worker should acknowledge the other good-byes and allow expression of feelings about the multiple endings. The worker may include the other endings when trying to make the good-byes different.

- *"I thought . . . but now . . ." discussions.* It is important to highlight the clients' growth as they end service. Workers can engage clients in expressing such observations by modeling a mode of sharing. This is easily accomplished through sharing an impression from earlier in service and then adding a present observation or feeling. For example, "You know, when you first came into the group I didn't think we would get along because I am much older than you. Now I am finding that I will miss you. I will especially miss the way you call me . . ." By reflecting first on the past and then on the present, the worker can bring the feelings and observations forward for discussion.

■ *Highlight resistance.* Given that people will often avoid the feelings associated with ending, workers can use expressions of their resistance to engage others in exploring sensitive feelings. For example, "You know, I hate good-byes so much that I am looking for ways to avoid saying good-bye. Do you ever feel like that?" Such statements can engage clients in discussions about what feelings they want to avoid.

■ *What I'll miss.* When the worker reflects on what they will miss in each member, themes of loss are introduced along with modeling expressiveness (Murphy & Dillon, 1998). Such expression helps the client(s) experience feelings of loss associated with endings. The items chosen to highlight in the statement also affirms aspects of the client's personality. If the worker can get others (especially in larger systems) to talk about what they will miss, a fuller discussion is possible.

■ *Evaluation.* As members are leaving service, it is helpful to have them evaluate their experience (Murphy & Dillon, 1998). This involves soliciting feedback about (1) what was helpful, (2) what was not helpful, and (3) changes they would recommend in any upcoming services. Evaluation allows clients to express feelings about service in a structured manner while introducing the inevitability of the future without service.

■ ***Case Example***   In the group described earlier, the worker wanted to get members to discuss current feelings. Although the group was going to continue with a new leader, there was still an ending of the group as it existed. (In a situation in which a group continues but the leader leaves, it is easy for members to avoid present feelings because only one person is leaving.) The worker felt it was important to attend to the ending given the turnover of people in the lives of the group members. The worker especially wanted to help the members explore abandonment feelings given their histories. The following excerpt demonstrates how the group struggled with the present issues.

> **WORKER:**   You know, you guys have all had such icky good-byes in the past. How can we make this good-bye better? *(try to focus on present and making it different)*
>
> **ROBERTO:**   This isn't really a good-bye for us; we are just getting rid of you.
>
> **ALL:**   (laughter)
>
> **WORKER:**   How will getting rid of me change the group? *(trying to engage rather than avoid)*
>
> **DENNIS:**   Well, Carmine is prettier than you.
>
> **ALL:**   (laughter)
>
> **WORKER:**   She is prettier . . . how will it change the way you guys act? *(still working on engagement)*
>
> **CLEVELAND:**   We'll act better.
>
> **ROBERTO:**   Yeah, we won't be able to make fun of her like we do with you.

ANTHONY: No

RAULF: No way.

WORKER: So really, the way you guys are acting will change plus the group will look better. Sounds like the group as you know it today will never be the same. *(reflecting on meaning and pushing engagement in dealing with the ending)*

ROBERTO: Yeah, I guess so.

WORKER: I know it sure will for me because I won't be there. You guys will be working with someone else. You know, I sometimes try not to even think about that because it is hard to think of this group without me as part of it. I am really going to miss you guys. *(reflecting on themes of loss)*

RAULF: Me too.

DENNIS: You are not going anywhere, Raulf.

WORKER: I think Raulf is saying that when the group changes that will be a bit of a loss . . . is that right? *(reflecting the meaning)*

RAULF: (nods)

DENNIS: I don't like thinking about the change either. I like the group the way it is.

ROBERTO: Yeah, I didn't always like it when you guys made me do things, but I kind of like the way things are now.

CLEVELAND: I am going to miss things.

WORKER: What about you, Anthony—what will you miss?

ANTHONY: I will miss the way we joke around with you.

ROBERTO: Yeah, most staff get mad when you tease them.

ALL: Uh huh.

WORKER: So you guys will have to learn new ways of getting along when Carmine comes into the group. Will it be hard to let go of the teasing and things that we do together? *(reflecting on meaning then exploring with questions)*

DENNIS: Yeah, that is half the fun of the group.

ROBERTO: Yeah, we should tell Carmine that that is one of the rules.

ALL: Uh huh.

WORKER: It does sound like it is ending—so you guys have been avoiding my question. How can we make this good-bye different? *(redirecting back to the issue)*

ROBERTO: You could come back! Not like those other staff.

DENNIS: Yeah, for the car wash.

WORKER: I could help with the car wash. *(negotiating how to be different)*

DENNIS: . . . and the coffee house too.

WORKER: I am willing to help out, but if you keep bringing me back, we won't have an ending will we? *(still negotiating and reflecting on the avoidance)*

DENNIS: No

WORKER: . . . and I will be graduating and having to move on to a new job. So we will have to make this ending a good one. I can do my part to help out on those things but what will you do differently this time? *(still stressing the meaning of the ending for all system members—pushing for the difference)*

ROBERTO: I usually swear at people when they are going, it is a fight.

WORKER: Can we do this one without fighting? *(negotiating the difference)*

ROBERTO: I'll try, but I get mad when people leave—I feel like they are leaving me.

RAULF: Yeah.

WORKER: When people have those sad feelings is it easier to fight? *(reflecting the feeling)*

ALL: Uh huh.

WORKER: When we fight, what feelings are we trying to avoid? *(exploring the feelings)*

CLEVELAND: Sad.

ANTHONY: Yeah, sad ones.

DENNIS: I hate good-byes.

EVERYONE: Me too.

WORKER: I find it really hard because I am the one to leave and I am being replaced. Carmine will get to have the fun with you guys now. *(reflecting the ending and orienting to the future)*

DENNIS: She better have fun and joke around, like you.

WORKER: That is one of the things you would like to keep, is it? Are there any other things about the group or how I was working in the group that you would recommend doing again in other groups? *(moving to evaluation)*

ROBERTO: I liked the cooking. I have a recipe book now.

DENNIS: I just liked the way that we got to decide on what to do . . . not like a staff or a teacher.

ANTHONY: I like that and the joking.

WORKER: What would you recommend never doing again? *(continued evaluation)*

CLEVELAND: Leaving.

ALL: Yeah.

WORKER: What else?

ROBERTO: I like the group. I wouldn't change anything.

WORKER: There is usually something. I wouldn't want to inflict others with the same mistakes I made here. *(continued evaluation)*

DENNIS: I think we could have a better room for the weeks that we are not cooking.

ROBERTO: That would be good.

WORKER: Okay.

In this example, see how busy the worker is at times directing the flow of discussion toward the present issues. One can also see how members will try to deny or minimize the endings to avoid their feelings. However, when the feelings surface, they tend to be safely processed among the group.

EXERCISE 15.2

Present-Oriented Responding

Based on the preceding example, think through the following questions and issues related to present-oriented responding.

1. What was the issue that seemed toughest to the worker and made him want to avoid discussing the ending?

2. What do you think might have been toughest for you if you were ending with this group?

3. Using your interactive tuning-in skills, what seemed to be the most critical issue for each of the members?

   a. Raulf:

   b. Roberto:

   c. Dennis:

   d. Anthony:

   e. Cleveland:

4. Identify three ways that group members tried to avoid talking about their feelings associated with the ending.

5. What was the statement that finally got the group members engaged in talking about their feelings associated with the ending?

6. When Dennis was negotiating with the worker about what to do differently, there seemed to be a feeling underneath his statements. Write a reflective statement that you would use in response to this theme.

7. Anthony and Cleveland seemed tuned into feelings when the worker asked them about what feelings were under the fighting. Write a question that you could use in response to help them explore their feelings.

Responding to Issues of the Future

The final time element strongly evident in ending is the future. Future-oriented issues are twofold. First, the members will go forward from the helping relationship with no further input from the worker. Even if they see each other, it will not be the same (Murphy & Dillon, 1998). The second element of the future is the client's ability to maintain and generalize the gains from service (Okun, 1997). Maintaining service gains is important because it focuses on prolonging the outcomes (Rzepnicki, 1991).

Anxiety is the dominant emotion in the future-oriented elements. Clients must move into the future without the support of the helping relationship to master problem situations on their own. This often creates anxiety, particularly if the client still credits the worker for his or her current success. It is important that workers help clients build confidence in their strengths and ability to succeed without support (Epston & White, 1995).

Workers use a combination of skills to orient clients toward the future. Although combinations of skill are used differentially depending on whether you are facilitating closure or projecting success forward, you will tend to use the following skills.

- *Tuning-in skills.* The worker needs to tune in to the individual fears and potential future risks of relapse for the client(s).
- *Thinking skills.* The worker uses prepositional thinking to predict which strengths should be reinforced to support success in light of the potential risks for relapse.

- *Engagement skills.* The worker engages clients in expressing their anxiety and in anticipating/planning for future challenges.
- *Reflection skills.* The worker often uses reflecting responses to capture client processing about the ending concurrent with reflecting strengths to promote confidence.
- *Sharing observations skills.* The worker shares observations of client growth and ability to help the client develop confidence and plan for future challenges. Effective workers share observed indicators of success to instill a sense that the tools for success have been achieved.

These skills are implemented through strategies and activities that occur in the last couple of meetings. Different strategies are used for the different future-oriented goals of ending. Some of the most common strategies are described here.

Carrying Relationship(s) into the Future.   The first challenge in responding to the future issues is to carry the influence of the helping relationship into the future as service ends. The helping relationship is an experience that clients can draw on in times of need. Some of the methods for helping clients carry the relationship into the future include:

- *Token gifts.* In helping the members put closure on the relationships, token gifts can be used so members take something concrete into the future symbolizing their successes in service. The token gifts ideally will reflect and build on an experience during service. The tokens do not need to be purchased gifts; homemade items such as certificates or cartoons serve this purpose. For example, a worker ending a children's group for child witnesses of spouse abuse used small bracelets with colored beads. In the last meeting, the worker would go through the bead colors and explain how each reminded him of the work done by the child. The child would then take the bracelet home after the last session.

- *"What I'll take with me."* Workers often promote closure on the relationship along with exploring the future by reflecting on what they will take with them as a result of the helping relationship. The worker then asks the clients what they will take with them to use in their lives. This strategy provides feedback about the helping relationship while promoting future postulations (Epston & White, 1995).

- *"When I see you next."* As relationships are ending, it is often helpful to talk about bumping into clients in the future and how they might talk with each other. Having members project such discussions introduces the changes in relationship and highlights future potentialities.

Maintaining the Gains.   The second challenge of intervention is to help the client system maintain the gains made through service (Perri, 1998). As clients move into the future from the helping relationship, there is a risk of relapse into problematic patterns. Consequently, workers focus on helping the client maintain mastery. Some of the common strategies for achieving this goal include:

- *Visualizing success.* When clients have achieved changes in their action systems, it is often useful to have them visualize challenging situations in which they successfully use their new skills (Epston & White, 1995). This helps them visualize success in the future and outside of the helping relationship.

- *Follow-up.* When clients have altered very difficult action systems, a follow-up system may be used to maintain the changes into the future (Okun, 1997). A schedule (diminishing over time) of additional contacts or meetings can monitor and support changes. In developing a follow-up plan, workers must still address the ending because the current helping relationship will end. Follow-up activities can create the illusion of continued service causing people to avoid exploration.

- *Planning relapse prevention.* It is useful to have members review high-risk situations prior to ending to think through how they can identify and respond to such situations (Brownell, Marlatt, Lictenstein, & Wilson, 1986). Effective workers use very realistic situations based on the client's history and life circumstances.

- *Paths back.* When ending, it can be useful to identify potential events that would necessitate re-engaging in service (Lebow, 1995). Identifying risk markers and methods of assessing situations helps clients know when more intervention is needed. Providing clients with a reconnection plan is important (e.g., coupons for free follow-up meetings). Even if clients do not reconnect, they will feel that there is a safety net.

- *"My voice will go with you."* Workers can help preempt relapse by predicting that there will be times of challenge when the client will recall discussions from service. The suggestion that the client will hear the worker's voice helping to solve a problem has been effective in helping clients move into the future with success (Rosen, 1982).

■ **Case Example.**   When ending with the group discussed in the previous two sections, the worker wanted to shift the focus to the future. The worker felt this was important given that there was to be a new person helping the group members. The following excerpt captures some of the exchange that occurred during the future-oriented discussions.

> **WORKER:**   You mentioned that you want to have fun when Carmine begins helping you with the group; what other things do you hope might happen?
>
> **RAULF:**   Eating.
>
> **WORKER:**   You want to keep the cooking part of the group?
>
> **RAULF:**   Yes.
>
> **WORKER:**   . . . and what else?
>
> **ROBERTO:**   Well, we want to keep on raising money so we can put on fun things for everyone.
>
> **DENNIS:**   Yeah, that is why we are together and we want to keep control of our own money.
>
> **WORKER:**   What will you say to her to convince her that these things are important to you.
>
> **ANTHONY:**   We'll just tell her that this is what we want.

WORKER: What room will you be meeting in? *(moving to visualize success)*

ANTHONY: This one.

WORKER: Where will she sit?

CLEVELAND: She can sit where you are.

WORKER: Okay, now picture her sitting here. What exactly will you say? *(continuing the visualization)*

ROBERTO: I can speak for the group. I will say, "Carmine, the group wants you to know the kinds of things we do. We get together and cook but while we eat we plan things that we can do for fun. We raise money so we can have dances and coffeehouses so everyone in the shelter can have fun."

DENNIS: . . . and because we raise the money, we are in charge of the money.

WORKER: You sound impressive to me. *(reflecting success)* Do you think she will go along with you?

ROBERTO: She better . . . or we will find someone else to help us.

In this exchange, notice how the group was able to orient to the future and begin to picture a successful discussion with the new staff member. The group was working cooperatively and was able to visualize themselves with the new person rather than with the leader who was leaving.

EXERCISE 15.3

Future-Oriented Responding

1. In tuning into the themes among the members in the previous excerpt, what seems to be the critical issue for the members as they add the new worker?

2. What do you think will need to happen in order for the group to stay together and succeed in the future?

3. What do you base this conclusion on?

4. What would you say to them to engage them in an exploration of what they need to do to make that happen?

5. Write a reflective statement that would indicate how important this is to the group's beliefs about success in the future.

6. What did you observe in the content themes of each member that identifies what is important to him?

   a. Roberto:

   b. Raulf:

   c. Cleveland:

   d. Anthony:

   e. Dennis:

Critical Chapter Themes

1. It is very common for people, including workers, to avoid the difficult feelings associated with endings. Workers must take control of their own feelings to help explore their reactions to ending service.
2. The power associated with endings comes from the convergence of past, present, and future in the act of ending. Workers must attend to all three times when helping clients with the ending.
3. Issues of the past include feelings associated with past difficult endings along with the ending of the service relationship. It is important to focus on both the personal past endings as well as the current ending.
4. Issues of the present include helping clients explore their feelings about ending along with evaluating their experience of service.

5. Future-oriented issues include helping clients to move out of service without undue anxiety and helping clients maintain their gains into the future.
6. Workers use different combinations of skill and strategies to help clients with the impact of each time element.

RECOMMENDED READINGS

Anthony, S., & Pagano, G. (1998). The therapeutic potential for growth during the termination process. *Clinical Social Work Journal, 26,* 281–296.

Boyer, S. P., & Hoffman, M. A. (1993). Counselor affective reactions to termination: Impact of counselor loss history and perceived client sensitivity to loss. *Journal of Counseling Psychology, 40,* 271–277.

Brownell, K. D., Marlatt, G. A., Lichtenstein, E., & Wilson, G. T. (1986). Understanding and preventing relapse. *American Psychologist, 41,* 765–782.

Epston, D., & White, M. (1995). Termination as a rite of passage: Questioning strategies for a therapy of inclusion. In R. A. Neimeyer & M. J. Manoney (Eds.), *Constructivism in psychotherapy* (pp. 339–354). Washington, DC: American Psychological Association.

Perri, M. G. (1998). The maintenance of treatment effects in the long-term management of obesity. *Clinical Psychology: Science & Practice, 5,* 526–543.

Rzepnicki, T. L. (1991). Enhancing the durability of intervention gains: A challenge for the 1990s. *Social Service Review, 65,* 92–109.

APPENDIX

Code of Ethics of the National Association of Social Workers

Approved by the 1996 NASW Delegate Assembly and revised by the 1999 NASW Delegate Assembly

PREAMBLE

The primary mission of the social work profession is to enhance human well-being and help meet the basic human needs of all people, with particular attention to the needs and empowerment of people who are vulnerable, oppressed, and living in poverty. A historic and defining feature of social work is the profession's focus on individual well-being in a social context and the well-being of society. Fundamental to social work is attention to the environmental forces that create, contribute to, and address problems in living.

Social workers promote social justice and social change with and on behalf of clients. "Clients" is used inclusively to refer to individuals, families, groups, organizations, and communities. Social workers are sensitive to cultural and ethnic diversity and strive to end discrimination, oppression, poverty, and other forms of social injustice. These activities may be in the form of direct practice, community organizing, supervision, consultation, administration, advocacy, social and political action, policy development and implementation, education, and research and evaluation. Social workers seek to enhance the capacity of people to address their own needs. Social workers also seek to promote the responsiveness of organizations, communities, and other social institutions to individuals' needs and social problems.

The mission of the social work profession is rooted in a set of core values. These core values, embraced by social workers throughout the profession's history, are the foundation of social work's unique purpose and perspective:

- service
- social justice
- dignity and worth of the person
- importance of human relationships
- integrity
- competence

This constellation of core values reflects what is unique to the social work profession. Core values, and the principles that flow from them, must be balanced within the context and complexity of the human experience.

Copyright © 1996, National Association of Social Workers, Inc.

PURPOSE OF THE NASW CODE OF ETHICS

Professional ethics are at the core of social work. The profession has an obligation to articulate its basic values, ethical principles, and ethical standards. The *NASW Code of Ethics* sets forth these values, principles, and standards to guide social workers' conduct. The *Code* is relevant to all social workers and social work students, regardless of their professional functions, the settings in which they work, or the populations they serve.

The *NASW Code of Ethics* serves six purposes:

1. The *Code* identifies core values on which social work's mission is based.
2. The *Code* summarizes broad ethical principles that reflect the profession's core values and establishes a set of specific ethical standards that should be used to guide social work practice.
3. The *Code* is designed to help social workers identify relevant considerations when professional obligations conflict or ethical uncertainties arise.
4. The *Code* provides ethical standards to which the general public can hold the social work profession accountable.
5. The *Code* socializes practitioners new to the field to social work's mission, values, ethical principles, and ethical standards.
6. The *Code* articulates standards that the social work profession itself can use to assess whether social workers have engaged in unethical conduct. NASW has formal procedures to adjudicate ethics complaints filed against its members.* In subscribing to this *Code*, social workers are required to cooperate in its implementation, participate in NASW adjudication proceedings, and abide by any NASW disciplinary rulings or sanctions based on it.

The *Code* offers a set of values, principles, and standards to guide decision making and conduct when ethical issues arise. It does not provide a set of rules that prescribe how social workers should act in all situations. Specific applications of the *Code* must take into account the context in which it is being considered and the possibility of conflicts among the *Code*'s values, principles, and standards. Ethical responsibilities flow from all human relationships, from the personal and familial to the social and professional.

Further, the *NASW Code of Ethics* does not specify which values, principles, and standards are most important and ought to outweigh others in instances when they conflict. Reasonable differences of opinion can and do exist among social workers with respect to the ways in which values, ethical principles, and ethical standards should be rank ordered when they conflict. Ethical decision making in a given situation must apply the informed judgment of the individual social worker and should also consider how the issues would be judged in a peer review process where the ethical standards of the profession would be applied.

Ethical decision making is a process. There are many instances in social work where simple answers are not available to resolve complex ethical issues. Social workers should take into consideration all the values, principles, and standards in this *Code* that are relevant to any situation in which ethical judgment is warranted. Social workers' decisions and actions should be consistent with the spirit as well as the letter of this *Code*.

In addition to this *Code*, there are many other sources of information about ethical thinking that may be useful. Social workers should consider ethical theory and principles generally, social work theory and research, laws, regulations, agency policies, and other relevant codes of ethics, recognizing that among codes of ethics social workers should consider the *NASW Code of Ethics* as their

---

*For information on NASW adjudication procedures, see *NASW for the Adjudication of Grievances*.

primary source. Social workers also should be aware of the impact on ethical decision making of their clients' and their own personal values and cultural and religious beliefs and practices. They should be aware of any conflicts between personal and professional values and deal with them responsibly. For additional guidance social workers should consult the relevant literature on professional ethics and ethical decision making and seek appropriate consultation when faced with ethical dilemmas. This may involve consultation with an agency-based or social work organization's ethics committee, a regulatory body, knowledgeable colleagues, supervisors, or legal counsel.

Instances may arise when social workers' ethical obligations conflict with agency policies or relevant laws or regulations. When such conflicts occur, social workers must make a responsible effort to resolve the conflict in a manner that is consistent with the values, principles, and standards expressed in this *Code*. If a reasonable resolution of the conflict does not appear possible, social workers should seek proper consultation before making a decision.

The *NASW Code of Ethics* is to be used by NASW and by individuals, agencies, organizations, and bodies (such as licensing and regulatory boards, professional liability insurance providers, courts of law, agency boards of directors, government agencies, and other professional groups) that choose to adopt it or use it as a frame of reference. Violation of standards in this *Code* does not automatically imply legal liability or violation of the law. Such determination can only be made in the context of legal and judicial proceedings. Alleged violations of the *Code* would be subject to a peer review process. Such processes are generally separate from legal or administrative procedures and insulated from legal review or proceedings to allow the profession to counsel and discipline its own members.

A code of ethics cannot guarantee ethical behavior. Moreover, a code of ethics cannot resolve all ethical issues or disputes or capture the richness and complexity involved in striving to make responsible choices within a moral community. Rather, a code of ethics sets forth values, ethical principles, and ethical standards to which professionals aspire and by which their actions can be judged. Social workers' ethical behavior should result from their personal commitment to engage in ethical practice. The *NASW Code of Ethics* reflects the commitment of all social workers to uphold the profession's values and to act ethically. Principles and standards must be applied by individuals of good character who discern moral questions and, in good faith, seek to make reliable ethical judgments.

ETHICAL PRINCIPLES

The following broad ethical principles are based on social work's core values of service, social justice, dignity and worth of the person, importance of human relationships, integrity, and competence. These principles set forth ideals to which all social workers should aspire.

Value: *Service*

Ethical Principle: *Social workers' primary goal is to help people in need and to address social problems.*

Social workers elevate service to others above self-interest. Social workers draw on their knowledge, values, and skills to help people in need and to address social problems. Social workers are encouraged to volunteer some portion of their professional skills with no expectation of significant financial return (pro bono service).

Value: *Social Justice*

Ethical Principle: *Social workers challenge social injustice.*

Social workers pursue social change, particularly with and on behalf of vulnerable and oppressed individuals and groups of people. Social workers' social change efforts are focused primarily on issues of poverty, unemployment, discrimination, and other forms of social injustice. These activities seek to promote sensitivity to and knowledge about oppression and cultural and ethnic diversity. Social workers strive to ensure access to needed information, services, and resources; equality of opportunity; and meaningful participation in decision making for all people.

Value: *Dignity and Worth of the Person*

Ethical Principle: *Social workers respect the inherent dignity and worth of the person.*

Social workers treat each person in a caring and respectful fashion, mindful of individual differences and cultural and ethnic diversity. Social workers promote clients' socially responsible self-determination. Social workers seek to enhance clients' capacity and opportunity to change and to address their own needs. Social workers are cognizant of their dual responsibility to clients and to the broader society. They seek to resolve conflicts between clients' interest and the broader society's interests in a socially responsible manner consistent with the values, ethical principles, and ethical standards of the profession.

Value: *Importance of Human Relationships*

Ethical Principle: *Social workers recognize the central importance of human relationships.*

Social workers understand that relationships between and among people are an important vehicle for change. Social workers engage people as partners in the helping process. Social workers seek to strengthen relationships among people in a purposeful effort to promote, restore, maintain, and enhance the well-being of individuals, families, social groups, organizations, and communities.

Value: *Integrity*

Ethical Principle: *Social workers behave in a trustworthy manner.*

Social workers are continually aware of the profession's mission, values, ethical principles, and ethical standards and practice in a manner consistent with them. Social workers act honestly and responsibly and promote ethical practices on the part of the organizations with which they are affiliated.

Value: *Competence*

Ethical Principle: *Social workers practice within their areas of competence and develop and enhance their professional expertise.*

Social workers continually strive to increase their professional knowledge and skills and to apply them in practice. Social workers should aspire to contribute to the knowledge base of the profession.

ETHICAL STANDARDS

The following ethical standards are relevant to the professional activities of all social workers. These standards concern (1) social workers' ethical responsibilities to clients, (2) social workers' ethical responsibilities to colleagues, (3) social workers' ethical responsibilities in practice settings, (4) social workers' ethical responsibilities as professionals, (5) social workers' ethical responsibilities to the social work profession, and (6) social workers' ethical responsibilities to the broader society.

Some of the standards that follow are enforceable guidelines for professional conduct, and some are aspirational. The extent to which each standard is enforceable is a matter of professional judgment to be exercised by those responsible for reviewing alleged violations of ethical standards.

1.   SOCIAL WORKERS' ETHICAL RESPONSIBILITIES TO CLIENTS

1.01   Commitment to Clients

Social workers' primary responsibility is to promote the well-being of clients. In general, clients' interests are primary. However, social workers' responsibility to the larger society or specific legal obligations may on limited occasions supersede the loyalty owed clients, and clients should be so advised. (Examples include when a social worker is required by law to report that a client has abused a child or has threatened to harm self or others.)

1.02   Self-Determination

Social workers respect and promote the right of clients to self-determination and assist clients in their efforts to identify and clarify their goals. Social workers may limit clients' right to self-determination when, in the social workers' professional judgment, clients' actions or potential actions pose a serious, foreseeable, and imminent risk to themselves or others.

1.03   Informed Consent

(a) Social workers should provide services to clients only in the context of a professional relationship based, when appropriate, on valid informed consent. Social workers should use clear and understandable language to inform clients of the purpose of the services, risks related to the services, limits to services because of the requirements of a third-party payer, relevant costs, reasonable alternatives, clients' right to refuse or withdraw consent, and the time frame covered by the consent. Social workers should provide clients with an opportunity to ask questions.

(b) In instances when clients are not literate or have difficulty understanding the primary language used in the practice setting, social workers should take steps to ensure clients' comprehension. This may include providing clients with a detailed verbal explanation or arranging for a qualified interpreter or translator whenever possible.

(c) In instances when clients lack the capacity to provide informed consent, social workers should protect clients' interests by seeking permission from an appropriate third party, informing clients consistent with the clients' level of understanding. In such instances social workers should seek to ensure that the third party acts in a manner consistent with clients' wishes and interests. Social workers should take reasonable steps to enhance such clients' ability to give informed consent.

(d) In instances when clients are receiving services involuntarily, social workers should provide information about the nature and extent of services and about the extent of clients' right to refuse service.

(e) Social workers who provide services via electronic media (such as computer, telephone, radio, and television) should inform recipients of the limitations and risks associated with such services.

(f) Social workers should obtain clients' informed consent before audiotaping or videotaping clients or permitting observation of services to clients by a third party.

1.04 Competence

(a) Social workers should provide services and represent themselves as competent only within the boundaries of their education, training, license, certification, consultation received, supervised experience, or other relevant professional experience.

(b) Social workers should provide services in substantive areas or use intervention techniques or approaches that are new to them only after engaging in appropriate study, training, consultation, and supervision from people who are competent in those interventions or techniques.

(c) When generally recognized standards do not exist with respect to an emerging area of practice, social workers should exercise careful judgment and take responsible steps (including appropriate education, research, training, consultation, and supervision) to ensure the competence of their work and to protect clients from harm.

1.05 Cultural Competence and Social Diversity

(a) Social workers should understand culture and its function in human behavior and society, recognizing the strengths that exist in all cultures.

(b) Social workers should have a knowledge base of their clients' cultures and be able to demonstrate competence in the provision of services that are sensitive to clients' cultures and to differences among people and cultural groups.

(c) Social workers should obtain education about and seek to understand the nature of social diversity and oppression with respect to race, ethnicity, national origin, color, sex, sexual orientation, age, marital status, political belief, religion, and mental or physical disability.

1.06 Conflicts of Interest

(a) Social workers should be alert to and avoid conflicts of interest that interfere with the exercise of professional discretion and impartial judgment. Social workers should inform clients when a real or potential conflict of interest arises and take reasonable steps to resolve the issue in a manner that makes the clients' interests primary and protects clients' interests to the greatest extent possible. In some cases, protecting clients' interests may require termination of the professional relationship with proper referral of the client.

(b) Social workers should not take unfair advantage of any professional relationship or exploit others to further their personal, religious, political, or business interests.

(c) Social workers should not engage in dual or multiple relationships with clients or former clients in which there is a risk of exploitation or potential harm to the client. In instances when dual or multiple relationships are unavoidable, social workers should take steps to protect clients and are responsible for setting clear, appropriate, and culturally sensitive boundaries. (Dual or multiple relationships occur when social workers relate to clients in more than one relationship, whether professional, social, or business. Dual or multiple relationships can occur simultaneously or consecutively.)

(d) When social workers provide services to two or more people who have a relationship with each other (for example, couples, family members), social workers should clarify with all parties which individuals will be considered clients and the nature of social workers' professional obligations to the various individuals who are receiving services. Social workers who anticipate a conflict of interest among the individuals receiving services or who anticipate having to perform in potentially conflicting roles (for example, when a social worker is asked to testify in a child custody dispute or divorce proceedings involving clients) should clarify their role with the parties involved and take appropriate action to minimize any conflict of interest.

1.07   Privacy and Confidentiality

(a) Social workers should respect clients' right to privacy. Social workers should not solicit private information from clients unless it is essential to providing services or conducting social work evaluation or research. Once private information is shared, standards of confidentiality apply.

(b) Social workers may disclose confidential information when appropriate with valid consent from a client or a person legally authorized to consent on behalf of a client.

(c) Social workers should protect the confidentiality of all information obtained in the course of professional service, except for compelling professional reasons. The general expectation that social workers will keep information confidential does not apply when disclosure is necessary to prevent serious, foreseeable, and imminent harm to a client or other identifiable person. In all instances, social workers should disclose the least amount of confidential information necessary to achieve the desired purpose; only information that is directly relevant to the purpose for which the disclosure is made should be revealed.

(d) Social workers should inform clients, to the extent possible, about the disclosure of confidential information and the potential consequences, when feasible before the disclosure is made. This applies whether social workers disclose confidential information on the basis of a legal requirement or client consent.

(e) Social workers should discuss with clients and other interested parties the nature of confidentiality and limitations of clients' right to confidentiality. Social workers should review with clients circumstances where confidential information may be requested and where disclosure of confidential information may be legally required. This discussion should occur as soon as possible in the social worker–client relationship and as needed throughout the course of the relationship.

(f) When social workers provide counseling services to families, couples, or groups, social workers should seek agreement among the parties involved concerning each individual's right to confidentiality and obligation to preserve the confidentiality of information shared by others. Social workers should inform participants in family, couples, or group counseling that social workers cannot guarantee that all participants will honor such agreements.

(g) Social workers should inform clients involved in family, couples, marital, or group counseling of the social worker's, employer's, and agency's policy concerning the social worker's disclosure of confidential information among the parties involved in the counseling.

(h) Social workers should not disclose confidential information to third-party payers unless clients have authorized such disclosure.

(i) Social workers should not discuss confidential information in any setting unless privacy can be ensured. Social workers should not discuss confidential information in public or semipublic areas such as hallways, waiting rooms, elevators, and restaurants.

(j) Social workers should protect the confidentiality of clients during legal proceedings to the extent permitted by law. When a court of law or other legally authorized body orders social workers to disclose confidential or privileged information without a client's consent and such disclosure could cause harm to the client, social workers should request that the court withdraw or limit the order as narrowly as possible or maintain the records under seal, unavailable for public inspection.

(k) Social workers should protect the confidentiality of clients when responding to requests from members of the media.

(l) Social workers should protect the confidentiality of clients' written and electronic records and other sensitive information. Social workers should take reasonable steps to ensure that clients' records are stored in a secure location and that clients' records are not available to others who are not authorized to have access.

(m) Social workers should take precautions to ensure and maintain the confidentiality of information transmitted to other parties through the use of computers, electronic mail, facsimile machines, telephones and telephone answering machines, and other electronic or computer technology. Disclosure of identifying information should be avoided whenever possible.

(n) Social workers should transfer or dispose of clients' records in a manner that protects clients' confidentiality and is consistent with state statutes governing records and social work licensure.

(o) Social workers should take reasonable precautions to protect client confidentiality in the event of the social worker's termination of practice, incapacitation, or death.

(p) Social workers should not disclose identifying information when discussing clients for teaching or training purposes unless the client has consented to disclosure of confidential information.

(q) Social workers should not disclose identifying information when discussing clients with consultants unless the client has consented to disclosure of confidential information or there is a compelling need for such disclosure.

(r) Social workers should protect the confidentiality of deceased clients consistent with the preceding standards.

1.08   Access to Records

(a) Social workers should provide clients with reasonable access to records concerning the clients. Social workers who are concerned that clients' access to their records could cause serious misunderstanding or harm to the client should provide assistance in interpreting the records and consultation with the client regarding the records. Social workers should limit clients' access to their records, or portions of their records, only in exceptional circumstances when there is compelling evidence that such access would cause serious harm to the client. Both clients' requests and the rationale for withholding some or all of the record should be documented in clients' files.

(b) When providing clients with access to their records, social workers should take steps to protect the confidentiality of other individuals identified or discussed in such records.

1.09   Sexual Relationships

(a) Social workers should under no circumstances engage in sexual activities or sexual contact with current clients, whether such contact is consensual or forced.

(b) Social workers should not engage in sexual activities or sexual contact with clients' relatives or other individuals with whom clients maintain a close personal relationship when there is a risk of exploitation or potential harm to the client. Sexual activity or sexual contact with clients' relatives or other individuals with whom clients maintain a personal relationship has the potential to be harmful to the client and may make it difficult for the social worker and client to maintain appropriate professional boundaries. Social workers—not their clients, their clients' relatives, or other individuals with whom the client maintains a personal relationship—assume the full burden for setting clear, appropriate, and culturally sensitive boundaries.

(c) Social workers should not engage in sexual activities or sexual contact with former clients because of the potential for harm to the client. If social workers engage in conduct contrary to this prohibition or claim that an exception to this prohibition is warranted due to extraordinary circumstances, it is social workers—not their clients—who assume the full burden of demonstrating that the former client has not been exploited, coerced, or manipulated, intentionally or unintentionally.

(d) Social workers should not provide clinical services to individuals with whom they have had a prior sexual relationship. Providing clinical services to a former sexual partner has the potential to be harmful to the individual and is likely to make it difficult for the social worker and individual to maintain appropriate professional boundaries.

1.10 Physical Contact

Social workers should not engage in physical contact with clients when there is a possibility of psychological harm to the client as a result of the contact (such as cradling or caressing clients). Social workers who engage in appropriate physical contact with clients are responsible for setting clear, appropriate, and culturally sensitive boundaries that govern such physical contact.

1.11 Sexual Harassment

Social workers should not sexually harass clients. Sexual harassment includes sexual advances, sexual solicitation, requests for sexual favors, and other verbal or physical conduct of a sexual nature.

1.12 Derogatory Language

Social workers should not use derogatory language in their written or verbal communications to or about clients. Social workers should use accurate and respectful language in all communications to and about clients.

1.13 Payment for Services

(a) When setting fees, social workers should ensure that the fees are fair, reasonable, and commensurate with the services performed. Consideration should be given to clients' ability to pay.

(b) Social workers should avoid accepting goods or services from clients as payment for professional services. Bartering arrangements, particularly involving services, create the potential for conflicts of interest, exploitation, and inappropriate boundaries in social workers' relationships with clients. Social workers should explore and may participate in bartering only in very limited circumstances when it can be demonstrated that such arrangements are an accepted practice among professionals in the local community, considered to be essential for the provision of services, negotiated without coercion, and entered into at the client's initiative and with the client's informed consent. Social workers who accept goods or services from clients as payment for professional services assume the full burden of demonstrating that this arrangement will not be detrimental to the client or the professional relationship.

(c) Social workers should not solicit a private fee or other remuneration for providing services to clients who are entitled to such available services through the social workers' employer or agency.

1.14 Clients Who Lack Decision-Making Capacity

When social workers act on behalf of clients who lack the capacity to make informed decisions, social workers should take reasonable steps to safeguard the interests and rights of those clients.

1.15 Interruption of Services

Social workers should make reasonable efforts to ensure continuity of services in the event that services are interrupted by factors such as unavailability, relocation, illness, disability, or death.

1.16 Termination of Services

(a) Social workers should terminate services to clients and professional relationships with them when such services and relationships are no longer required or no longer serve the clients' needs or interests.

(b) Social workers should take reasonable steps to avoid abandoning clients who are still in need of services. Social workers should withdraw services precipitously only under unusual circumstances, giving careful consideration to all factors in the situation and taking care to minimize possible adverse effects. Social workers should assist in making appropriate arrangements for continuation of services when necessary.

(c) Social workers in fee-for-service settings may terminate services to clients who are not paying an overdue balance if the financial contractual arrangements have been made clear to the client, if the client does not pose an imminent danger to self or others, and if the clinical and other consequences of the current nonpayment have been addressed and discussed with the client.

(d) Social workers should not terminate services to pursue a social, financial, or sexual relationship with a client.

(e) Social workers who anticipate the termination or interruption of services to clients should notify clients promptly and seek the transfer, referral, or continuation of services in relation to the clients' needs and preferences.

(f) Social workers who are leaving an employment setting should inform clients of appropriate options for the continuation of services and of the benefits and risks of the options.

2. SOCIAL WORKERS' ETHICAL RESPONSIBILITIES TO COLLEAGUES

2.01 Respect

(a) Social workers should treat colleagues with respect and should represent accurately and fairly the qualifications, views, and obligations of colleagues.

(b) Social workers should avoid unwarranted negative criticism of colleagues in communications with clients or with other professionals. Unwarranted negative criticism may include demeaning comments that refer to colleagues' level of competence or to individuals' attributes such as race, ethnicity, national origin, color, sex, sexual orientation, age, marital status, political belief, religion, or mental or physical disability.

(c) Social workers should cooperate with social work colleagues and with colleagues of other professions when such cooperation serves the well-being of clients.

2.02 Confidentiality

Social workers should respect confidential information shared by colleagues in the course of their professional relationships and transactions. Social workers should ensure that such colleagues understand social workers' obligation to respect confidentiality and any exceptions related to it.

2.03 Interdisciplinary Collaboration

(a) Social workers who are members of an interdisciplinary team should participate in and contribute to decisions that affect the well-being of clients by drawing on the perspectives, values, and experiences of the social work profession. Professional and ethical obligations of the interdisciplinary team as a whole and of its individual members should be clearly established.

(b) Social workers for whom a team decision raises ethical concerns should attempt to resolve the disagreement through appropriate channels. If the disagreement cannot be resolved, social workers should pursue other avenues to address their concerns consistent with client well-being.

2.04 Disputes Involving Colleagues

(a) Social workers should not take advantage of a dispute between a colleague and employer to obtain a position or otherwise advance the social workers' own interests.

(b) Social workers should not exploit clients in disputes with colleagues or engage clients in any inappropriate discussion of conflicts between social workers and their colleagues.

2.05 Consultation

(a) Social workers should seek the advice and counsel of colleagues whenever such consultation is in the best interests of clients.

(b) Social workers should keep themselves informed about colleagues' areas of expertise and competencies. Social workers should seek consultation only from colleagues who have demonstrated knowledge, expertise, and competence related to the subject of the consultation.

(c) When consulting with colleagues about clients, social workers should disclose the least amount of information necessary to achieve the purposes of the consultation.

2.06 Referral for Services

(a) Social workers should refer clients to other professionals when the other professionals' specialized knowledge or expertise is needed to serve clients fully or when social workers believe that they are not being effective or making reasonable progress with clients and that additional service is required.

(b) Social workers who refer clients to other professionals should take appropriate steps to facilitate an orderly transfer of responsibility. Social workers who refer clients to other professionals should disclose, with clients' consent, all pertinent information to the new service providers.

(c) Social workers are prohibited from giving or receiving payment for a referral when no professional service is provided by the referring social worker.

2.07   Sexual Relationships

(a) Social workers who function as supervisors or educators should not engage in sexual activities or contact with supervisees, students, trainees, or other colleagues over whom they exercise professional authority.

(b) Social workers should avoid engaging in sexual relationships with colleagues when there is potential for a conflict of interest. Social workers who become involved in, or anticipate becoming involved in, a sexual relationship with a colleague have a duty to transfer professional responsibilities, when necessary, to avoid a conflict of interest.

2.08   Sexual Harassment

Social workers should not sexually harass supervisees, students, trainees, or colleagues. Sexual harassment includes sexual advances, sexual solicitation, requests for sexual favors, and other verbal or physical conduct of a sexual nature.

2.09   Impairment of Colleagues

(a) Social workers who have direct knowledge of a social work colleague's impairment that is due to personal problems, psychosocial distress, substance abuse, or mental health difficulties and that interferes with practice effectiveness should consult with that colleague when feasible and assist the colleague in taking remedial action.

(b) Social workers who believe that a social work colleague's impairment interferes with practice effectiveness and that the colleague has not taken adequate steps to address the impairment should take action through appropriate channels established by employers, agencies, NASW, licensing and regulatory bodies, and other professional organizations.

2.10   Incompetence of Colleagues

(a) Social workers who have direct knowledge of a social work colleague's incompetence should consult with that colleague when feasible and assist the colleague in taking remedial action.

(b) Social workers who believe that a social work colleague is incompetent and has not taken adequate steps to address the incompetence should take action through appropriate channels established by employers, agencies, NASW, licensing and regulatory bodies, and other professional organizations.

2.11   Unethical Conduct of Colleagues

(a) Social workers should take adequate measures to discourage, prevent, expose, and correct the unethical conduct of colleagues.

(b) Social workers should be knowledgeable about established policies and procedures for handling concerns about colleagues' unethical behavior. Social workers should be familiar with national, state, and local procedures for handling ethics complaints. These include policies and procedures created by NASW, licensing and regulatory bodies, employers, agencies, and other professional organizations.

(c) Social workers who believe that a colleague has acted unethically should seek resolution by discussing their concerns with the colleague when feasible and when such discussion is likely to be productive.

(d) When necessary, social workers who believe that a colleague has acted unethically should take action through appropriate formal channels (such as contacting a state licensing board or regulatory body, an NASW committee on inquiry, or other professional ethics committees).

(e) Social workers should defend and assist colleagues who are unjustly charged with unethical conduct.

3.   SOCIAL WORKERS' ETHICAL RESPONSIBILITIES IN PRACTICE SETTINGS

3.01   Supervision and Consultation

(a) Social workers who provide supervision or consultation should have the necessary knowledge and skill to supervise or consult appropriately and should do so only within their areas of knowledge and competence.

(b) Social workers who provide supervision or consultation are responsible for setting clear, appropriate, and culturally sensitive boundaries.

(c) Social workers should not engage in any dual or multiple relationships with supervisees in which there is a risk of exploitation of or potential harm to the supervisee.

(d) Social workers who provide supervision should evaluate supervisees' performance in a manner that is fair and respectful.

3.02   Education and Training

(a) Social workers who function as educators, field instructors for students, or trainers should provide instruction only within their areas of knowledge and competence and should provide instruction based on the most current information and knowledge available in the profession.

(b) Social workers who function as educators or field instructors for students should evaluate students' performance in a manner that is fair and respectful.

(c) Social workers who function as educators or field instructors for students should take reasonable steps to ensure that clients are routinely informed when services are being provided by students.

(d) Social workers who function as educators or field instructors for students should not engage in any dual or multiple relationships with students in which there is a risk of exploitation or potential harm to the student. Social work educators and field instructors are responsible for setting clear, appropriate, and culturally sensitive boundaries.

3.03   Performance Evaluation

Social workers who have responsibility for evaluating the performance of others should fulfill such responsibility in a fair and considerate manner and on the basis of clearly stated criteria.

3.04   Client Records

(a) Social workers should take reasonable steps to ensure that documentation in records is accurate and reflects the services provided.

(b) Social workers should include sufficient and timely documentation in records to facilitate the delivery of services and to ensure continuity of services provided to clients in the future.

(c) Social workers' documentation should protect clients' privacy to the extent that is possible and appropriate and should include only information that is directly relevant to the delivery of services.

(d) Social workers should store records following the termination of services to ensure reasonable future access. Records should be maintained for the number of years required by state statutes or relevant contracts.

3.05 Billing

Social workers should establish and maintain billing practices that accurately reflect the nature and extent of services provided and that identify who provided the service in the practice setting.

3.06 Client Transfer

(a) When an individual who is receiving services from another agency or colleague contacts a social worker for services, the social worker should carefully consider the client's needs before agreeing to provide services. To minimize possible confusion and conflict, social workers should discuss with potential clients the nature of the clients' current relationship with other service providers and the implications, including possible benefits or risks, of entering into a relationship with a new service provider.

(b) If a new client has been served by another agency or colleague, social workers should discuss with the client whether consultation with the previous service provider is in the client's best interest.

3.07 Administration

(a) Social work administrators should advocate within and outside their agencies for adequate resources to meet clients' needs.

(b) Social workers should advocate for resource allocation procedures that are open and fair. When not all clients' needs can be met, an allocation procedure should be developed that is nondiscriminatory and based on appropriate and consistently applied principles.

(c) Social workers who are administrators should take reasonable steps to ensure that adequate agency or organizational resources are available to provide appropriate staff supervision.

(d) Social work administrators should take reasonable steps to ensure that the working environment for which they are responsible is consistent with and encourages compliance with the NASW Code of Ethics. Social work administrators should take reasonable steps to eliminate any conditions in their organizations that violate, interfere with, or discourage compliance with the Code.

3.08 Continuing Education and Staff Development

Social work administrators and supervisors should take reasonable steps to provide or arrange for continuing education and staff development for all staff for whom they are responsible. Continuing education and staff development should address current knowledge and emerging developments related to social work practice and ethics.

3.09 Commitments to Employers

(a) Social workers generally should adhere to commitments made to employers and employing organizations.

(b) Social workers should work to improve employing agencies' policies and procedures and the efficiency and effectiveness of their services.

(c) Social workers should take reasonable steps to ensure that employers are aware of social workers' ethical obligations as set forth in the NASW Code of Ethics and of the implications of those obligations for social work practice.

(d) Social workers should not allow an employing organization's policies, procedures, regulations, or administrative orders to interfere with their ethical practice of social work. Social workers should take reasonable steps to ensure that their employing organizations' practices are consistent with the NASW Code of Ethics.

(e) Social workers should act to prevent and eliminate discrimination in the employing organization's work assignments and in its employment policies and practices.

(f) Social workers should accept employment or arrange student field placements only in organizations that exercise fair personnel practices.

(g) Social workers should be diligent stewards of the resources of their employing organizations, wisely conserving funds where appropriate and never misappropriating funds or using them for unintended purposes.

3.10   Labor–Management Disputes

(a) Social workers may engage in organized action, including the formation of and participation in labor unions, to improve services to clients and working conditions.

(b) The actions of social workers who are involved in labor–management disputes, job actions, or labor strikes should be guided by the profession's values, ethical principles, and ethical standards. Reasonable differences of opinion exist among social workers concerning their primary obligation as professionals during an actual or threatened labor strike or job action. Social workers should carefully examine relevant issues and their possible impact on clients before deciding on a course of action.

4.   SOCIAL WORKERS' ETHICAL RESPONSIBILITIES AS PROFESSIONALS

4.01   Competence

(a) Social workers should accept responsibility or employment only on the basis of existing competence or the intention to acquire the necessary competence.

(b) Social workers should strive to become and remain proficient in professional practice and the performance of professional functions. Social workers should critically examine and keep current with emerging knowledge relevant to social work. Social workers should routinely review the professional literature and participate in continuing education relevant to social work practice and social work ethics.

(c) Social workers should base practice on recognized knowledge, including empirically based knowledge, relevant to social work and social work ethics.

4.02   Discrimination

Social workers should not practice, condone, facilitate, or collaborate with any form of discrimination on the basis of race, ethnicity, national origin, color, sex, sexual orientation, age, marital status, political belief, religion, or mental or physical disability.

4.03   Private Conduct

Social workers should not permit their private conduct to interfere with their ability to fulfill their professional responsibilities.

4.04   Dishonesty, Fraud, and Deception

Social workers should not participate in, condone, or be associated with dishonesty, fraud, or deception.

4.05   Impairment

(a) Social workers should not allow their own personal problems, psychosocial distress, legal problems, substance abuse, or mental health difficulties to interfere with their professional judgment and performance or to jeopardize the best interests of people for whom they have a professional responsibility.

(b) Social workers whose personal problems, psychosocial distress, legal problems, substance abuse, or mental health difficulties interfere with their professional judgment and performance should immediately seek consultation and take appropriate remedial action by seeking professional help, making adjustments in workload, terminating practice, or taking any other steps necessary to protect clients and others.

4.06   Misrepresentation

(a) Social workers should make clear distinctions between statements made and actions engaged in as a private individual and as a representative of the social work profession, a professional social work organization, or the social worker's employing agency.

(b) Social workers who speak on behalf of professional social work organizations should accurately represent the official and authorized positions of the organizations.

(c) Social workers should ensure that their representations to clients, agencies, and the public of professional qualifications, credentials, education, competence, affiliations, services provided, or results to be achieved are accurate. Social workers should claim only those relevant professional credentials they actually possess and take steps to correct any inaccuracies or misrepresentations of their credentials by others.

4.07   Solicitations

(a) Social workers should not engage in uninvited solicitation of potential clients who, because of their circumstances, are vulnerable to undue influence, manipulation, or coercion.

(b) Social workers should not engage in solicitation of testimonial endorsements (including solicitation of consent to use a client's prior statement as a testimonial endorsement) from current clients or from other people who, because of their particular circumstances, are vulnerable to undue influence.

4.08   Acknowledging Credit

(a) Social workers should take responsibility and credit, including authorship credit, only for work they have actually performed and to which they have contributed.

(b) Social workers should honestly acknowledge the work of and the contributions made by others.

5.   SOCIAL WORKERS' ETHICAL RESPONSIBILITIES TO THE SOCIAL
     WORK PROFESSION

5.01   Integrity of the Profession

(a) Social workers should work toward the maintenance and promotion of high standards of practice.

(b) Social workers should uphold and advance the values, ethics, knowledge, and mission of the profession. Social workers should protect, enhance, and improve the integrity of the profession through appropriate study and research, active discussion, and responsible criticism of the profession.

(c) Social workers should contribute time and professional expertise to activities that promote respect for the value, integrity, and competence of the social work profession. These activities may include teaching, research, consultation, service, legislative testimony, presentations in the community, and participation in their professional organizations.

(d) Social workers should contribute to the knowledge base of social work and share with colleagues their knowledge related to practice, research, and ethics. Social workers should seek to contribute to the profession's literature and to share their knowledge at professional meetings and conferences.

(e) Social workers should act to prevent the unauthorized and unqualified practice of social work.

5.02   Evaluation and Research

(a) Social workers should monitor and evaluate policies, the implementation of programs, and practice interventions.

(b) Social workers should promote and facilitate evaluation and research to contribute to the development of knowledge.

(c) Social workers should critically examine and keep current with emerging knowledge relevant to social work and fully use evaluation and research evidence in their professional practice.

(d) Social workers engaged in evaluation or research should carefully consider possible consequences and should follow guidelines developed for the protection of evaluation and research participants. Appropriate institutional review boards should be consulted.

(e) Social workers engaged in evaluation or research should obtain voluntary and written informed consent from participants, when appropriate, without any implied or actual deprivation or penalty for refusal to participate; without undue inducement to participate; and with due regard for participants' well-being, privacy, and dignity. Informed consent should include information about the nature, extent, and duration of the participation requested and disclosure of the risks and benefits of participation in the research.

(f) When evaluation or research participants are incapable of giving informed consent, social workers should provide an appropriate explanation to the participants, obtain the participants' assent to the extent they are able, and obtain written consent from an appropriate proxy.

(g) Social workers should never design or conduct evaluation or research that does not use consent procedures, such as certain forms of naturalistic observation and archival research, unless rigorous and responsible review of the research has found it to be justified because of its prospective scientific, educational, or applied value and unless equally effective alternative procedures that do not involve waiver of consent are not feasible.

(h) Social workers should inform participants of their right to withdraw from evaluation and research at any time without penalty.

(i) Social workers should take appropriate steps to ensure that participants in evaluation and research have access to appropriate supportive services.

(j) Social workers engaged in evaluation for research should protect participants from unwarranted physical or mental distress, harm, danger, or deprivation.

(k) Social workers engaged in the evaluation of services should discuss collected information only for professional purposes and only with people professionally concerned with this information.

(l) Social workers engaged in evaluation or research should ensure the anonymity or confidentiality of participants and of the data obtained from them. Social workers should inform participants of any limits of confidentiality, the measures that will be taken to ensure confidentiality, and when any records containing research data will be destroyed.

(m) Social workers who report evaluation and research results should protect participants' confidentiality by omitting identifying information unless proper consent has been obtained authorizing disclosure.

(n) Social workers should report evaluation and research findings accurately. They should not fabricate or falsify results and should take steps to correct any errors later found in published data using standard publication methods.

(o) Social workers engaged in evaluation or research should be alert to and avoid conflicts of interest and dual relationships with participants, should inform participants when a real or potential conflict of interest arises, and should take steps to resolve the issue in a manner that makes participants' interests primary.

(p) Social workers should educate themselves, their students, and their colleagues about responsible research practices.

6. SOCIAL WORKERS' ETHICAL RESPONSIBILITIES TO THE BROADER SOCIETY

6.01 Social Welfare

Social workers should promote the general welfare of society, from local to global levels, and the development of people, their communities, and their environments. Social workers should advocate for living conditions conducive to the fulfillment of basic human needs and should promote social, economic, political, and cultural values and institutions that are compatible with the realization of social justice.

6.02 Public Participation

Social workers should facilitate informed participation by the public in shaping social policies and institutions.

6.03 Public Emergencies

Social workers should provide appropriate professional services in public emergencies to the greatest extent possible.

6.04 Social and Political Action

(a) Social workers should engage in social and political action that seeks to ensure that all people have equal access to the resources, employment, services, and opportunities they require to meet their basic human needs and to develop fully. Social workers should be aware of the impact of the political arena on practice and should advocate for changes in policy and legislation to improve social conditions in order to meet basic human needs and promote social justice.

(b) Social workers should act to expand choice and opportunity for all people, with special regard for vulnerable, disadvantaged, oppressed, and exploited people and groups.

(c) Social workers should promote conditions that encourage respect for cultural and social diversity within the United States and globally. Social workers should promote policies and practices that demonstrate respect for difference, support the expansion of cultural knowledge and resources, advocate for programs and institutions that demonstrate cultural competence, and promote policies that safeguard the rights of and confirm equity and social justice for all people.

(d) Social workers should act to prevent and eliminate domination of, exploitation of, and discrimination against any person, group, or class on the basis of race, ethnicity, national origin, color, sex, sexual orientation, age, marital status, political belief, religion, or mental or physical disability.

REFERENCES

Adams, J. F. (1997). Questions as interventions in therapeutic conversation. *Journal of Family Psychotherapy, 8,* 17–35.

Alissi, A. (1980). *Perspectives in group work practice.* New York: Research Press.

Allcorn, S. (1995). Understanding organizational culture as the quality of workplace subjectivity. *Human Relations, 48,* 73–96.

Allcorn, S., & Diamond, M. A. (1997). *Managing people during stressful times: The psychologically defensive workplace.* Westport, CT: Quorum Books.

Allen, J. G., Coyne, L., Colson, D. B., Horwitz, L., Gabbard, G. O., Frieswyk, S. J., & Newson, G. (1996). Pattern of therapist interventions associated with patient collaboration, *Psychotherapy, 33,* 254–261.

Allen, J. G., Gabbard, G. O., Newsom, G. E., & Coyne, L. (1990). Detecting patterns of change in patients' collaboration within individual psychotherapy sessions. *Psychotherapy, 27,* 522–530.

Anderson, J. (1997). *Social work with groups.* New York: Longman Publishing.

Anderson, N. B., & Armstead, C. A. (1995). Toward understanding the association of socioeconomic status and health: A new challenge for the biopsychosocial approach. *Psychosomatic Medicine, 57,* 213–225.

Angell, B. G. (1996). Neurolinguistic programming theory and social work treatment. In F. J. Turner (Ed.), *Social work treatment: Interlocking theoretical approaches* (4th ed., p. 480–502). New York: Free Press.

Anthony, S., & Pagano, G. (1998). The therapeutic potential for growth during the termination process. *Clinical Social Work Journal, 26,* 281–296.

Arthur, N. (1998). Counsellor education for diversity: Where do we go from here? *Canadian Journal of Counselling, 32,* 88–103.

Badger, D. (1985). Learning for transfer: A further contribution. *Issues in Social Work Education, 5,* 63–66.

Baenninger-Huber, E., & Widmer, C. (1999). Affective relationship patterns and psychotherapeutic change. *Psychotherapy Research, 9,* 74–87.

Bagarozzi, D. A., & Anderson, S. A. (1989). *Personal, marital, and family myths—theoretical formulations and clinical strategies.* New York: W. W. Norton.

Bandler, R., & Grinder, J. (1975). *The structure of magic.* Palo Alto, CA: Science and Behavior Books.

Banks, S. (1998). Professional ethics in social work—what future? *British Journal of Social Work, 28,* 213–231.

Baron, J. (1994). *Thinking and deciding* (2nd ed.). Cambridge, UK: Cambridge University Press.

Berlin, S. B., & Marsh, J. C. (1993). *Informing practice decisions.* New York: Macmillan.

Bernstein, S. (1976). Conflict and group work. In S. Bernstein (Ed.), *Explorations in group work* (pp. 72–106). Boston: Charles River Books.

Berry, G. W., & Sipps, G. J. (1991). Interactive effects of counselor–client similarity and client self-esteem on termination type and number of sessions. *Journal of Counseling Psychology, 38,* 120–125.

Betancourt, H., & Lopez, S. R. (1995). The study of culture, ethnicity, and race in American psychology. In N. R. Goldberger & J. B. Veroff (Eds.), *The culture and psychology reader* (pp. 87–107). New York: New York University Press.

Beutler, L. E., & Clarkin, J. F. (1990). *Systematic treatment selection: Toward targeted therapeutic interventions.* San Francisco: Brunner/Mazel.

Biringen, Z. (1990). Direct observation of maternal sensitivity and dyadic interactions in the home: Relations to maternal thinking. *Developmental Psychology, 26,* 278–284.

Bischoff, M. M., & Tracey, T. J. G. (1996). Client resistance as predicted by therapist behavior: A study of sequential dependence. *Journal of Counseling Psychology, 42,* 487–495.

Bloom, M., Fischer, J., & Orme, J. G. (1995). *Evaluating practice: Guidelines for the accountable professional* (2nd ed.). Boston: Allyn & Bacon.

Boverie, P. E. (1991). Human systems consultant: Using family therapy in organizations. *Family Therapy, 18,* 61–71.

Bowen, M. (1978). *Family therapy in clinical practice*. New York: Jason Aronson.

Boyer, S. P., & Hoffman, M. A. (1993). Counselor affective reactions to termination: Impact of counselor loss history and perceived client sensitivity to loss. *Journal of Counseling Psychology, 40,* 271–277.

Bozarth, J. D. (1997). Empathy from the framework of client-centered theory and the Rogerian hypothesis. In A. C. Bohart & L. S. Greenberg (Eds.), *Empathy reconsidered: New directions in psychotherapy* (pp. 81–102). Washington, DC: American Psychological Association.

Brookfield, S. D. (1987). *Developing critical thinkers: Challenging adults to explore alternate ways of thinking and acting*. San Francisco: Jossey-Bass.

Broome, B. J. (1991). Building shared meaning: Implications of a relational approach to empathy for teaching intercultural communication. *Communication Education, 40,* 235–249.

Brown, J. E. (1997a). Circular questioning: An introductory guide. *Australian & New Zealand Journal of Family Therapy, 18,* 109–114.

Brown, J. E. (1997b). The question cube: A model for developing question repertoire in training couple and family therapists. *Journal of Marital and Family Therapy, 23,* 27–40.

Browne, N. M., & Hausmann, R. G. (1998). The friendly sound of critical thinking. *Korean Journal of Thinking and Problem Solving, 8,* 47–53.

Browne, N. M., & Keeley, S. M. (1994). *Asking the right questions: A guide to critical thinking* (4th ed.). Englewood Cliffs, NJ: Prentice-Hall.

Brownell, K. D., Marlatt, G. A., Lichtenstein, E., & Wilson, G. T. (1986). Understanding and preventing relapse. *American Psychologist, 41,* 765–782.

Buttny, R. (1996). Clients' and therapist's joint construction of the clients' problems. *Research on Language and Social Interaction, 29,* 125–153.

Byng-Hall, J. (1988). Scripts and legends in families and family therapy. *Family Process, 27,* 167–179.

Cameron, G., & Wren, A. M. (1999). Reconstructing organizational culture: A process using multiple perspectives. *Public Health Nursing, 16,* 96–101.

Carpenter, J., & Treacher, A. (1989). *Problems and solutions in marital and family therapy*. Oxford, UK: Basil Blackwell.

Cartwright, D., & Zander. A. (1968). *Group dynamics* (3rd. ed.). New York: Harper & Row.

Chang, P. (1994). Effects of interviewer question and response type on compliance: An analogue study. *Journal of Counseling Psychology, 41,* 74–82.

Clark, C. (1998). Self-determination and paternalism in community care: Practice and prospects. *British Journal of Social Work, 28,* 387–402.

Collins, D. (1995). Death of a gainsharing plan: Power politics and participatory management. *Organizational Dynamics, 24,* 23–38.

Conger, J. A. (1998). The dark side of leadership. In G. R. Hickman (Ed.), *Leading organizations: Perspectives for a new era* (pp. 250–260). Thousand Oaks, CA: Sage.

Corcoran, K. (1998). Clients without a cause: Is there a legal right to effective treatment? *Research on Social Work Practice, 8,* 589–596.

Corey, G., Corey, M. S., & Callahan, P. (1998). *Issues and ethics in the helping professions* (5th ed.). Pacific Grove, CA: Brooks/Cole.

Corey, G., & Herlihy, B. (1996). Client rights and informed consent. In B. Herlihy & G. Corey (Eds.), *ACA ethical standards casebook* (5th ed., pp. 181–191). Alexandria, VA: American Counseling Association.

Cormier, S., & Cormier, B (1998). *Interviewing strategies for helpers: Fundamental skills and cognitive behavioral interventions* (4th ed.). Pacific Grove, CA: Brooks/Cole.

Courtright, J. A., Millar, F. E., Rogers, L. E., & Bagarozzi, D. (1990). Interaction dynamics of relational negotiation: Reconciliation versus termination of distressed relationships. *Western Journal of Speech Communication, 54,* 429–453.

Crits-Christoph, P., Demorest, A., & Connolly, M. B. (1990). Quantitative assessment of interpersonal themes over the course of psychotherapy, *Psychotherapy, 27,* 513–521.

Croxton, T. A., Churchill, S. R., & Fellin, P. (1988). Counseling minors without parental consent. *Child Welfare, 67,* 3–14.

Daley, J. M., Wong, P., & Applewhite, S. (1992). Serving on the boards of mental health agencies: The experiences of Mexican American community leaders. *Administration and Policy in Mental Health, 19,* 353–365.

Davitt, J. K., & Kaye, L. W. (1996). Supporting patient autonomy: Decision making in home health care. *Social Work, 41*, 41–50.

Dawes, R. M. (1988). *Rational choice in an uncertain world.* San Diego: Harcourt Brace.

Dean, H. E. (1998). The primacy of the ethical aim in clinical social work: Its relationship to social justice and mental health. *Smith College Studies in Social Work, 69*, 9–24.

DeJong, P., & Berg, I. K. (1998). *Interviewing for solutions.* Pacific Grove, CA: Brooks/Cole.

DeJong, P., & Miller, S. D. (1995). How to interview for client strengths. *Social Work, 40*, 729–736.

de Luynes, M. (1995). Neuro linguistic programming. *Educational and Child Psychology, 12*, 34–47.

Denby, R., & Alford, K. (1996). Understanding African American discipline styles: Suggestions for effective social work intervention. *Journal of Multicultural Social Work, 4*, 81–98.

Devaux, F. (1995). Intergenerational transmission of cultural family patterns. *Family Therapy, 22*, 17–23.

Dickson, D. T. (1998). *Confidentiality and privacy in social work: A guide to the law for practitioners and students.* New York: Free Press.

Dolgoff, R., & Skolnik, L. (1996). Ethical decision making in social work with groups: An empirical study. *Social Work with Groups, 19*, 49–65.

Dowd, E. T., & Sanders, D. (1994). Resistance, reactance, and the difficult client. *Canadian Journal of Counselling, 28*, 13–24.

Dozier, R. M., Micks, M. W., Cornille, T. A., & Peterson, G. W. (1998). The effect of Tomm's Therapeutic questioning styles on therapeutic alliance: A clinical analog study. *Family Process, 37*, 189–200.

Dunn, W. N., & Ginsberg, A. (1986). A sociocognitive network approach to organizational analysis. *Human Relations, 39*, 955–975.

Durana, C. (1998). The use of touch in psychotherapy: Ethical and clinical guidelines. *Psychotherapy, 35*, 269–280.

Edwards, J. K., & Bess, J. M. (1998). Developing effectiveness in the therapeutic use of self. *Clinical Social Work Journal, 26*, 89–105.

Elkind, S. N. (1992). *Resolving impasses in therapeutic relationships.* New York: Guilford Press.

Ellis, A. (1996). Thinking processes involved in irrational beliefs and their disturbed conse-quences. *Journal of Cognitive Psychotherapy, 9*, 105–116.

Epston, D., & White, M. (1995). Termination as a rite of passage: Questioning strategies for a therapy of inclusion. In R. A. Neimeyer & M. J. Manoney (Eds.). *Constructivism in psychotherapy* (pp. 339–354). Washington, DC: American Psychological Association.

Evans, D. R., Hearn, M. T., Uhlemann, M. R., & Ivey, A. E. (1998). *Essential interviewing A programmed approach to effective communication* (5th ed.). Pacific Grove, CA: Brooks/Cole.

Falicov, C. J. (1998). *Latino families in therapy: A guide to multicultural practice.* New York: Guilford Press.

Fischer, L., & Sorenson, G. P. (1996). *School law for counselors, psychologists, and social workers* (3rd ed.). New York: Longman.

Fiske, S. T. (1995). Controlling other people: The impact of power on stereotyping. In N. R. Goldberger & J. B. Veroff (Eds.), *The culture and psychology reader* (pp. 438–456).

Ford, F. R. (1983). Rules: The invisible family. *Family Process, 22*, 135–145.

Forgatch, M. S. (1989). Patterns and outcome in family problem solving: The disrupting effect of negative emotion. *Journal of Marriage and the Family, 51*, 115–124.

Freedman, J., & Combs, G. (1993). Invitations to new stories: Using questions to explore alternative possibilities. In S. G. Gilligan & R. Price (Eds.), *Therapeutic Conversations.* New York: W. W. Norton.

Freeman, J. B. (1993). *Thinking logically* (2nd ed.). Englewood Cliffs, NJ: Prentice-Hall.

Gambrill, E. (1990). *Critical thinking in clinical practice: Improving the accuracy of judgments and decisions about clients.* San Francisco: Jossey-Bass.

Gambrill, E. (1994). What critical thinking offers to clinicians. *The Behavior Therapist, 17*, 141–147.

Gambrill, E. (1997). *Social work practice: A critical thinker's guide.* New York: Oxford University Press.

Garland, J. A., Jones, H. E., & Kolodny, R. L. (1976). A model for stages of development in social work groups. In S. Bernstein (Ed.), *Explorations in group work* (pp. 17–71). Boston: Charles River Books.

Gaston, L. (1990). The concept of the alliance and its role in psychotherapy: Theoretical and empirical considerations. *Psychotherapy, 27*, 143–153.

Gaston, L., Marmar, C. R., Thompson, L. W., & Gallagher, D. (1988). Relation of patient pretreatment characteristics to the therapeutic alliance in diverse psychotherapies. *Journal of Consulting and Clinical Psychology, 56*, 483–489.

Gelso, C. J., & Hayes, J. A. (1998). *The psychotherapy relationship: Theory, research, and practice.* New York: John Wiley.

Gibbs, L. E. (1991). *Scientific reasoning for social workers.* New York: Macmillan.

Gibbs, L. E. (1994). Teaching clinical reasoning. *The Behavior Therapist, 17*, 1–6.

Gibbs, L. E., & Gambrill, E. (1999). *Critical thinking for social workers—Exercises for the helping profession.* Thousand Oaks, CA: Pine Forge Press.

Godwin, D. D., & Scanzoni, J. (1989). Couple consensus during marital joint decision-making: A context, process, outcome model. *Journal of Marriage and the Family, 51*, 943–956.

Goldin, E., & Doyle, R. E. (1991). Counselor predicate usage and communication proficiency on ratings of counselor empathic understanding. *Counselor Education and Supervision, 30*, 212–224.

Goodyear, R. K., & Sinnett, E. R. (1984). Current and emerging ethical issues for counseling psychology. *Counseling Psychologist, 12*, 87–98.

Greenblatt, M. (1986). "End runs" and "reverse end runs": A note on organizational dynamics. *American Journal of Social Psychiatry, 6*, 114–119.

Greene, G. J., Lee, M., Mentzer, R. A., Pinnell, S. R., & Niles, D. (1998). Miracles, dreams, and empowerment: A brief therapy practice note. *Families in Society, 79*, 395–399.

Gummer, B. (1994). Managing diversity in the work force. *Administration in Social Work, 18*, 123–140.

Hall, A. S., & Jugovic, H. J. (1997). Adolescents' self-determination: Assuming competency until otherwise proven. *Journal of Mental Health Counseling, 19*, 256–267.

Hare, A. P. (1982). *Creativity in small groups.* Beverly Hills, CA: Sage.

Harris, G. A. (1996). Dealing with difficult clients. In F. Flash (Ed.), *The Hatherleigh guide to psychotherapy.* (pp. 47–61). New York: Hatherleigh Press.

Hartman, A. (1978). Diagramatic assessment of family relationships. *Social Casework, 59*, 465–476.

Harvey, J. B. (1988). The Abilene Paradox: The management of agreement. *Organizational Dynamics, 17*, 17–34.

Hedges, L. E. (1992). *Interpreting the countertransference.* Northvale, NJ: Jason Aronson.

Helms, J. E. (1995). Why is there no study of cultural equivalence in standardized cognitive ability testing? In N. R. Goldberger & J. B. Veroff (Eds.), *The culture and psychology reader* (pp. 674–719). New York: New York University Press.

Hendrick, S. S. (1988). Counselor self-disclosure. *Journal of Counseling and Development, 66*, 419–424.

Henry, W. P., Schacht, T. E., & Strupp, H. H. (1990). Patient and therapist introject, interpersonal process, and differential psychotherapy outcome. *Journal of Consulting and Clinical Psychology, 58*, 768–774.

Herlihy, B., & Remley, T. P. (1995). Unified ethical standards: A challenge for professionalism. *Journal of Counseling and Development, 74*, 130–133.

Hess, P. M., & Hess, H. J. (1998). Values and ethics in social work practice with lesbian and gay persons. In G. P. Mallon (Ed.), *Foundations of social work practice with lesbian and gay persons* (pp. 31–46). New York: Harrington Park Press.

Hillyer, D. (1996). Solution-oriented questions: An analysis of a key intervention in solution-focused therapy. *Journal of the American Psychiatric Nurses Association, 2*, 3–10.

Hoenderdos, H. T. W., & van Romunde, L. K. J. (1995). Information exchange between client and the outside world from the NLP perspective. *Communication and Cognition, 28*, 343–350.

Horton, J. (1998). Further research on the patient's experience of touch in psychotherapy. In E. W. L. Smith & P. R. Clance (Eds.), *Touch in psychotherapy: Theory, research, and practice* (pp. 127–141). New York: Guilford Press.

House, S. (1994). Blending NLP representational systems with the RT counseling environment. *Journal of Reality Therapy, 14*, 61–65.

Huber, C. H. (1994). *Ethical, legal, and professional issues in the practice of marriage and family therapy* (2nd ed.). Columbus, OH: Merrill.

Hynan, D. J. (1990). Client reasons and experiences in treatment that influence termination of psychotherapy. *Journal of Clinical Psychology, 46*, 891–895.

Isaacs, M. L., & Stone, C. (1999). School counselors and confidentiality: Factors affecting professional choices. *Professional School Counseling, 2*, 258–266.

Ivey, A. E., & Ivey, M. B. (1998). Reframing DSM-IV: Positive strategies from developmental counseling and therapy. *Journal of Counseling and Development, 76*, 334–350.

Jackson, Y. (1998). Applying APA ethical guidelines to individual play therapy with children. *International Journal of Play Therapy, 7*, 1–15.

Jennings, L., & Skovholt, T. M. (1999). The cognitive, emotional, and relational characteristics of master therapists. *Journal of Counseling Psychology, 46*, 3–11.

Johnson, D. W. (1997). *Reading out: Interpersonal effectiveness and self-actualization.* Boston: Allyn & Bacon.

Johnson, S. M. (1996). *The practice of emotionally focused marital therapy: Creating connection.* New York: Brunner/Mazel.

Kahane, H. (1992). *Logic and contemporary rhetoric: The use of reason in everyday life* (6th ed.). Belmont, CA: Wadsworth.

Kassierer, J. P., & Kopelman, R. I. (1991). *Learning clinical reasoning.* Baltimore: Williams & Wilkins.

Kopp, R. R. (1995). Metaphor therapy: Using client generated metaphors in psychotherapy. New York: Brunner/Mazel.

Lafferty, P., Beutler, L. E., & Crago, M. (1989). Differences between more and less effective psychotherapists: A study of select therapist variables. *Journal of Consulting and Clinical Psychology, 57*, 76–80.

Lansberg, I. (1988). Social categorization, entitlement, and justice in organizations: Contextual determinants and cognitive underpinnings. *Human Relations, 41*, 871–899.

Lebow, J. L. (1995). Open-ended therapy: Termination in marital and family therapy. In R. H. Mikesell & D. Lusterman (Eds.), *Integrating family therapy: Handbook of family psychology and systems theory* (pp. 73–86). Washington, DC: American Psychological Association.

Leigh, A. (1998). *Referral and termination issues for counsellors.* London, UK: Academy of Hebrew Language.

Link, B. G., & Phelan, J. (1995). Social conditions as fundamental causes of disease. *Journal of Health and Social Behavior, (Extra Issue)*, 80–94.

Lowy, L. (1976). Decision-making and group work. In S. Bernstein (Ed.), *Explorations in group work* (pp. 107–136). Boston: Charles River Books.

Lum, D. (1992). *Social work and people of color: A process-stage approach.* Pacific Grove, CA: Brooks/Cole.

Mallinckrodt, B. (1993). Session impact, working alliance, and treatment outcome in brief counseling. *Journal of Counseling Psychology, 40*, 25–32.

Manthei, R. J. (1997). The response-shift bias in a counsellor education program. *British Journal of Guidance and Counselling, 25*, 229–237.

Marlin, E. (1989). *Genograms: The new tool for exploring the personality, career, and love patterns you inherit.* Chicago: Contemporary Books.

McCollum, V. J. C. (1997). Evolution of the African American family personality: Considerations for family therapy. *Journal of Multicultural Counseling and Development, 25*, 219–229.

McGoldrick, M., Gerson, R., & Shellenberger, S. (1999). *Genograms: Assessment and intervention.* New York: W. W. Norton and Sons.

McGovern, M. P., Newman, F. L., & Kopta, S. M. (1986). Metatheoretical assumptions and psychotherapy orientation. *Journal of Consulting and Clinical Psychology, 54*, 476–481.

McKay, N., & Lashutka, S. (1983). The basics of organization change: An eclectic model. *Training and Development Journal, 37*, 64–69.

McKay, M. M., Nudelman, R., McCadam, K., & Bonzales, J. (1996). Evaluating a social work engagement approach to involving inner-city children and their families in mental health care. *Research on Social Work Practice, 6*, 462–472.

McLennan, J., Culkin, K., & Courtney, P. (1994). Telephone counsellors' conceptualizing abilities and counselling skills. *British Journal of Guidance and Counselling, 22*, 183–195.

McPherson, J. M., Popeilarz, P. A., & Drobnic, S. (1992). *American Sociological Review, 57*, 153–170.

Meichenbaum, D. (1997). The evolution of a cognitive-behavior therapist. In J. K. Zeig

(Ed.), *The evolution of psychotherapy* (pp. 95–104). New York: Brunner/Mazel.

Miller, R. (1999). The first session with a new client: Five stages. In R. Bor & M. Watts (Eds.), *The trainee handbook: A guide for counselling and psychotherapy.* London, UK: Sage.

Miller, S. D. (1994). Some questions (not answers) for the brief treatment of people with drug and alcohol problems. In M. F. Hoyt (Ed.), *Constructive therapies.* New York: Guilford Press.

Miller, W. R., Benefield, R. G., & Tonigan, J. S. (1993). Enhancing motivation for change in problem drinking: A controlled comparison of two therapist styles. *Journal of Consulting and Clinical Psychology, 61,* 455–461.

Minuchin, S. (1974). *Families and family therapy.* London, UK: Tavistock.

Montague, J. (1996). Counseling families from diverse cultures: A non-deficit approach. *Journal of Multicultural Counseling and Development, 24,* 37–41.

Moosbruker, J. (1983). OD with a community mental health center: A case of building structures patiently. *Group and Organization Studies, 8,* 45–59.

Murphy, B. C., & Dillon, C. (1998). *Interviewing in action process and practice.* Pacific Grove, CA: Brooks/Cole.

Najavits, L. M., & Strupp, H. H. (1994). Differences in the effectiveness of psychodynamic therapists: A process-outcome study. *Psychotherapy, 31,* 114–123.

Neimeyer, G. J., Macnair, R., Metzler, A. E., & Courchaine, K. (1991). Changing personal beliefs: Effects of forewarning, argument quality, prior bias, and personal exploration. *Journal of Social and Clinical Psychology, 10,* 1–20.

Nelson, M. L., & Neufeldt, A. (1996). Building on an empirical foundation: Strategies to enhance good practice. *Journal of Counseling and Development, 74,* 609–615.

Nixon, R., & Spearmon, M. (1991). Building a pluralistic workplace. In R. L. Edwards & J. Yankey (Eds.), *Skills for effective human services management* (pp. 155–170). Silver Springs, MD: NASW Press.

Northen, H. (1998). Ethical dilemmas in social work with groups. *Social Work with Groups, 21,* 5–18.

Okun, B. F. (1997). *Effective helping: Interviewing and counseling techniques.* Pacific Grove, CA: Brooks/Cole.

Omer, H. (1997). Narrative empathy. *Psychotherapy, 34,* 19–27.

Palazzoli-Selvini, M., Boscolo, L., Cecchin, G., & Prata, G. (1980). Hypothesizing-circularity-neutrality: Three guidelines for the conductor of the session. *Family Process, 19,* 3–12.

Panagua, F. (1995). *Assessing culturally diverse clients.* Thousand Oaks, CA: Sage.

Patalano, F. (1997). Developing the working alliance in marital therapy: A psychodynamic perspective. *Contemporary Family Therapy: An International Journal, 19,* 497–505.

Patterson, G. R., & Forgatch, M. S. (1985). Therapist behavior as a determinant for client noncomplaince: A paradox for the behavior modifier. *Journal of Consulting and Clinical Psychology, 63,* 846–851.

Patton, M. Q. (1980). *Qualitative evaluation methods.* Beverly Hills, CA: Sage.

Paulson, R., Herinckx, H., Demmler, J., Clarke, G., Culter, D., & Birecree, E. (1999). Comparing practice patterns of consumer and non-consumer mental health service providers. *Community Mental Health Journal, 35,* 251–269.

Peile, C. (1998). Emotional and embodied knowledge: Implications for critical practice. *Journal of Sociology and Social Welfare, 25,* 39–59.

Penn, P. (1982). Circular questioning. *Family Process, 21,* 267–280.

Perri, M. G. (1998). The maintenance of treatment effects in the long-term management of obesity. *Clinical Psychology: Science and Practice, 5,* 526–543.

Pritchard, C., Cotton, A., Bowen, D., & Williams, R. (1998). A consumer study of young people's views on their educational social worker: Engagement as a measure of an effective relationship. *British Journal of Social Work, 28,* 915–938.

Prout, S. M., DeMartino, R. A., & Prout, H. T. (1999). Ethical and legal issues in psychological interventions with children and adolescents. In H. T. Prout & D. T. Brown (Eds.), *Counseling and psychotherapy with children and adolescents: Theory and practice for school and clinical settings* (3rd ed.) (pp. 26–48). New York: John Wiley.

Quintana, S. M., & Holahan, W. (1992). Termination in short-term counseling: Comparison of successful and unsuccessful cases. *Journal of Counseling Psychology, 39,* 299–305.

Raw, S. D. (1998). Who is to define effective treatment for social work clients? *Social Work, 43,* 81–86.

Ray, R. D., Upson, J. D., & Henderson, B. J. (1977). A systems approach to behavior: III. Organismic pace and complexity in time–space fields. *Psychological Record, 27,* 649–682.

Reamer, R. G. (1998). Clients' right to competent and ethical treatment. *Research on Social Work Practice, 8,* 597–603.

Reandeau, S. G., & Wampold, B. E. (1991). Relationship of power and involvement to working alliance: A multiple-case sequential analysis of brief therapy. *Journal of Counseling Psychology, 38,* 107–114.

Rennie, D. L. (1994). Clients' accounts of resistance in counselling: A qualitative analysis. *Canadian Journal of Counselling, 28,* 43–57.

Ridgway, I. R., & Sharpley, C. F. (1991). Multiple measures for the prediction of counsellor trainee effectiveness. *Canadian Journal of Counselling, 24,* 165–177.

Robbins, S. P. (1993). *Organizational behavior: Concepts, controversies, and applications* (6th ed.). Englewood Cliffs, NJ: Prentice-Hall.

Rober, P. (1999). The therapist's inner conversation in family therapy practice: Some ideas about the self of the therapist, therapeutic impasse, and the process of reflection. *Family Process, 38,* 209–228.

Rollnick, S., & Morgan, M. (1996). Motivational interviewing: Increasing readiness for change. In A. M. Washton (Ed.), *Psychotherapy and substance abuse: A practitioner's handbook* (pp. 179–191). New York: Guilford Press.

Rosen, S. (1982). *My voice will go with you: The teaching tales of Milton Erickson.* San Francisco: Brunner-Mazel.

Rothman, J. C. (1999). *Self-awareness workbook for social workers.* Boston: Allyn & Bacon.

Rowe, C. E. Jr., & MacIsaac, D. S. (1989). *Empathic attunement: The "technique" of psychoanalytic self psychology.* Northvale, NJ: Jason Aronson.

Rusbult, C. E., Johnson, D. J., & Morrow, G. D. (1986). Impact of couple patterns of problem solving on distress and nondistress in dating relationships. *Journal of Personality and Social Psychology, 50,* 744–753.

Rzepnicki, T. L. (1991). Enhancing the durability of intervention gains: A challenge for the 1990s. *Social Service Review, 65,* 92–109.

Sabourin, S. (1990). Problem-solving, self-appraisal and coping efforts in distressed and nondistressed couples. *Journal of Marital and Family Therapy, 16,* 89–97.

Safran, J. D., Crocker, P., McMain, S., & Murray, P. (1990). Therapeutic alliance rupture as a therapy event for empirical investigation. *Psychotherapy, 27,* 154–165.

Saleebey, D. (1997). The strengths approach to practice. In D. Saleebey (Ed.), *The strengths perspective in social work practice* (2nd ed., pp. 49–57). New York: Longman.

Samstag, L. W., Batchelder, S. T., Muran, J. C., Safran, J. D., & Winston, A. (1998). Early identification of treatment failures in short-term psychotherapy: An assessment of therapeutic alliance and interpersonal behavior. *Journal of Psychotherapy Practice and Research, 7,* 126–143.

Santa Rita, E. Jr. (1998). What do you do after asking the miracle question in solution-focused therapy? *Family Therapy, 25,* 189–195.

Satterfield, W. A., & Lyddon, W. J. (1998). Client attachment and the working alliance. *Counselling Psychology Quarterly, 11,* 407–415.

Scannapieco, M., & Jackson, S. (1996). Kinship care: The African American response to family preservation. *Social Work, 41,* 190–196.

Schaap, C., Bennun, I., Schindler, L., & Hoogduin, K. (1993). *The therapeutic relationship in behavioural psychotherapy.* Chichester, UK: John Wiley.

Schmidt, J. J. (1987). Parental objections to counseling services: An analysis. *School Counselor, 34,* 387–391.

Schwebel, M., & Coster, J. (1998). Well-functioning in professional psychologists: As program heads see it. *Professional Psychology: Research and Practice, 29,* 284–292.

Sells, J. N., & Hays, K. A. (1997). A comparison of time-limited and brief time-limited group therapy at termination. *Journal of College Student Development, 38,* 136–142.

Shaw, M. E. (1971). *Group dynamics.* New York: McGraw-Hill.

Shilts, L., & Gordon, A. B. (1996). What to do after the miracle occurs. *Journal of Family Psychotherapy, 7,* 15–22.

Shulman, L. (1985/6). The dynamics of mutual aid. *Social Work with Groups, 8,* 51–60.

Shulman, L. (1999). *The skills of helping individuals, families, groups and communities* (4th ed.). Itasca, IL: Peacock.

Slonim-Nevo, V. (1996). Clinical practice: Treating the non-voluntary client. *International Social Work, 39,* 117–129.

Smith, D., & Fitzpatrick, M. (1995). Patient-therapist boundary issues: An integrative review of theory and research. *Professional Psychology: Research and Practice, 26,* 499–506.

Smith, K. J., Subich, L. M., & Kalodner, C. (1995). The transtheoretical model's stages and processes of change and the relation to premature termination. *Journal of Counseling Psychology, 42,* 34–39.

Smith, K. K., Kamistein, D. S., & Makadok, R. J. (1995). The health of the corporate body: Illness and organizational dynamics. *Journal of Applied Behavioral Science, 31,* 328–351.

Sommers-Flanagan, J., & Sommers-Flanagan, R. (1997). *Tough kids, cool counseling: User-friendly approaches with challenging youth.* Alexandria, VA: American Counseling Association.

Sonkin, D. J. (1986). Clairvoyance vs. common sense: Therapist's duty to warn and protect. *Violence and Victims, 1,* 7–22.

Spurling, L., & Dryden, W. (1989). The self and the therapeutic domain. In W. Dryden & L. Spurling (Eds.), *On becoming a psychotherapist* (pp. 191–214). London, UK: Tavistock/Routledge.

Staller, K. M., & Kirk, S. A. (1998). Knowledge utilization in social work and legal practice. *Journal of Sociology and Social Welfare, 25,* 91–113.

Stein, R. (1995). The role of affects in the process of change in psychotherapy. *Israel Journal of Psychiatry and Related Sciences, 32,* 167–173.

Stein, R. H. (1990). *Ethical issues in counseling.* Buffalo, NY: Prometheus Books.

Sue, D. W., Ivey, A. R., & Pedersen, P. B. (1996). *A theory of multicultural counseling and therapy.* Pacific Grove, CA: Brooks/Cole.

Sue, D. W., & Sue, D. (1990). *Counseling the culturally different* (2nd ed.). New York: John Wiley.

Talley, P. F., Strupp, H. H., & Morey, L. C. (1990). Matchmaking in psychotherapy: Patient–therapist dimensions and their impact on outcome. *Journal of Consulting and Clinical Psychology, 58,* 182–188.

Tansey, M. J., & Burke, W. F. (1989). *Understanding countertransference: From projective identification to empathy.* Hillsdale, NJ: Analytic Press.

Thyer, B. A., & Myers, L. L. (1998). Supporting the client's right to effective treatment: Touching a raw nerve? *Social Work, 43,* 87–91.

Tjosvold, D., Andrews, I. R., & Struthers, J. T. (1991). Power and interdependence in work groups: Views of managers and employees. *Group and Organizational Studies, 16,* 285–299.

Tokar, D. M., Hardin, S. I., Adams, E. M., & Brandel, I. W. (1996). Clients' expectations about counseling and perceptions of the working alliance. *Journal of College Student Psychotherapy, 11,* 9–26.

Tomm, K. (1987). Interventive interviewing: Part II. Reflexive questioning as a means to enable self-healing. *Family Process, 26,* 167–184.

Tomm, K. (1988). Interventive interviewing: III. Intending to ask lineal, circular, strategic, or reflexive questions? *Family Process, 27,* 1–15.

Triandis, H. C. (1995). The self and social behavior in differing cultural contexts. In N. R. Goldberger & J. B. Veroff (Eds.), *The culture and psychology reader* (pp. 326–365). New York: New York University Press.

Tyron, G. S., & Kane, A. S. (1990). The helping alliance and premature termination. *Counselling Psychology Quarterly, 3,* 233–238.

Tryon, G. S., & Kane, A. S. (1993). Relationship of working alliance to mutual and unilateral termination. *Journal of Counseling Psychology, 40,* 33–36.

Uhlemann, M. R., Lee, D. Y., & Martin, J. (1994). Client cognitive responses as a function of quality of counselor verbal responses. *Journal of Counseling and Development, 73,* 198–203.

Vallis, T. M., Shaw, B. F., & McCabe, S. B. (1988). The relationship between therapist competency in cognitive therapy and general therapy skill. *Journal of Cognitive Psychotherapy, 2,* 237–249.

Walborn, F. S. (1996). *Process variables: Four common elements of counseling and psychotherapy.* Pacific Grove, CA: Brooks/Cole.

Waldron, H. B., Turner, C. W., Barton, C., Alexander, J. F., & Cline, V. B. (1997). Therapist defensiveness and marital therapy process and outcome. *American Journal of Family Therapy, 25,* 233–243.

Watt, J. W., & Kallmann, G. L. (1998). Managing professional obligations under managed care: A social work perspective. *Family and Community Health, 21,* 40–49.

Watzlawick, P., Beavin, J. H., & Jackson, D. D. (1967). *Pragmatics of human communication: A study of interactional patterns, pathologies, and paradoxes.* New York: W. W. Norton.

Weaver, H. N., & White, B. J. (1997). The Native American family circle: Roots of resiliency. *Journal of Family Social Work, 2,* 67–79.

Webb, A., & Wheeler, S., II (1998). A social dilemma perspective on cooperative behavior in organizations: The effects of scarcity, communication, and unequal access on the use of a shared resource. *Group and Organizational Management, 23,* 509–524.

Wesley, C. A. (1996). Social work and end-of-life decisions: Self-determination and the common good. *Health and Social Work, 21,* 115–121.

Wheelan, S. A., McKeage, R. L., Verdi, A. F., Abraham, M., Krasick, C., & Johnston, F. (1994). Communication and developmental patterns in a system of interacting groups. In L. R. Frey (Ed.), *Group communication in context: Studies of natural groups* (pp. 153–178). Hillsdale, NJ: Lawrence Erlbaum.

White, M. (1986). Negative explanation, restraint, and double description: A template for family therapy. *Family Process, 25,* 169–184.

White, M. (1988). The process of questioning: A therapy of literary merit? *Dulwich Centre Newsletter.* Dulwich Centre, NZ.

Wiseman, H., & Rice, L. N. (1989). Sequential analyses of therapist-client interaction during change events: A task-focused approach. *Journal of Consulting and Clinical Psychology, 57,* 281–286.

Worrell, M. (1996). An existential-phenomenological perspective on the concept of "resistance" in counselling and psychotherapy. *Counselling Psychology Quarterly, 10,* 5–15.

Wubbolding, R. E. (1996). Professional issues: The use of questions in reality therapy. *Journal of Reality Therapy, 16,* 122–127.

Yalom, I. D. (1995). *The theory and practice of group psychotherapy* (4th ed.). New York: Basic Books.

INDEX